JAMIE H SCRUTTON

THE DEVIL MAKES WORK FOR CREATIVE HANDS

(COLLECTED SCRIBBLINGS 2008 - 2021)

I dedicate this book to my incredible family, friends, my beautiful partner Marc and everyone who has supported and had me perform at their events. For their patience, virtue and open-mindedness. I also want to say a huge thank you to my friend Danny Lane, for taking the time to proofread this manuscript at first hand.

— Much love and appreciation —

ISBN 978-1-78222-855-4

Book layout and production management by Into Print
www.intoprint.net
01604 832149

PROLOGUE

It is currently 10:15pm on Monday 21st December 2020 and I am literally on the verge of launching this fucking laptop across my room, imminently close to a breakdown, which is ironic because this book is predominantly based around my own personal experiences with mental health and during the aftermath of any given manic episode.

This book allows me to share the underlying theme of oppressive mental health issues, that are hidden in my work amongst the sugar-coated subjects of my whimsy musings. I have spent the whole of this month, simultaneously working on an animation commission and this book, which is put together in the form of a written montage of excerpts from my journal. Luckily, thanks to my journals, I haven't really had the ominous task of rewriting the past thirteen years from scratch.

What happened approximately fifteen minutes ago, I had reached the point of completing this project. I went to save the document and the final ten pages of this book had completely erased itself, without my permission. I could feel the adrenaline seething within me and I nearly stuck two fingers up at everything around me with a vehement scream of "FUCK OFF!" But I didn't. Do you know why? There is always a solution. I have managed to rewrite aspects the missing document, so I am asking myself and you, what is the point of raging over something which is rectifiable? Everything will be okay. I am somewhat calm to an extent, even though I can feel my veins pumping with unreleased serotonin but I am here, I am breathing and I have everything that I need. There is a pandemic erupting at this minute but I am well.

I have been urging to write this book for the past year. The whole concept of doing this is to express myself openly through this form, other than live poetry performance or a physical film. Many people have advised me to publish my work, particularly my whimsical anecdotes, as a way of furthering myself in the field of writing and becoming an established poet. I have always been hesitant about publishing my work in print because I usually write to perform it live. Then I thought, if I were to do this project, why not have a "Greatest Hits" compilation if you like, of absolutely everything which I have expressed through my own journals and previous artistic projects, and bring them together in one book, accompanied by a selection of my whimsical anecdotes.

I have always admired certain types of writers who have produced work in a similar style, such as the prolific Alan Bennett and the genius Pam Ayres. I am always drawn to books which contain unusual collections of works. I have had the brilliant opportunity of performing and showcasing my work at various gigs throughout the UK during the past thirteen years. The magic of this is meeting the ordinary to the bizarre, wonderfully outlandish characters along the journey.

I am very open about my mental health, so hopefully this book will provide readers an understanding of my personal experiences and to help those who might feel they are delusionally functioning differently to everyone else at times. I do not think of this book as a memoir because it isn't. It is just an overview showing how I have adapted and developed over the years and who I have become during my struggles throughout my twenties and early thirties. I have condensed the hellish parts of this book and filled some of the pages with a splurge of whimsy too.

I want you all to have some acknowledgement to feel that it is okay to not be okay and that you can heal from the hellion within you, because life gets better with patience, practice and virtue. Everyone has some physical response to mental health although some individuals experience the condition on more debilitating levels through intrusive thoughts and most often PTSD. Please do not isolate yourself away from the people who truly care about you and most importantly do not feel that you are burdening anyone with your battles. People generally would rather stick their kettle on and are happy to listen, advise and offer support. There is nothing worse than being a victim in a dystopian world with self-harm being the only answer to obliterate your existence. Trust me, I have been there. It is fucking crippling and I wouldn't recommend it to anyone.

I have many attributes which give me strength whenever depression and anxiety unfolds. My strongest one is my passion to create and experiment with different art forms. I also have a fanatical enthusiasm for thrill-seeking. I am a huge advocate for anything which can safely plunge me into the realms of danger, conveniently distracting me from the pressures of reality. I experienced my first Skydive back in May 2015 and it was also my first time on a plane – isn't this rock n' roll or what?! This incredible experience did initially cure my mental ailment temporarily. The internal feeling of oppressiveness had been obliterated for a good couple of months. I felt like a complete sane human being. Following this, I developed a bucket list of adventures and made 2020 the year of 'mind-conquering' activities (obviously pre-COVID-19.) Bungee jumping was one of the thrills which I decided on pursuing. After quite an abundance of rescheduled dates, due to the infamous global pandemic, I experienced two immense jumps in Tatton Park, Cheshire and Salford Quays, with the support of my boyfriend Marc. He, my family, friends, psychiatric professionals, as well as these physical activities and fantastic visits to my second home at Blackpool Pleasure Beach, has helped me to suppress my mental health issues in as many ways possible.

I am extremely apprehensive about releasing my own personal reflections about my manic episodes here, but modern-day society is becoming more accepting and aware of the grievous mental issues that people have to tolerate and are possibly powerless to defeat by themselves. These people live as warriors who fight against this relentless 'Satan' that dwells within themselves. There is an uninvited behemoth in everyone, which most often thrives on us to express ourselves candidly and this is why I have titled this book *The Devil Makes Work for Creative Hands.*

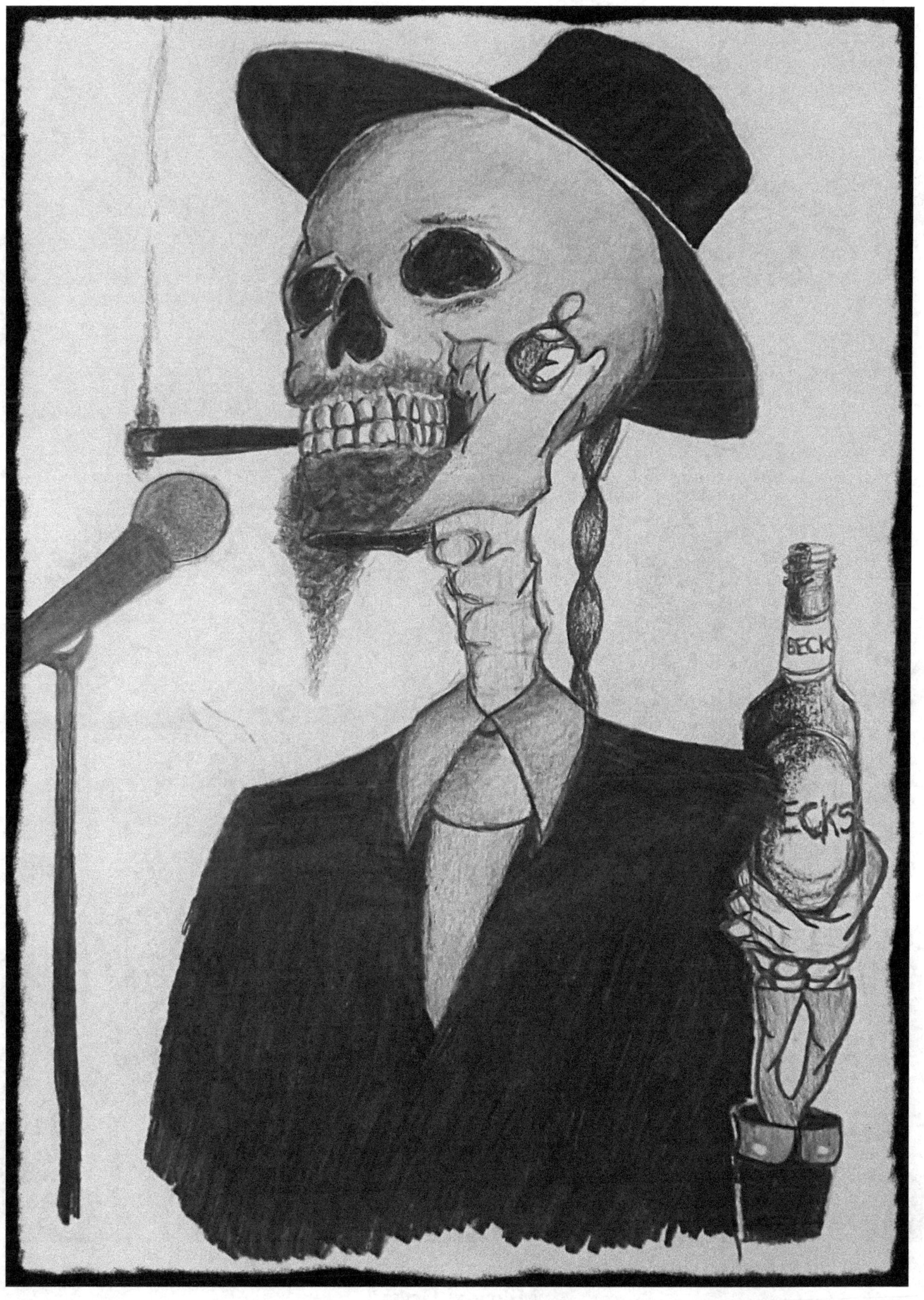

"A Supposed Punk Poet"
February 2021

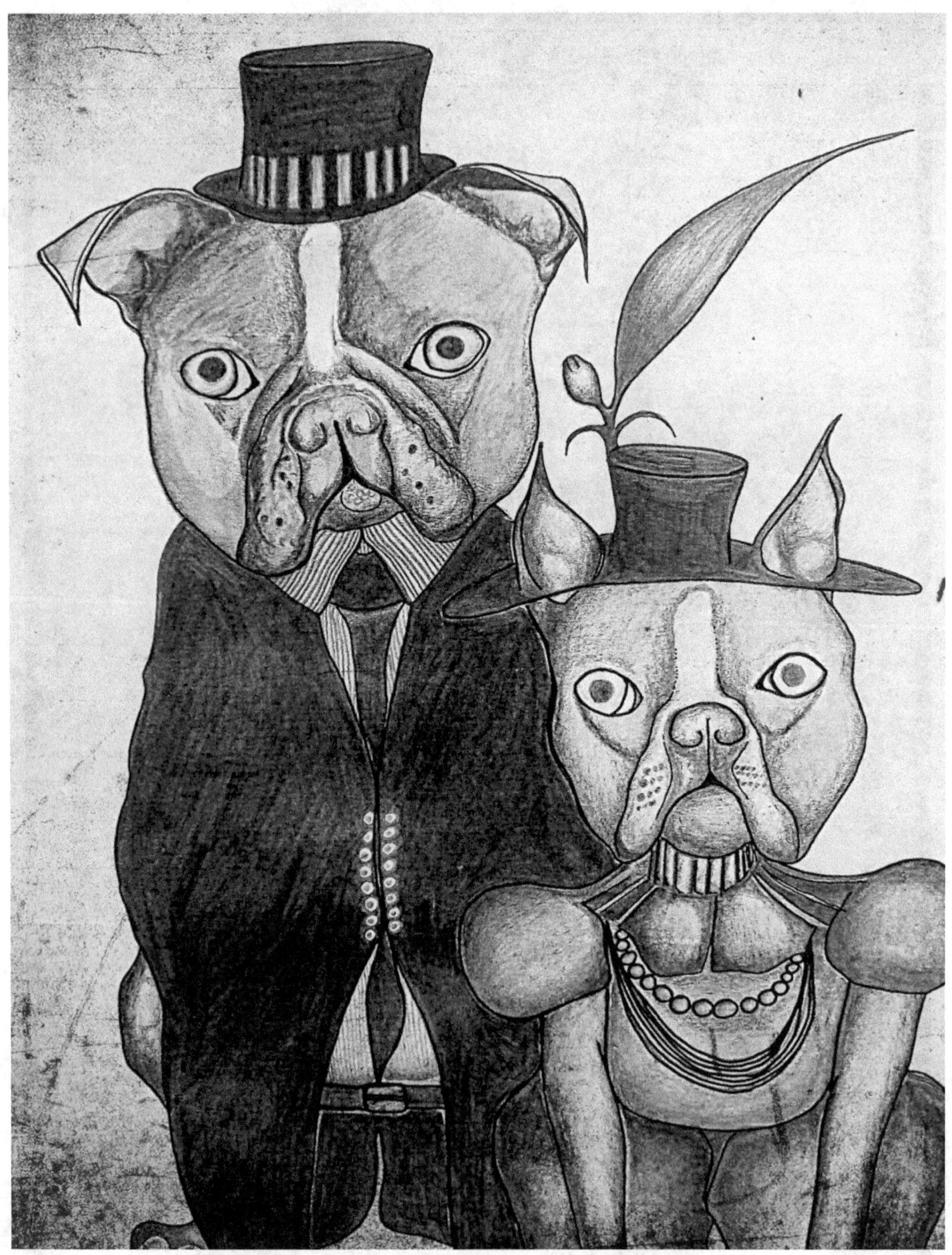

"Milo and Jarvey"
Commissioned A4 Pencil Sketch - 3/2/2021
Remastered as this print - 14/3/2021

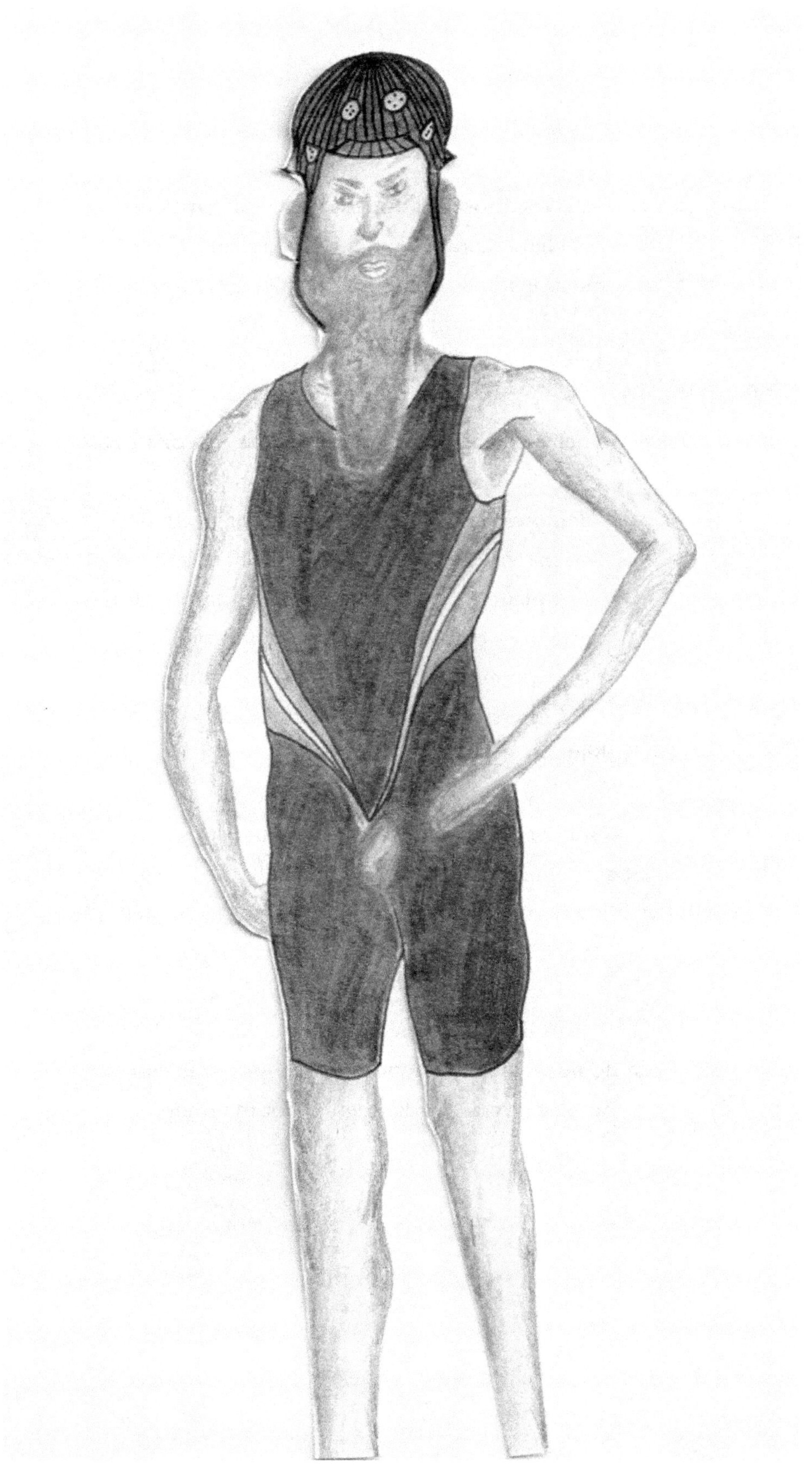

"I have never liked the taste of male testosterone, for those who dress in lycra."

Lycra

Lyrcra is the most unattractive piece of garment,
That could be modelled on a man.
Some individuals find it provocatively alluring,
But personally, I am not a fan!
It is skimpy, it is offensive, it is revolting,
It is incredibly, unnecessarily tight.
It is extremely revealing in the most private of constitutes,
My, oh my, lycra is such a sight!
It is definitely not suitable for the faint-hearted,
For me visually, it is too much to handle.
I have seen plenty of the unmentionables in my time,
You know, parts which swing and dangle!
Some people, materially, find it arousing,
Others use it as a carnal embrace,
But I think it should be kept to what it is designed for,
A safety shield in a cycle race.
It contributes to a heap of implications,
It accumulates an abundance of bollocks sweat,
Lyrca is an invention that I wouldn't want to befriend,
It is a demon that I would rather forget!
I ain't criticising people's fetishes,
Whatever fabric excites the skin.
I just do not see the attraction that propels this fantasy,
Because, lycra, my darlings, is not my thing!

Wednesday 24th October 2018

Whilst working with two beauties in the Leeds Playhouse box office on Eastgate, Lynn and Terri inspired me to write an original whimsical anecdote from their perspective of men wearing lycra. I made Lynn and myself a cup of tea, settling down at my workstation for the afternoon shift, when I overheard their witty conversation. "Sweaty bollocks!" Lynn cackled. This man she was referring to happened to religiously wear lycra. Their conversation continued and that was when I began quietly write the lycra poem on the computer, when the phone bookings went quiet. I then emailed the anecdote through to them both, subsequently brightening up their day.

I use everyday life experiences and observations to help me create sketches or stories and I'm also tempted to adapt them because I have a fruity imagination. I continue to perform this anecdote at many events around the United Kingdom, as it seems to cast a charm on audiences. I made my debut performance of this poem in January 2019. It was at an event called "Scriptstuff" in a quirky venue named Temperance in Leamington Spa.

Wednesday 30th January 2019

This evening, I performed at an event called 'Scriptstuff' based in a lukewarm cafe named Temperance in Leamington Spa. I met with Scott aka Danger Mouse and his female acquaintance, Amber, whilst getting off the number 11 bus from Coventry. The event was held downstairs in a room known as 'The Magic Lantern', which showcases short film screenings as well as the poetry nights. A tall middle-aged man was telling me about this venue as he served me a petite, traditional English tea. I mentioned to him that I also specialised in filmmaking.

"Hand drawn stop motion animations," I replied, after he asked me what style I worked in.

The man said that he had a friend who specialised in 3D Animation, using various objects, including clay modelling.

The audience capacity was bursting this evening, in the dimly lit 'Magic Lantern' room. Hosted by Mike Tuck, 'Scriptstuff' began at 7:30pm and concluded at 10pm. Danger Mouse was the opening poet to take the mic. I was the fourth poet to grace the mic with a whimsical anecdote of mine titled "Lycra." I wasn't championed the poet of the month but really, who cares? It was all about participation and creative bonding. The headliner for the evening was the LGBTQ poet and activist, Nicola Wylde, who read out original poems from the ink of her notebook. She spoke about acceptance from the perspective of a gay woman who went to church, and about the minority of people who opposed same sex relationships. Nicola was interesting to listen to, although personally, free verse isn't my preferred style. It was brilliant to see Tim Jenkins, who I had previously met at a "Roots To Shoot" film night in Coventry on a couple of occasions.

I arrived back at The Highcroft Guest House Hotel in Coventry at approximately 11:30pm. At midnight, I reached the new decade of my life; the thirties.

Thursday 21st February 2019

After a long tedious 10 'til 5 shift at the box office, Terri picked up Lynn and myself on the opposite side of the road to take us to the LS6 Cafe in Headingly. We were going to an event called "Outspoken," where I was scheduled to perform on the open mic section in the second half. When Steve Clarkson, the compere, called me up to the microphone upstairs in the Terrace room, I introduced my first anecdote to a lively audience, which was "Lycra" followed by an archived piece titled "Thirty Pence to Have a Piss?!" I received a thriving reception and so did Laurence Inman aka Lence, who performed his spoken word rap in the second half.

Unfortunately, Terri's daughter, Simone, had to dash off during the interval as her boyfriend was waiting for her outside the LS6 Cafe. It was nice to sit down to a meal in the venue before the event commenced with Simone, Lynn and Terri. It was such a buzzing night overall, as the spoken word event was happening upstairs and there was a quiz event which occurred simultaneously downstairs. Adele Baran was also in attendance. She is a good friend of mine as we used to work together at the Playhouse. She greeted me with a hug and pleaded for me to perform another one of my anecdotes titled "Have a Good Life Bellend." I had forgotten a few words for this, but I did promise to perform it at a subsequent event when she attends.

This gig was part of an LS6 mini Leeds tour which I took part in during the Spring. I performed a 'Greatest Hits' collection consisting of my current and archived anecdotes, which were locally based. I was approached by a quirky looking girl there, with extremely short orange hair by the name of Anne. She asked me if I performed a poem about feeling sombre but unfortunately, I didn't. She then highly recommended her friend's preferred barber to me near the Hyde Park Picture House, who charges £5.00 for a haircut. She also suggested that I should join her for tea and cake at her house afterwards. I thought she was quite unique!

The final open mic performer had a tote bag hanging on his left shoulder. His name was Trevor Wainwright. He introduced his name, then without performing any form of a poem, he hurried out of the room. I later befriended Trevor and appeared on his radio show on Sunday 4th August 2019 in Pontefract. I spoke about all things whimsy and then performed a few of my anecdotes.

Big Knickers Rule!

Doreen has heard, they have returned in vogue,
They are back to being cool,
They may not be visually flattering in any sense,
but big knickers rule!
She can't be doing with all this provocative lingerie,
They are nothing but a strand of string,
They are only good for (you know what,)
And that is a needless fling.
She would rather feel adequately serene,
It is more than she can say for some,
For women who want to feel fabulous,
With material stuck up their bum!
They slide between the orifice,
They make an uncomfortable grind,
There is always a policy of keeping your unmentionables intact,
and that is to be kind to your behind.
So ladies, never mind trying to impress your fellas, or girls
You have to be kind to be cruel,
They may not be visually attractive in any sense,
but by god, don't big knickers rule!

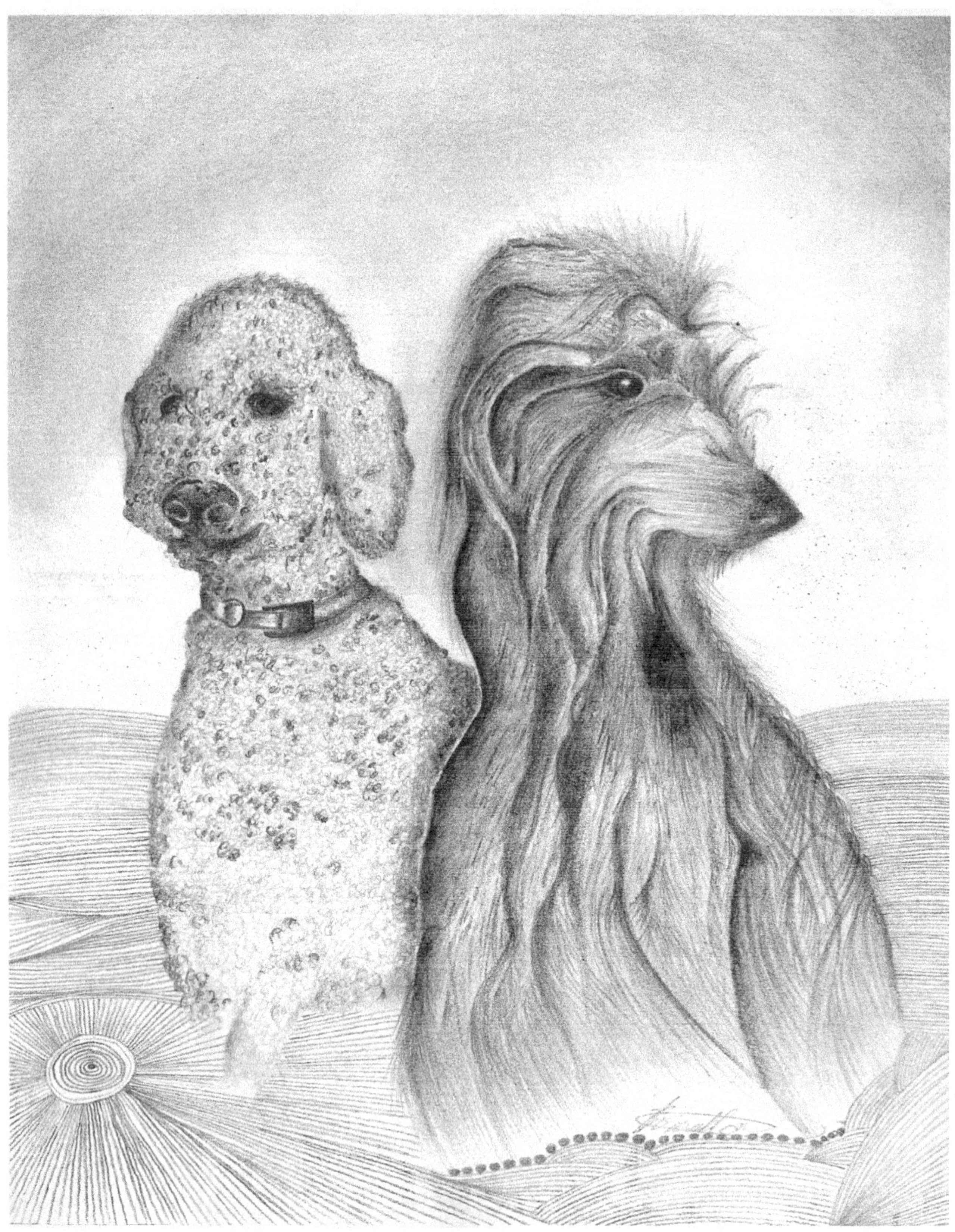

"Rosie and Daisy"
A4 Pencil Sketch - January 2021

I Fancy a Woodchopper

Oh, I do say Ave Marie,
I fancy myself a woodchopper today.
Never mind the trees withering and the leaves getting blown,
He is certainly fanning me away!

My partner was fascinated by the new garden prospect,
I was witnessing a completely different view.
My, oh my, that woodchopper has definitely adjusted my attention.
My eyes are stuck to him like glue!

Dear Mercy, he knows how to drill a thing or two,
He knows how to work up a sweat.
He knows how to manhandle a trunk so vigorously,
He is the perfect good-natured asset.

Oh, I do say Ave Marie,
This morning, I fluttered my lashes as I pray.
The woodchopper can fumble with my garden any time,
He can maintain my trunk any day!

Monday 18th January 2021

I wrote a new anecdote this afternoon which is primarily based on four strapping woodchoppers who were preserving the neighbour's garden, next to Marc's cottage. We were both briefly glancing out of the bedroom window and Marc was appreciating how the view onto the street 'looked more open.' However, I was drooling over the men attentively.

Danny, a friend of ours, giggled when I told him there were woodchoppers working outside.

He teased "Ooh I bet you would fancy a woodchopper!"

Immediately, I wrote the poem in five minutes after him feeding me with this phrase. I love how amusing concepts based on real life events inspire me to write nonsensical verses and how they make people chuckle. You will come to read more about this about later on in the book.

At approximately 3:45pm, Marc and I drove to Castle Hill, Huddersfield where I performed my woodchopper poem, whilst holding my journal. I stood on a wall with the vast, sweeping Yorkshire landscape surrounding me as my only audience. The weather was incredibly bitter with the winter mist was congregating in the air. We both took a stroll around the historic landmark, before heading back to the car.

I Ran Off With the Local Vicar

Me' mam told me t' find a man of me' own,
Any type but not too particular,
I've told that I have packed my bags,
T' run off with the local vicar.

Oh, he's a handsome, charming gent,
"I LOVE THEE!" I happily protest,
Oh, I cannot wait for Sunday to arrive and I toddle to the Chapel,
T' see him in his Sunday best!

Oh, how I gaze into his eyes with merriment,
As I shroud with passion t' the Hymns
I peek over the bible t' see his dazzling smile,
As I give him t' repent t' me' sins!

Oh, how I could be married to a vicar,
One day this magnificent church will be mine,
Living the life in religious matrimony,
and access to unlimited holy wine!

Me' mam and me' friends would disapprove.
They would snare and think of me as odd.
But I could actually shout with pride,
That I have got me' own personal sex God!

Me' mam told me t' find a man of my own,
I have one in particular,
That is why I have packed my bags and I've ordered the cab,
T' run off with the local vicar!

This anecdote is to be narrated by a juvenile twenty-ish year old woman.

Long Johns

He has such a sensuous appearance,
Still, after 20 years of being wed,
But when he wears his long johns,
I ban him from the bed!

They are such a repulsive garment,
They are such a ghastly sight,
They don't particularly arouse me,
They give me such a fright!

Oh, fancy seeing your husband,
With his wobbly, knobbly knees,
His thighs and shins the size of twigs,
Oh no thank you please!

He has his champion features,
It's his legs that I cannot bear,
I would rather see him in his tighty-whities,
And thermal underwear!

My personal inner thoughts of him in them,
Are completely obstruse,
With him lying next to me in bed wearing the long johns,
I strictly refuse!

It prevents him from the bitter winter, I shall give him that,
But the material is frantically coarse,
He needs to burn the long johns,
Otherwise I am filing for a divorce!

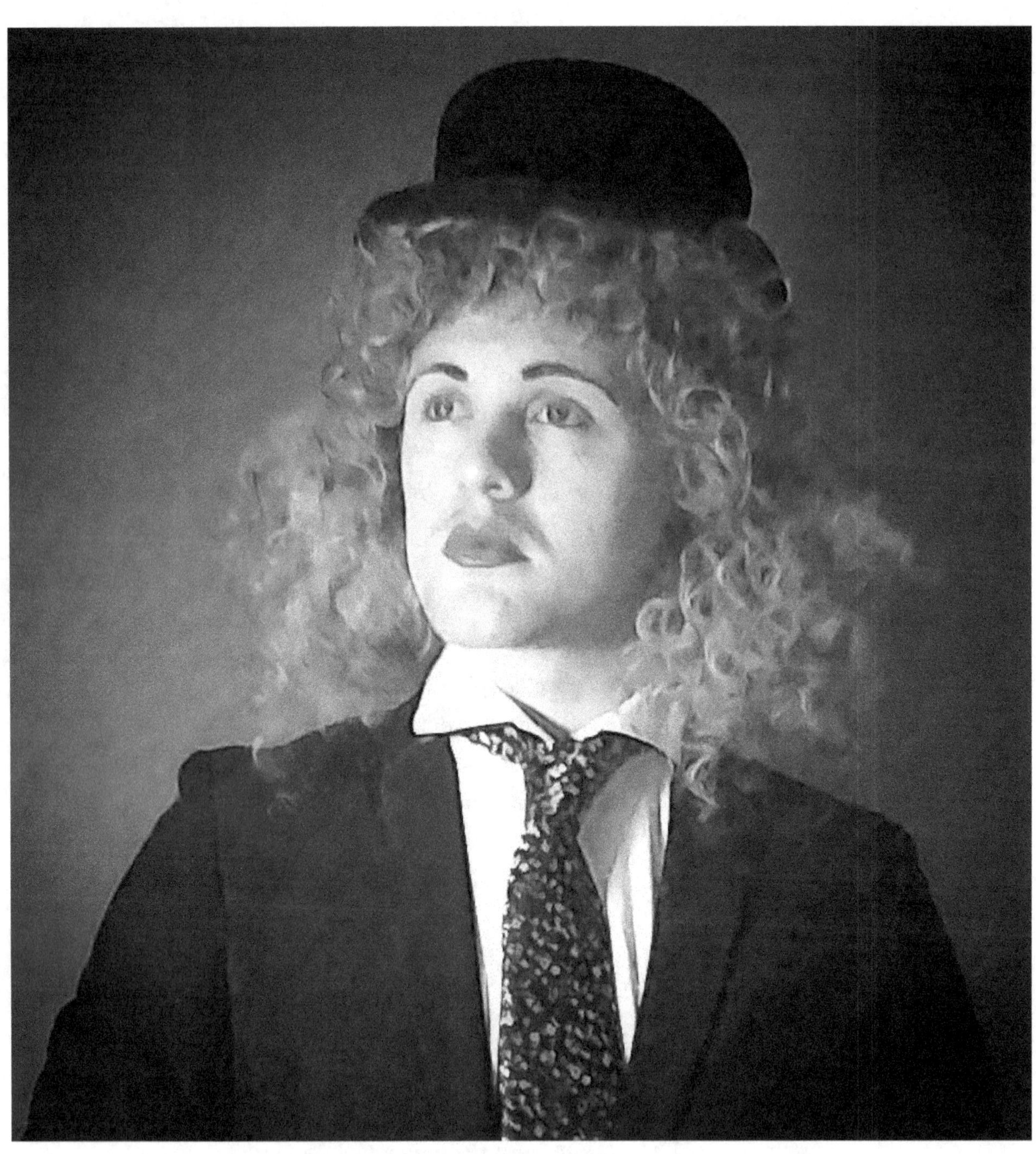

"They wore their strange beauty like war paint-"

\- Quoted by Holly Black

A Reflective Generation

I have an artistic family history, which includes my great, great grandad, Herbert Schofield. He used to perform ventriloquism and the spoons in the Yorkshire music halls from 1909 by the stage name of Herbert Rowland. He was locally known as a popular comedian, wooing audiences with his whimsical genius. He composed Yorkshire and Lancashire's award-winning war song titled 'That was the Widow's Prayer.' This song was later performed by a pianist in 2003, when my mum and grandma ventured to London to appear on Derek Acorah's 'Antique Ghost Show,' which was broadcasted on Living TV. Derek attempted to channel great, great grandad with his animated hypnotic presence, as my mum and grandma watched with nostalgic smiles on their wooden chairs. Great, great grandad always looked immaculate on stage, sporting shiny spat shoes and a top hat. Women were drawn to his charm, they idolised him and he knew it. My great, great grandma would joke that she was going to kill him because of his womanising traits.

He also had a prolific background in alternative medicine and worked as a magnetic healer, herbalist and masseur, curing patients of various forms of ailments around the country.

"Is he in?" smiled this woman in a high-pitched tone, upon entering his surgery on Warwick Street in Batley Carr.

"Oi! Is he in!" repeated my great, great grandma with a sarcastic tone.

Giddy women would be phoning him every hour.

When patients died back in those days, they used to wrap corpses up in rugs and place pennies on their eyelids to keep them closed. This was the procedure that Herbert used, as opposed to now, when you have an open casket in a public ceremony.

He was the first person to own a car in Batley, West Yorkshire, which he idolised, although it wasn't very reliable. The vehicle was so slow and he had a couple of minor crashes with other passing cars.

His sister, Dolly, was an elegant, vigorous, independent woman just short of five foot in height. She resided in London with prominent, bleached hair, glowing red lips and an alluring "hey darlings" squeaky tone. She adored her makeup as much as she loved her cigarettes and lived the life of luxury.

I recall my grandma walking me past great, great granddad Schofield's house when I was a teen, indulging me in stories about our superior family history. I have always envisaged Aunty Dolly to being similar to Dolly Parton because of the way grandma described her. These stories of the relatives that we look up to will be forever treasured with pride.

Spirituality also had an influential part in the lives of our family members for generations. My mum and my grandma use their spiritual gifts to aid health and provide guidance to various people who visit their healing room from around the UK and overseas. They are both renowned for their ability to tune into the spirit world and for their compassion for others.

Spiritual remedial has helped me to overcome many episodes that I've had with my mental health. It has also helps me to feel guided on my path enables me to thrive and achieve. I have physically seen and experienced things myself, making me a huge advocate of spirituality and the afterlife, as all of my family are.

My great grandma, Mary, was affectionately known by my immediate family members as 'Taxi grandma,' because we used to travel in a taxi every Sunday to her bungalow in Thornhill Edge, Dewsbury. She admired theatre and had an ingenious love for writing in the same sense that I do. I remember her having what used to call a "magical bookshelf" at the age of six in her flowery wallpapered living room. I would borrow books written by various authors including Catherine Cookson and Daphne du Maurier and take them home in Batley, then return them the week after.

The fascination which I developed for storytelling was inspired by these novels. I began to imagine my own stories and express them through various art forms, including live performance poetry. I am not an actor by any standard but I'm open-minded about performing the roles of different characters and it helps me develop my self-confidence. I am an Aquarius, so I have always had the eccentricity within me to be able to try it! I had the habit of gallivanting around the house with a t-shirt on my head, pretending to be Roald Dahl's Veruca Salt or Alanis Morissette at the age of seven.

I identify myself as a man but every now and then I love to tap into my feminine side and become someone of the opposite sex for a temporary moment. I believe it is completely healthy to transition yourself into any possible living form of nature. It doesn't matter what your sexual orientation is. The mysteriousness of wondering what a mental and physical attribute could feel like is fascinating. For example, I sometimes wonder what the sensory experience of a woman is like whilst she is having sexual intercourse with a man. And what the ethereal experience of death would be like too. I also wonder what it would be like to be completely free from mental health struggles, where the psyche is no longer fabricating fucked up irrational thoughts and forcing us to live under false pretences.

I think we all take in the realities of everyday life in our own individual ways, yet still feel vulnerable and inquisitive about the unknown. The realms of spirituality and the arts are forces to be reckoned with. Those platforms can indeed challenge perceptions of ourselves, the outside world and beyond.

Since theatre has been a big part of my family's lives through generations, it's been a privilege to carry on this tradition through my own performances. It's also a brilliant way to honour those who have passed, particularly my great, great grandad and my great grandma.

Here are the lyrics to my great, great grandad's song and sheet music, which won the Yorkshire and Lancashire Song contest. It is about a mother grieving after sending her son to war.

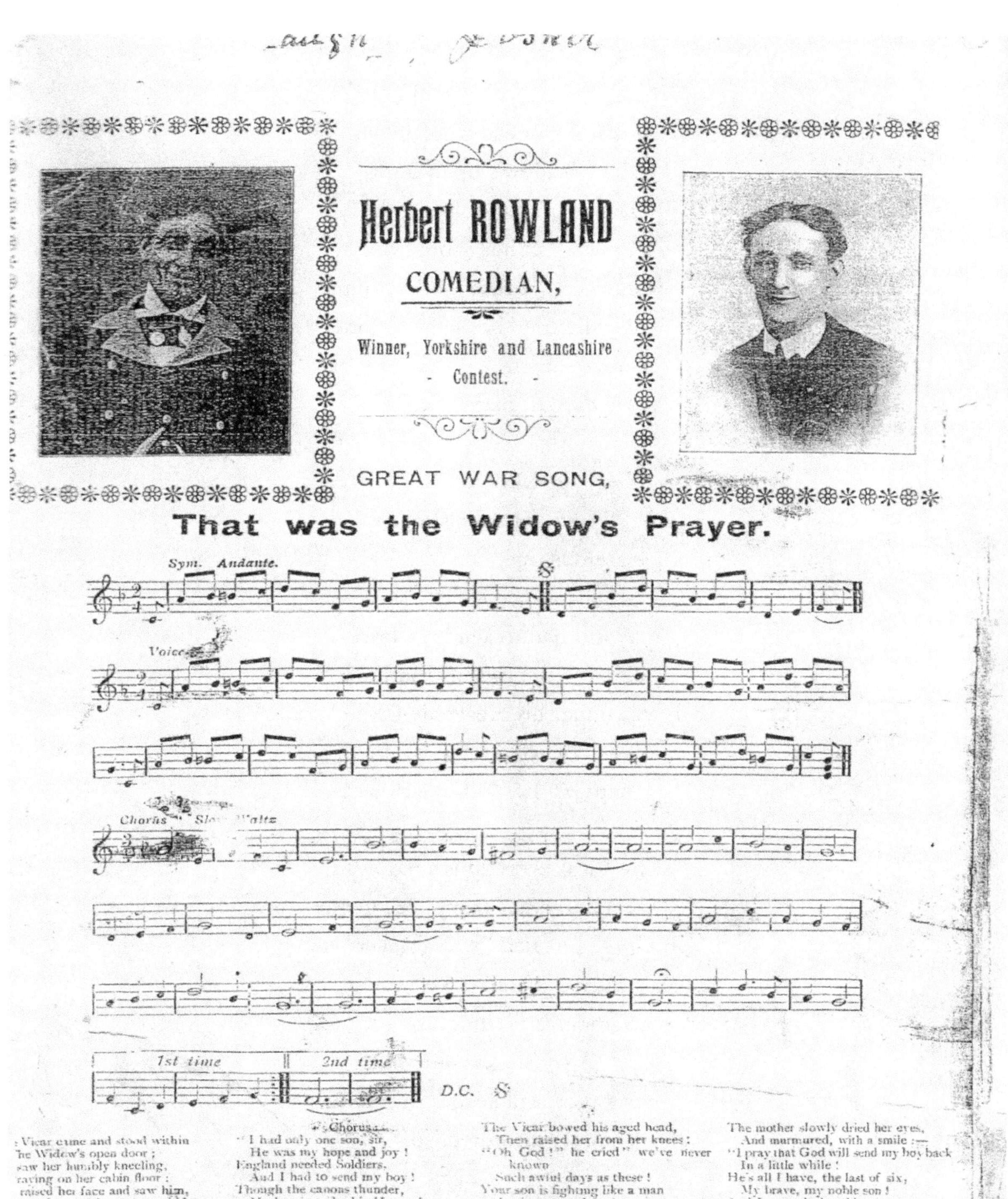

(Above) The original Music Sheet

That was the Widow's Prayer

The Vicar came and stood within
The Widow's open door,
He saw her humbly kneeling,
Praying on her cabin floor;
She raised her face and saw him,
Then she tried her tears to hide,
"Forgive me, sir, for weeping, but
'Tis hard to bear!" she cried:

Chorus:
"I had only one son, sir,
He was my hope and joy!
England needed Soldiers,
And I had to send my boy!
Though the canons thunder,
My boy is under his Heavenly Father's care;
Oh Lord! Thy will, not mine, be done!"
That was the Widow's Prayer.

The Vicar bowed his aged head,
Then raised her from her knees:
"Oh God!" he cried "we've never known
Such awful days as these!
Your son is fighting like a man
Against a cruel foe!
And God will keep him safe!"
The Widow murmured, soft and low:

Chorus:
"I had only one son, sir,
He was my hope and joy!
England needed Soldiers,
And I had to send my boy!
Though the canons thunder,
My boy is under his Heavenly Father's care;
Oh Lord! Thy will, not mine, be done!"
That was the Widow's Prayer.

The mother slowly dried her eyes,
And murmured, with a smile:
"I pray that God will send my boy back
In a little while!
He's all I have, the last of six,
My brave, my noble son!
And I can only humbly pray,
Oh God! Thy will be done!"

Chorus:
"I had only one son, sir,
He was my hope and joy!
England needed Soldiers,
And I had to send my boy!
Though the canons thunder,
My boy is under his Heavenly Father's care;
Oh Lord! Thy will, not mine, be done!"
That was the Widow's Prayer.

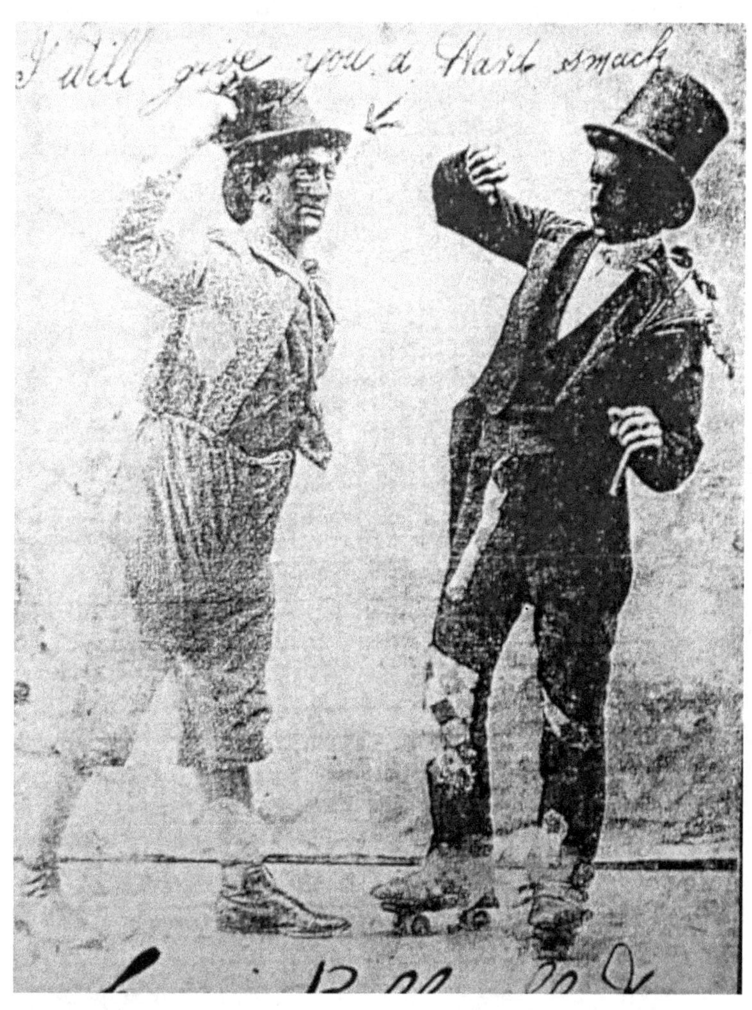

Great Grandad Herbert performing on a UK Music Hall Stage.

OH ALAN TITCHMARSH!

Oh! Fancy a man like Alan Titchmarsh revamping my lawn,
A bedazzling surprise at the sudden crack of dawn,
To pull back your curtains and witness the man,
Rejuvenating my garden to the best that he can!

I never knew he could make me blush with his agricultural powers,
Shovelling the earth with a blanket of flowers,
Oh, he can mow my garden any day of the week,
The fun and the frolics with his agrarian streak!

How I have admired him since the peak of his career,
The compulsion and the obsession and the loving revere,
How I made my husband file for a divorce,
Since the moment I saw Alan on the vintage Ground Force!

Oh Alan, how you ferment me, if only you know,
The way you plough my crops, with your long garden hoe,
You are my agronomist, my florist and intellectually wise,
With your draconian grin and those big iris eyes!

Oh Alan! You are my world! You are so brawny and strong,
Having a gentlemen like you, how can I go wrong?
The way you fondle and regravel my dried up dead weeds,
and the knowledge of satisfaction with my gardening needs!

Oh Alan Titchmarsh! Please make me your wife!
You are my gardening monarch, you are the love of my life!
Marry me under your prickly fir tree,
Oh Alan Titchmarsh, you are the only man for me!

Thursday 6th September 2018

I arrived at 'The Big Comfy Bookshop' in The Fargo Village in Coventry at 7:30pm for this evening's poetry event called 'Fire and Dust'.

"Do you know where 'The Big Comfy Bookshop' is?" I asked a beautiful black girl named Miloni, with glitter glossed lips literally standing outside the homely, quirky venue. The bookshop's intimate interior is a utopia for dedicated bookworms. Almost like a shrine filled to the brim with eclectic books written by the greatest pioneers of literature. A bookshop of distinctive value.

"It is literally there." Miloni answered, pointing with a smile.

I would subsequently sit with her and her male friend at the front table for the evening. Miloni was the third last poet to grace the open mic spot during the second half after the brilliant guest poet, Adam Smith, delivered his material. Miloni actually lives here in Coventry but studies Politics at Manchester Metropolitan University.

I was the sixth or seventh performer to grace the microphone, showcasing my material to an adequately large audience. I performed my two anecdotes "Oh Alan Titchmarsh" and "My Husband Has Booked Our Funeral." My material seemed to have been well received by the Coventry crowd. A couple of enthusiastic middle-aged women approached me during the interval with a smile and commended me for my whimsy material. I appreciated their compliments.

A senior Poet named John concluded the first half with a twenty-minute guest set of his material which was predominantly inspired by the prolific writer Phillip Larkin.

"Fire and Dust" is a brilliant poetry event compered by an extremely welcoming man named Rafael. It commenced at 8pm and concluded at 10:15pm.

I returned to The Highcroft Guest House Hotel at approximately 11pm. I headed back to Yorkshire the following day on the National Express coach, changing at Birmingham.

FLEAS!

I have discovered my inner independence again,
Today is the move,
I am going to reside in the city in a terraced house,
Based on Wellington Grove,
The top loft room is an advantage,
It is perfectly quintessential,
For a mature, developing adolescent,
This is a sweet little residential,
My housemates are admirable,
My outlook is an analogue.
The first couple of February lukewarm evenings,
I slept comfortably like a log,
But the "too good to be true" statement appeared,
It wasn't the perfect, amicable dream.
Things started to slope into despair,
They weren't as homely as they seemed,
The previous resident I am subletting from,
He previously had a cat,
The perfection of living.
Well, everything ended at that,
When I exerted my independence,
When life was becoming a breeze.
Now I am covered with blistering bites,
THE HOUSE IS FULL OF FLEAS!
I haven't slept well, for four whole nights,
My skin has become a feast,
The irritable scratching at the bites,
Which are now the size of a beast.
I have tried every repellent in existence,
To attempt to decrease the godforsaken gout,
I have blitzed the whole house, twice every day,
Just to get the bastards out!
6pm the infestation manifests,
I am living with this unbearable itch,
Infuriated with the devilish pests,
These fleas are such a bitch!
There is always a reasonable policy,
Of a strict no pet zone,
Because of intrusive predicaments like this happen,
When I am bitten to the bone!

I can't be having this with the time that I am here,

I can't be doing with this until June,

I don't expect to pay my well-earned money,

On a flea infested room!

The Predicament would be subsequently resolved,

The fleas have perished in vain,

Now, I can eventually reside in this terraced house,

To begin from "scratch" again!

Monday 18th February 2019

In the late afternoon, I left the little working-class town of Batley to reside in the nearby bustling city of Leeds. This would be my final day at the house where I had lived for the past fourteen years, excluding the three years when I was studying at university. My parents split up in June 2018, so I had no choice but to move out. My dad allowed me to decorate my parent's living room wall with my grand artistry. I made a gallery of sketches from my notebook for the next residents to enjoy. I stayed with my sister, Chloe, at her flat for a couple of weeks then moved into 11 Pennington Grove, Woodhouse, Leeds.

I had a fabulous four months living there with the beautiful Meghan and Andre. There were a lot of laughs along the way. And there were a couple of memorable moments including the drama of bailiffs turning up unannounced due to Meghan's bank account being overdrawn.

On the evening of Monday 8th April 2019, I performed my anecdote, "The Day My Gran Rode a Rollercoaster", at an event called 'Soundbite'. This was held at 'The Headingley Enterprise and Arts Centre' in Leeds. On returning home, I picked up a box of teabags and essentials from the local shop and snapped my key in half in the front door lock. How the hell I managed to do this is completely beyond me. I couldn't even say that it snapped. It melted like a Caramac bar in a child's sweet tooth cavity.

I was stood outside howling at the front door for a response from my housemates. Meghan thought it was the bailiffs banging at the door as she timidly walked towards the window, phoned me up and cautiously asked "Hello?"

"Hello," I replied and explained what had happened.

Meghan was cackling in her bedroom because Andre was on the phone cursing his brother to come over and repair the lock in his Romanian native accent. I couldn't help cackling to myself downstairs and choked on my Cheerios to avoid being obviously amused at what had happened. Anyhow, the key situation was resolved when Andre's brother cycled all the way from Harehills to rectify this predicament.

All went well that ended well, until we discovered a flea infestation which was left behind by the guy I was sub-letting from. My anecdote "Fleas" was based on a passage which I had written in my journal and adapted into a rhythmical rhyming verse. I sat up in bed virtually on the edge of breaking down as I wrote a section of the poem at 11:30pm on Sunday 24th February 2019. I completed it during a shift at the box office the following Thursday and read it out to Meghan and Andre when I returned home. They both loved it. Andre chuckled away in the kitchen.

We did everything we could to obliterate the pests. Andre fumigated the whole house with a mixture of white spirit and water, but this didn't resolve the issue. A week or two later, the fleas disappeared thanks to the help of Pest Control. I forced the previous tenant to foot the bill as he ran off with my rent money. Although, without this unique experience, I wouldn't have had the inspiration to write my anecdote and create an animation film. I commenced work on my animation project during September 2019 in the basement flat that I moved into at North Lodge House, on the morning of Saturday 24th August 2019.

Monday 16th September 2019

Today I embarked on a new animation project. My mind was buzzing with concepts of what I should create but being the undecisive artist that I was, I had no idea what to do.

At approximately 8pm, I changed into my black top and shorts ready to shoot several stills of myself looking perturbed. I sat on my chair posing in front of the camera on a tripod in my basement room. I was going to rotoscope for much of this project. Rotoscoping (for any readers who are unaware,) is a term where animators capture live action footage, then replicate this frame by frame as a traced drawing, which is then put together to be viewed as animation. It is tediously time-consuming, but the result is epic.

I sat down at my workstation, underneath the window, to sketch out a rough depiction of Pennington Grove. This visual didn't make the final edit, although an intricate portrayal of 'a terraced house' looked far more appealing.

Tuesday 17th September 2019

At 8am, I resumed work on the current project. I decided to retrace the image of Pennington Grove, as I wasn't satisfied with the original illustration, which is now pinned up on the wall beneath my window. At 10am, I took a break to find a repair shop for my laptop, which had decided to break down. Without having any luck repairing it, the wonderful heroic IT Technician at the Playhouse, Ross Bownes, had the device up and running again by mid-October.

Later on in the afternoon, I photographed a sequence of images commencing with the window of my room then navigated my camera towards my bed. I then filmed myself in character climbing onto my bed at long shot and at head on frontal view. Following this, I changed to side angle showing the character asleep in bed, until he turns slightly onto his back and gradually sits up upright. Returning to long shot and frontal view, he would slightly look to the left then take his focus to the right. An improvised performance takes place at that point, of a cat climbing up and descending from his bed. This sequence was created using four free hand drawings of a cat silhouette which was cut out. They were chronologically placed onto the visuals of the character sat upright in bed, then played back to show movement.

Saturday 21st September 2019

Shot by shot, I created the animation depicting the gradual linear development of a bird cage. I rotoscoped two individual birds, by creating separate templates of wings moving up and down. This was designed to create a moving sequence of birds flying. Once the cage was in full view, I placed a bird in the middle of it. The bird was fading in gradually, and I did this by filming sequences of its image, which appeared to look darker on three separate sheets of tracing paper. The bird would ascend from its cage, so I used three templates for this. I thought it would look good to have my left hand appearing and opening the cage door to let the bird fly out, so I did. I worked on this sequence from 8:45am until 11:40am.

Sunday 22nd September 2019

Mid-afternoon, I reproduced the image of the bird cage and erased the sketch in each frame, to create the illusion of it fading out. I did attempt to create a silhouette of the Leeds sky-line but felt that the image didn't work well with the overall project. It didn't provide counterbalance and didn't marry up well with the accompanying visuals. I have also reached the conclusion not to use the original drawing of Pennington Grove and decided to go with a frontal view of a terraced house, which I drew free hand. I made this fade in using the same techniques that I used for the opening bird cage scene.

Monday 23rd September 2019

Between 9:30am and 10:20am, I sat down at my workstation to resume my animation project. I placed a piece of tracing paper over the surface of the laptop screen and traced five different photographs of my startled expression. This sequence will be used simultaneously with the following line -

"THE HOUSE IS FULL FLEAS!"

Once the drawings were complete, I embedded the visuals onto a key frame, to see if they would marry together as a motion visual and they did. I then headed out for a run, returning home at 11:50am.

I spent a good hour, from 2pm, working on the 'startled expression' sequence. I had an idea to add a swarm of fleas crawling out of my ears. I made a handful of black one-inch square cut outs and laid them out on the table. I captured them on my camera and moved the squares a fraction and took another shot to generate the impression of a moving swarm. It didn't work well though, so I subsequently scrapped this idea.

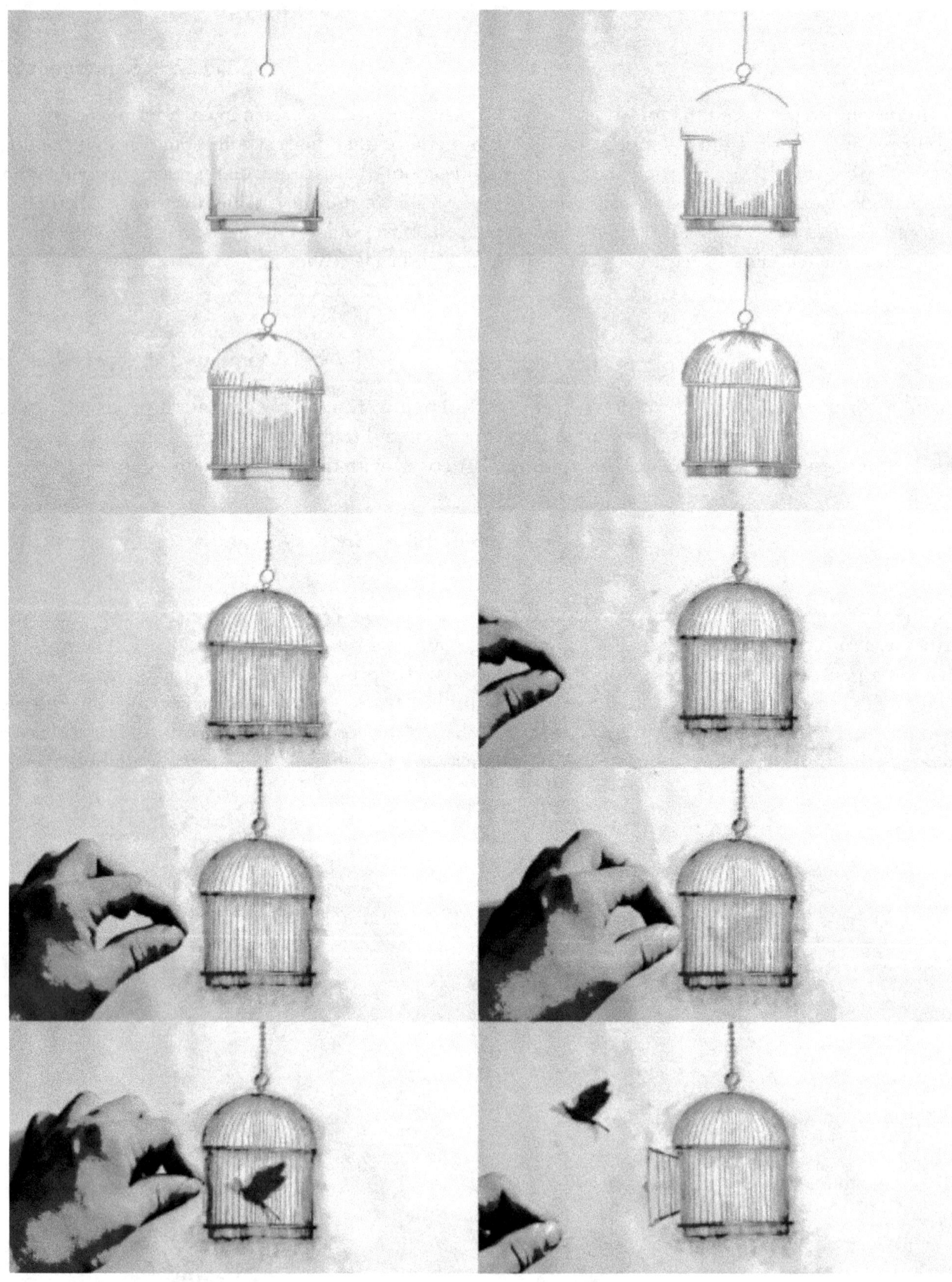

"The birdcage sequence"

Tuesday 24th September 2019

Between 10:30am and 1:05pm, I reverted to a half-drawn sketch, which was a template of a bedroom; the bay window was positioned centrally with a view of the rooftops on the opposite side of the road. A bird would comfortably perch on the outside ledge, twitching its head from left to right. I drew the furnishings separately the next day. This allowed me to show the room evolving gradually in the animation using separate photographs. I wasn't initially taken by the sequence but grew to like it more later on.

Friday 27th September 2019

I continued with the animation for an hour or so this evening, collating the photographic images from last Tuesday. I carried out a screen test to grasp a sense of what the end-result would look like. I was confidently satisfied.

Over the course of the following weekend, I took the opportunity to connect the sequences together. And whilst editing the visuals on my mobile phone, I opted for a cartoon effect and filtered the brightness and saturation levels. I transferred the edits back onto the laptop again, to form 30 second GIF clip then put this back onto my phone… This sounds all too technical I know, but it was around this time when I wanted to provide the viewer with something a little different in comparison to my previous projects. The subtle cartoon effect allowed me to do this. Three hundred and seventy-three photos have been collated so far for this developing project. I'm feeling optimistic after seeing the evidence of how it may look like a final edit. It encouraged me to progress with the project even further.

Saturday 28th September 2019

I sketched out a flea replicate, which was copied from the original template. I also drew a replicate of drawer to make it look like it was opening. Two devilish Fleas would appear in pairs.

Tuesday 1st October 2019

I recorded the narration of the "FLEAS" anecdote, sat at my workstation in the basement room, at approximately midday. This required several takes in order to achieve a perfect vocal tone.

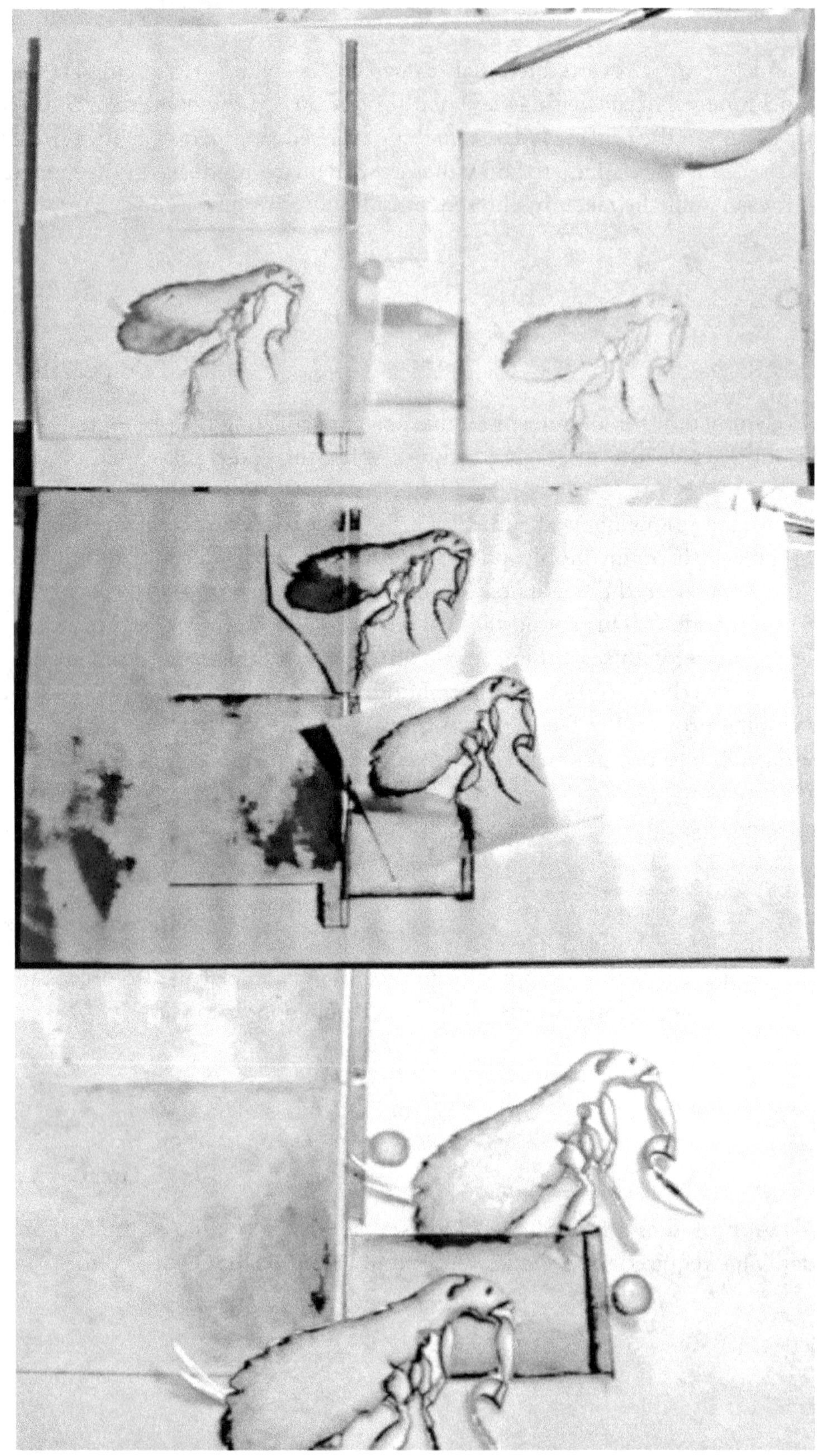

Developing the scene for when the flea's creep out from the drawers.

Tuesday 8th October 2019

Between 10:30am and 12:15pm, I traced a film clip of me performing "The Granny Zimmer Frame Race" poem. This footage was made at a gig of called 'Word of Mouth,' based at The Leeds Student Union, in March of this year. I tied the resulting animation with the line: -

"My outlook is an analogue."

I wanted to show myself being content living in the city again and venturing around locally, doing what I do best and that is to perform. There were just over 30 frames of drawings prepared for this two second segment. I photographed the frames in the correct order on my workstation and played back the images to see how effective the resulting animation was. It was comfortably effective.

Wednesday 9th October 2019

I extended the sequence from yesterday and added some improvements. I also re-photographed the 'poetry performance' sequence at my workstation. I felt a little apprehensive of what the clip played back, but after looking at it with a new perspective, I grew more confident that I could work on it and make it better.

Thursday 17th October 2020

I rotoscoped a linear image of the city, to go in the opening section of the animation. A train cattle truck would rattle along the tracks, as farm animals pass by. This train would then veer out of view to lead the way for the city visual to appear. I decided to change my mind about using the city image later on and re-placed this with a scrolling sign saying "Welcome to Leeds."

Sunday 20th October 2019

I spent much of my time dipping in and out of the project throughout the course of today. I produced a rotoscoped visual looking up at The LS6 Cafe, to place before the sequence of me performing. This was the venue I performed at on Thursday 21st February 2019 which the flea fiasco happened. I wanted the animation to have an autobiographical feel to it and capture what actually happened during that time. I kept delving into my journal to check on what was occurring then and to help me jigsaw the narrative together. I personally felt more hopeful about what I could do as an artist now, that I have worked on this project.

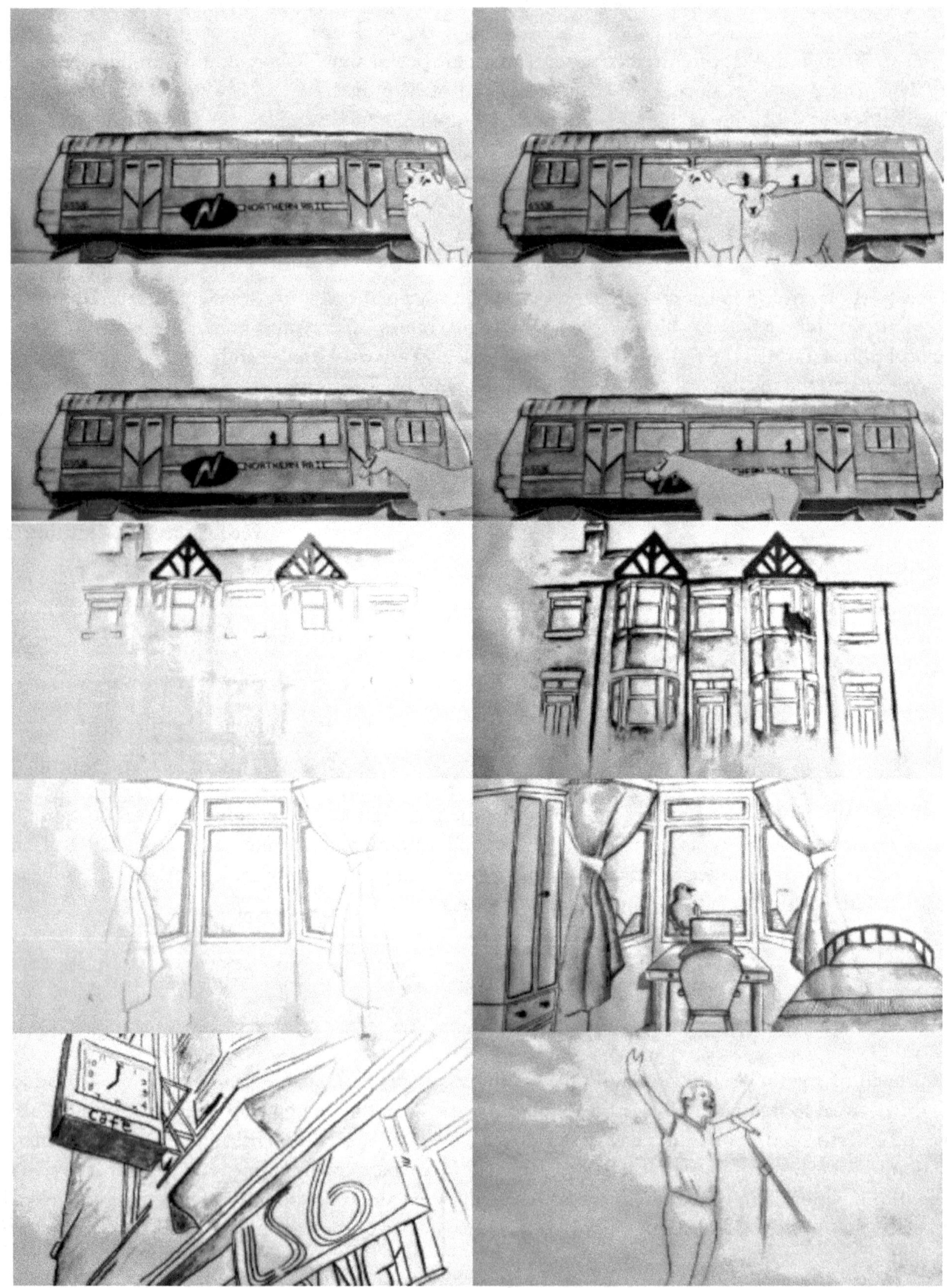

Verse 1 and Verse 2 -

1 - "Welcome to Leeds" scene
2 - Animation sequence of the exterior and interior appearing visuals
3 - LS6 Cafe "My outlook is an analogue"

Monday 21st October 2019

I made ten photocopies of the side profile of a flea, to use for this evening's sequence which portrayed the first appearance of the demonic fleas. The idea was to show one of them scrambling out from a bottom drawer of a cupboard and another creeping in view on the floor below. By key framing, I made the fleas look as if they were slowly swaying from side to side, which helped to add more interest whilst the background was completely at a standstill. Whilst the second flea scurried over to the right-hand side of the screen and out of view, the first flea crawled back into the drawer and vanished out of sight. In order to achieve the flea's disappearing act, I literally cut away parts of the flea, to give the viewer the impression that this pest is heading back into hiding. To overlap live action footage with animation, I keyframed my right hand closing the drawer. At 8:20pm I concluded work on the animation.

Tuesday 22nd October 2019

Between 9pm until midnight, I spent my time editing the "Fleas" animation. The screen test sequences which I merged as a Gif Video has now been compiled into MovAvi. I synced the clips together in MovieMaker, then transferred the keyframing video onto the professional editor. I then adjusted the contrast, brightness and gamma. I also added a Vignette 7 value, an old age film effect, to enhance the overall visual quality of the clip. This brief animation which I have produced so far links with the first verse of my poem. Verse two is about the flea manifestation of a bedroom and the LS6 Cafe where the character performs on stage. Verse Three refers to the cat strutting on the bed and the character being asleep. Fast forwarding to verse nine, this focusses on a victorious looking clock, where two fleas, position themselves glancing up at the antique at either side until a pair of menacing eyes emerge from the bottom of the screen. Some of these scenes will have overlapping visuals using a half grade opacity tool. This will give the overall clip a vintage appearance and make it more appealing.

Wednesday 23rd October 2019

I edited the photos on my phone that I had compiled earlier to create a sequence of a pest control van called "Good Riddens", slowly pulling up and parking outside of the victorious looking terraced house. I completed this the next day.

Later, I created a scene of war between a tight gathering of fleas and a bottle of pesticide. I visualised this scene in my head, thinking this would be effective. Using a photocopier, I made ten copies of a flea drawing the other morning whilst in the box office. I cut out around eight of them. Two of the fleas would take the ultimate lead in the battle scene, protecting themselves with a riot shield. The remaining fleas would huddle together and march behind their leaders. A bottle of flea killer would appear from the right-hand side of the screen and the battle would commence as soon as the pesticide is sprayed. A flea would leap up onto the spray lever, swinging consistently from side to side to banish the conflict.

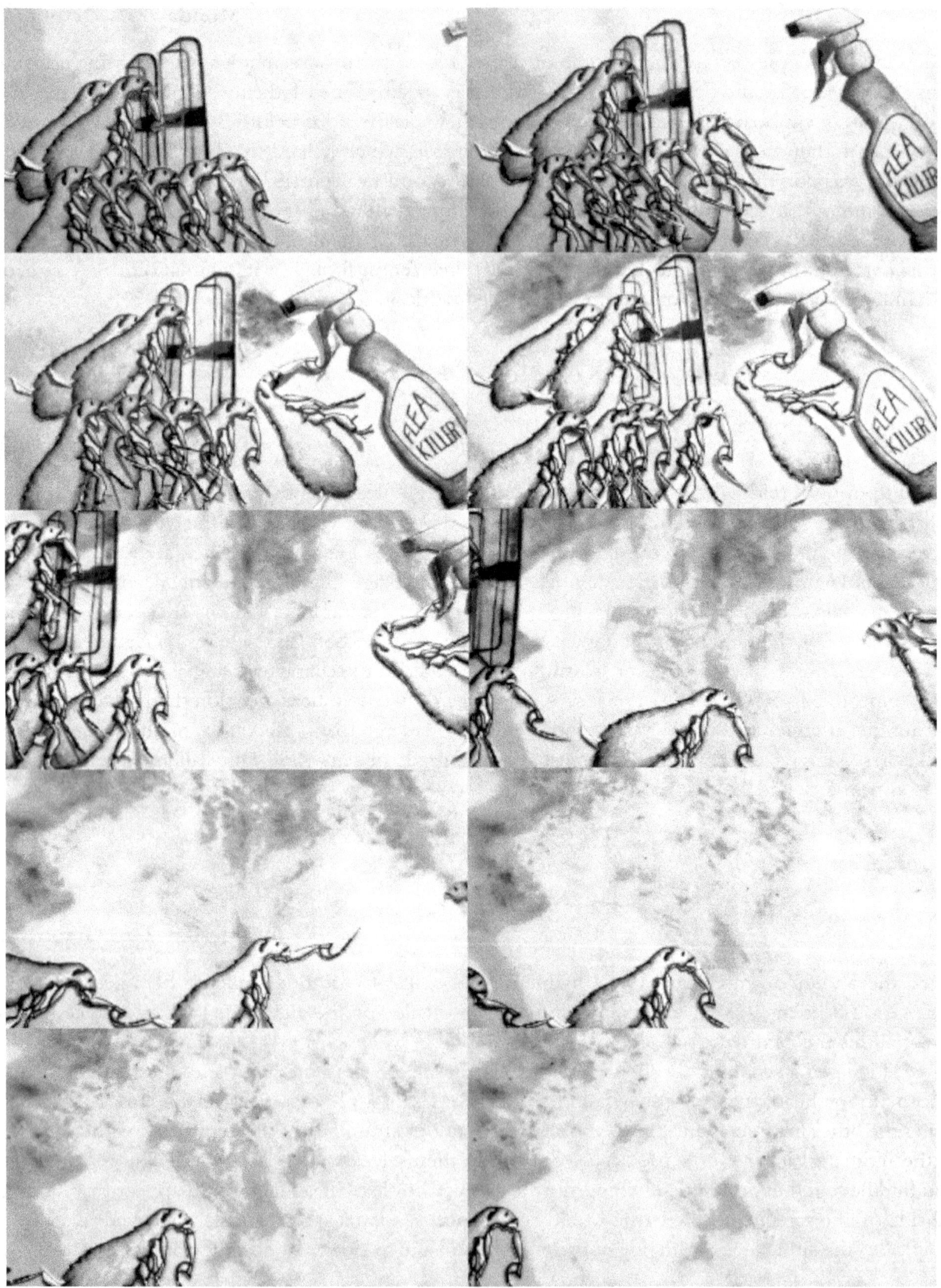

"The bleach war sequence"

I completed half of this sequence at my workstation, later editing the visuals on my phone then transferred them onto MovAvi. I completed the entire war scene, on the evening of Friday 25th October 2019, after experiencing a surge of experimental creativity. I also finished embedding the line -

"THE HOUSE IS FULL OF FLEAS!"

I created the portrait of the character's apprehensive expression and overlapped this with visuals of fleas, scattered all over his face. The terraced house would faintly appear within the same scene. I subsequently recorded the voice-over using some of the "Fleas" poem and added this to the relevant sections of the animation before returning to bed at midnight.

Wednesday 30th October 2019

I headed out for a run between 9am and 9:50am, had a shower, then resumed work on my animation. I concentrated on embedding the following lines:

"There is always a reasonable policy,
For a strict No Pet Zone,
Because intrusive predicaments like this happen,
When I am bitten to the bone!"

I key framed a flea using the force of its legs rolling a "No Pets" sign from the left-hand side of the screen to the right. I did this by making two separate cut outs of the flea and the sign. I also photographed a head-on frontal view of a character's apprehensive looking face, which I rotoscoped as an animation template.

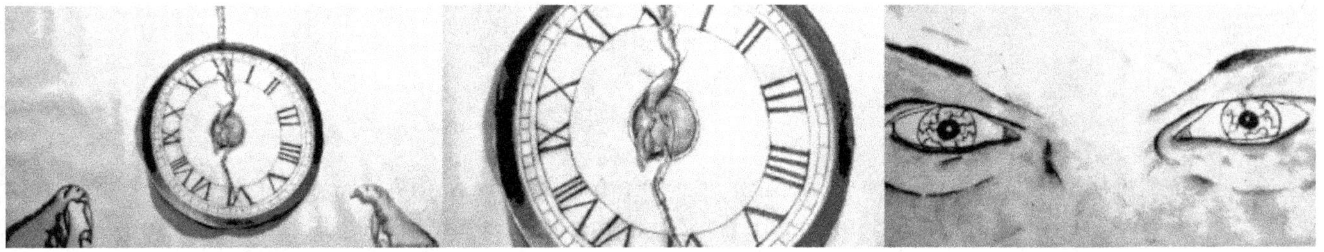

(Above) *"6pm the infestation manifests"*

I then made a cut out of his skull as I planned to have a herd of fleas gnawing at the character's flesh. This would link metaphorically with the accompanying narrative: "bitten to the bone". The eventual scene would play out with the cranium rolling to the right and out of view.

Thursday 31st October 2019

I resumed work on my animation at 9pm and prepared the templates for the following lines -

"I haven't slept well for four whole nights,
My skin is becoming a feast."

An initial concept was to have the character's corpse on display at a meat market stall, owned by fleas titled "Get Your Flesh Here!" Even though it seemed a good idea at first, I didn't feel it would be effective enough. Alternatively, I filmed myself slightly turning away from the camera in my bed, to represent the above narrative. I also took photographs of my abysmal facial expression, so that I can use this opportunity to add animated eyes. Using three recordings, I rotoscoped the visuals and merged them together to create this scene.

Saturday 2nd November 2019

After two months, which at times were strenuous, I pushed on with this much invested project and completed "Fleas" this evening at 8:30pm. I added finishing touches to some of the clips to give the overall film the important finished look. I inserted sound effects to add a extra sense of realism in certain parts. I completed the final scene where the fleas create havoc in the bedroom. Two are destroying the space and a third one is bouncing erratically on the bed. Simultaneously, I added the following lines:

"I can't be doing with this until June,
I don't want to spend my well-earned money,
On a flea infested room!"

The soundtrack which I used for the animation, is by Funny Background Music, titled "Curious Tip Toe." The mischievous macabre sound complimented the wittiness and whimsy feel of this animation.

On its completion, I sent the animation to my very good friends, Laurence Inman and Lisa Boardman, to critique. They were absolutely impressed with it, which made me feel more optimistic about the overall result. I was very excited about releasing this at various film festivals around the UK.

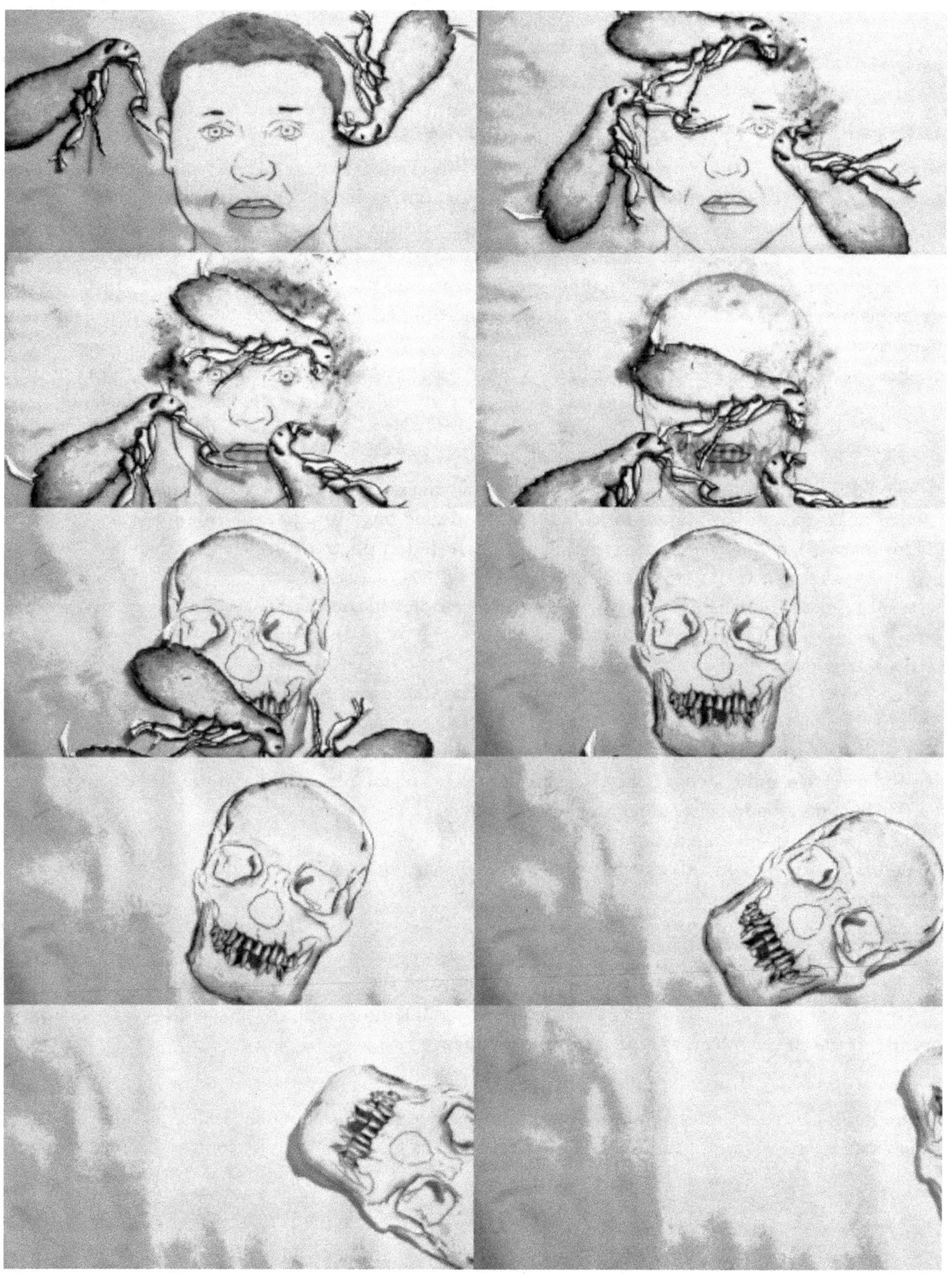

The sequence for "Bitten to the bone!"

Saturday 9th November 2019

I arrived in a very dark, autumnal London on a Megabus at 4:45pm, with soaking rain throwing down from the bipolar Siberian sky. I journeyed the 2.2 mile radius by foot from London Victoria to The Cinema Museum based in Elephant and Castle. I was heading for this evening's event "The Exploding Cinema" where "Fleas" was on the screening bill. It was the fourth short film to be shown in the second half.

On arrival, I was asked by an artist named Dennis da Silva if I was interested in dressing up and performing as a gay Portuguese seahorse, as part of his live performance this evening accompanied by a short film. He approached me whilst we waited for the doors to open at the Cinema Museum. The reason being was that his main actor apparently walked out on him at the last hurdle. I declined. His live visual performance was titled "Tamesis."

It was lovely to see my animation being played on a big screen in front of a bunch of film enthusiasts. When this clip lasting three minutes and thirty-one seconds ended, Adam, the host for the evening, invited me onto the stage for an informal Q&A.

"Hello," I spoke into the microphone, getting somewhat comfortable on the platform.

Adam in his snazzy hat, smiled from his podium beside me. "OK Jamie," Adam began. "It's a lovely little film there. Erm, it seems to me that you are interested in poetry as well as filmmaking. There seems to be a connection between words and images in this film, is that right?"

"Yes." I replied, "Normally, I link my whimsical anecdotes to my animations and at certain events, I do perform alongside them as a live recital. That is what I love to do - narrating them live." I answered, whilst my arms became animated during my speech.

"OK, yeah …" he said "you could probably do that here sometime if you wanted?"

"Yeah", I smiled, "that would be great. We could figure it out."

"So yeah…" Adam asked with a curious pause, "Is this based on a real-life experience?" In order not to repeat the narrative and concept behind the anecdote, I explained to Adam and the audience of the crisis that I, Meghan and Andrei encountered when residing in the house full of fleas.

"And you turned your experiences into a film?" Adam asked.

"Yes, I did." I answered, adding that they were first written as a poem, which I then decided to adapt into an animation.

"OK, that was one of the things I was interested in." Adam smiled. He subsequently opened the floor for questions from the audience.

I talked about making the tenant pay for the pest control fees and about the processes I used to create the project with including rotoscoping and manipulating 2D and 3D cut out images. I was thanked for my time and left the stage with an applause from the audience.

"Exploding Cinema" commenced at 7:10pm and ended at approximately 10:30pm. With the help of Google's satellite navigation, I returned to London Victoria Coach Station by foot.

Saturday 11th January 2020

"Fleas" was selected along with seventeen other films, to be screened this evening, as part of "The Leamington Film Festival" based at The Temperance in Leamington Spa. The Festival was sold out. I was making my way there on the bus, when I missed the e mail from Adrian Gaines, the festival and venue owner, stating that I may have to attend the next day after. But he did manage to squeeze me in to the petite Magic Lantern room when I got there. My animation was the tenth film to be showcased, during the second half. They were also some other interesting films scheduled within the three-hour programme, including a fifty-one minute documentary titled "I Am Dyslexic," directed by a Thom Davies, depicting the personal experiences of five people living with dyslexia.

My attendance led me to meet Mandy Kerr, the Executive Director of a theatre organisation called Heartbreak Productions. They were celebrating thirty years of working in the arts. She sat beside me during the event with her husband and kindly treated me to a lemon drizzle cake during the fifteen-minute interval. When the evening ended, she gave me one of her business cards.

Brian Harley, the founder of "Roots to Shoot" film night, where I have screened my work many times, kindly agreed to put me up for the night as a cheeky last-minute favour.

Wednesday 22nd January 2020

I arrived at the Birmingham Digbeth Coach Station at approximately 2:35pm and headed over to a nice Moroccan cafe called Kabura, just a little further up, on the opposite side of the road for a bite to eat and a cup of tea. I then walked 3.9 miles to The Artefact Cafe to attend "The Magic Cinema" event that was taking place this evening. My animation "Fleas" had been selected to be screened as part of an eclectic programme of short films showcased in the café's small back room. The event opened with an animated music video produced by a local filmmaker named Ben, who I sat with and spoke to as well as his girlfriend. "Fleas" was the second film to be shown during the first half. I stood up from my seat and introduced the animation with a very brief speech describing the inspiration behind it. It was very well received by the audience.

I befriended another Filmmaker by the name of Richard Rowbottom who screened his short film titled "Harpoon." This film was about the discovery of an octopus living in his basement room. It was also good to see Andy Howlett again, who was then curating "The Magic Cinema."

Upon exiting the cafe, a young Birmingham based animator briefly introduced himself to me. His name was Josh Leech. We got talking about our approaches in animation work whilst walking for a good two or three minutes. He recommended a social animation evening called "OverLeap" which was also based here in Birmingham. Josh had to leave for the nearby train station as I made my way back to Birmingham Digbeth coach station.

I thoroughly enjoyed performing "Fleas" as a stand-alone piece. It is one of the most fascinating anecdotes to perform on the poetry circuit, inspired by an unexpected experience which is fun to share with the audience.

Monday 2nd December 2019

Zoe, a student with shoulder length hair and red ringlets, welcomed me onto the stage in the basement space at The Hyde Park Book Club in Leeds. I performed my anecdotes "Fleas" and "Thirty Pence to Have a Piss?!" to a crowd of students. This was part of the LUU Spoken Word Society event, in aid of "Homeless" Charity. It was a fantastic experience to deliver a four-minute set of whimsies to a public gathering. There were some fascinating poets who shared their verbal splurge of artistry during this glacial December evening. I had a few senior doctors congratulate me for my performances, whilst I was ordering myself a brew from the bar upstairs. I eternally thanked them and mentioned they could find my animation "Fleas" online.

Zoe closed the event with a few of her personal witty observational poems, shortly before 9pm. Afterwards, I took the ten-minute walk back to North Lodge House, via Woodhouse Lane.

"Fleas" Further showings:

In Other Words (A live recital) - The Crowd of Favours - Leeds, (2019)
In Other Words (A live recital) - Gulivers, NQ, Manchester (2019)
The Walthamstow International Film Festival - Walthamstow, (2021)

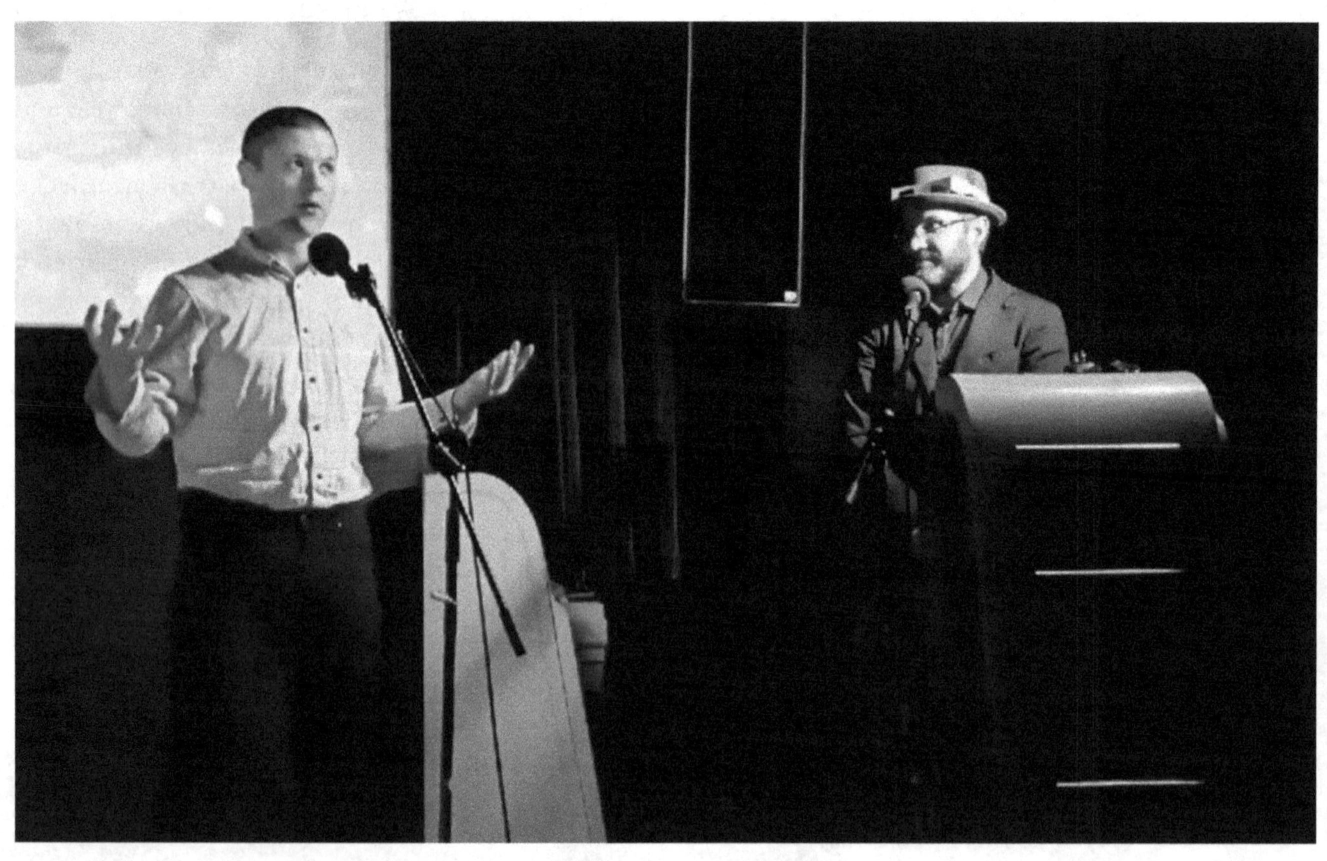

During a Q&A session after the screening of "FLEAS!"
Exploding Cinema, The Cinema Museum, London - 9/11/2019

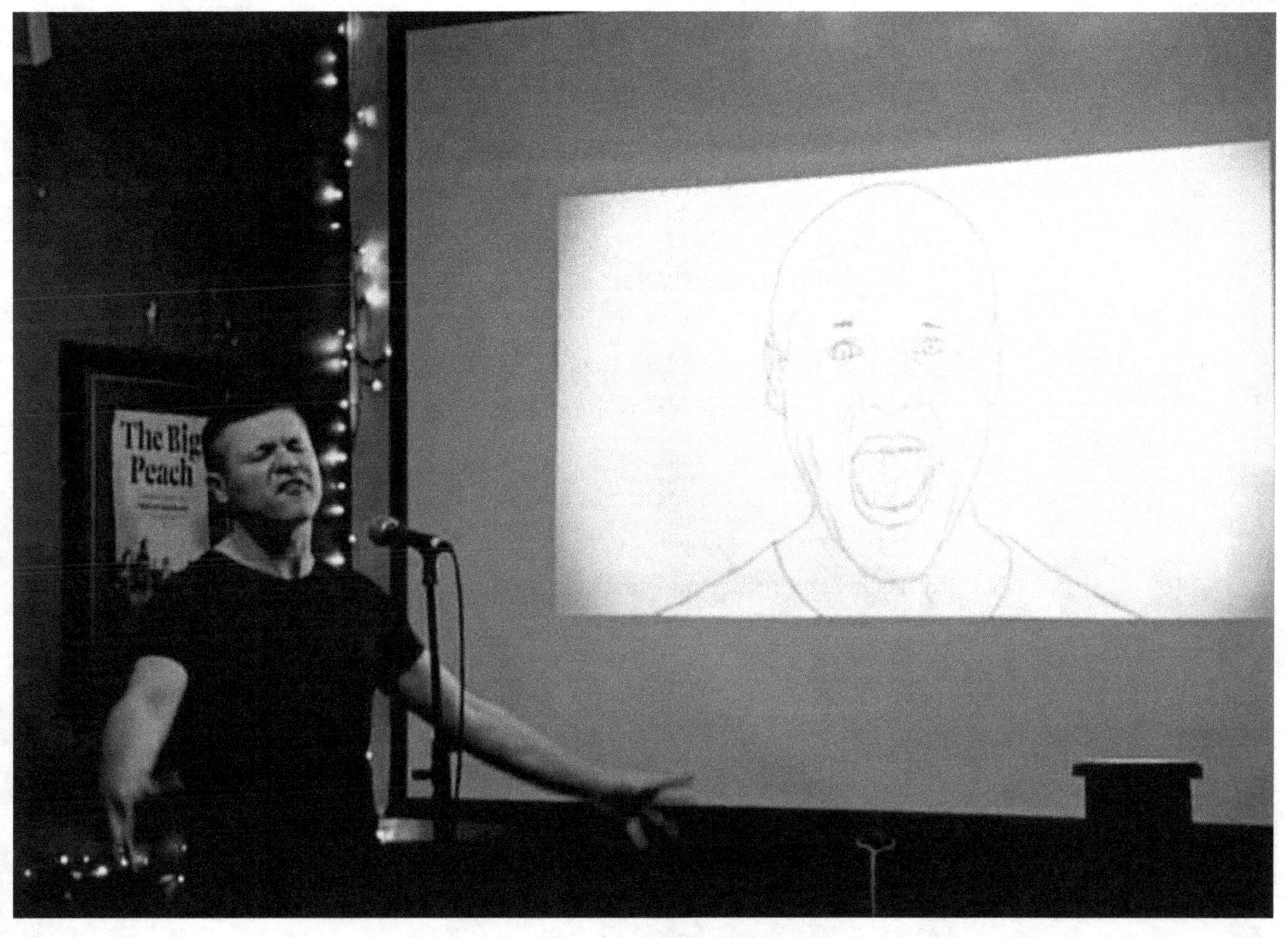

In Other Words - December 2019 edition
Performing alongside my Animation "FLEAS" based at Gullivers, NQ - Manchester
Photo courtesy of Lisa Boardman

The Fabulous Tom Ford

Whenever I am feeling gravely oppressed,
and my day is rather calamitous,
I take a trip to John Lewis and I sprinkle myself,
With Tom Ford's Fucking Fabulous.

I am always approached by a smiling assistant,
As if spraying a tester bottle is a sin,
But I need Tom's exotic, fruitful aroma positioned on my physique,
No other scent turns me on like him.

I get a flutter of excitement just admiring the bottle,
Every time my skin goes into dehydrated thirst,
But Mr Ford has every droplet of Fucking Fabulous in one little ounce,
His passion makes my armpits burst!

No other perfume gives me that arousing effect,
I have tried Tommy Hilfiger to Jimmy Choo,
But there is something about Mr Ford that lifts me with elation,
He tantalises me whenever I am feeling blue.

I have never sensed a scent as invigorating as his,
His bottle of exotic fusions has got me floored,
No other scent makes me sweetly stench like him,
No other brand does it like Tom Ford!

This Anecdote is narrated from the perspective of a lavish lady, who adores Tom Ford's new exotic perfume. "Fucking Fabulous" is the actual brand name. My lovely friend, Jo, and I used to take a trip to the John Lewis store based in The Victoria Quarter in Leeds, when we were on a lengthy break from the Playhouse. We would directly head straight to the perfume department and smother ourselves with the available tester. The name of the scent, for censorship reasons, was covered with a black sticker. We used to rip off the sticker and walk away. We are like two schoolgirls when together. The inspiration for this poem, came from our little trips, although the lavish lady, I feel, was more mature than what we are but still had our wit. I then introduced the brand to a beautiful friend, god bless her, named Sandy. We were just as mischievous, experimenting with all the latest trends, just before work and whenever we met in town. Again, observational perspectives and experiences, allow me to channel my inner poet, and to give birth to anecdotes like these.

Two Ladies On A Train

Monday 28th September 2020

I caught the 5:22pm Northern Service train back to Leeds from Blackpool North, where I briefly spoke with two middle-aged ladies by the names of Denise and Margy. They were getting off at Bradford Interchange. Well, they accidentally missed their stop as the train began heading towards Leeds.

"Here, where are we going now? The train is going the other way?" Margy curiously piped up, as they both ascended from their seats.

"Excuse me, you didn't let us off! Hello? You didn't let us off! We need Bradford!" Denise projected, as she made her path to the conductor's door, to project her panic.

"This is Bradford. You have just missed it." A man with headphones, calmly spoke. "Yeah we want Bradford!" Margy said, looking at Denise, who was still senselessly talking to a door.

Anyhow, the problem was resolved when they both alighted at New Pudsey and had to commute back to Bradford Interchange on the next expected service. Well, they sort of "alighted." Margy was already out standing on the platform with her abundance of suitcases, waiting for Denise to alight with her belongings too, until the door's started to close on her, nearly shipping her friend to Leeds.

"What the bloody hell is happening now?" Denise projected, as the doors closed. When Denise eventually alighted onto the platform, she made sure that the conductor was known as an "ARSEHOLE!"

I just sat there laughing, throughout the whole whimsical ordeal. I arrived home at approximately 9pm.

A Peculiar Imagination

I have always enjoyed the freedom of observing and interpreting existences in life through my own perspective. Since childhood, performing anecdotes has led me to being the kind of artist that I am today. There are different qualities in everyone. Mine is my own peculiar imagination. When I create new work, I experiment on my ideas in an improvisational manner as opposed to having a rigid plan to begin with. I feel restricted when methods of working are contained in strict frameworks. I have had many experiences where the result of my work has been the complete opposite to what I originally expected. It's remarkably compelling not knowing how my accomplishments will turn out.

Putting together my journal entries along with a collection of photographs and whimsical anecdotes, is a way for me to demonstrate my mental health experiences and how I like to express myself through art and everything in between.

Monday 19th March 2018

I have made a series of drawings to help build up my self-confidence today. I invested in an A4 hardback sketchbook this morning, as the current book that I have been dipping in and out of is literally crumbling apart. Sitting in the living room from midday to 8pm, I made three intricate and elaborate drawings in this new sketchbook. The first drawing, I titled "The Hellion Within Me," was an interpretation of the state of my own mental health. The second piece had an elderly lady's head, floating in the middle of the sea. She had a pensive look on her face as a small boat sailed on by. The third drawing was of a skull with a crow perched on top of it. None of these pieces had a narrative behind them. I just wanted to create which I did. I have been feeling a little apprehensive about myself as an artist, so this rapid sketching exercise helped me to pause and check if my work was good enough and continue my passion. Requiring reassurance is one of the main symptoms of anxiety and this is what I have been experiencing. I am satisfied with my drawings. I just need to start believing in myself.

Wednesday 21st March 2018

I decided to experiment with a drawing that I made in my new sketchbook. I had the idea of animating the elderly looking skeleton that had a crow standing on its head. I wanted to stretch my skills in animation. I don't think that the clip will become an important animation piece. It was purely for experimentation.

Using the same image of the skull in full frontal view. I drew another two versions which displayed changes to the crow's movements; one with its wings raised and another with its wings in a lower position. This enabled me to create a flying sequence. Frame by frame, the bird glided past the skull and eventually landed on the top of its head. The skull would then have a trail of sweat, trickling down its apprehensive looking face. I was going to have the crow pecking away at the skull until there was nothing left of it by this was yet to be completed.

Friday 23rd March 2018

I completed this very short animation which I started a couple of days ago and titled it "Come Dine with Me." The crow landed on the skull and subsequently pecked away at it. A second crow appeared from the left-hand side of the screen and began pecking simultaneously at the side of the skull. Both crows were made using hand drawn 2D cut outs, which I moved a couple of inches to achieve the appropriate motion frame by frame as a collection of photographic stills. I gradually erased sections of the skull to show that it was disappearing. Using a bold charcoal pencil, I made distinctive marks to portray the crumbs chipping off from the skull. The completed experimental animation lasted forty seconds in length and consisted of approximately ninety-seven photographs. I overlapped this with sound effects including loud caws and erratic noises of wings flapping to make the creatures appear more real. For the soundtrack, I used a royalty-free track composed by Kevin McLeod called "Chase Pulse," which was an excellent accompaniment for the two hungry crows.

I just wanted to experiment and bring my drawings to life and to see how they would form and marry as part of an animation. I had a vague idea of animating the whole of my sketchbook and combining my drawings as a short piece. I am still undecided about this concept. I was also undecided about whether to publicly screen "Come Dine With Me" to a live audience, or just keep it as a reference for future work. I'll figure it out, depending if I become immune or not to this small piece of work.

Saturday 24th March 2018

I drew another illustration in my sketchbook this evening as I relaxed in the living room when everyone was in bed. This piece was of a female rabbit holding a cigarette in her right hand. I decided to turn this into a twenty-second animation piece the next day. It took me approximately five hours to compose. This clip would begin with the rabbit appearing gradually as a still. I traced a replicate of the rabbit's arm from the original sketch, which I cut out so that I could make this move into different positions. A second cut out of a hand holding a burning match moves in from the left-hand side of the screen to light up a cigarette. The 'femme fatale' looking rabbit would inhale the smoke from the cigarette. Obscure ringlets of smoke would billow out from its ears. This smoke effect was simply created by adding charcoal to the image and erasing it repeatedly frame by frame. This consistent process made it look realistically like smoke. I then fused the photos together as a sequence in Moviemaker and extracted the video onto MovAvi Editor, to help sharpen the filter.

I thought about marrying up a dozen of my sketchbook drawings together to create a short animation film. This film would be different to the ones that I make with the inclusion of whimsical anecdotes like 'Fleas', but it would allow me to showcase my craftmanship, using different techniques. I have always been inspired to bring my drawings to life. Video art or short film is an effective way to achieve this.

Monday 26th March 2018

This afternoon, I begun to bring alive another sketch in animation format. This piece was called "The Hellion Within Me." Using the same process, I produced a template tracing an original illustration in my sketchbook. I photographed variations of this template. I was a little sceptical about whether my combined sketches would work well within one single animation.

As a working title for the Animation, I have decided on simply "Sketchbook."

This evening, I placed a royalty free soundtrack called Cabaret Noir onto the rabbit clip which was titled simultaneously as "She Must Be Proud." This helped to lift the mood.

Saturday 31st March 2018

Since midday, I have been experimenting on how to interpret my sketchbook illustrations in animation format. I used Visual Stop Motion Animation for this. Last night, whilst lounging on the couch at my Aunty Jenny's house, I drew a skeleton kneeling down on a jagged hilltop during a lightning storm. Rain was falling down from the grotesque, grey clouds. I decided to make an animation sequence for this. The cut out of the skeleton that I made was detached into sections, so that I could manipulate the movements of its individual parts and portray the skeleton climbing to the top of the hilltop. Using a rubber, graphite stick and pencil, I managed to draw the rain with various textures and ended the scene with the skeleton standing upright.

I went downstairs to edit what I had produced so far. I wasn't really taken by it at the time. I considered having butterflies flying out of the skeleton's mouth so I made various mediocre sized cut outs of the butterflies. I photographed their different movements, frame by frame, and checked this as a run through. Again, I still wasn't taken by this effect.

I completed the hand-drawn opening title - "The Hellion Within Me" and included a bolt of lightning from the top right-hand side of the screen. I abandoned this experimentation at 7:30pm. I wasn't excited about what I had created throughout the course of the day.

I felt overwhelmed not understanding what I was trying to achieve, even though it was part of an experimental exercise. I didn't want to end up with random, obscure sketches. Although this was the way to go in order to create an experimental film. The whole concept of the experimental film genre is about pushing creative boundaries and stepping out of the norms of creative practice and produce a moving picture which doesn't necessarily follow a structured narrative. There is a lot more freedom in running a project like this. "Sketchbook" is definitely opening me up as study of mine. It is stimulating, overwhelming and challenging but it does teach me to grasp ideas, adapt them and maintain my stamina.

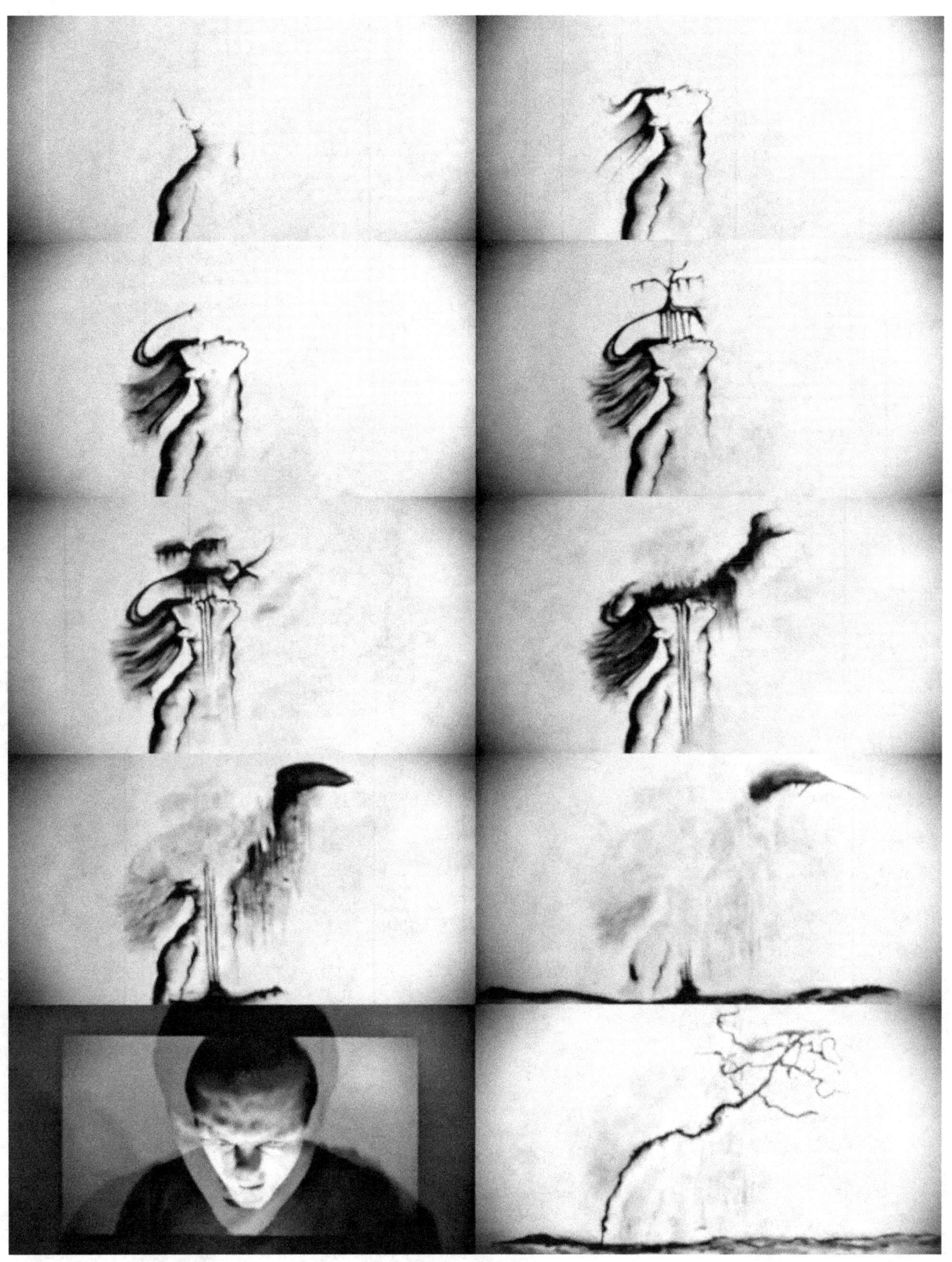

"The Hellion Within Me"
Animated sequence

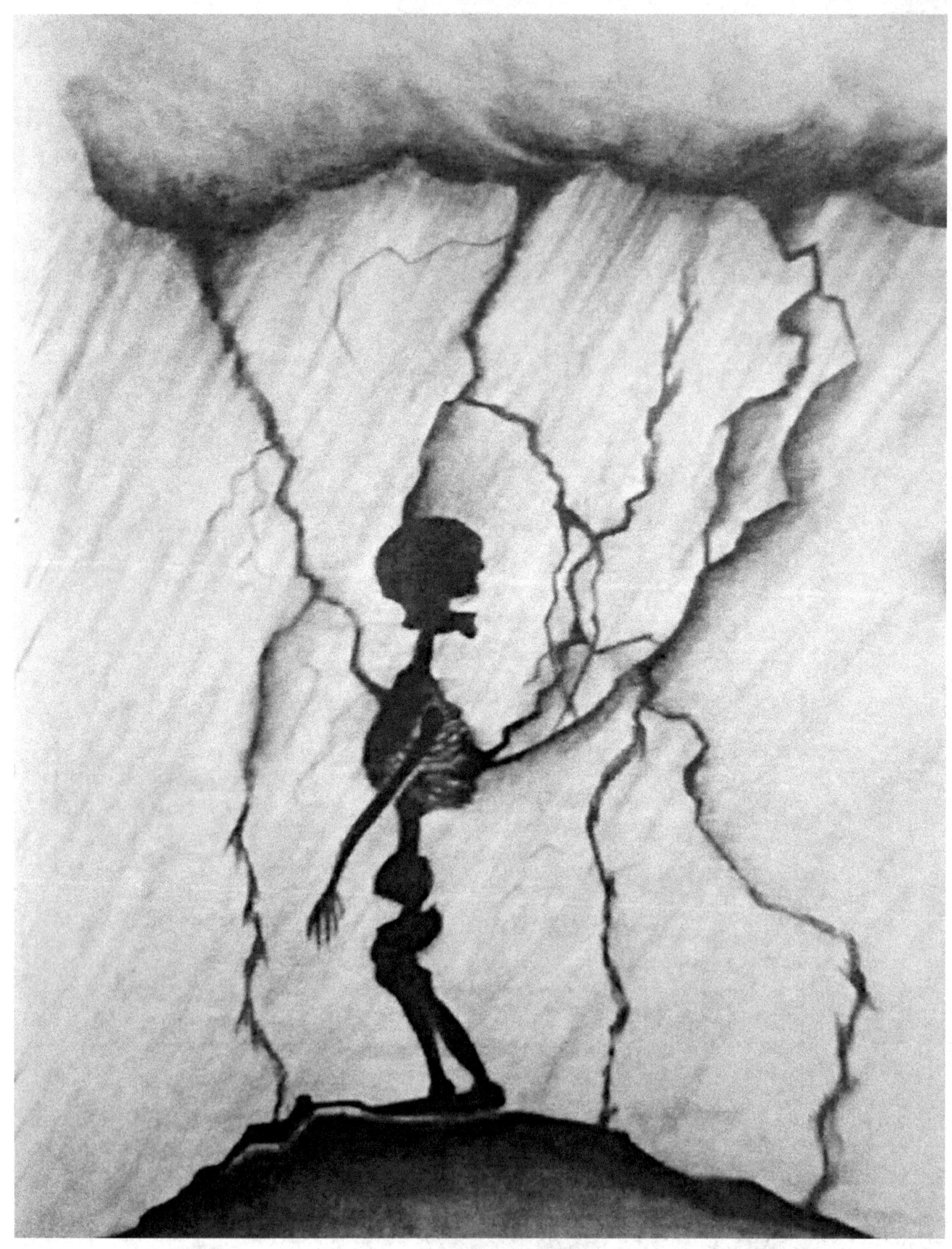

"Skeleton Resurrection"
A4 Pencil Sketch

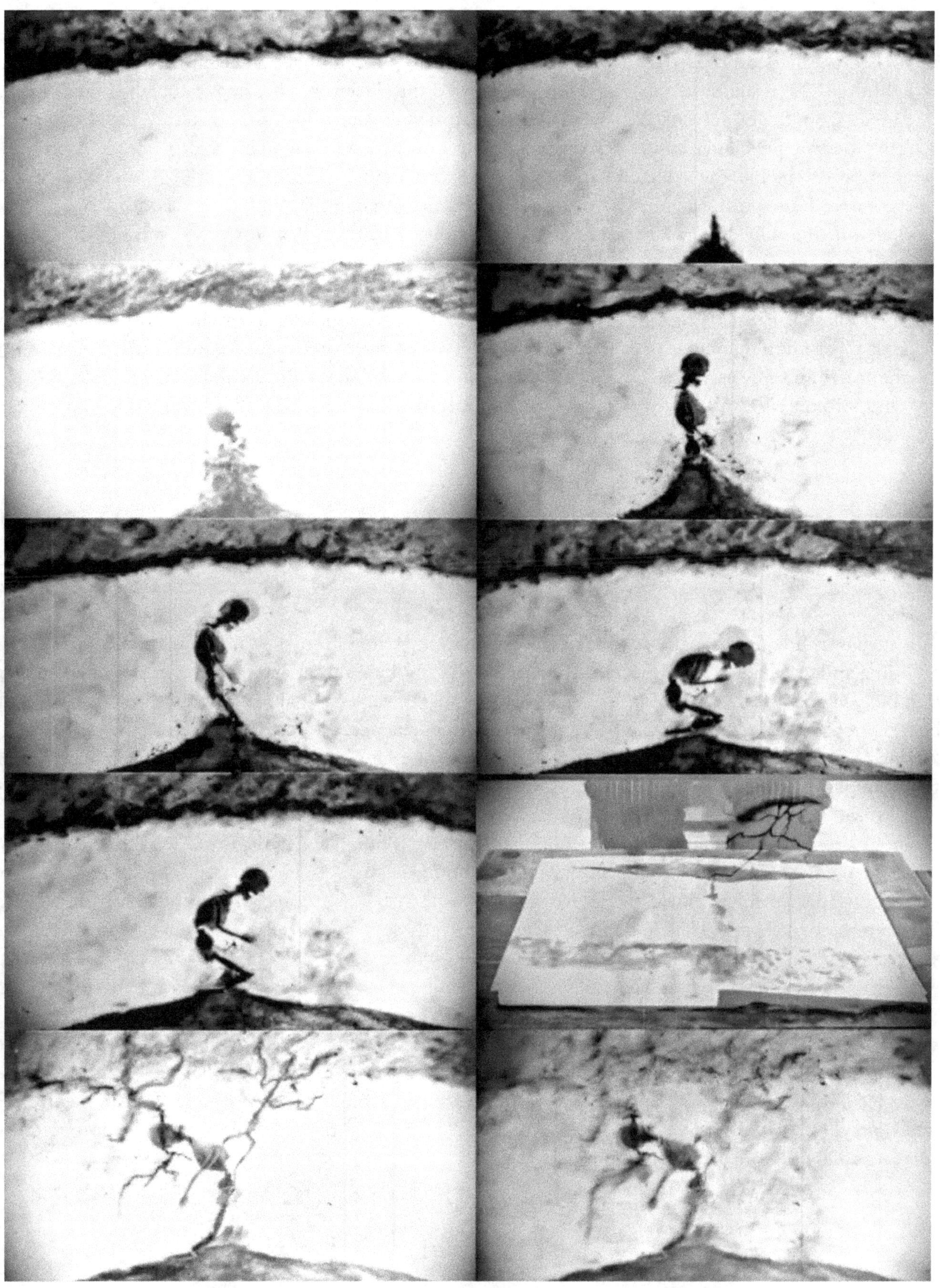

"**Skeleton Resurrection**"
Animated sequence

Sunday 1st April 2018

I returned to my bedroom at 10am to rework the sketch of a silhouetted skeleton being struck by a bolt of lightning. The resulting animation sequence showed the skeleton appearing gradually, as the jagged hill rose eerily from the bottom of the screen. The skeleton woke up, whilst its appearance flashed in the dark. I rubbed out the pencil markings and reapplied them frame by frame to achieve this effect. Upon reaching the summit of the hill, the skeleton bended forward with an arched spine and the lightning struck directly on its frame. I altered the brightness using three contrasts, ranging at half of a second for each tone, to produce the lightning effect. This turned out to be quite realistic as if a storm was surging.

In the evening, I recommenced my work on the "Come Dine with Me" short animation piece, and included live film footage. When the crow disappeared from the scene at the right-hand side of the screen, I made it look as if it was flying past my bewildered looking face. I glanced at my sketchbook to find another piece of illustration to include in this animation. Because of the experimental nature of this project, it gave me the freedom to be as diverse as I wanted with my skills and ideas and I enjoyed converting my original sketches into moving images. I was inspired and excited by all the creativity that I worked with during much of this day.

Monday 2nd April 2018

I decided to retitle the animation "A Peculiar Imagination" when I returned home from the coffee bar with grandma and grandad. Today, I developed work on the smoking rabbit clip. In here, I developed an interaction between myself and the rabbit. I was conscious that it was essential to show the contrast of the rabbit being a fictional character and me being a non-fictional character. I decided to depict the rabbit dragging my face onto the sketchbook with a candy cane stick for a cheeky peck on the lips. On the following day, I continued with this sequence. I posed in front of the camera in my bedroom, taking shots of myself to capture my overwhelmed reaction to the rabbit's seductive advances. I attached these photographic stills to an email, so that I could print them out at the library. The scale of my figure looked small compared to the size of the rabbit, so I had to redraw the rabbit as a smaller version. I cut out six photographs of myself and placed them beside the provocative creature, so that I could create the animated interaction between the two characters. The resulting scene, showed me turning to the rabbit in astonishment, before she extended her neck directly towards me for a cheeky peck on the lips. During the edit, I decided to add some colour, to add some passion to the kiss. The rabbit's neck extended from the sketchbook. I managed to achieve this effect by mounting a second sketch of the rabbit's head on a piece of raised foamboard. I completely changed my mind and scrapped this concept and decided to have my face being hauled onto the sketchbook next to the alluring rabbit. I think this worked well realistically.

I placed the camera on a tripod facing a miniature oak table which I positioned in the centre of the bedroom. The sketchbook was laid on top and I placed myself in the scene sitting on a chair to witness the surreal activity that was emerging on the open pages.

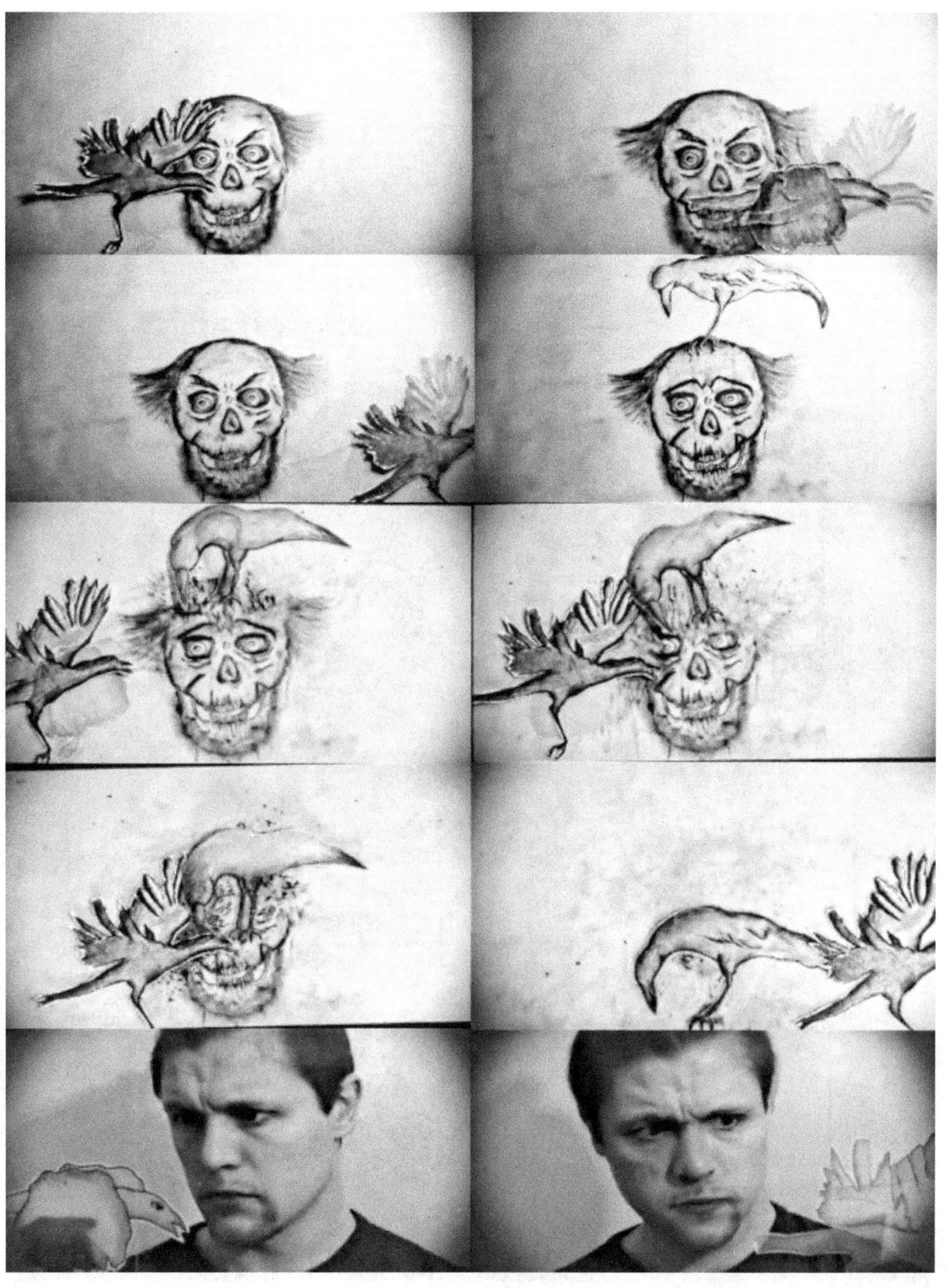

"Come Dine With Me"
Animation sequence

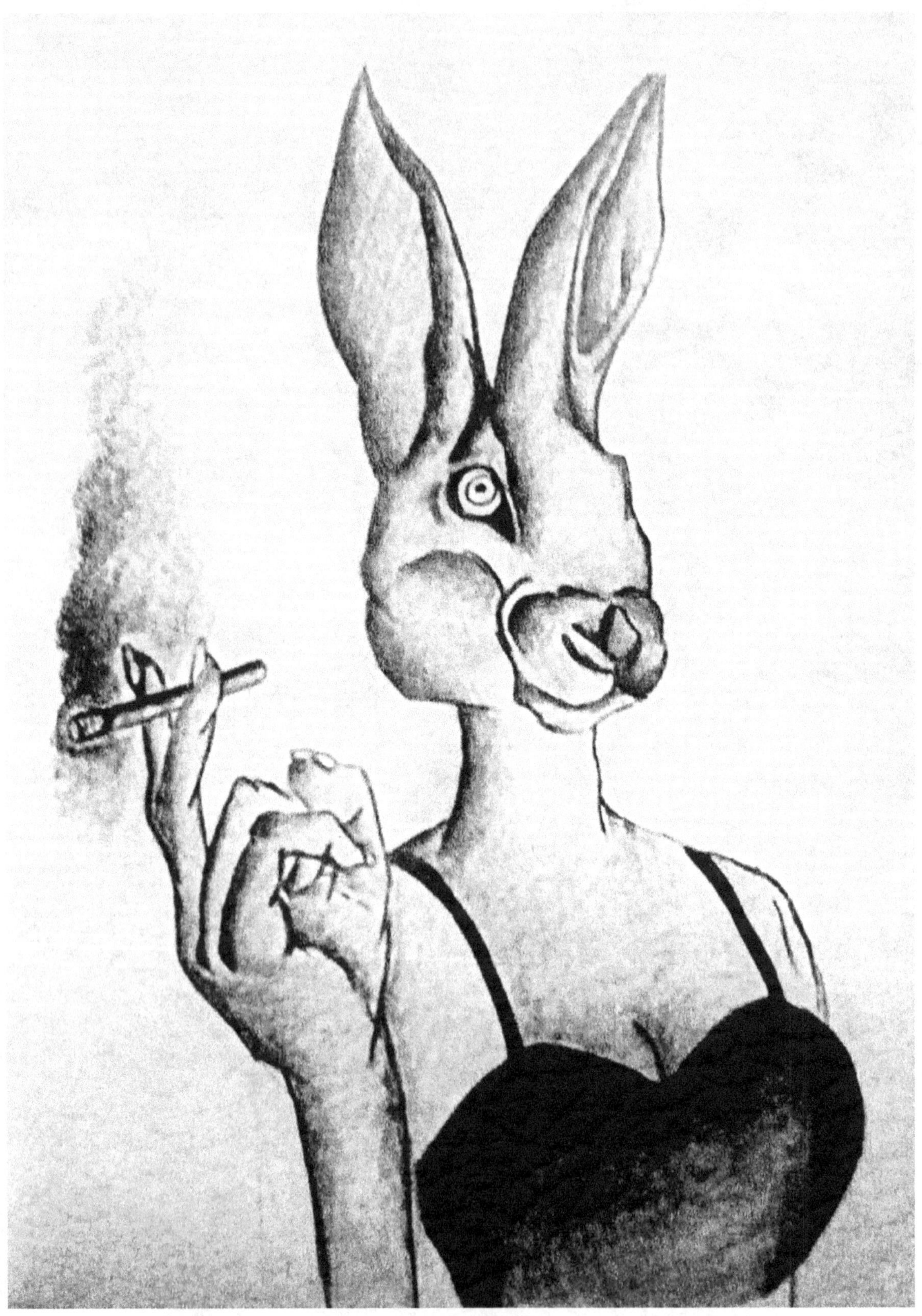

"Smoking Rabbit"
Remastered A4 Sketch (2018)

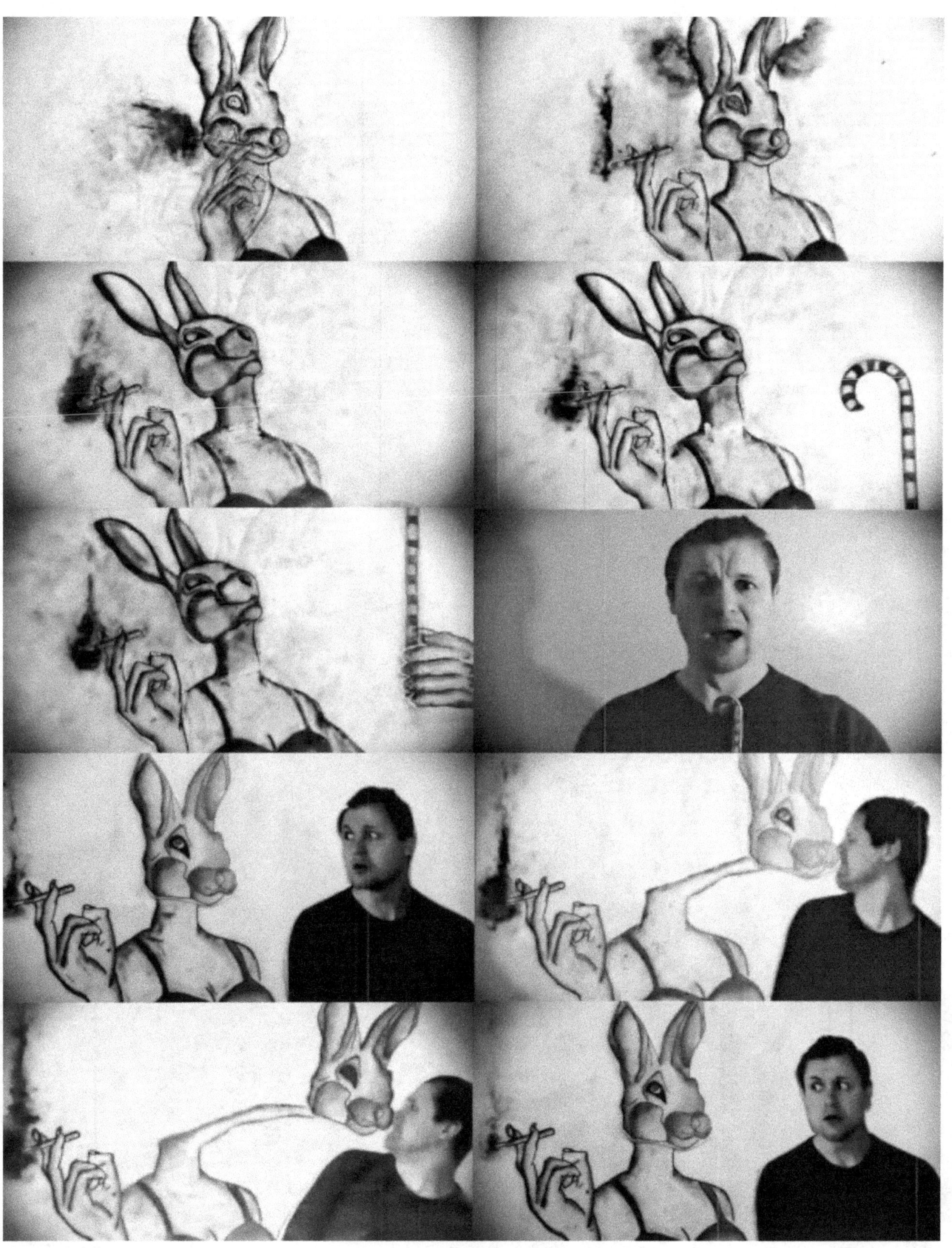

"Smoking Rabbit"
Animation sequence

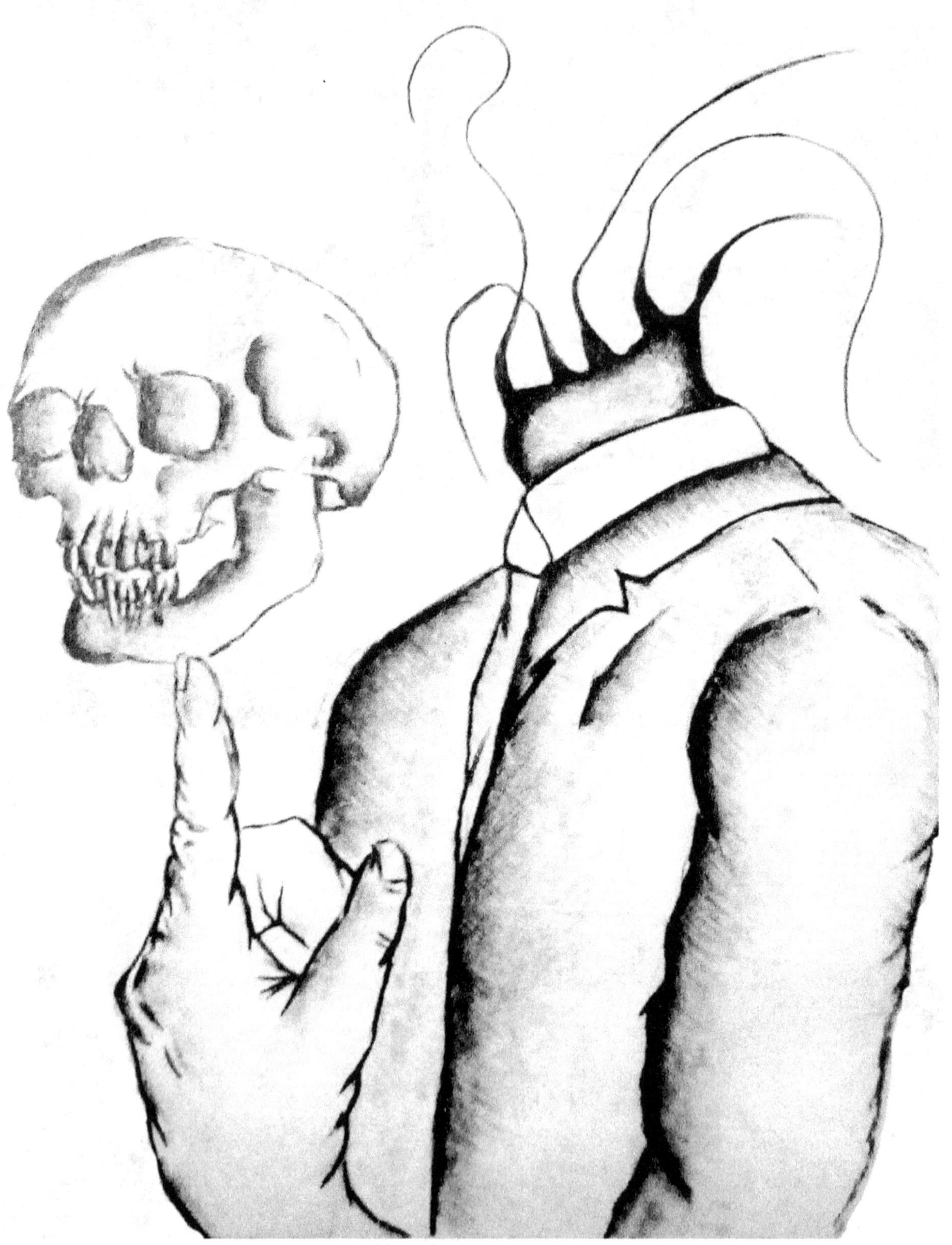

"Headless Skeleton"
Remastered A4 Pencil Sketch

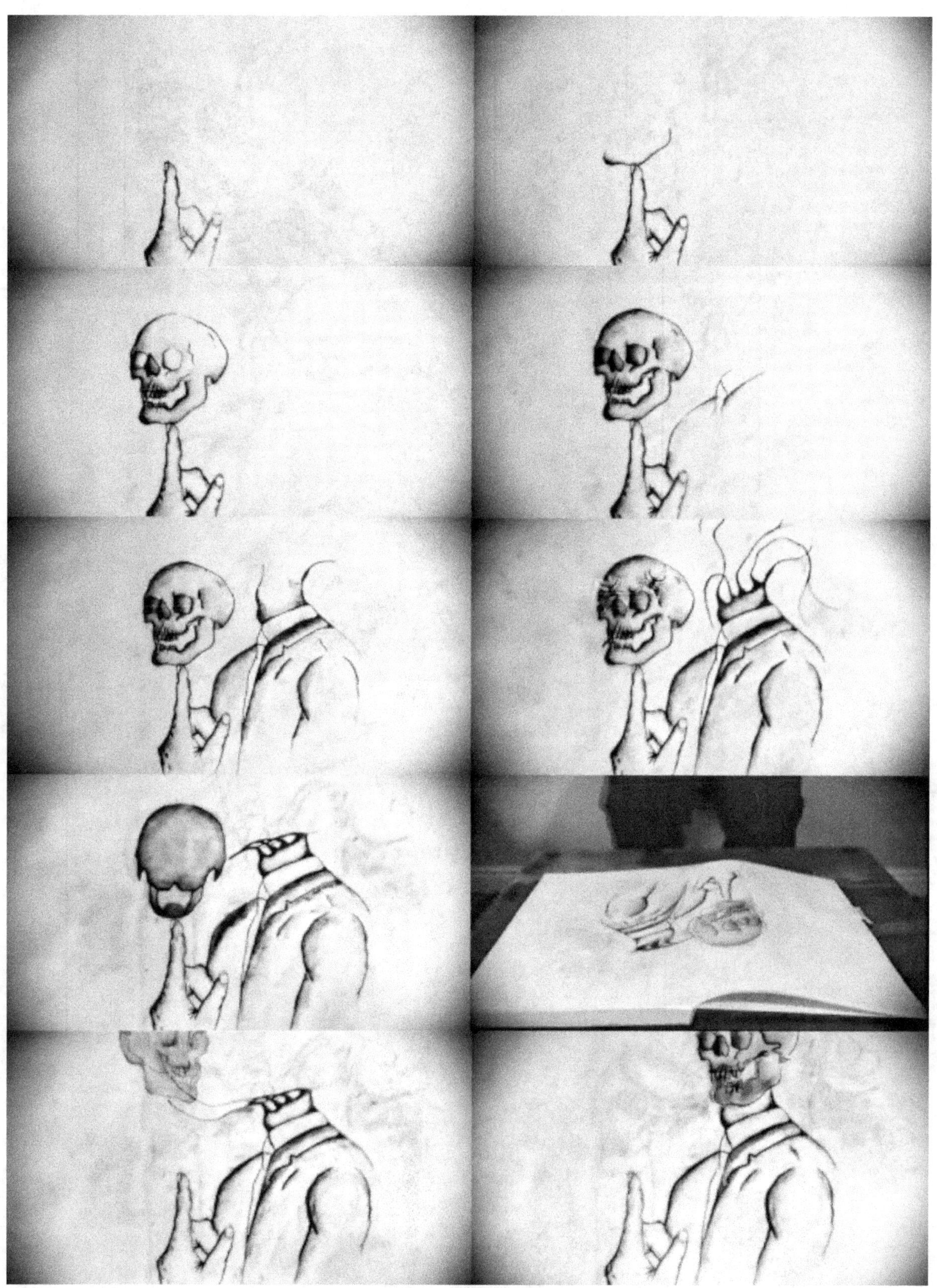

"Headless Skeleton"
Animation sequence

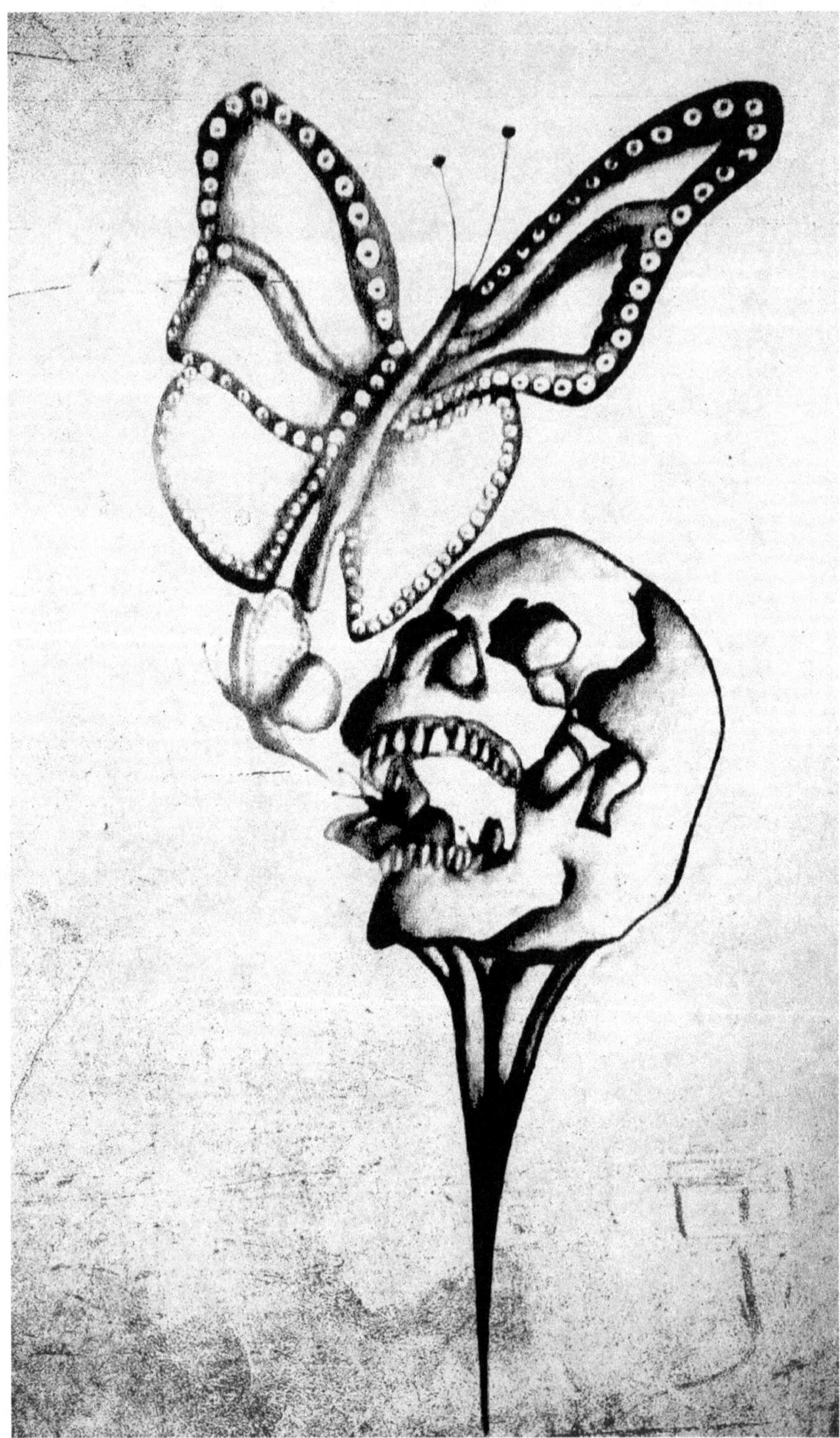

"Butterfly Effect"
A4 remastered Pencil Sketch

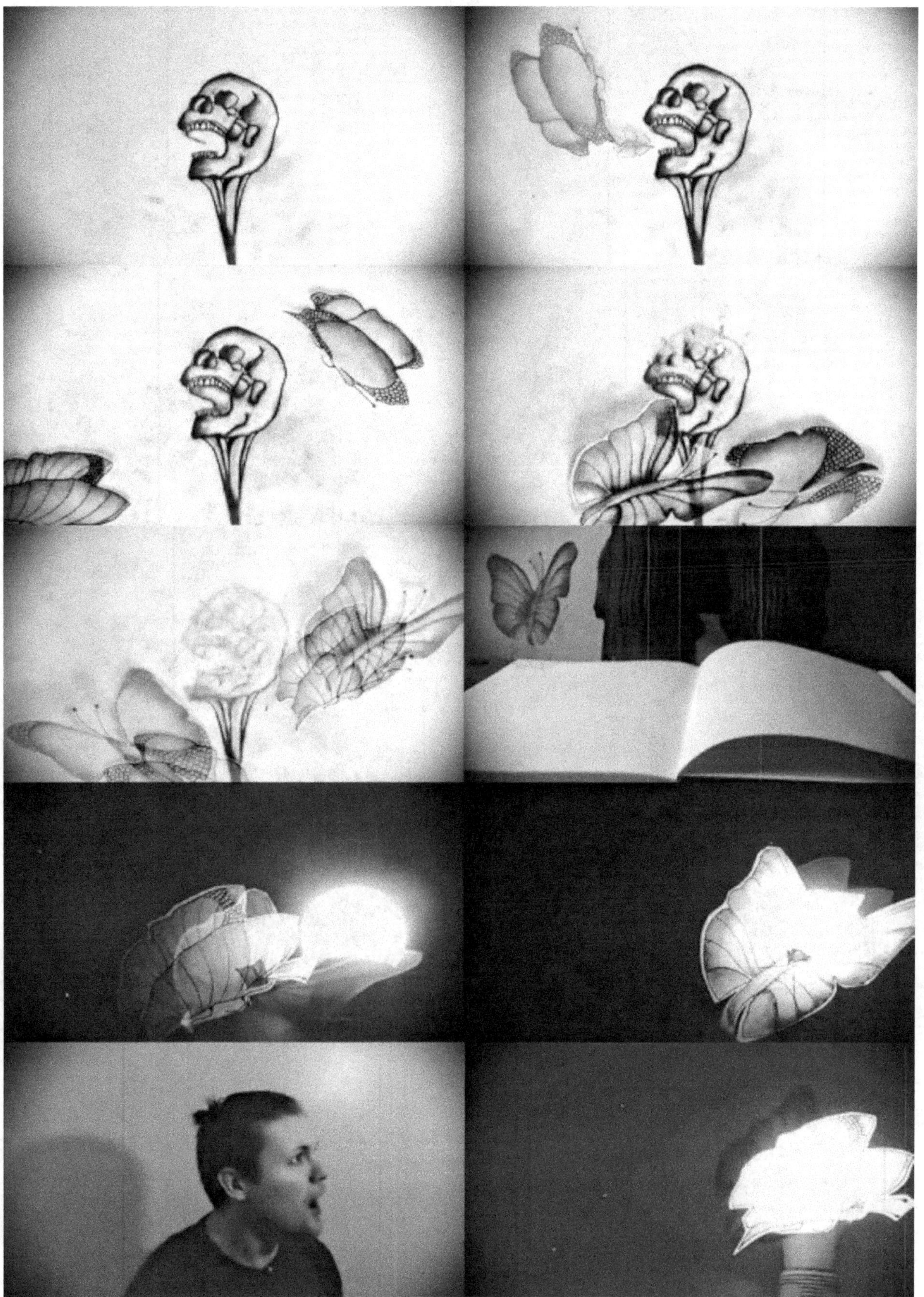

"Butterfly Effect"
Animation stills

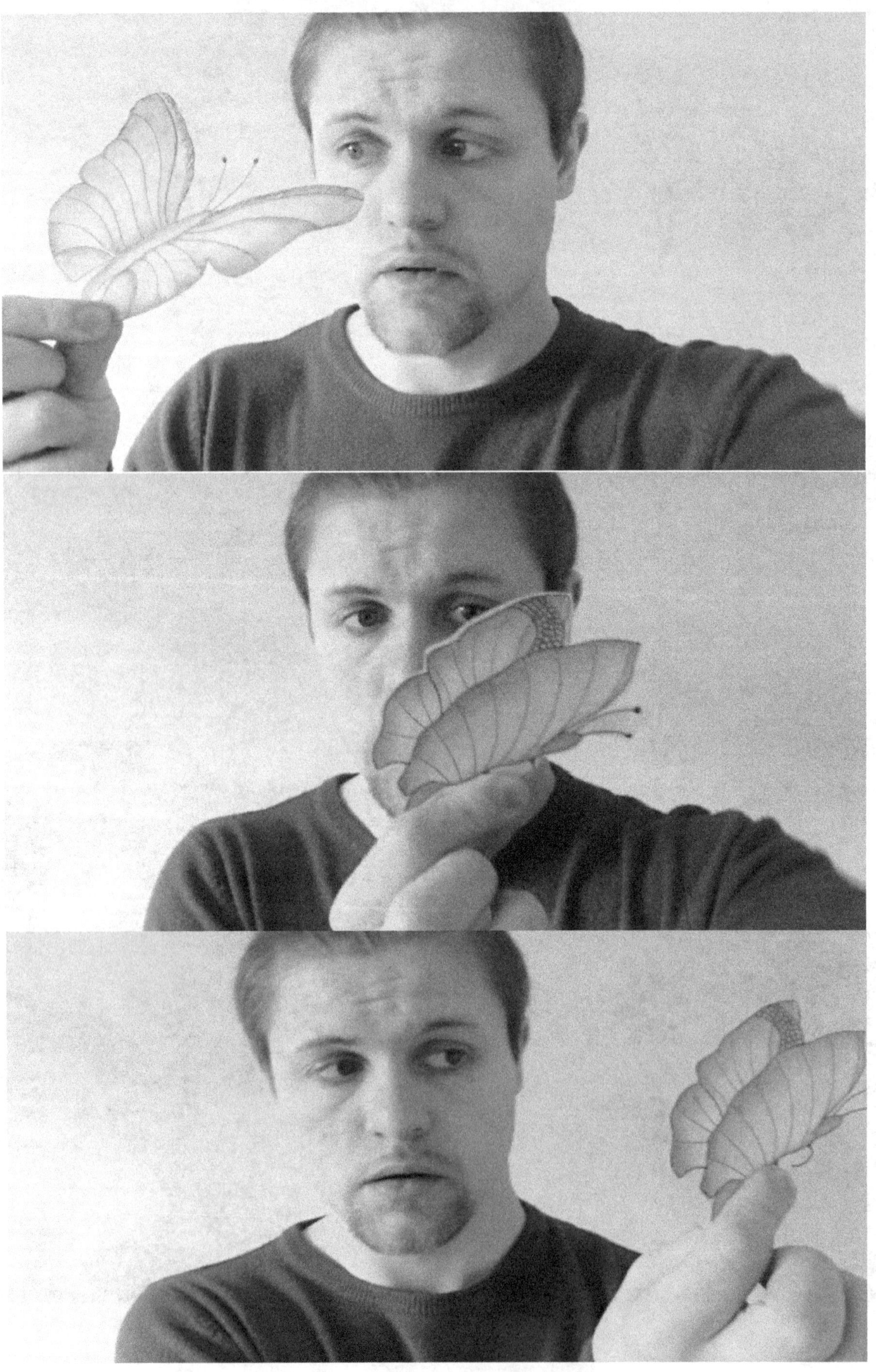

I would often hold a piece of "character" by the fingertips, or place them onto a 10cm thin wire, when interacting animation with live action.

I placed a template of the rabbit drawing on the sketchbook and used this to make an animation with as part of a running film clip of my bedroom. I wanted to combine realism with surrealism in the animation, which was an experimental move compared to what I have done in my previous animation work.

Towards the end of the evening, I traced the outline of another sketch depicting a headless skeleton spinning his own head on the tip of his finger. I developed the sequence for this on the following Friday, to create the effect of a skull spinning 360 degrees in clockwise motion. I made three cut outs of the skull in different positions so that I could create the impression of it spinning. During the animation, the skull appeared to rise and reattach itself to its scraggly neck. At the closing of the sketch "The Hellion Within Me," I added a sudden thunder bolt, which gave it a bewitching feel.

Tuesday 10th April 2018

I completed the current project, at approximately 3:30pm. The animation concludes with a pitiful looking butterfly heading towards a naked light, next to the artist, and dying of electrocution. To create this effect, I used two versions of a butterfly cut out, to create the sequence of it flying. Both templates were attached to piece of silver magnetic wire, which can be extremely flimsy to handle. I used this material to support the butterfly mounting up from the sketchbook, propelling it at a height, past my peculiar expression on the film. Frame by frame, I moved the butterfly towards the luminous target, alternating between both templates, to create a sense of movement. It took a good few retakes to make this right, due to either the animated movement not being in sync, or due to the photographed image appearing blurry in the photographs.

This animation has been an intriguing but challenging journey, which allowed me to extend my usual creative boundaries and realise new prospects which I learned would either work or didn't. I used a quote at the end of the project, taken from the prolific Genevan philosopher, writer and composer, Jean-Jacques Rousseau —

"The world of reality has its limits; the world of imagination is boundless."

Why? Because the imagination is an endless source of wondrous and enchanting possibilities, which can enter, affect and evolve in any aspect of real-life existence. There is an infinite spectrum of inventions extraordinaire to be conjured and experimented with. Art is a beautiful craft which helps to unearth mysterious concepts.

The exciting part, when a project is completed, is getting in touch with festivals. "A Peculiar Imagination" had an incredible tour around the United Kingdom and even overseas at "The Pugnant Film Series" based in both Athens and Greece. Although I wasn't able to attend the screenings. The animation alongside a catalogue of my previous projects was featured at an event called "The Creative Pie." It was screened at The Northern Quarter Bar (formerly known as The Hand Drawn Monkey) based on Wood Street in Huddersfield. It was a brilliant event. Other artists on the bill included a local photographer named Adrian Evans who presented his work via a projector and talked about it on stage. A poet named Rosa Lucy performed her ode to a female pianist and friend who had sadly passed away. She accompanied her compelling narrative with a piano recording playing at the same time. A physical performance group called Make Do Theatre gave a performance of a work in progress exploring the issue of homelessness. There were a couple of other artists too who shared their artistic creations.

Tuesday 15th May 2018

I arrived in Sheffield at 8:15pm, heading directly towards the Showroom Cinema Complex. I met Rob Speranza, a filmmaker and this evening's curator, in the bar space. He introduced me to Alice Ramsey, the Executive Director and Producer for Film Hub North. She finished her meal as I sat down and joined her. We spoke about what processes I use to develop my animations and what my aims were for the future. Alice was approaching a diverse range of filmmakers, to offer them commissions using Arts Council funding. Alice mentioned that she had a long day of meetings with filmmakers, hence the reason she left at the interval. It was a pleasure to meet her.

My animation "A Peculiar Imagination" was the fourth short film to be screened during the second half. Filmmakers were invited to introduce their work before the screenings commenced. I spoke about how I wanted to make an experimental animation, which physically involved myself, as the "artist" interacting with my own illustrations that emerged from my own sketchbook. I thought the animation was well received by the audience.

There were a couple of films which I was particularly drawn to. One being "Run Rabbit Run" made by Eleanor Smith, a twenty-year old student filmmaker. It was a brilliantly crafted film noir styled short, depicting a 1920's gangster tale. Eleanor was only eighteen at the time of creating the project. The second Film was the highlight of the evening, titled "Absent from our Wedding," directed by Debbie Howard. This twenty-minute short film documented a double proxy wedding, based in Montana, USA. It was a legal ceremony, where both the bride and groom have proxies standing in for them, as the ceremony is performed. This documentary actually inspired me to become a proxy myself, marrying in the place of an absent couple. The ceremony was so intriguing. I wasn't sure if the United Kingdom allowed to proxy wedding ceremonies but I thought it would be brilliant to introduce couples to something alternative, as opposed to your standard traditional white wedding.

Saturday 26th May 2018

"I started making stop motion animation back in the summer of 2016," I answered, standing behind a microphone after the screening of my animation "A Peculiar Imagination." I was stood on the stage at The Horse Hospital in Bloomsbury, London during an Exploding Cinema event. I went on to explain the creative method that I used to create my animations with.

"Did you specifically draw the illustrations purposely for the film, or were they stand alone pieces?" A man would ask from the corner of the room.

"I used my sketchbook to create illustrations with. The headless skeleton with his skull spinning around on the tip of his finger was intended for this animation but the previous three or four drawings, I decided on adapting into an animation." I answered, squinting directly at him, through the lights that beamed from the spotlights on the ceiling.

Another filmmaker on the front row asked how technical it was to create the butterfly electrocution.

"It was created by turning my camera flash on and off repeatedly to achieve that effect" I said.

He was impressed by the hand-drawn typography of the opening title and I received some positive inspiring feedback from the audience.

A woman by the name of Dimple approached me, as I was about to leave The Horse Hospital, during the interval. She commended me for my animation, adding how visually fantastic it was. I felt extremely honoured by her words. Dimple was a Filmmaker too. I couldn't really hear her because an quirky band called "The Connie Faggotts" was performing during the interval. We exchanged phone numbers to keep in contact with each other. She asked me to collaborate on a current global project of hers based solely on psychology. I mentioned that I am always commuting to London, as she asked me where I was based.

"Ah Leeds," She vaguely smiled, as she initially thought I was based in the capital.

Unfortunately, I had to leave to catch National Express coach back to Yorkshire. I could hear the faint bustling uproar of shouts from the football fans in the bar opposite The Horse Hospital.

Thursday 30th August 2018

I arrived at London Victoria coach station at approximately 3:10pm with the sun radiantly beaming over the capital. I headed to Angel by foot, whilst the streets were overwhelmingly congested with humans. I took the route past the historic Trafalgar Square, through the prolific Covent Garden market and Drury Lane. I was approached by a lovely black lady in her mid-forties, wearing a Shelter charity jacket. She was welcoming the tourists and luring them in. Her name was Maureen. She complimented me on how nice my long brown, shoulder length hair was, which was combed to the left-hand side of my face. Then she described how much she loved my charismatic Yorkshire dialect.

"You're not from around here are you?" Maureen smiled.

"Leeds," I answered, even though I was Batley-based. It was much easier to name a well-known city nearby as opposed to a small working-class town that no one had ever heard of.

She asked me what brought me here.

"I'm screening an animation this evening in Angel." I pleasantly smiled.

The conversation progressed onto subject of how expensive it was to rent accommodation in London. We agreed that the extortionate rent price of nine hundred pounds a month was shocking compared to what we paid in the north.

At 6:50pm, I made my way into the basement studio of The Candid Arts Trust based in Angel, for this evening's edition of "Kino 98." I was the first filmmaker to arrive and introduced myself to Dustin as well as another American male curator, who I forgot the name of.

A rather handsome barman with a top knot hairstyle and rugged stubble was present too, preparing the mini bar before the arrival of the audience. There was a good-sized audience turning up for this evening's event.

It was lovely to see Molly Brown and her new animation "Snake Charmer." She brought three of her friends along this evening; Hannah, who narrated Molly's short film and whom I had already met at the Exploding Cinema event. Then there was Desree, an Australian filmmaker, who showcased her experimental piece titled "Dolls" based on an unpublished short story written by Daphane Du Maurier. Desree asked for the audience's feedback, due to the project being unfinished. I appreciated her film as an experimental, rugged piece. "Dolls" was the final film that was shown during that evening.

My animation "A Peculiar Imagination" was the second short film to be screened. I was invited to the microphone to introduce my work as it was the rule to do this if your film was being shown at Kino London. Another rule, was that the filmmaker had to be present at the event, otherwise it wouldn't be screened. A previous rule, which had been scrapped, was that if any films didn't contain the Kino logo, the filmmakers had to create a film in response to an audience's chosen theme. The deadline to complete the challenge was a month, in order for the film to be screened at the following event. Anyhow, back to this evening, I returned to the couch where we all sat down. The animation was showcased to the audience and was very well received.

A young Indian woman approached me to say that she "really, really, really, really" enjoyed my film and wondered if it was available online. I gave her my name, mentioning that it was available on my YouTube channel. Desree also complimented me on my talent and how beautiful my animation was. I thanked her for her kind words. It was brilliant to see Marie Andrews too, a regular documentary filmmaker. She arrived during the second half after travelling on a train and accidentally missing the first half.

The event ended at approximately 9:20pm as I said my goodbyes to everyone and headed by foot back to London Victoria coach station. I caught the 11:30pm National Express coach arriving in Leeds at 5:20am. I then caught the 223 bus at 6am back to Batley.

Wednesday 26th September 2018

I headed to The Now Serving Bar, based in Wakefield this evening, where "A Peculiar Imagination" was scheduled to be screened at their Mini Indie Film Festival. The event was part of The Wakefield Art Walk.

I met three men gathered outside of the bar. One of them being Nathan Birkinshaw who was the curator of the event. He shook my hand and greeted me with a smile. I mentioned that I was one of the Filmmakers.

"Oh, which is your film?" Nathan asked.

"A Peculiar Imagination." I answered. He complimented me for my animation as he led me into the dark venue and introduced me to two Mancunian filmmakers named Axel and Shaun. They both lived together creating projects as a filmmaking duo. One of their short films was on the bill this evening. They were both extremely good friends with Nathan, hence the invitation to screen here tonight. Shaun mentioned that "A Peculiar Imagination" was by far his favourite film in the entire showcase, which filled me with pride. I gave them my name so that we could keep in contact with each other and hopefully see them again at a future event. An interesting array of eclectic films were screened this evening.

I said goodbye to Nathan in the toilets, thanking him for screening my animation. He said he would contact me for further submissions.

Saturday 29th September 2018

At approximately 2:15pm, I arrived at the petite Deptford Cinema based in London and entered the vintage bookshop. I was welcomed by a middle-aged female librarian with long grey hair and round spectacles. She was managing the artsy bar area.

"Is this where the Film Festival is?" I asked.

"It is yes. The first section of the Experimental Films is still screening but you are more than welcome to sit in our bar or go down to the cinema room. Charlotte the organiser is down there, most probably sat at the back. She has fine short hair." She smiled, with a soft tone in her voice.

I mentioned that I am one of the filmmakers, showcasing during the second half at 3pm and the reason that I am early is that I have travelled down from Leeds by coach.

"You have travelled all the way down from Leeds?" She asked, impressed by my commitment.

I made my way down the narrow wooden staircase where I was met by a thick black curtain, shielding the light from upstairs. Upon my entry, I was quietly greeted by Charlotte, who I could hardly see due to the darkness that obliterated the view of the underground, retro cinema room. Fairy lights decorated the stage underneath the projection screen, exposing the brick wall interior and adding character to the space. I managed to catch a few of the Experimental Films during the first batch.

Molly Brown, a credulous animator, and her partner Brandon arrived during the intermission. We greeted each other as they sat down beside me. The second half of the festival commenced at 3:15pm and "A Peculiar Imagination" was the first film to be screened. I made sure that I stayed for Molly's one minute animation called "Rush," which documented the pandemonium of London's rush hour. As always, her work was brilliant!

I had to leave at 4:45pm to catch the 6:30pm coach service back to Leeds. I took the tube train from Deptford to Lewisham. Then changed here to go to London Canon Street, then went from there directly to London Victoria.

On Sunday 16th September 2018, my animation was nominated for The Golden Trellick award, at The Portobello Film Festival based at The Westbank Studio Gallery, in Ladbroke Grove. It was shortlisted within the low budget horror and sci fi category, although it wasn't championed the winner. I didn't attend this specific award ceremony evening.

As I mentioned in a previous journal entry, "A Peculiar Imagination" was experimental compared to my whimsical shorts. I had always been inspired by experimental filmmaking since I discovered this during my fine art degree course at De Montfort University in Leicester. Even then, I never thought about graduating as a filmmaker. I did often wish that I had been introduced to animation during my degree, as showcasing my work and my eccentric imagination would have been brilliant and I would have enjoyed the flexibility of exploring different materials. There was a reason why I happened to discover the medium of animation in the summer of 2016, and what a great introduction it was when I created "Man Bun."

Making this animation allowed me to express myself creatively and at free will. It gave me the opportunity to develop my work as a non-mainstream genre. Anyone can reinterpret an idea in any way they wish and go completely off the spectrum of how the artist originally devised their work. "A Peculiar Imagination" was once reviewed by The Framelight Film Festival, back in February 2019. They wrote:

"This intriguing animated short deals with themes familiar to us all from birth, to death and everything in between, situating the audience within the artist's considerations of his own mortality. The film thematically weaves us through his psyche and fantastical perception of the values of love and the aspects of re-birth and their impact, before we reach the inevitable final moment in our lives, demonstrated by using clever visual cues and motifs within a stop motion animated framework. The primary goal by the film's denoument, with the reality - verses - imagination thesis, placed front and centre of its narrative structure."

On reflection, my initial intention was to produce a moving image, which would seamlessly bring to light the hidden themes that were tucked away within my sketchbook. The whole project was mainly about experimentation without requiring the usual narrative to validate it. I do not start a project with preconceived plan. I just tend to find my way into it naturally and allow the piece to grow and breathe freely. And when completed, I present it to audiences in the hope that they will be able perceive it, critique it or enjoy it in their own individual ways or to even feel challenged to stretch their own imaginations.

"A Peculiar Imagination" Further showings:

Chapel FM Open Mic Night - Chapel FM, Seacroft, Leeds (2018)
Big Poetry - The Blue Walnut Cafe, Torquay (2018)
In Other Words - Temple of Boom, Leeds (2018)
Live and Animated - The Slocken, Leeds (2019)
Gingerlicous Nights - The Old Post Office Cafe, Silsden (2019)
The Dunbobbin Film Festival - Online - *(Winner of the 1-5 minute Experimental Category)* (2021)

I taught myself the process of making stop motion animation during the summer of 2016. I wanted to bring something unique to this genre, using my fine art background. My previous films, prior to animation was a portrayal of me, imitating a self-created extravagant character. I wanted to shy away from this comfort, by expressing my narrative through a different scope. My first Animation "Man Bun" allowed me to do this.

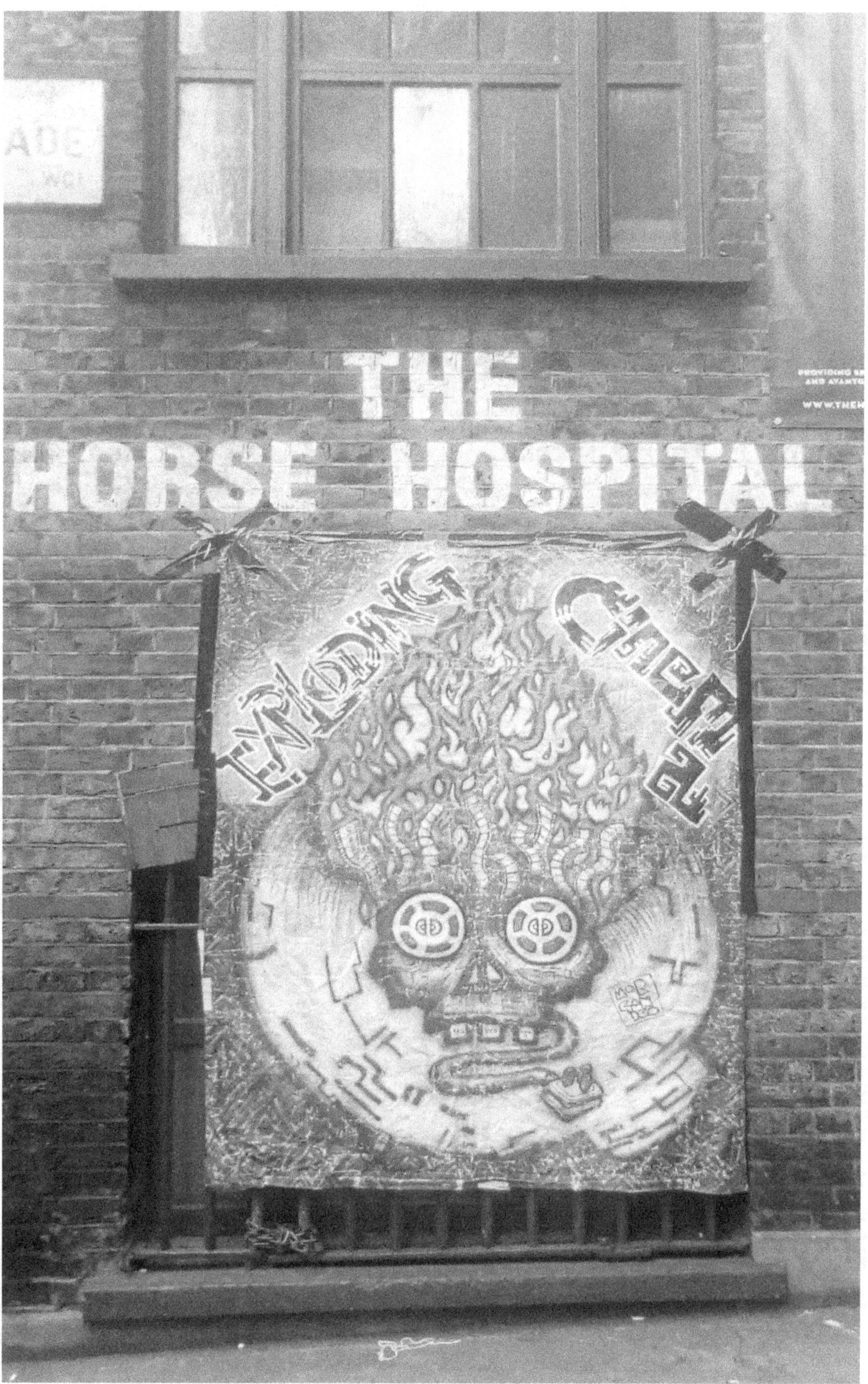

Exploding Cinema - The Horse Hospital
26/4/2018

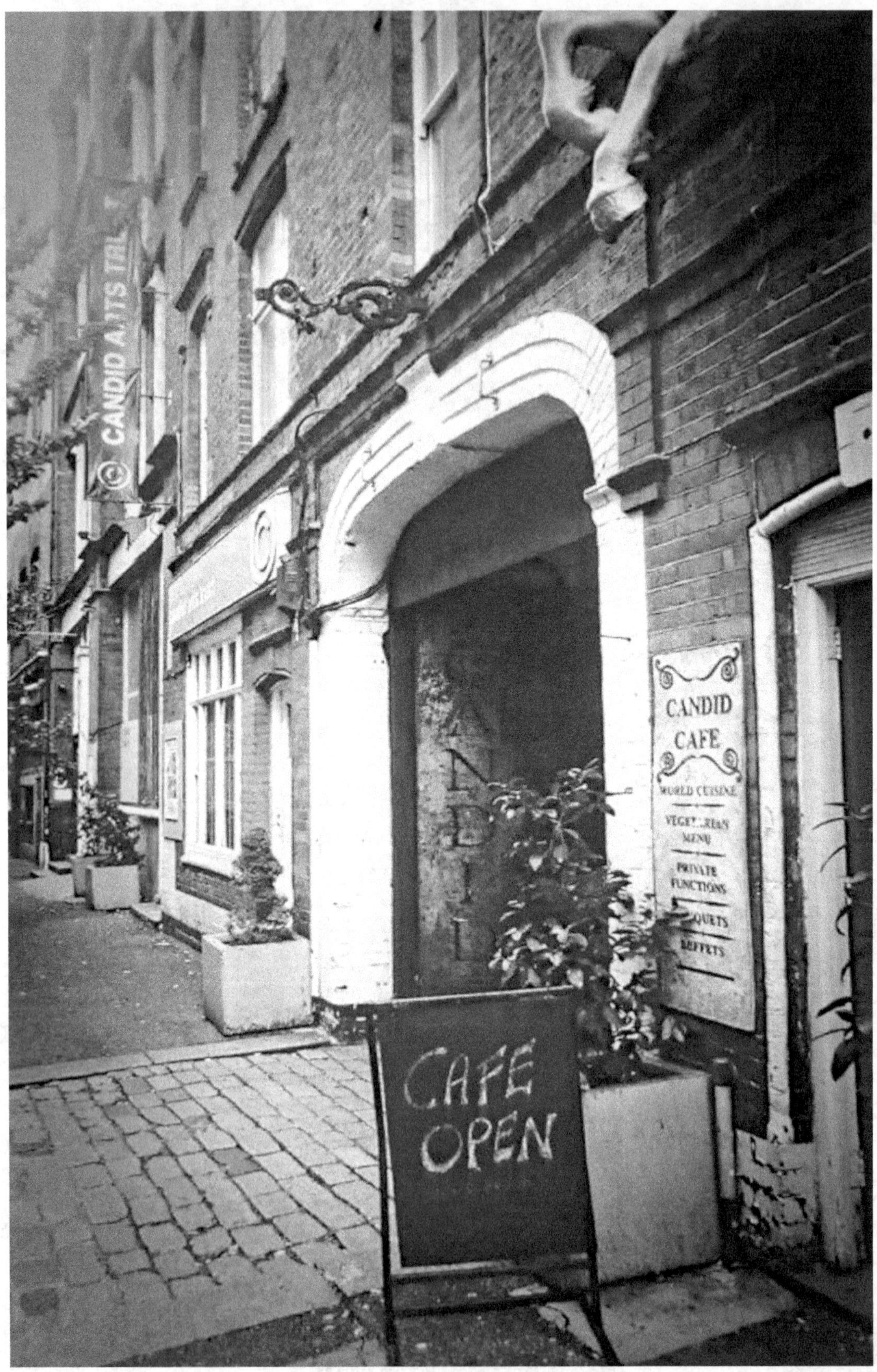

The Candid Arts Trust - Angel, London
Home to "Kino London" Short Open Mic Film Night

Mr Kipling

Mr Kipling knows how to comfort me,
On a Siberian, winter's night,
With his scrumptious fondant fancies,
and those Battenburg cake delights.
He grants me with satisfaction,
He converts me into a sweat,
His candid toothsome treats,
Gives me the time that I will never forget!
Those succulent lemon layer slices,
and a piece of treacle tart,
Combines to create a euphoria,
To excite and melt my heart.
I have never felt so much affection,
From a gentleman to workmanship and adore,
His bundles of delectable desserts,
Makes me crave and confide in more.
As I lay in ecstasy in bed,
And I indulge in that final bite,
Mr Kipling knows how to comfort me,
On a Siberian, winter's night.

This anecdote is written from a lady's perspective. Whenever I perform this poem, I always imagine her to be a little bit plump, as she lays comfortably on a four post bed, indulging in a box of Mr Kipling treats next to the radiant orange glow of a fire.

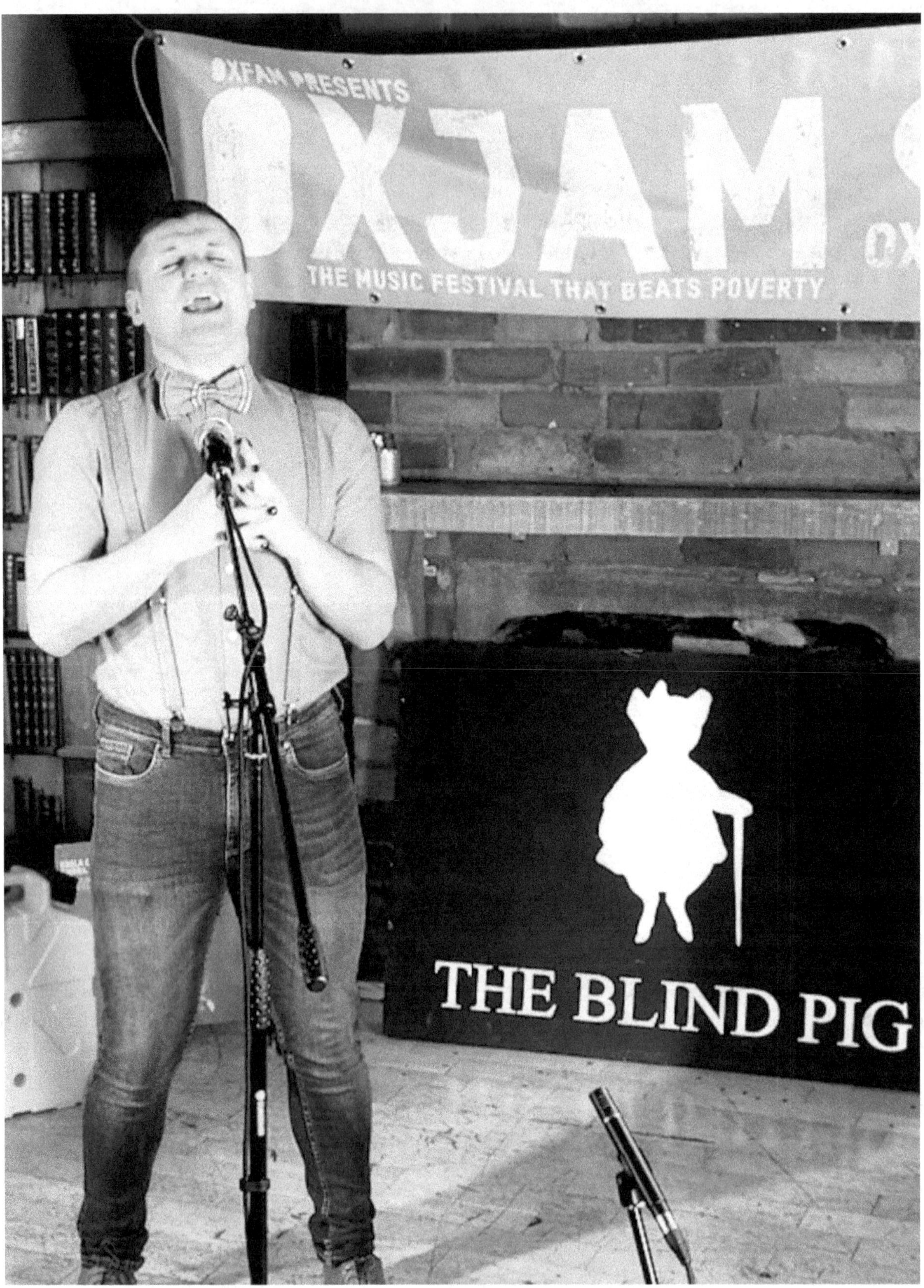

Performing my anecdote "Mr Kipling" as part of The Oxjam Bridge Music Festival sessions.
The Blind Pig, Sowerby Bridge - 18/10/2020

Manbun

I want to grow a man bun,
I want to get in with the groove,
But the only predicament I have,
Is that my wife doesn't approve.
Yes I am a middle-aged fella,
I have discovered this sudden phase,
I want to fit in with the modern society,
And get in with this craze.
My wife reckons I would look "HORRENDOUS!"
But how the hell does she know?
If she won't let me experiment with my style,
And let the damn thing grow?
My roots are in adequate good condition,
I have a brilliant head of hair,
I don't want to sit at home,
With a shaven scalp,
It is a trend that I cannot bare!
I'm prepared for my new appearance,
I am stored up with lacquer and gel,
But my wife is still against the idea,
It is going to make her life hell!
Oh yes darling, I want to grow a man bun,
I want to get in with the groove,
But this will never be a conclusion,
Because my wife doesn't approve!

This whimsical anecdote was inspired by a middle-aged man who wanted to grow a man bun. I was working at the West Yorkshire Playhouse based in Leeds and was checking the audience tickets for a show, which I have forgotten the name to. I had a full-length man bun as my then style. This man became really enthusiastic about this new modern trend. His wife was beside the auditorium door, obviously against the idea. Whether the man went ahead with his newly found hairstyle I will never know, but I only have him to thank for this anecdote. I wrote the poem within ten minutes of starting my shift, when the audience settled into their seats. I then subsequently adapted this into a stop motion animation piece.

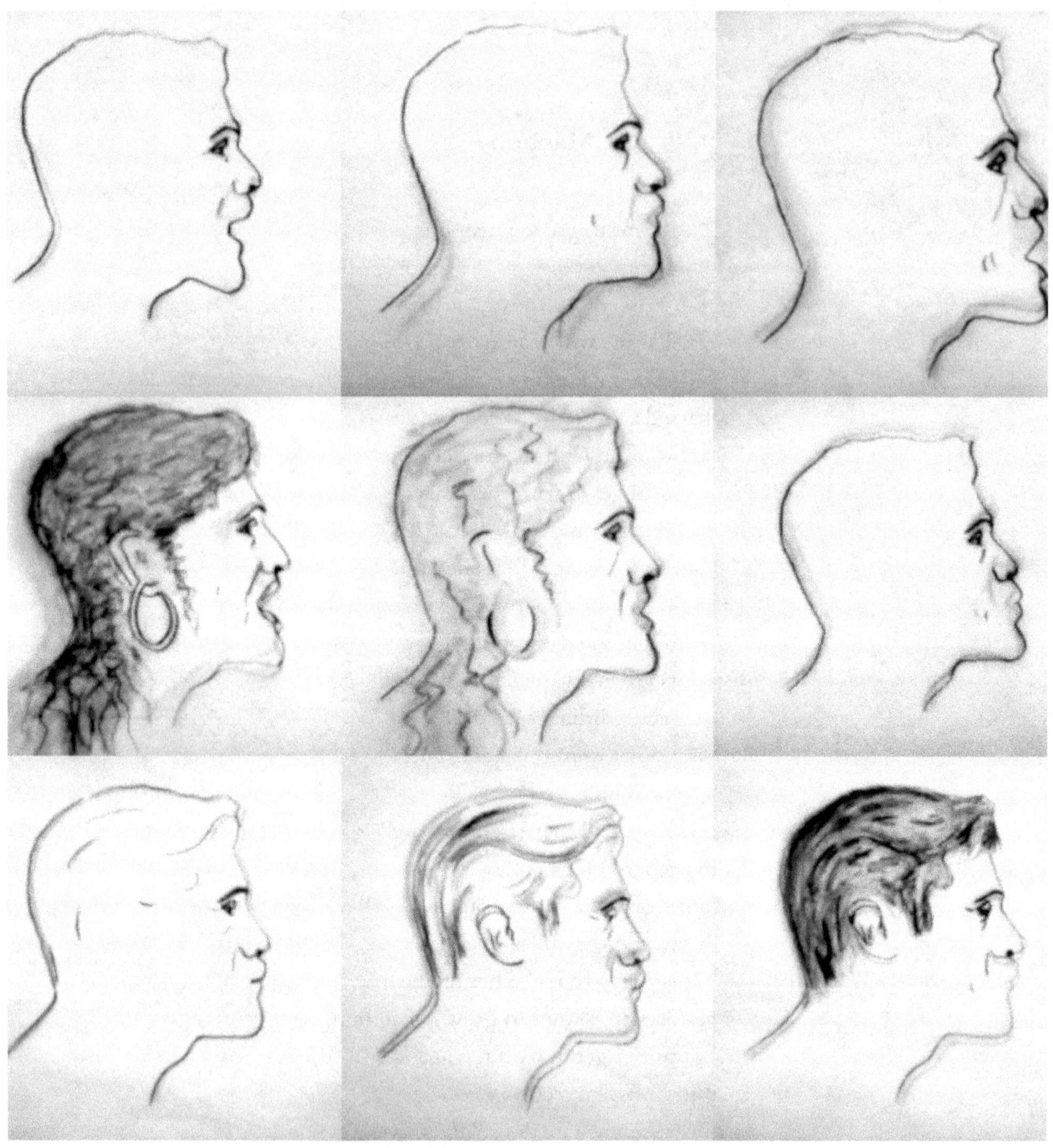

"Manbun" Animation stills.
Duration: 01:26

During August 2016, I was intensely involved in creating two hand-drawn animations. The extremely repetitive process of developing these projects was a tedious, stressful challenge but result was satisfying. These were the two films which I eventually became honoured to call my own.

I commenced work on "Man Bun" in late August. I immediately knew that I wanted to take new direction. I had this intriguing concept of making the film more like an animated 2D drawing, as opposed to focussing on realism. It would be a repetitive week of constantly making rotoscoped drawings. I made a film recording of a side shot of my own head narrating the 'Man Bun' anecdote. It then took approximately 900 drawings to export this into a hand-drawn animation piece. I discovered a new dynamic style bringing my own art work to life through this art form. The animation brought nostalgic memories to some people, comparing my style to the A-HA Music Video "Take On Me."

My working schedule consisted of nine-hour full days running consecutively and occasionally evenings. I was often seated on the edge of my bed, hunched over my laptop as I rotoscoped every second, frame by frame. The good old retro MovieMaker was my own editing software I could only afford at the time. This software was incredibly frowned upon by aspiring filmmakers but I thought it was completely ideal for producing stop motion animation projects. It was affordable and simple. As you will have previously read, I began to use another type of software by the name of MovAvi, which was genius for animating. I did use MovieMaker but this was only during the process of a rough cut edit, and then I would perfect this in MovAvi.

A couple of weeks after completing "Man Bun," I had a surge of creative energy and began producing a second animation titled "Hurricane George" which was an adaptation of another whimsical anecdote of mine. Told through the perspective of a wife, who was tired of her husband's revolting farts, I used the same processes like I did for "Man Bun," though the sequences were composed of rotoscopes and hand-drawn 2D cut outs. It still gave me the ability to broaden my newly found skills in this genre.

"Hurricane George" would later become my less favoured animation. A few people described me as being demonic, when I shared how intensively I work in animation. When I revealed that I literally drew everything by hand, the question that they usually proposed to me was - "Why put yourself through that much pressure, when you have modern software which can virtually do everything for you?" I believed that illustrating everything myself meant I was sharing entirely my own artistic abilities and processes and that I was conveying everything in my own style. There is a uniqueness, when I draw, for example, portraits and other parts of the anatomy. I can never capture the realism that many credulous artists manage to achieve, but this is what makes my work original.

The reason why I choose to work in black and white is because it adds character and makes my images appear more distinctive. Since childhood, I have always been drawn to classic black and white film, before the magic of technicolour began. I do often use a colour in certain films. When the prolific Disney animations first appeared on our TV sets on the 16th October 1923, these were based entirely on the practice of drawing by hand. I was inspired to do the same in my own work.

I premiered my debut animation "Man Bun" at The Hyde Park Book Club, based in Leeds, during an "Open Mic Night Film Event" in late August. The Film was also screened at The Coventry International Film Festival on Saturday 12th November 2016 at The Ego Arts Performing Centre. I suspected that the animation category had an evening preview a couple of days prior to my visit, as there was only myself and another audience member present at the Saturday matinee. Weirdly amiable as it was but I would have preferred much more of a crowd to be there.

On the evening of Monday 25th September 2017, I headlined a brilliant event by the name of "Stanza Extravaganza" at The Artizan Gallery in Torquay. The night was hosted by the fabulous Robert Garnham who was renowned as the Professor of Whimsy. He was incredible. I first met him in February 2015, where he headlined a poetry night called "Evidently" at The Kings Arms in Salford. I performed my whimsical anecdote at the same event called "I've Fallen in Love with Mr Muscle!" We briefly spoke after wards and this was when he invited me to perform in Torquay in the following December. The second time I saw him was September 2017. My Aunty Jenny gave me the idea of performing a live narration whilst my animations were playing on a projector screen at the same time. To my own fascination, I did this. I hadn't really seen anything marry together like this before, particularly on the poetry circuit, so this allowed me to present another angle of who I was as an artist. Most often, I explained my practice as an animator at poetry events and explained my practice as a poet at a film Festival. During the subsequent years ahead, I continued to perform alongside my animations at various events throughout the United Kingdom.

On Thursday 8th November 2018, I headlined "Big Poetry" based at The Blue Walnut also in Torquay, which was compered by Robert Garnham and another fabulous friend of mine Samantha Boarer. My set was a live recital alongside my animations. We were all huddled inside the petite cinema room as I sat on a chair narrating my whimsy visuals to the audience.

Tuesday 1st November 2016

I arrived at The Tin Tin Art Centre, based in Coventry at 7:20pm where a barge slept contently on a canal dressed in autumnal leaves. A man wearing glasses and holding a glass of pure orange juice stood inside the doorway.

"Is it open to go into the Roots To Shoot Film event?" I asked the man.

"Yes it is," He politely answered.

We both then went into the venue and stood in a dim lit corner.

"I'm showing a Film." I said.

He is too. We spoke about our passion and enthusiasm through filmmaking for a good couple of minutes. I then asked if a Brian Harley was present (The event curator.)

"Yes. He is just around there. He is wearing a snazzy blazer." The man directed me to the main room, where tonight's cinematic showcase was taking place. The space was only lit by small candles. A bowl of popcorn was positioned on each table.

"Hey Jamie, how are you?" Brian smiled, shaking my hand and welcoming me with a hug.

"I'm good, thank you," I answered.

He sat on a wooden stool next to a tall table, where the tickets were being sold. We spoke a little, before he introduced me to another filmmaker by the name of Phoenix Morrisey, who had purple locks that were illuminous and dazzling. She was sat on the other side of the room with her supportive parents. They had commuted from Crewe by car and seemed to be nice people.

The event commenced at 8:20pm. A selection films that had produced from around the country were being shown. The opening short film was a Pixar produced piece, titled "Borrowed Time." My animation "Man Bun" was the final short film to be shown before the intermission. I introduced the film from my seat before it was shared with the audience. Brian mentioned that he would be sharing more of my films on the Roots to Shoot website and social media pages.

I had to get off to catch the 9:42pm train service back to Yorkshire, via Birmingham New Street and Manchester Piccadilly. I took a wrong turn during my walk to Coventry train station, through a couple of underpass tunnels. A young man politely asked me if I had any weed to give him.

"No, I am not from around here." I said.

"Do you know anyone who has? Anyone in Birmingham?" He asked.

"No," I answered.

"Where are you from, if you don't mind me asking?"

"Leeds."

"Oh, it doesn't matter." He said, walking off in the opposite direction. The reason I have added this conversation, is that you will get a general idea, of the characters I attract, whilst commuting to various destinations. I must fit the absolute perfect criteria of a dealer, amongst many other attributes, but what is a journal if you don't attract the misfits?

I received an email from "The First Rule of Film Club Presents," requesting a download to the animation "Man Bun," whilst I sat and had a tall hot chocolate at 2:05am at Manchester Piccadilly Station.

Friday 11th November 2016

I travelled to Widnes by train this evening to see "Man Bun" being screened at "The First Rule of Film Club Presents Indie Showcase." The event was based in a venue named "The Studio." I met with the curators of the event, Peter McKerion and Rod Hay. Peter mentioned that he appreciated artists who contribute their work which includes stop motion animation. He had a female friend who specialised in this genre, but with lego, so he knew how tedious and repetitive the process was to create a project. The screening of "Man Bun" went well tonight, as did an array of seventy-eight hand-picked films from around the world.

I was given a lift back home by Dave Gilbank, who also screened two of his films this evening. He was a Creative Director of his own production company based in Bradford. A really pleasant and genuine man. We spoke about a variety of subjects, predominantly focused on film, as we drove down the dimly lit motorway. He provided me with some good advice about subtitling "Man Bun" in Spanish. He had a friend in Spain, who could provide this service, at the rate of fifty pounds. He told me that experimental work like this may appeal to film festivals overseas. Dave also added that he would pitch me a brief to see how good my editing skills are, in order to work within his production company. He used to be a film festival judge himself. There were numerous films which would not grab his attention. The films which were shortlisted for an award was, in his own words, "diabolically bollocks!" A short film should be approximately six minutes or less in length to appeal to his taste. I had forgotten the title to this particular film which appealed to him but I remembered him saying that it had a sophisticated quality to it, which urged him to write to the director, to commend them for their naturally pure, satisfying abilities. I was glad I had the opportunity to network with Dave on an informal level. He dropped me off outside my house at approximately midnight as he drove back home to Bradford.

Monday 14th November 2016

Tonight, I screened two of my stop motion animations - "Man Bun" and "Hurricane George" at an event called The Shag, based at The Exhibit in Balham, London, which was curated by the wonderful artist Sam Hacking. Sam arrived five minutes after me as I sat at a table opposite a snazzy bar. A couple of audience members who arrived later started sniggering, when they asked the bar tenders if The Shag was upstairs; a joke I would always chuckle about. I received some complimentary feedback from the audience during the Q & A after the screenings had finished. Sam admired how I developed my work, which meant a lot to me, as I previously wrote that the juxtaposition from one genre to another, allowed me to have flexibility in my projects.

I met with other fantastic artists tonight, including Sam Holloway who screened his comical short film titled "The Girl who Shouts at Birds." Amy Gwillam also screened a political short film portraying the distorted ways of living in this constituency, titled "Frankie From Balham." Each artist had an opportunity of speaking about their work processes, concepts and future ambitions, as an opportunity of sharing ideas and inspire audience members.

I had to leave at 10:20pm, to commute back to Yorkshire by train.

Sunday 29th January 2017

Me and my then partner at the time, Gray, arrived in a very rainy Kingston Upon Thames, at approximately 2:30pm. We caught the Virgin East Coast Service from Leeds to London Kings Cross and then took a replacement coach to Surbiton, where a rather annoying man kept on repetitively grunting in a vulgar manner opposite to us. "Man Bun" had been selected to be screened as a finalist, as part of a competition at "The Muybridge Film Festival," based at The Rose Theatre. Despite not winning that night, the screening went well. The show commenced at 3pm and ended at approximately 5pm. Post screening, there was an award ceremony. We later had a drink in the bar, as there was a variety comedy performance happening in the Auditorium. We both stayed overnight in a luxurious Premier Inn, a mile or two away from the Theatre.

We returned back to Leeds the following day, stopping for a drink at London Kings Cross station before catching the train.

Tuesday 25th July 2017

I caught the National Express coach service from Leeds bus station to London Victoria. I set off at 1pm and arrived in the capital at approximately 5:40pm. I was screening "Man Bun" at the Kino Open Mic Film Night, based at The Bill Murray Comedy Club in Angel. I arrived at the venue after asking people for directions to the location. I experienced an almighty sense of apprehension which clawed my gut just before the event. My anxiety propelled during the summer of 2017 and this was one of many episodes. Molly Brown greeted me at the front entrance. It was brilliant to see her again. Molly brought along her friends Stuart and Ann-Marie, who ran a film festival in Hull called "The Tea Break Film Festival," although she was based in Leeds. The Kino event had been on hiatus for a good year, so tonight was the return of it. The turnout was incredible. "Man Bun" was screened after the interval in front of a thriving audience. Like all filmmakers, I was invited up onto the stage to briefly introduce the animation. I was always going to screen at Kino London, as it was a fantastic night for any given film enthusiast.

Saturday 18th May 2019

I screened "Man Bun" this evening at an event called "Say it with Your Chest," based at The Open Source Arts, just off Kirkstall Road in Leeds. Tai invited me to submit an animation of mine, the night before, so I accepted. The event programme consisted of live performances and films. "Man Bun" was the second film to be showcased. Adekola subsequently invited me to the mic for a brief interview about my practice as an artist, my primary inspirations and how long I had been creating animations for.

"This December will be my tenth year of working in film, eleven years in performance poetry and three years working in animation. Observing life is the main thing that I am inspired by. Pam Ayres is another influence too."

There was an array of politically charged poets during the rest of the evening, which did feel like an extremely heavy weight on my mind by end of the event. As always, Laurence delivered a fantastic feature set. I met a few friendly faces this evening, including a Bradford-based poet named Taihra, who recited her poetry as the final open mic performance. Also a Canadian senior gentlemen and Daz who resided in Holborn Towers in Woodhouse and owns an allotment on Woodhouse Moor.

Laurence and I returned to the city centre by foot, delving in creative conversation. He became inspired by the bedazzling neon lights, which were staged buildings that we passed along Kirkstall Road. He recorded footage of these illuminated buildings for a music video that he was producing, and we walked up to Woodhouse Moor, where we embraced each other to say goodnight. He then caught the bus home at approximately 11:15pm.

Since my teenage years, I have suffered immensely with my mental health. When I first became aware of it as a young adolescent at sixteen, I found it extremely debilitating and could not comprehend what my psyche was spontaneously unravelling. The reason I am discussing my periodic condition now, is that it fits comfortably with my then episode at Kino London and throughout the summer of 2017 which I will tell more about in the next section of this book.

"Manbun" Further showings:

Jackanory (A live recital) - Westgate Studios, Wakefield (2017)
Live and Animated (A live recital) - The Slocken, Leeds (2019)
Gingerlicous Nights (A live recital) - The Old Post Office Cafe, Silsden (2019)

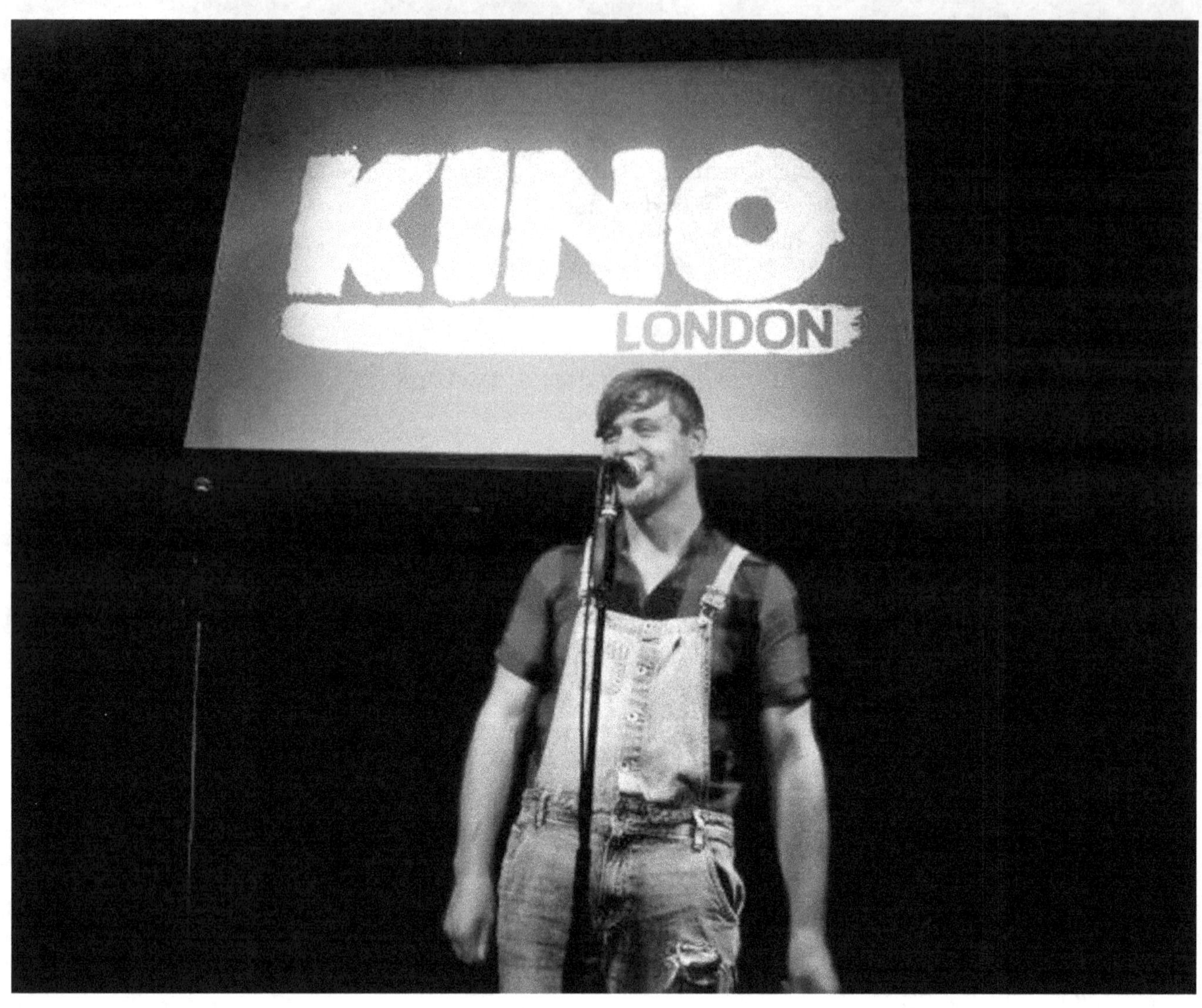

Introducing "Manbun" at Kino London.
The Bill Muray Comedy Club, Islington (July 2017)

The Walking Group

I've joined a Thursday morning walking group,
I thought, a little bit of exercise, then tea,
Well, I didn't half get the wrong end of the stick
My oh my, it nearly killed me!

I thought the over-60s had a life of pleasure,
I thought that this would be something I'd like,
Well, I'm telling you would I have opposed,
If I knew it was a ten-mile hike!

I was up to my neck in mud,
My anatomy ached as I felt the wrath,
The other women had a giggle at my expense,
Even the cows had a laugh!

My legs used muscles which I have never worked before,
As I ploughed up countless hills,
It didn't have destroy my inner dignity,
It didn't half bloody kill!

The other women nattered and laughed with joy,
Admiring the shoddy countryside,
Well, I was ready to hibernate in the nearest pub,
To drink a gin and feel fortified!

But on that evening, I returned home,
Blister's eradicated my feet,
So I cheered myself up, I went to the fridge,
I got myself a treat.

Then I decided that walking groups are not for me,
The sessions are nothing but a sin,
They are the devil's advocate on my precious senior health,
So I have gone and packed them in!

(This Anecdote is to be recited from a senior lady's perspective.)

The Granny Zimmer Frame Race

They are ready to rocket the hurdle,

Exhilaration pasted on their face,

They are in for the crown,

The granny zimmerframe race.

It is every senior to their own,

The competitiveness in their eye,

The biddies are in for the win,

But who will qualify?

The shroud of a gun,

They are off on their way,

Who will plunge for the finish?

Who will save the day?

Number 2 is scuttling up,

She is about to overtake Number 3,

But Number 1 could have a chance,

My, oh my,

Who could it be?

Number 4 has fuel in her legs,

She is in it the utmost,

But Number 2 is not far behind,

Who will be the first to reach the post?

Number 3 is the favourited,

As she buckles upon her stride,

But Number 1 is taking no chances,

As she haggles at the side.

It is an extremely epic call,

An inch between their span,

Number 3 is at the joyride,

She is doing the best that she can.

Of course Number 1,

Has graced the first place,

She is the first champion to grace,

The granny zimmer frame race!

Monday 15th October 2019

I arrived at The Queenies Coffee House in Huddersfield at approximately 6:35pm, opening up the entrance door with a ring in its bell. I saw Rose Condo, a Canadian poet and compere for this evening's event. She welcomed me into the homely, lukewarm venue with a hug and a pleasant smile, saying how glad she was for me to attend this evening. I was actually the first member of the public to arrive. Rose looked and seemed extremely well. We delved into conversation about everything creative about the arts. She has moved to Salford now, adding that the Spoken Word event "Evidently" which was curated and compered by the Mancunian Poet Kieron King, will be going on hiatus this December being the final event. Rose then asked me what I had been up to. I told her about my upcoming guest slot at The Blue Walnut Cafe based in Torquay on the 8th November, presenting my set with a live recital of my whimsical animations. She hinted that there could be a possibility to showcase at an event here at Queenies. It would be brilliant if I could. I subsequently met Lyndsey Price, who was going to be the first guest poet to deliver a beautiful set. Her poems were based on her place within the Poetry Society, the surroundings around her, observations on life and her analytical study of the modern ego that we are enveloped in today. She is based in Liverpool working as a theatre practitioner, creatively involved specifically within this role, as opposed to a performance poet. Ash Dickinson was the second guest poet of the evening, huddled together with an array of fine eclectic open mic performers. I was the third poet in the first half to perform my whimsical anecdote "The Granny Zimmer Frame Race," which was received very well by the audience. I spent the majority of the afternoon rehearsing the poem, as I walked around the house, in order to present a faultless delivery. Lyndsey mentioned that senior people using zimmer frames really do compete against one another in a bid to become champions. She used to work in a care home, so has witnessed this happening. A second female poet who performed on the open Mic, added that she has witnessed this occur too, as she worked in a care home. The seniors would place netting down onto the floor to represent the finish line. My anecdote resonated with them both.

"Did you smoke weed when you wrote it?" The female poet asked, with a laugh.

"I don't think so," I answered, laughing at the wisecrack.

The event concluded with a twenty-five minute set from Ash Dickinson. The event ran at 7:30pm until 9:15pm. I made my way back to the bus stop, opposite Huddersfield train station, to catch the 229 Arriva service back to Batley. A man named Stuart Swayde, who also performed this evening, joined me on the bus journey, getting off at Bradley.

Thursday 8th November 2019

I had an absolute enthralling experience, performing as a headline act at Big Poetry, based at The Blue Walnut Cafe in Torquay, this evening. It was arguably the biggest gig of 2018 for me, which Robert Garnham had invited me down to perform for the Devonians. It was a privilege. I travelled since 4:50am on the Megabus from Leeds, changing at Bristol and then Exeter Park and Ride. Then it was to Newton Abbott at 3:45pm. Samantha Boarer kindly let me stay over at her home which was based in a rural area. Her parents were away touring America for three weeks, so it worked out perfectly for me to stay. I did profusely thank her for my stay. She mentioned that it was no problem at all.

Samantha and I arrived at The Blue Walnut Cafe in Torquay at approximately 7:15pm in the delightful presence of Robert Garnham. The event commenced at 8pm and ended at 10pm. The open mic performers tonight were brilliant. Robert compered the first half and Samantha compered the second. She began with a poem about her historic love for bread which she had to abandon due being glucose intolerant. Robert introduced me in the final half, when everyone gathered in the petite twenty-three seater cinema room for my twenty minute set. It was an extremely intimate setting. I sat on a chair in the corner of the cinema room directly under the projection screen. I opened up my set with two standalone whimsical anecdotes of mine titled "The Walking Group" and "The Granny Zimmer Frame Race" before cuing in the man who operated the projector. He pressed play on the DVD, where I delivered a live recital of my stop motion animations, including "A Peculiar Imagination."

I concluded my set with a rendition of the humorous verse written by the brilliant inspiring Pam Ayres, titled "Mixed Ward." The audience's response to my delivery was brilliant. Robert mentioned that I had earned myself a herd of new fans, particularly a woman named Louise, who suggested that I should move to Torquay to provide the Devonians with more of my witty material.

I provided Mr Projectionist with a copy of my animations to thank him for allowing me to perform at The Blue Walnut Cafe. Samantha mentioned to me that she had recommended my animations to a lecturer at the Bath University who was looking for filmmakers to introduce to her drama students. Apparently, the students were in awe of my animations. I really appreciated this and felt very honoured to be recommended. It's a pleasure to be able to express myself, spreading wit and whimsy to enthusiastic audiences up and down the nation.

Friday 9th November 2018

Samantha drove me to the Newton Abbott train station for 7:40pm, where I caught the National Express coach service to Exeter Sidwell Street. I stopped off at a lovely Cafe, as I had a good two hour and a half hour wait to kill before the 10:20am Megabus service from here to Leeds.

I sat at a table with my laptop and uploaded a portion of my performance from last night on my social media pages. I had a small creamy latte and a chocolate croissant. The eleven-hour journey back to Leeds was bearable, considering it could have been extremely tedious. The Megabus was involved in a minor collision with a wall as it left from Birmingham to Sheffield. I arrived into Leeds for 6:50pm, managing to catch the 229 Bus Service back to Batley. I had a brilliant time in the English Riviera, seeing and meeting an array of fabulous talent too.

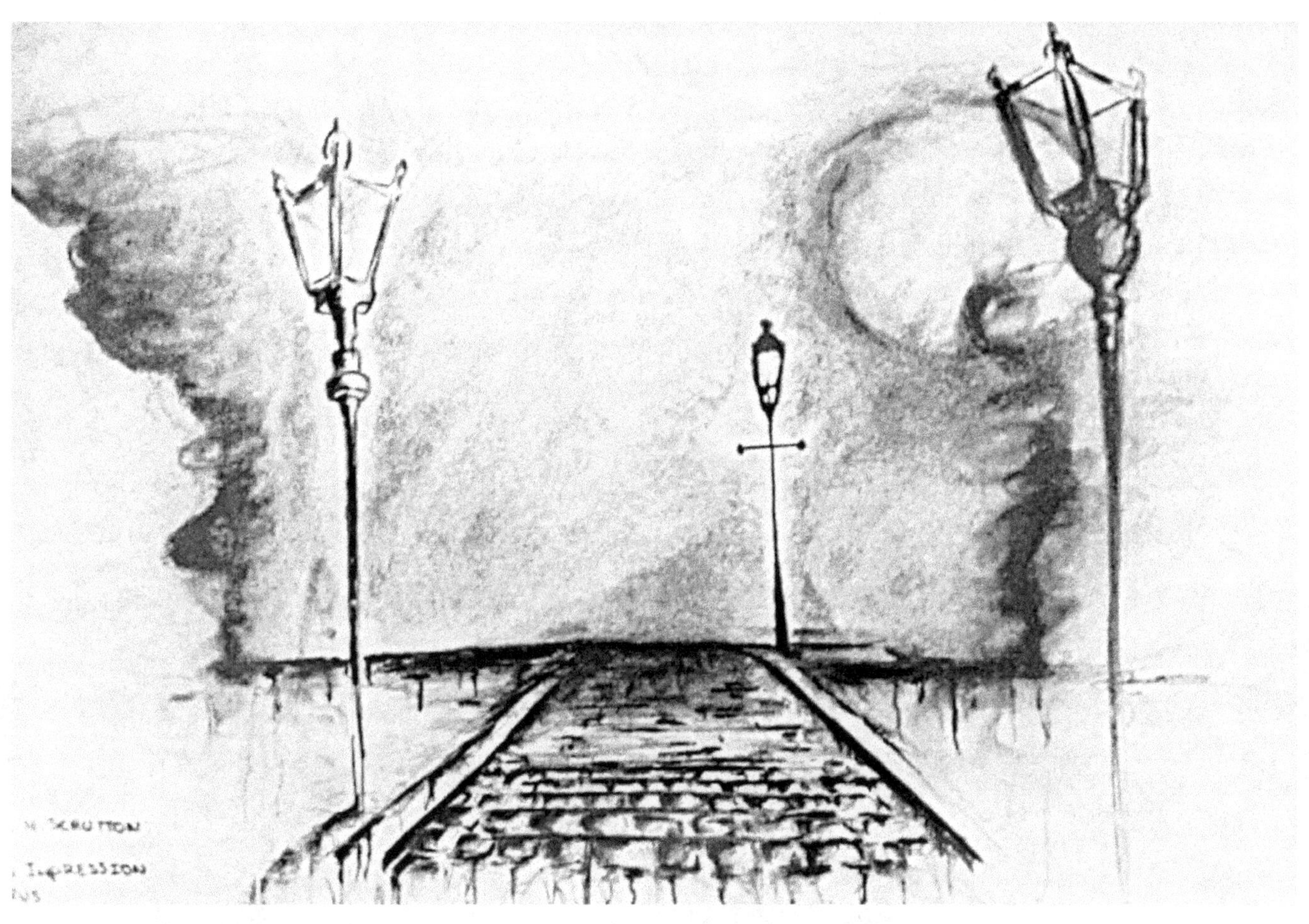

"Midnight Pretences"
A print from the original A4 Pencil Sketch
April 2018

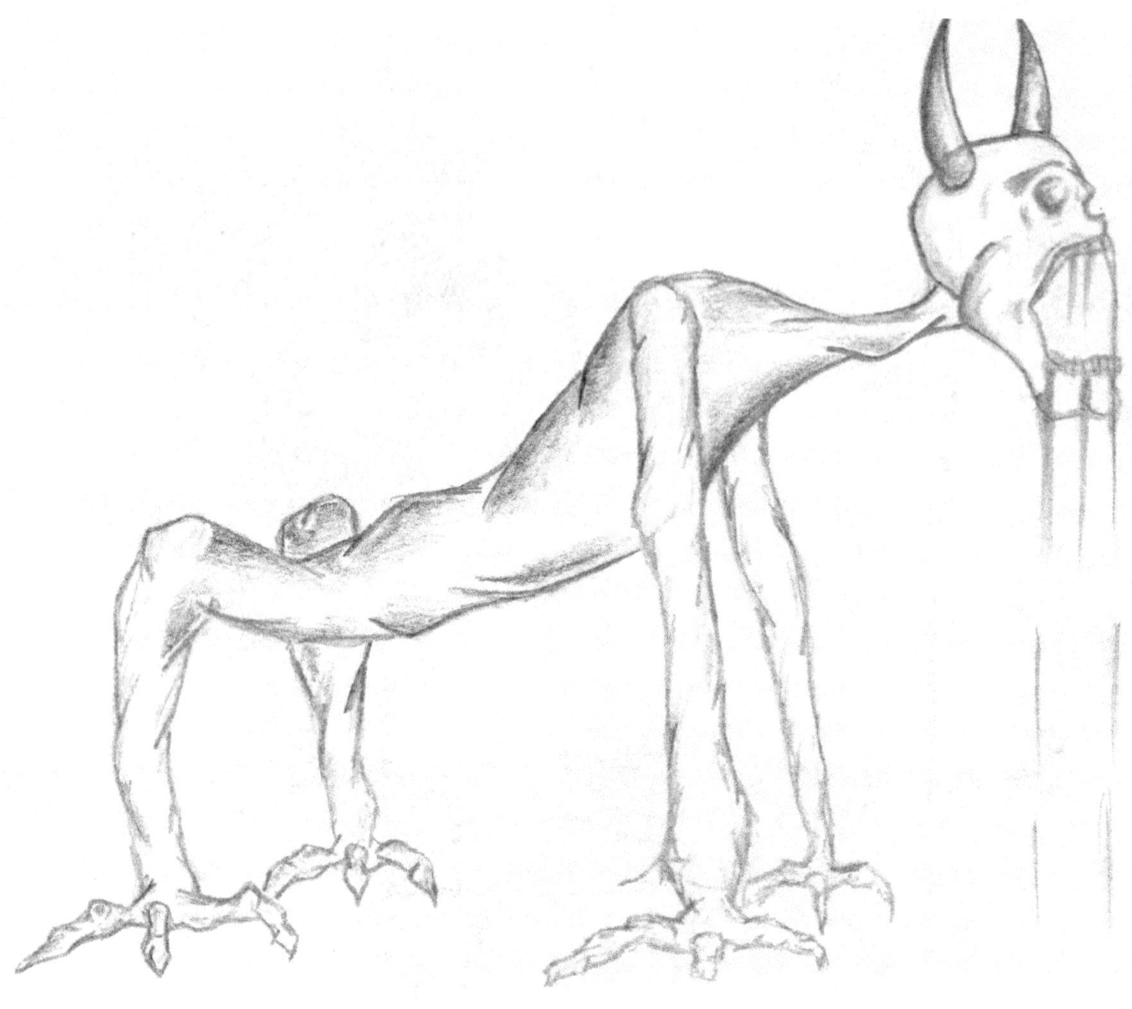

"The Nightcrawler"
A quick A5 Pencil Sketch - 15/3/2021

Also known as the Frenso Alien, the Nightcrawler is a North American cryptid. They are known to have an extremely petite anatomy, knees bent backwards and most often faceless.

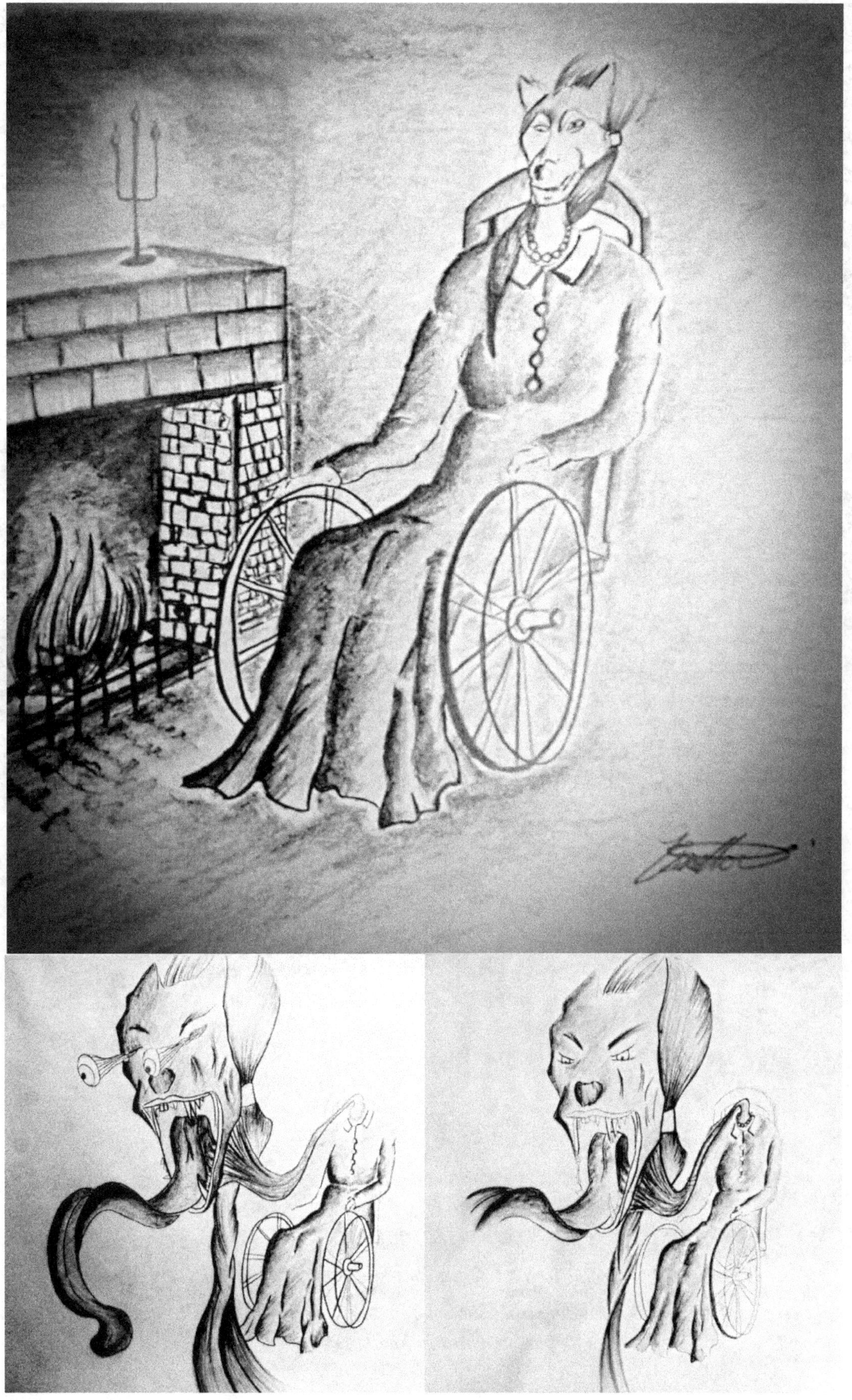

"Little Red Riding Hood"
Working Animation concept - unreleased (November 2017)

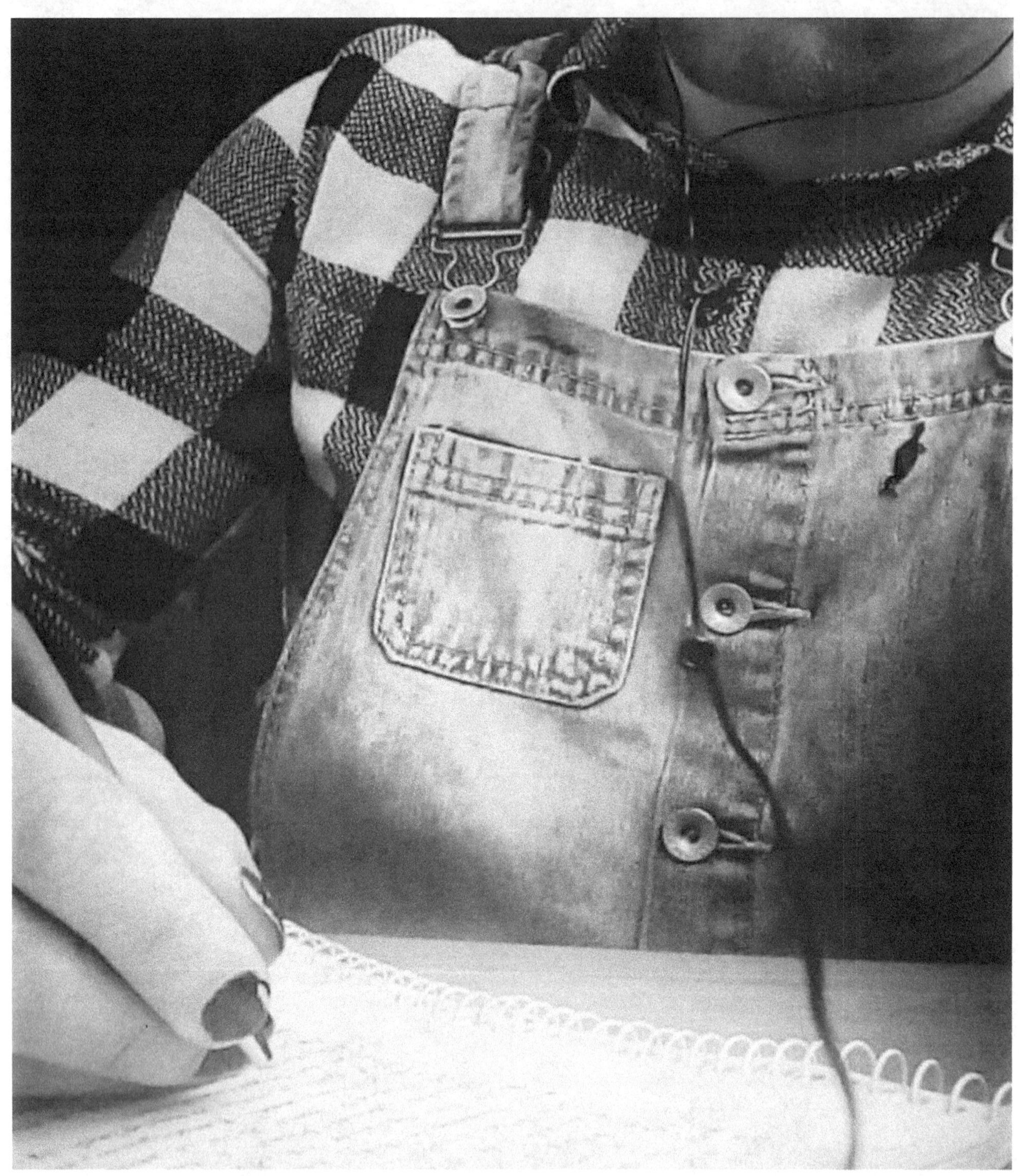

- 6/3/2017
A little bit of scribbling whilst I de-tour to London on an East Coast train service.
In the evening, I performed my Whimsical Anecdotes in an intimate lukewarm candlelit cabin, in a back garden, based in South London.

Director's Cut

A brilliant Wigan-based poet by the name of Eva Curless, approached me to adapt a compelling poem of hers into an animation. It was based on her own experience with mental health. I gladly agreed as it would allow me to express my own perspective on a condition which affects many people every day. What you will read below, are some ideas that I had for the opening of the Eva's poem "Director's Cut".

The narrative opens up with the questionable line:

"Facebook asks her "What's on your mind?" Watched as her walls crumble down with every blind comment. Every reminder that she was ugly, worthless, irrelevant - "

The whole animation was produced with a single sheet of A3 tracing paper and using the same techniques as mentioned in my previous projects. The opening scene began with a faint looking cloud, which formed itself into these following words:

"Facebook ask's her, what's on your mind?"

The hand-written text then transformed itself into the outline of the woman. Teardrops poured from her perplexed eyes, with a spider's web of turmoil appearing behind her. A good sixteen shots after, the web faded out and the following text appeared on her head: "ugly" and "worthless". The woman and the text appeared to crumble simultaneously into a heap of oppression, and then the image Zoetrope faded in. The object would rotate displaying expressionless faces.

The toy then crumbled again, into a heap of ash, before reprising into the scene of an isolated, forgotten place. A tree sprouted up from the ground and spread its branches during the narrative: "... Leaves of driftwood smiles." A bed then appeared, showing the woman lying down in desolation. I added a gritty texture to the contours of her body to show her experience of neurotic anxiety. The leaves descended from the tree branches onto the woman and at the right-hand side of the screen. The trees would then form a merciless silhouette of a distinctive face, intending to "swallow her up during the new winter trends - "

A congregation of three trolls would then peer intensely into a laptop screen, the woman coming into contact with the trolls and sensing their demonic, grotesque personalities, a troll's neck extending and hovering over her and peering back with its demonic eyes, a tenacious sea wave surging upwards as the woman suffers with bouts of apprehension. A teardrop builds up in the woman's eyes, to form a catastrophic flood. This would represent one of the lines from the poem:

"Then push her out like a paper boat through the same stormy weather - "

Instead of having the literal portrayal of a boat, her physical presence being the "boat" drowning in the attacks of abuse. Life is an endless high tide of day to day pressures which we all unfortunately have to sail through and I feel it is extremely important to represent this.

The troll would now be seen holding a gun. The woman then kneeled down with her head in her hands. Her black hair was flowing downwards and touching the ground. The gun disappeared and the troll knelt down and overshadowed her from behind. The troll's neck once again began to extend, as the woman swayed irritably as a result of its bullying presence. The image of the troll disintegrated and abandoned the anguished woman who was propelled with fear.

We would then see the medical professionals repairing the lives of their patients by, I quote from the poem, "gluing lives back together" after the woman "swallowed the trolls lies with a bottle of pills" in a bid to self harm.

She would then sit isolated on the edge of a jagged cliff looking towards the moon. This scene would fade out, frame by frame, into the perspective of looking out from a bedroom window, with the moon still present behind the glass panes.

The animation ended with the woman being exposed to the sadistic trolls who were sat in the auditorium of a theatre. Her fearless presence was apparent as she stood stalwart on a stage. This imposing theatre setting represented her internal strength and her healing soul. The camera would gradually out focus from the woman on stage. To evident this, I used the lines, I quote from the poem -

"You didn't notice that her joy was staged,
The scriptwriting in which her life engaged,
But when the encore's done and the curtain's shut,
The skin isn't thick enough, for the director's cut -"

This was an absolutely beautiful reflection of how the woman had healed from the abuse that she had experienced, even though the scars were present mentally. I used a royalty free soundtrack by Kevin McLeod, to accompany this powerful scene. I also used sound effects to help enhance some of the other scenes such as the storm surge.

It was a fantastic honour to have Eva inviting me to adapt her poem into an animation. She loved the final edit and added that it was perfect in every way.

Being involved in the poetry circuit, provides me the opportunity to networking an array of fabulous poets of differing styles. Meeting Eva at the Verbal Remedy Poetry Night in Leeds enabled me to collaborate with her and express the subject of mental health through the medium of animation.

Rob Speranza screened the animation at "Showroom Shorts" on Tuesday 23rd January 2018, which went extremely well. Research indicates that in England, mental illness is a silent predator, which affects one in four people each year. One in six people report experiencing a common mental health problem such as anxiety and depression in any given week. I imagine these figures to have catapulted into double figures as a result of the Covid-19 global pandemic.

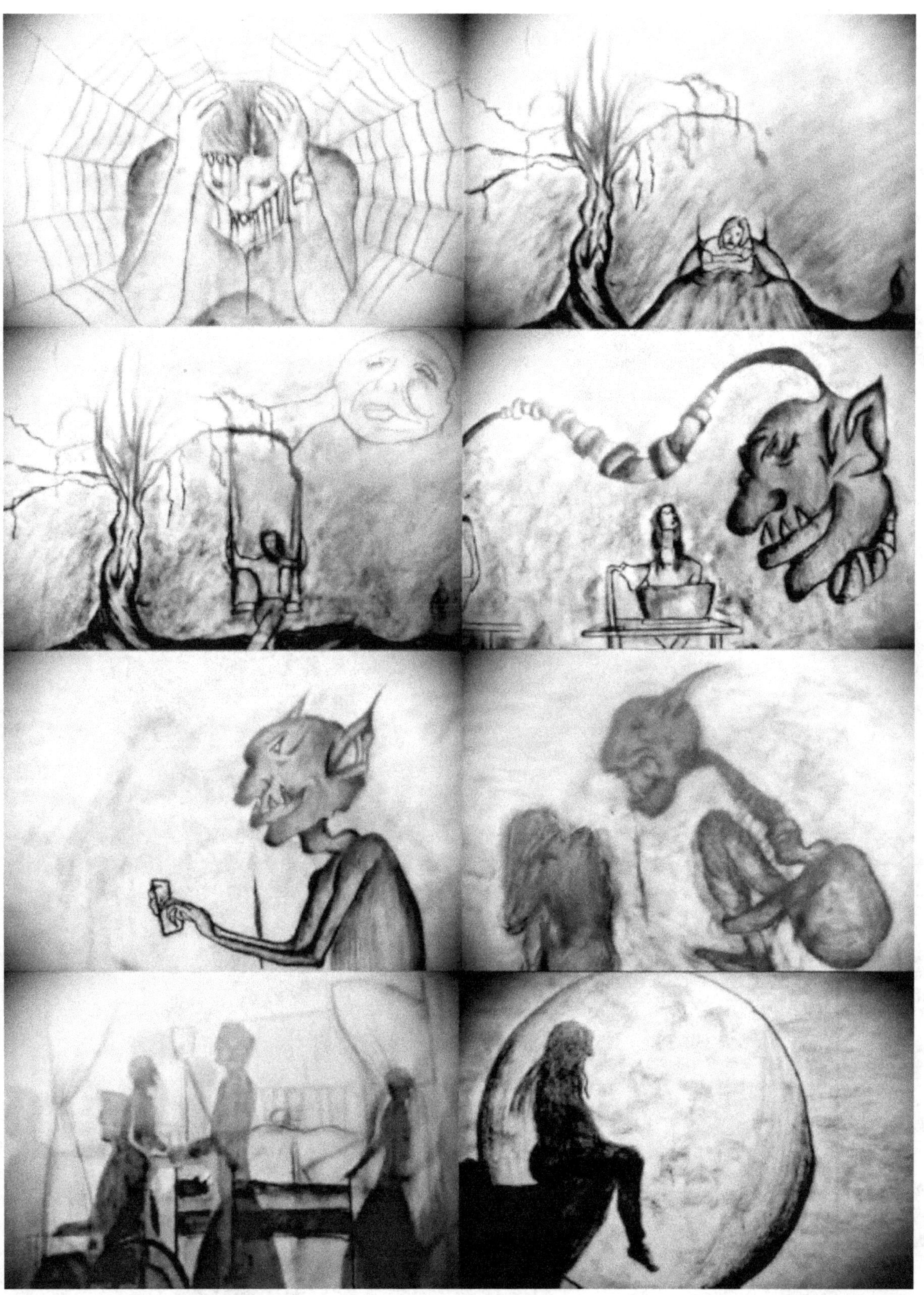

"Director's Cut" - Animation stills.
Duration: 03:42

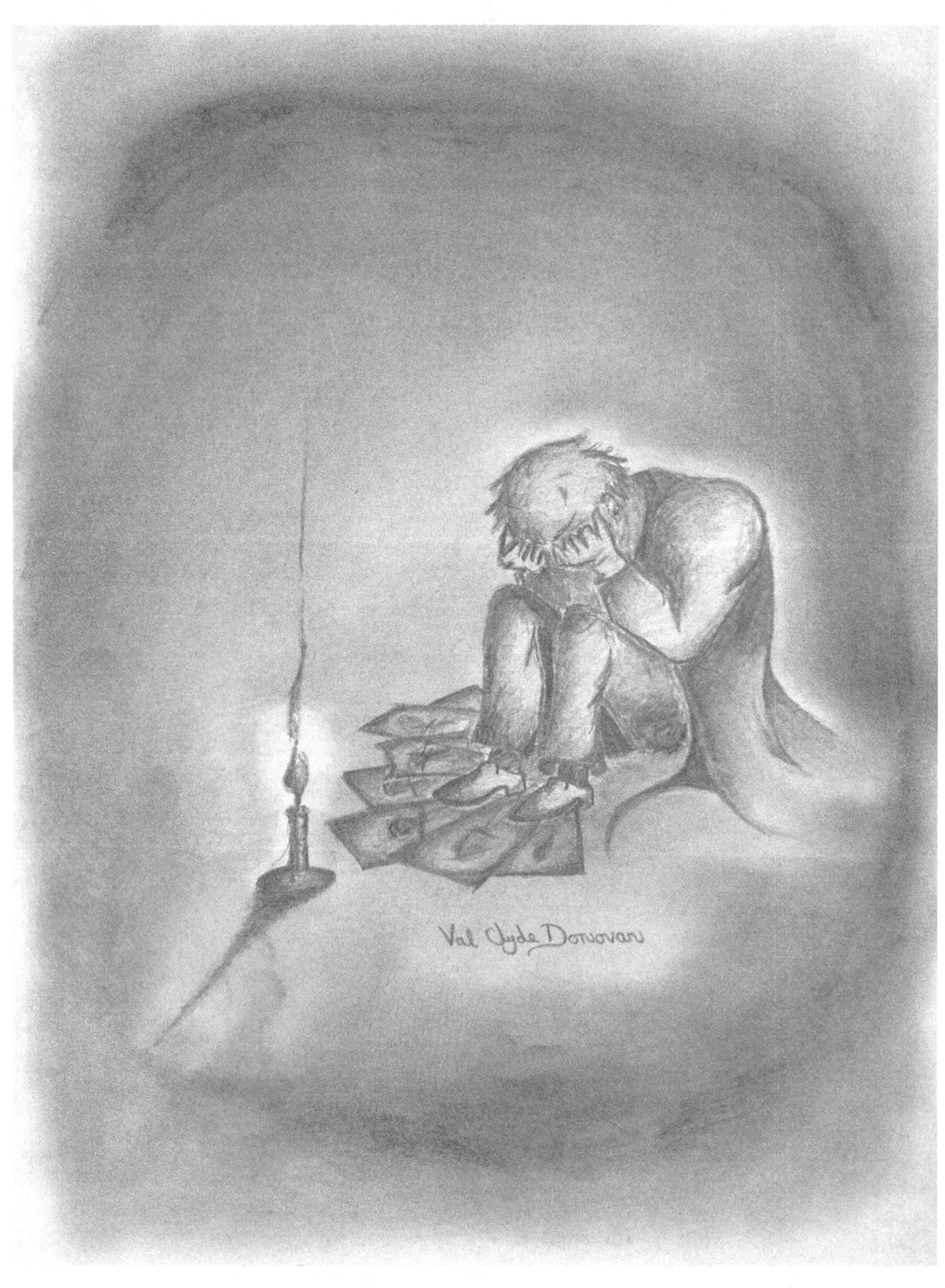
Val Clyde Donovan

Beyond Imagination

During the autumn of 1989, there was an extravagant looking house stood in the Yorkshire moors. It was a well-known structure, which once claimed its fortune from faming over many generation's, but now there is nothing left but history which has faded and left behind a concrete brittle form of architecture. During the evenings, the house settles as a silhouette with a history of a sinister dynasty on the peak of a hill. The house belonged to a fifty something year old, dejected artist by the name of Val Clyde Donovan. Val was a tall, angular looking gentleman. He had a Dickensian grey beard and wore a suit, which was once exquisite to the eye, but now is nothing but a victim to his wiry figure. He was dreadfully thin due to malnutrition. His haggard skin appeared to be sucked into his stern, lurid face, allowing his cheek bones to stick out. As a young man he was extremely self-conscious, but now he is fighting with a relentless demon in his mind. He was the only child birthed to reclusive parents. They never involved themselves in any activity with anyone. They kept themselves to themselves. He has spent the majority of his life, sat skittish on his chair, twiddling his fingers on the arm rest, cross legged and rocking side to side in a seamless motion. This happened when he was secluded in his dreary, bitter attic, with nothing there apart from multiple paintings hanging unbalanced on the decomposed walls.

Every now and then, there was the pattering of the rain, splashing relentlessly onto the roof, which was the perfect metaphor for his mental state of mind. The birds which made themselves at home perched on the chimney, were divergent interpretations of Val's childhood. This house had never been cleaned for so long. This territory represented his state of mind; turbulent and herculean. The repulsive stench of damp penetrated his surroundings. The yellow cobwebs were twined from pillar to post, like a spirit, haunting its presence around him. The Georgian window, above the charred mantelpiece, which once shone the radiant euphoria of the sun, was now nothing but a boarded up black out, disguising the evidence of anyone even living there. Rodents scuttled timidly from corner to corner, creaking the floorboards, and made a irritable cacophony with their feet. Val was far too distant in mind to be concerned about the little creatures that lived with him. He was immobilized from being conscious of his surroundings since he dwelled his second home, which was his psyche. He was agoraphobic, having an uncomfortable fear of the outside. Being locked away in his candle lit attic, this was the only place that felt like a sanctuary. Darkness was his only consoling friend, which he felt adequately safe to be in, but it didn't stop the monster that he lived with every second of the day.

This space would be a nightmare for any OCD sufferer. His condition was a form that was never spoken about in the open. Nowadays the term OCD is often portrayed as a compulsive cleaning disorder. The OCD which Val had was his tendency to repetitively ruminate on thoughts that seemed real but were in fact entirely false. Every painting of Val's represented the destruction of his mental health. He used his painitngs to reassure himself that his thoughts were nothing more than make belief. Anyone would compare him to the prominent abstract expressionist Mark Rothko, in the manner of how they both become captivated by their tortured minds. Val was prone to believe that he was responsible for a brutal assassination of an innocent soul. Nothing was going to help him overcome this anxiety, more than the paintings which hung around him. The more he attempted to suppress his thoughts, the more they became believable. Making paintings which depicted his troublesome fears was an aid for him. It helped to counsel him in a way that he could logically understand them. Little did he know that his work would be eventually cause his disappearance.

Val's psychosis instantly began after the death of his mother and the sentencing of his father and the estranged upbringing that he had with them. He was always an outcast at school and an introvert in comparison to his peers. He was persecuted for not fitting in with the bracket of ordinariness; even his professors had their doubts about his unorthodox identity. He didn't share his thoughts of his own life behind closed doors; he kept them secretly hidden away in his delusional mind. One day, Val ran up to the attic to flee from the fracas between his parents, locking the door shut and curling up into a ball with his hands shielding his ears. The commotion suddenly stopped with silence. He released his hands from his ears, timidly looking down to the floor, noticing a small serrated stone at his feet. Picking it up, he used the rock to scribble out his afflictions on the surface. The drawings weren't anything that ranked themselves as a masterpiece, but they portrayed the environment he was capsuled in. No elemental detail was there in the drawings, Val just made linear, candid sketches of a hostile family. A tear fell from his fledgling eyes and diluted his depictions. He channelled his emotions, expressing them by drawing illustrations on the ground. Val discovered his vocation as an artist during his infancy, which allowed him to acknowledge his melancholy on paper as well as the ground. Val witnessed unimaginable things, too delicate for any child to see. Creativeness was the only outlet for him to comprehend and face his demons. His drunken father resented the idea of his son receiving more attention from his mother than he did. At the age of six, Val's father killed his wife in jealous revenge. He was sentenced to life in prison and Val was left to look after himself, alone in the attic. Since childhood, he rarely exposed himself to daylight, hence the reason why his skin has wreck over the years. The only time he did was by keeping himself occupied, consistently producing paintings in order to promote his art to enthusiastic art buyers. His persistent dedication as an artist deteriorated, as he developed a fear of the outdoors. He never succeeded at earning a living as a professional artist due to this, although he did continue with his practice, portraying the science of anxiety, which he suffered with, every day. Something out of the ordinary entered his mind, which became a mental catalyst.

One Siberian November evening, ten or so years prior to 1989, he overheard a stranger outside speak about a volatile lady, who was strangled violently as she slept. The assassin was a male companion of hers, who lived two doors down. The news subsequently affected Val. Within a second, pessimistic voices in his head told him that he was the suspect to her murder and that he should be sentenced for this malicious crime. Although he knew he was innocent, his mind made him believe that he wasn't. This was the beginning of his psychosis. Val could not understand why he was experiencing these callous thoughts. Attempting to obliterate them from his unparalleled mind was futile. They would remain vigorously and more powerfully inside his intellect. Val was aware of the term intrusive thoughts. He briefly experienced episodes of these when he turned eighteen. He became threatened by a thought that he was the suspect of a woman's rape, even though he wasn't. This thought eventually dissolved from his mind in a matter of weeks.

This current obsession was something that he had never experienced before. These thoughts that he had felt seemed extremely sincere, which lead him to believe undeniably that they were true. The only way he could expose these thoughts, was through his artistry. He painted on large canvases, so that he could study his own thoughts at face value, as opposed to re-enacting them subconsciously. He stood before a blank canvas on an easel, slowly pulling back its dusty sheet. The dust evaporated in the air like white butterflies fluttering away into the midst. There it was the first of six canvases that he had never touched. Black charcoal was used as a base for the linear sketch that appeared, which was ideal, because the rough textures represented his disorientated way of thinking. He dipped his paintbrush in a bucket of dirty water, that was collected in the rain. He swept his brush over the charcoal to create a raisin black silhouette of the woman that he thought he had assassinated. He produced another painting which reassured him of his innocence. This time he began to add a little more definition, understanding his cognitive behaviour. After the completion of each piece, he exhibited his own delusions on his wall, as an indication of what he was thinking. Studying the depictions, Val felt extremely at ease knowing that his subjects were no important than just thoughts. He was elated, he was able to reflect and evaluate his misconceptions, by observing these illustrations. A grin appeared on his face, which hadn't been seen for at least ten years. It wasn't a grin of gladness; it was a sign of the hidden mania he sensed in the pit of his stomach. It was invisible to the eye but physical within him.

As he sat for a couple of hours or so in his ligneous chair, on a somewhat balanced wavelength, the paranoia would immediately return, occupying his mind with vengeance. He violently rocked back and forth in his chair, grasping his head with the palm of his clammy hands. He experienced flashbacks of the killing of his mother when he was younger. These thoughts appeared more frequently throughout this manic episode, he began to regard his paintings as if they were deceiving him. As he became more sedentary, with a fiery shudder throughout his body, Val stood up and made his way over to an empty canvas to perform his rituals again. In the same process – as an attempt to defeat the hellion that dwelled within him. He produced identical copies his original paintings, in order to make them authentic, but this ritual had perturbing consequences. With Val overanalysing his thoughts, they however became stronger and unrelentless in his mind. He felt the need to confess to the murder of the woman which he had not committed. He erratically painted himself as the suspect, confessing his sins, in order for someone to come and witness his deeds, once he had placed a scalpel to his throat. Somehow, he managed to prevent himself from making the "confession" and viewed it as something based on nothing but a crippling anxious thought. This brutal depiction became a prominent piece, which led him to wonder "what if" his thoughts were true. Seeing sense of his cognition, settled his compos mentis slightly but it did not cure him of his OCD. He glanced over to the putrid timber door, that was once a shield for him to hide behind, away from his violent father. He saw himself as a defenceless child, his head tucked between his knees, masking away the reality that he was living in. Val held out his right hand to his imaged younger self at the door, as an attempt to comfort his past. There was no response from the child. Val quickly rubbed his eye with the tip of his finger, realising that that moment was a delusion. A sickening sound of static resonated in his ears, as the child disappeared. The sound of crows cawing repetitively on the roof broke the silence of Val's grief. The eerie wind wailed through the cracks of the boarded up Georgian window and oozed its way in uninvited, as Val's grey hair gently whisked to and fro. He closed his eyes, feeling the tenderness of the sclera. Tears formed, reddening his gaunt face as he tightly closed his eyes. He relaxed and opened his eyes a second or two later, composing himself to face reality again.

As days, weeks, and months pass by, Val became a hoarder to his own artistry. His weight is deteriorating rapidly. His grey hair is dying gradually and his hygiene is paradise for the rodents he lives with. The flies even decline to hover around him. The attic is quilted with endless hours of analytical paintings, in order to logically see a conclusion to his mania. The walls, ceiling and floorboards became victimized to his possessive scribblings. Some days he discovered a realm of understanding, but other days he didn't. He found it onerous to swim in his temperamental high tides, attempting to reach the shores. He wasn't always dependent through his art. Often he would find it hard to concentrate, due to the over hypersensitivity of his obsessive thinking. Some days he would have frequent loss of energy. He spent this time curled up in to a ball and sleeping, besides a flickering candle, the mind too unconscious to dwell on any thoughts. When awakening, he experienced unbearable apprehension. His body would jitter, his face felt paralysed. All he yearned was to break free from his skin and feel ordinary like any other person. When he was somewhat free from the intrusive thoughts, he would then ruminate of how deficient he personally feels as an Artist, as well as an individual. He has never found the adoration or respect for himself, whether he is highly renowned or not. He believes his expression through art, comes directly and explicitly from the heart and it has never been forced in any form or dimension. He is extremely grateful for the gifted talent he has been given from a life source, primarily helped to express his mental health through artistic composition. The loft became a museum of the goblins in his sanity. The alienation stifled his personal space. He was the jury to his own self-deprivation, attempting to make a verdict to which side of ruminations to believe; his mind or his paintings.

A couple of briskly evenings pass by, Val sits hunched up in his chair, nibbling away at his fingernails, which are stump and gritty. His body trembles, to the rhythm of his palpitating heart, channelling off from his Anxiety. He merely has hair and his skeletal anatomy, is like a canvas frame but without the fabric. He subsequently rises from the chair and nervously makes his way forward to the canvas, like he is stepping towards the unknown of his own death. He picks up a matted paintbrush, which rests tiresomely in a pallet and makes his first mark on to the canvas, revisiting his mental capacity. Within ten minutes, he recreates the same painting. An eclectic variation of Venetian, Rossi Corsa, Oxblood and rustic reds perform a collaboration of shades, to represent the massacre in the work, expressed rather erratically with the rugged edge of the paintbrush. He profusely sweats, as he is delving back into his mind, to play out the thought, physically seeing sense of his factious thinking. He drops the paintbrush, clenches his hands and then grips his saggy skin in horror. In a moment of fury, he picks up a scalpel laying on the floor besides his feet, violently sabotaging the paintings, which pose as victims before him. Dropping the instrument, he gradually steps back from the demonic painting, collapsing to the ground in a state of apprehension. He huddles up into a foetal position, cowing frantically at his misdemeanours. His nullifying energy prevails the ambience throughout the attic, and in to the paintings which are ravaged on the walls. Inch by inch, metre by metre, his pessimistic work fuses itself together into a duvet of his revulsions. The paintings begin to animate and perform the sadistic thoughts out around him, as he screams in anguish, begging them to stop. Second by second, the pieces disintegrate in to fragments of his imagination, the attic roof becoming shredded by the overwhelming force of his frantic mind, erupting upwards, in to the monstrous evening sky. The rumble of the floor shuddered, cracks began to form on the ground around him. Then a hand of an infant stretches out from beneath the foundation of the ground, vigorously pulling at his arm. A second adulescent arm appeared. Then a third, then a forth, then a fifth, then a sixth, until an assemble of human remains beseiged him. The female victim in the paintings breaks free from the canvas plain-woven fabric, clutching to the last strands of his fickle grey hair, in a desperate bid to be rescued from the savages of the earth. He fights her off in a bid to abseil from the affliction. She becomes possessive for him to save her, but he wants to obliterate her from his neurotic mind, cleansing himself from the thoughts. Val is stretched beyond recognition from his head to his feet, his skin peeling away by the force of the entities. He is sinking in to the swamps of the ground, screaming for mercy. The painting hauls the woman back in, festering away in to the sky. Brick by brick, tile by tile, dust by dust, scared thoughts by scared thoughts, everything is swept up in to the unknown. A final swoosh of a shroud pierces through his ears, as he is swallowed up by the terrain and then … Nothing.

The house has completely banished, not a spec of evidence remains on the site. Not an existance of Val anywhere. Not even a flurry of medievel entities haunt the Yorkshire moors like they used to. Complete emptiness. All that remains is the thirsty grass, waiting for the next droplet of rain to harness the greenery back in to the land. Each year on the anniversary of the spook, a small fragment of woollen fabric would seep through the twiggy arms of the trees, coming to rest in the centre of Val's decay. The material slept for ten minutes, subsequently dispersing in to the swampy earth. Anxiety is the key element to Intrusive thoughts, of how our minds reflect on a particular situation to obliterate the physical symptom. No one can predict whenever anxiety strikes. It is a ticking bomb, waiting to detonate. Sometimes mental health has a fantasy of condemning a person, in order to challenge their strength, to see if they have the will power to defeat the confliction within the mind. It is a brilliant feeling to have the ruminations stripped bare from the mind, allowing yourself to breathe again. Val was defeated by his mind, until the bitter end. Mentally he had the courage to suppress his thoughts, but physically he was too powerless to try. The hollow spot became a mortuary. Overgrown weed burying the space, in order to deflect history. The spindly trees, mourned the land of Val's necropolis. His corpse is entombed ten feet underground, just enough depth for the earth creatures to feed their appetite amongst his enfeebled flesh. Not a soul has visited the area, nor hiked passed its tracks in a bid to reach the other side of the Moors. No birds home their prays there like they used to. All is forbidden. Our mental faculties are grotesque in making us think, feel and act the way we do. No matter how sincere of a person you are, no matter how far you stretch to great lengths by giving your service to another individual in need, no matter how jubilant and blessed in life you are, your mentality will come to consume you. Whatever entity assailed Val the way it did, is completely beyond imagination.

"I'm not an abstractionist. I'm not interested in the relationship of color or form or anything else. I'm interested only in expressing basic human emotions: tragedy, ecstasy, doom, and so on."

- As quoted from Mark Rothko.

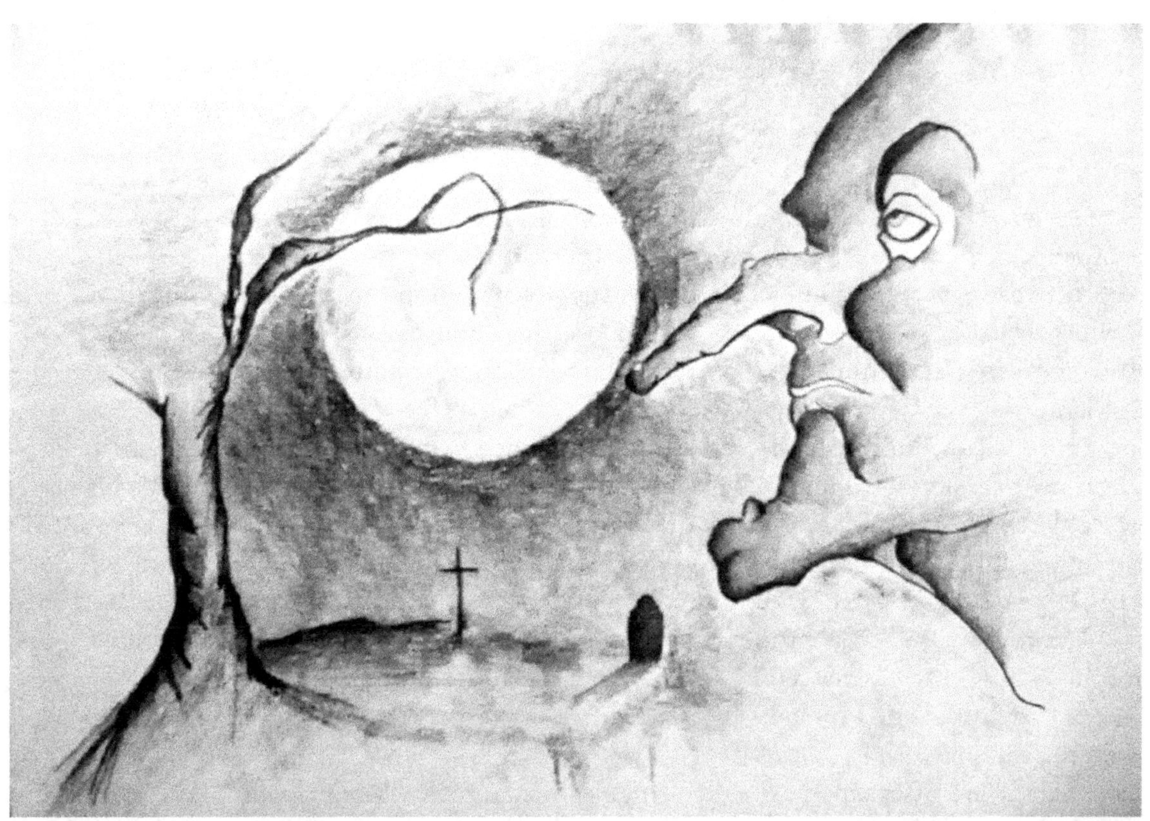

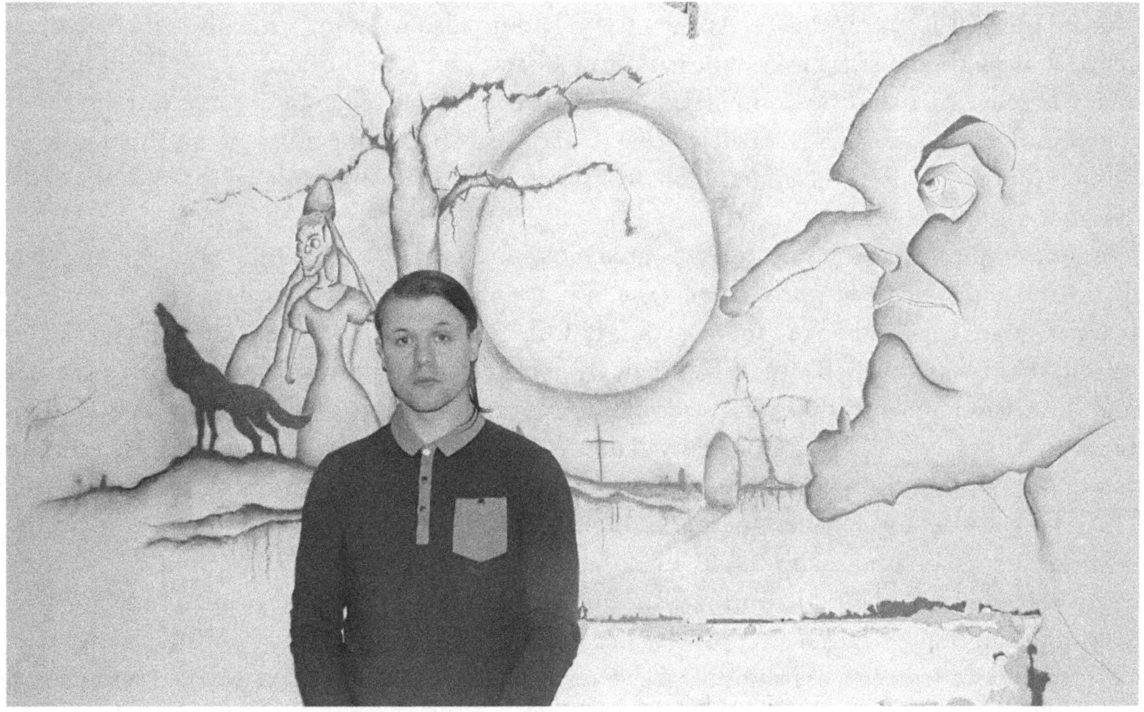

"The Witch"
(**Above**) A4 Pencil Sketch - April 2018.
(**Below**) "The Witch" transferred onto my old living room wall - January 2019.

The Uninvited

"Mental illness marked by periods of great excitement or euphoria, delusions and overactivity." This is a quote from an internet source which describes my manic episodes perfectly.

I do capture my own personal mental health struggles within my art, as well as my library of archived journals, which I am completely obsessed with. I use these journals as a way of explicitly recording my personal struggles in their entirety as an attempt to understand the pattern of an episode when they spontaneously manifest.

When I am sedated on medication such as sertraline, they help me to supress the make-belief illusions that occur in my mind and turn into intrusive thoughts. I am an extremely creative individual and my psyche is always alert with some form of innovative idea. So, when a thought unexpectedly pops into my head, it is a crippling feeling. The more I attempt to drown out this thought, the more my anxiety propels. I then have to reassess a certain real-life situation that affected me so that I can settle my cognitive behaviour. As much as I perform rituals such as producing drawings, I find that it helps me to make a logical and believable sense of what I had experienced in life. But because I tend to obsessively ruminate, this is when the internal battle of contradicting thoughts commence. An overwhelming feeling of jitters takes over me and this is when the shit gets real.

I first became aware of my mental health struggles when I was just sixteen years of age. It happened in December 2005 when I was an art Student at the Batley Art and Design College. I had crippling thoughts that convinced me that I was an abuser. At the time, I had no idea what intrusive thoughts were. But when these occurred, it made me socially distant from my surroundings and detached me from understanding what was a true sense of reality. I was in afraid of my surroundings being an imminent trigger to intrusive thoughts. Around this time, I had a further thought that I was becoming a murderer, threatening me with disillusionment and animosity. This stemmed from watching a TV programme based on the infamous murderers of the 1970's and 80's.

I was in college the following day and this anxiety spontaneously seeped into my thinking which was extremely distressing. When I was around seventeen years of age, I was suffocated with the gruelling concept that I was going to smother my mum with a pillow. The reality was that I knew this was completely fabricated and that I wasn't capable of doing that. I was anguished with distress and agitation and couldn't understand the reasoning to this fear. This thought did eventually disappear naturally. A couple of weeks after graduating from De Montfort University, I developed irrational thoughts about my mum again. The horror was centred around the delusion that I was going violently wound her with a knife. I didn't speak anything of this because it was never going to happen. Again, these thoughts disappeared over the course of a few weeks and I didn't have any experience of these thoughts again.

I had my first physical breakdown in the summer of 2008, a few weeks prior to starting University. Routines were changing for me, so my psyche became overwhelmed by my new surroundings. I found that anxiety had wicked way of rearing its ugly head when my mind was over-worked and this was what happened in 2008. I was plagued again with sexual intrusive thoughts, which I attempted to supress. I discovered that the more I fought these thoughts, the more of a tempest they had become. At approximately 6pm on the evening of Wednesday 20th August 2008, I attempted to take my own life with a concoction of paracetamols. A postman came to my aid when I was walking up Scotchman Lane towards Morley, in a state of confusion. It was a deliberate act of yearning for someone to help relieve me of this overacting heinous mind. I really didn't want to end my life. The postman called an ambulance for me and I was taken to Staincliffe hospital. I didn't do much harm to myself, except for a few minor chest pains. I was conscious throughout the whole ordeal and was later placed into a hospital cubicle whilst the crisis team assessed my condition. I never had any repeated sessions with them so it didn't solve the issue of my mind imagining things.

I had a second physical relapse on the evening of Saturday 3rd October 2010, when I commenced my third year at university. I hid myself away in my room, surrounding myself with an array of family photos. I placed myself on my bed as I self-harmed on tablets. Jess, a friend, came knocking on my door to ask me for a catalogue. I let her in and this was when she noticed what was going on. She gently led me to the toilet to be physically sick before an ambulance arrived. It was a selfish moment of crying out for help. I recall not even seeing the crisis team during that evening at the royal infirmary. I decided to discharge myself and we made our own way back home in the early hours of the bitterly cold October night.

I returned to Batley for a week to recuperate. One evening, my mum mentioned that she had seen a nun standing at her bedroom door whilst she was in bed. Even though she didn't know anything of my vulnerable state until I told her the next morning, spirituality had a way of bringing people closer to you with their love and guidance.

I became somewhat more aware of the term intrusive thoughts in September 2011, when I did my own research online, which is the worst thing to do in any given situation. A sense of relief overcame me but I had an erupted sense of fear the following day. I was experiencing irrational thoughts thinking I had sexually harmed someone and this sense of anxiety began to become extreme. Day after day I performed ritals as I sat naked in the bath, even though I knew that these thoughts were completely irrational. The ruminating became so debilitating that I knew there was no alternative other than to self-harm. I planned to jump from a bridge over the M62 near Morley, as I knew this would be a quick end to this persistent pain.

I hibernated in bed for the majority of my days to avoid experiencing any further episodes. I hid two packets of paracetamols down the side of my bed in case I needed them. My mum eventually suspected that I was hiding pills and demanded that I handed them over, which I did. One evening, I became a demonically possessed human being, lying across the bedroom floor battling helplessly with conflicting perceptions of reality and bipolar logic.

My mum and grandma attempted to send spiritual healing through me which worked temporarily but then I was back wanting to banish my existence. It seemed the only way to put a permanent end to this suffering. On Saturday 6th October 2012, I locked myself away in my bedroom and consumed myself with half a bottle of antifreeze which I purchased from a DIY shop that morning. My mum found me, tucked up in bed, disillusioned when I awoke with her screaming. My dad immediately drove me to hospital, as I violently coughed up blood, into a plastic bag in the back passenger seat. I remember being taken into the accident and emergency department, but I do not recall any other form of activity. I woke up later in a hospital bed dressed in a nightgown, connected to a catheter and a drip. Fomepizole was being pumped into my system to dilute the poisonous substance from me as I continued to vomit blood in cardboard bowls.

I was a hairpiece away from death and needed immediate medical help. Initially the medical professionals were considered eradicating the antifreeze by pumping vodka into my blood but it didn't come to this. I spent a whole gruelling week being medically treated by the brilliant NHS team in a high dependency ward based at Staincliffe hospital. The medics guessed that my survival rate was borderline during the first few days of being admitted. The hospital never had an incident concerning antifreeze poisoning so the only answer was to contact The Royal Hallamshire Hospital based in Sheffield for immediate medical advice. I just cannot thank the NHS enough for their unwavering support. Still naive at the time, I didn't entirely comprehend the jeopardy I had put myself or my family in.

I remember the hospital being a safe haven for me, as I felt protected from my intrusive thoughts and any other peril which came with this. Two days prior to my discharge, I glanced out of the hospital window witnessing the foggy scene of the car park and feeling once again threatened by the menacing triggers of the outside world. Upon hearing that I had to stay an extra night for my blood levels to stabilise, it was a relief and I felt safe again.

The following morning after I was discharged, I had the first of many home treatment sessions with Emma, a brilliant psychiatrist, who provided me with a better understanding of my own psychosis. Another young woman also came along with Emma, as a nurse on work placement. She gave me an explanation, from a professional perspective, what the term intrusive thoughts meant as opposed to what I had previously learned on an online forum. She also booked me in for an appointment at the Priestly Unit, based at the hospital, for a pre-CBT assessment on my delirium. This assessment did heal me to the extent that it helped me to cope and strengthen my stamina in battling with my demons. The professional who explained in great detail of my recent manic episode, spoke of a man who was experiencing the same thing as what I had. He was 99.9% cured after an extensive recovery programme. A daily dose of fluxetine and diazepam elevated my mood, although the trepidation did seep back in.

On Saturday 10th November 2012, I decided to decrease the dose of my diazepam, after following advice from Emma. I had no tendency of ruminating by the end of 2012. I was due another CBT home visit session in January 2013, by a male professional. I decided that I didn't need any more psycho analysis from professionals, feeling I had the strength to transition back to my normal self again. I did experience a minor intrusive thought in fear that I would purposely cut my throat with a razor blade. This thought became rooted in my mind as I casually shaved my facial stubble. It was disturbing. I had to distance myself from the razor blade just in case my mind controlled me to do it.

When I was approximately 16 years of age, I remember being stood at my skylight window in my bedroom, experiencing thoughts of pushing my tongue to the back of my throat. The urge was persistent, hurling me into this spiral of dismay and worrying what the consequential effects would be if I swallowed my tongue. I have experienced an array of peculiar concepts when it comes to intrusive thoughts. I completely abandoned my love of creating artwork, whilst alienating myself from the world. I did return to the mic in the December of 2012, as I performed a couple of my anecdotes at a gig called "Guitar and Verse" based at Gullivers NQ, in Manchester.

Tuesday 6th January 2015

I developed a kind of manic OCD thinking they was something wrong with my teeth, whilst I brushed them this morning. My gums were bleeding and I instantly began to panic. My anxiety accumulated throughout the following couple of weeks. I had been overworking myself, during the Christmas period at The Playhouse, as well as sending my work off to different festivals. I think this triggered a sense of panic, whilst I was in a tired and vulnerable mindset. Day after day, my mind felt preoccupied with worry, dissolving everything that I had a passion for. I cancelled my gig at "Propaganda," a cabaret event based in London which I was scheduled to perform at on Friday 16th January 2015. My enthusiasm for running faded out completely and I experienced a couple of panic attacks a couple of times during the mornings, feeling the need to not want to get out of bed. The thought of breathing another day of apprehension felt unbearable but I fought and fought for will power and determination. I would subsequently venture out for a short run during several days in January. I repeatedly pushed myself to the extreme, to try and reach out for my own voice and enthusiasm to become creative again. I experienced symptoms which I learned about by researching online forums:

Hysteria.

A minor form of delirium. The bane of believing in illusions to the point of becoming a fantasist.

Hypomania. I am experiencing this less frequently now but it used to be excessive.

Hypersexuality. This is moderately normal for me as I do have a high sex drive. Often this elevates when I'm feel unaffected by other symptoms.

Heightened expression of thoughts.

Hyperactivity. I develop an abundance of ideas but don't seem to develop them due to lack of enthusiasm.

During the autumn of 2016, I was bullied by the irrational thinking again. This episode escalated due to the overwhelming stress that I experienced at the time when I was completing three animations in the space of two months. I had also just commenced work at The Playhouse, so my diary was full and it sucked me into overdrive. During the final week of August of that year, I was housesitting for Aunty Jenny whilst she was on holiday for a couple of weeks in Cornwall. Every night, I barricaded the back door with wooden dining chairs and any other door which led upstairs. I was convinced that this house was being burgled. On the final evening, my mum and dad brought me back home as I was too paranoid of being alone in the house. Mentally, everything seemed to feel perfectly logical but irrational thoughts plagued me with anxiety.

My animation "Hurricane George" was screened at an Exploding Cinema event at The Cinema Museum in London on Saturday 1st October 2016. I stayed over for a couple of nights in the capital at The European Hotel. I was burdened with a rather oppressive and overreactive psyche. My coordination derailed during the two day visit and my physical function was not in sync with reality. I awoke during the night lying in my own bed sweat which formed from the jitteriness I was experiencing during sleep. Returning home on the afternoon of Monday 3rd October, I felt somewhat calm but this was only a temporary state. I considered self-harming but I chose to seek immediate help. On the morning of Monday 10th October 2016, I had an appointment with my GP. She listened to me as I told her of the intrusions which afflicted my mind. The GP prescribed me Sertraline and booked me in for an appointment to see the Single Point of Access team based in Dewsbury. This was a different team, as opposed to having the professionals that visited me back in 2012. I remember sitting down in a room, as I told a female professional everything which was bullying my mind and how it had mentally and physically affected me. Firstly, she asked me about my childhood and pretty much my life, to seek some evidence of history which might have caused the spike in my mental health struggles. I explained to her that I had a brilliant childhood and that my adult life wasn't any different.

Being overly ambitious and trying to strive for the best opportunities for an awarding career comes at a price. You have to focus with a consistent drive in order to seize the prize. The mind can only take on a certain amount of pressure before the journey of ambition dissolves in a tornado of doom. After persisting with my medication and regular exercises, I felt like I was getting back in touch with reality again.

The previous year, I had a bout of apprehension that I thought my teeth were falling out, which was bizarre. Again, this was the cause of anxiety. The most unexpected situations can trigger off anxiety. Being rejected along my career path would really affect me during my twenties because I didn't know how to deal with not being accepted. I had a couple of gigs now and again, but still wondered if I was capable enough of being an artist.

In the spring of 2013, I performed my anecdotes at The Duple Working Men's Club in the south of Blackpool. I stood on the stage wearing a pink wig, a bonnet, a pair of spectacles and a belvia bra and I belted out the lines of my poem called "Me' Beautiful Belvia Bra." As soon as I began to perform a piece about being scared of a man's penis, I was asked to leave the stage in a rather direct manner, by a middle aged, pretentious female singer. This was in front of elderly working men who were gathered at their tables for a pint and a catch up on the latest football results. Being escorted from the microphone was expected, particularly in a Working Men's Club. I remember getting changed in the small dressing room before sitting back down beside Chloe, my sister who came along to offer me support. I was in floods of tears. The woman advised me to tone my material down.

Shortly afterwards, a middle-aged man took the stage, prancing about in nothing but a Borat mankini with half of his testicles on display for the world to see. They loved that! When I look back at the embarrassment that I experienced back that, I laugh about it now. It doesn't affect me in any way but when you are trying to flourish in the performing arts industry, particularly in your early twenties, it does have a detrimental effect on your mental health. In the summer of 2014, I performed a fifteen-minute set of anecdotes as part of the Pure Performance festival, based at The Trispace Gallery in Bermondsey. This was the most humiliating gig I had ever done. My material was immediately disliked by two blonde women who were sat at the front row. They were snarling and heckling at me all the way through my set, and this affected an uproar from the rest of the audience. They were more enthralled by a heavy metal duo prior to my performance, practically having sex with each other. Thinking about it now, I should have just whipped out my penis poem for them all. This poem did go down extremely well at the Manchester based gigs in the summer of 2012, including "Bang Said The Gun" at The Old Nags Head and "Openmind" at The Taurus Bar on Canal Street.

In April 2018, I became overwhelmed by a debilitating episode of anxiety, when I worked with my good friend Jo, as part of a tour called "The Damned United," which was run by the Leeds Playhouse at the time. Jo and I had so many laughs together when we visited different communities in Leeds. During the two-week tour, we were accompanied by David, a lovely, genuine, Geordie man. He was also the Senior Associate Producer at The Playhouse assisting us with stage management, amongst other things. We did casually date. In a state of naivety at the time, I became immensely attracted to him, partly due to his looks but most of all his personality. I was spurred into thinking that I may be on the verge of committing to a serious relationship with him. I had days when I became paranoid, thinking that he didn't see me in a physical sense, and on other days I became extremely eager to see him during our shifts when we could communicate with each other. But the paranoia persisted. I recall having a brief discussion about my mental health with Tiffany (Leeds Playhouse security) and my good friend Rachel. I told them that I had this overwhelming fear of becoming fond of David, but overthinking nonsensical things. I tended to allow depression to get the better of me. I suggested that I should ask him if we could just be friends because my anxiety was too overpowering. Rachel advised me not to do this as it meant that my depression would win.

A couple of evenings previously, the sensitive subject of mental health was discussed between myself and David when we sat down for a drink in the Playhouse bar. He was like a therapist, attempting to take me back to the days when I was verbally and physically bullied at secondary school. I told him that I never looked back at the moments which caused me distress. It is hard for anyone to decipher where mental health conditions can root from. They can be brought on as part of a traumatic experience, but in some cases it can be described simply as a genetic condition. Depression can suddenly burden you with distressing feelings that you cannot control. I completely allowed my anxiety to hurdle to the winning line by baring everything to David.

On Monday 23rd April 2018, we decided to stay firm friends, as opposed to becoming partners. We both sat opposite each other in The Hedonist Bar on Lower Briggate in Leeds, where I confessed that I was falling for him at such a rapid pace. David mentioned how amazing I was as an individual and how brilliant our first date was, a week prior to this evening. I did tear up but I also held back from crying. My anxiety did slightly diminish, when I laid my cards out on the table, mentioning that our friendship contributed to the uneasiness which I physically experienced.

"I know that I will never have a relationship because the way I emotionally am," I said.

"How do you feel about that?" He asked.

I was silent for a second or two. "Upset but I have the comfort of my family and friends." I answered.

During the following couple of weeks, I overanalysed everything from that particular evening. But as the years went on, I learned to value, credit and discover the love that I needed for myself, before I could love anyone else. With the increased doses of my sertraline medication, I found my soul healing to an extent.

However, during the spring of 2019, I became preoccupied with of being oppressed. I wasn't bullied by any intrusive thoughts, the sense of bleakness that I was brought on due to working countless shifts, as well as forming my own schedule of gigs. This grotesque feeling was overbearing. I did have thoughts of obliterating my own existence, but I resisted and persisted to heal myself.

On Saturday 11th May 2019, I attended a workshop which was led extremely professionally by a man named Laurence. This workshop was part of the Found Fiction Writing Festival founded by the brilliant poet Steve Clarkson, based at The Leeds Library. During my visit, I personally didn't feel comfortable being there, as I didn't feel like I belonged. I was questioning myself at the time, whether I was good enough to be an artist. I was reaching the point of ending my aspirations of becoming an artist. Everyone in attendance appeared to be outstanding as artists and I felt like shit. I confided in Laurence on Monday 13th May 2019 when he took me out for a meal at a restaurant called Estabulo based in The Light, in Leeds. We headed to the Headley Verity where I bought him a drink to thank him of his support and for the mutual friendship that we already had. It was here when we both opened up to each other about the challenges that we were both experiencing. Laurence spoke of how unique and distinctive I was as an artist and that I should never allow any speck of adversity to overshadow the talents I had. At that time, I wasn't receiving any form of feedback or creative support.

We interestingly bumped into a friend of ours named Annie and her quirky companion called Anne, who I had previously met at the Outspoken gig. Although she didn't remember meeting me then as she was pissed. Laurence and I ended up having a drink with them both at The Library pub based on Woodhouse Lane. Annie and Anne had a minor disagreement with a man in spectacles named Wallace Runnymede. He apparently resented the autistic community even though he had autism himself. He compared the condition to having AIDs or cancer which was completely insensitive of him. He was only with us for a good ten minutes before he left the building. Annie was then worried about the fact that he, this Nazi, had kissed her once in the past. It was an interesting evening, in comparison to the day that I had earlier when I was feeling oppressed with worry.

In February 2020, I met my future partner Marc Hartley. He was a beautiful genius in every respect. His British sign language interpreter (and our close mutual friend,) Keren introduced us, when I was selling him a ticket for a production of "Oliver Twist" whilst working at the box office. I was immediately attracted to his ambience. Marc invited me out for a coffee at Pret Manger in The Victoria Quarter, Leeds and then onto Bella Italia, on the evening of Tuesday 18th February 2020. We dated for a few weeks before deciding to officially commit ourselves to a relationship. He came along to a couple of my gigs, including "In Other Words" based at The Brunswick in Leeds, where I performed alongside my animation titled "Smoggy Spectacles" on Friday 28th February 2020. As Marc is profoundly deaf, I tried my best to introduce him to all the poets using British Sign Language. My interpretation skills weren't fantastic at the time but they did dramatically improve over time according to Marc. There are no communication barriers between us at all. Our conversations are extremely fluent and understandable. Marc has seen the deterioration of my mental health during 2020.

My mental health struggles burdened me during the summer. That year was a turbulent whirlwind for the whole planet, due to the Covid-19 pandemic and the lockdowns preventing us from meeting up with our nearest and dearests. In July 2020, I began to sell my artwork as after being persuaded by people to make it available to buy online. I accepted this peculiar American man's invitation to sell him one of my pieces. As anyone would be at the time, I was overwhelmed with excitement that someone overseas wanted to display one of my pieces in their home. To cut a long story short, I provided him with all the details which he needed in order to purchase one of my prints. I accidentally sent him a link in my email which he then used as an opportunity to send out scam e mails across the nation, requesting payment for an expiring TV licence. I became a victim of fraud. Four days later, the problem was resolved. My anxiety propelled me into a relapse of intrusive thoughts and my inner demon began to overhaul me. I was travelling back and forth from North Lodge House to Marc's cottage, as my flat was oppressive and made me feel more worse than I could have imagined. It was unbearable. Thoughts of self-harm intruded my psyche on the evening of the next dated Journal entry.

Sunday 26th July 2020

I wasn't in the brightest of places psychologically. The experience has been hell. This entrapment of anxiety took me to the most foreboding place mentally, especially this morning. I was contemplating putting an end to it all either through an overdose or by drowning myself in the Leeds canal, numbing the pain beforehand with a bottle of vodka. In the early mornings, I woke up with abdominal cramps and irrational thoughts. I was capsized persistently within my own psyche. I was unable to convince myself that things would eventually be fine and this is what depression and anxiety does to you.

I am currently sat on the couch at Marc's house. The time is currently 6:25pm. He has been sorting things out in the back garden but he is now talking to a friend on facetime.

On Saturday 25th July 2020, Marc drove Danny and myself to John's house based in Rotherham, arriving at approximately 3:30pm. My anxiety was persistent throughout the day, although I felt more at ease during the journeys there and back. My appetite had slightly improved, compared to what it was like last Friday evening at Marc's cottage, when I was struggling to finish my meal, which isn't like me. My mind wasn't mentally in control as it was ruptured with anxiety. However, we did had a lovely time. We sat down for a meal, followed by a "gay trifle," and sat down for a chat, before arriving back in Huddersfield at 8:40pm. I was extremely tired because of all of the anxiety I was experiencing throughout this week. So, I relaxed on the couch with a blanket and briefly fell asleep.

It was a very surreal week of victimisation and worry, which I never saw coming the week before. At 7:10pm, I had brief bouts of anxiety during the previous fifteen minutes or so. A ten minute meditation video, followed by a Kalms tablet took the edge off it. Marc has been been brilliantly supportive, just being there for me. He asked me when we drove to Danny's house today, if my anxiety was going affect our relationship. Nothing will detach our love for each other, no matter how overwhelming things can mentally get for me. I absolutely love him too much. I am dreading returning home in Leeds tomorrow, to be myself within my own thoughts. I do know I will get through this manic episode.

Tuesday 28th July 2020

The time is currently 11:15am and I am sat on Marc's couch, feeling heavy eyed and slightly apprehensive. It is disturbing my connection with reality. I am terrified of being alone at the moment, so Marc has allowed me to stay here. I have a lot to thank him for. He has been incredibly amazing. I am just putting on an ordinary face on for him as I really do not want to destroy this brilliant relationship that we both have. He is my beacon of light.

I managed to achieve at least five hours sleep last night, which is better than I did the previous night. My persistent tendency to ruminate and my bouts of crippling anxiety have made me become an insomniac. Kalms tablets are somehow helping me to heal but the apprehension is still there. I am going to have a lavender bath soak now, to see if this makes an improved difference.

My GP prescribed me a dose of amitriptyline on Thursday 30th July 2020, to help cure my anxiety. I was hoping to be medicated on Sertraline but anything is a godsend if it helps to eradicate this burden. On Saturday 1st August 2020, I relapsed with intrusive thoughts of hurting loved ones again, which fuelled another a manic episode.

Saturday 1st August 2020

Last night, I hurled myself into bed, closed my eyes and tried to distract my mind from the current threat of my email account being hacked.

At 8:05pm I arrived at my mum and Nigel's house to stay there for the next couple of nights. I felt incredibly inclined to self-harm today, due to ruminating persistently. Because I was the only tenant living at North Lodge House, I felt extremely vulnerable to ending my life. I phoned up the Leeds based Single Point of Access team, as an aid of saving me from self harm.

I am feeling more at ease at this minute, as I sit with my mum and Nigel around a small fire in the back garden, whilst the sun descends and sleeps for the night. My psyche has been constantly under a lot of uninvited stress. I've been trying to defeat it and still am. I just need to plough through this battle and rise above it like a phoenix, but sometimes I become desperate. I personally feel that I did the correct thing by visiting my mum and Nigel, as opposed to destructing myself on my own.

Monday 3rd August 2020

It is currently 8:20pm and I am sat on the couch at Marc's cottage. I have experienced numerous bouts of intrusive thoughts throughout the weekend, ruminating one delusional thought after the other. This is the highest level of manic delusions that I have encountered in any episode. I have medicated myself back on sertraline, to help reduce the ruminations and debilitating anxiety. I am just not ready to return to North Lodge House and settle back into my own space just yet. Even though I do feel that I am a burden on people in need of support and comfort, I feel more at ease. I don't have the urge to self-harm like I previously did. Uninvited intrusions and irrational beliefs had sprawled and cemented their way into my mind and made the last couple of weeks feel like torture, all because of my email account being compromised. I began to think that I was going to get prosecuted for something that was imposed on me and completely out of my control. I don't know if it is my anxiety dictating me, but I feel that Leeds isn't the haven for me anymore. I could happily settle here at Marc's cottage with my soulmate for life. It has been such a bastard of a year and this current episode of mine is just the icing on the bittersweet cake.

This afternoon, mum and I went for a walk through Briar woods and then through Howley. I left my mum and Nigel's house at 5pm to collect my Sertraline prescription from the Batley based pharmacy on Wellington Street, queing outside for a good fifteen minitues due to the ongoing social distancing measures of Covid-19. I then commuted on the slightly delayed 6:01pm Transpennine Express service to Huddersfield where Marc picked me up from the train station and then ate fish and chips at his warm cottage. Marc has been incredible to me throughout the past couple of weeks and I shall forever be grateful for that.

Throughout the weekend, my anxiety fluctuated, resulting in an abundance of sensations from being completely sedated with calmness, to becoming overwhelmed with my delusional thoughts which at times felt like a tsunami out of my control. The more you try and supress those thoughts, the more aggravating they become and this is where the anxiety takes hold. My mind is currently swinging in different places at this minute. 2020 has been a fucking turbulent rollercoaster, like many people, I cannot wait to see the back of it.

I feel trapped at times when I go through my thoughts in an attempt heal at this frightening time. Attempting to overcome this internal brute, whilst confined in my basement room with little natural light, isn't the healthiest way to overcome my depression.

Wednesday 5th August 2020

I experienced countless bouts of anxiety throughout the course of yesterday. I think it is the medication that is sedating me, as side effects start to persist when first taking them. Recuring thoughts are persistently whirling around in my head. I went with Marc to a car showroom in Rochdale, as he was collecting a new magnetic blue Peugeot 308, which he is absolutely ecstatic about. We then headed into Huddersfield town centre to sit down for a sandwich and a pot of tea at a coffee shop that we often visit. My appetite has dramatically decreased, being a side effect of the anti-depressants that I was taking, and so has my sex drive. We both do still have sexual intimacy, though the sensation feels temporarily numb for me. These side effects normally last for four or so weeks after first taking the antidepressants.

Marc drove us both to Holmfirth in the afternoon, to visit Sid's Cafe from the world-renowned Yorkshire-based comedy "The Last Of The Summer Wine." We didn't have a drink and a bite to eat due to the cafe closing early as they had run out of food. Despite my persistent anxiety, I had a lovely afternoon with Marc. We returned home at approximately 4:20pm.

Thursday 6th August 2020

I had a slight bout of anxiety this morning when awakening, due to my persistent intrusive thoughts aggravating my psyche. These episodes returned sporadically throughout the day. My current condition hasn't been as crippling due to understanding that it is all completely psychological and not real. When I was a lot younger, self-harm was the only answer to end these irrational intrusions circulating in my mind, but now I have matured and educated myself about intrusive thoughts and what causes them. I am more familiar now with the pattern and rhythm of my intermittent episodes.

Marc has been out to visit his friend Pat in Leeds for the whole afternoon and will be returning home soon. I am just lounging on the couch. This is another symptom of anxiety. Not having the willpower or energy to do anything, generates a habit of lethargy. All you want to do is quilt yourself up under a duvet, no matter how sweltering or bitter the weather is. It provides you with some form of haven. The time is currently 8:10pm.

Friday 14th August 2020

My psyche has been occupied with delusional thoughts throughout the course of today, which I didn't allow myself to pay much attention to. I returned home from Marc's cottage at midday yesterday. I was initially at ease but subsequently became slightly apprehensive as the afternoon ticked by. In the evening I felt quite normal. Reading back at my previous journals, allowed me to understand my thought processes and helped me to feel reassured. I already knew that what I was thinking was purely psychological and not real. But when I am living through a manic episode, the imagination has a clever talent of distorting irrational thoughts and making them so real. It causes anxiety.

This morning, I awoke with a very little sense of apprehension, but this changed within an hour or so. I just needed to accept these thoughts that were occurring and allow them to come and go when they please which I do. But the concentration of trying to not give them the fuel to erupt is fucking harder than that it seems. Marc is urging me to move out from North Lodge House, in order to heal. There is a mediation centre that will be letting rooms, as soon as the lockdown eases within the Kirklees district. The centre is based in Huddersfield. I did actually sleep there one evening, back in February 2017, when I performed at "The Hand Drawn Monkey" open mic night. Claire L lived there at the time. It was pure serenity. The only concern I have about going back there is when I do fully heal, I will be yearning to breathe in the city life again.

I returned home from Ryman Stationary, based in The Merrion Centre, with pieces of A1 pure white card, to make professional mounts of a print of mine titled "The Owl and The Pussycat." This was to be sold to Jan O. Jan parked up her car at North Lodge House and I gave her the print. We then headed to The Library pub for a drink. I also had a bite to eat which Jan kindly bought me. It was brilliant to see her again and to catch up on the old times. She looked vibrantly well.

It is currently 11:25pm and I am feeling somewhat at ease, though I am feeling mildly delusional. My mind has a repetitive habit of bouncing from thought to thought, as a way to try and get a reaction out of me but I am not giving it the satisfaction.

Sunday 16th August 2020

At 3:10pm, I have just returned from Leeds. I am having a debilitating day with my delusional overthinking which is slightly paralysing me with silent anxiety. I am currently on week two of taking the Sertraline, so I am aware of the possible side effects which comes with taking the medication. I am not trying to resist the delusions, as this is the worst solution anybody could do. I am just allowing them to come and go like I previously stated. I have not yet suffered with any overthinking when based here in Leeds. The serotonin chemicals within my psyche, must have started to disintegrate when I became overwhelmed with stress working at The Playhouse, the national lockdown as you will soon come to read and my animation practice thereafter. I know that I will eventually return back to some form of normality and all of this will be a nonsensical distant memory. But the only way to heal is to fight and then rise like a phoenix.

I went to San CoCo Cafe for a decaffeinated tea and a toasted sandwich in order to have breath of fresh air from North Lodge House. There was some sort of protest near Leeds town hall in a bid to "Save Our Children" or something along those lines.

My anxiety propelled soon after meditating. My mum phoned me just before finishing the meditation session. My ruminating completely overwhelmed me with its unshiftable presence. My mum is sending healing over to me, hence the reason I am feeling a sudden sensation of heat simmering throughout me, as I sit on the edge of my bed. The time is now 9:10pm. I am going to stay with Marc for a little while, as my basement room is not helping me to heal one bit. He will be picking me up shortly, even though I do appear to be at ease and composed.

The time is currently 10:25pm. I am sitting at the wooden table in the communal kitchen at North Lodge House. Marc is on his way to pick me up. He is absolutely brilliant in every retrospect and I am tremendously grateful for his sympathy, compassion and understanding throughout my current episode. I cannot thank or love him anymore for the support he has provided me with.

Wednesday 19th August 2020

Slight anxiety and delusions have been present but I have had a better day. I met two more of Marc's deaf friends shortly after midday - Hazel and Angela. We dined in the Wimpy restaurant based in Huddersfield town centre for a good couple of hours. They are both incredibly lovely ladies. They also know how to have a dirty joke or two. Marc went to view a number of houses with Jane today, as she is looking to move out of Wakefield to an area near Marc's cottage. They both returned home at approximately 7:20pm with a takeaway Chinese, bought kindly by Jane. I submitted my animation "Fleas" to The Kingston Upon Thames Film Festival this evening but unfortunately wasn't selected for screening.

My current mental health episode slowly eased off, allowing me to be free with some form of normal life. At the beginning of September 2020, new residents had arrived at North Lodge House. Two Brazilians, Vinnie and Taina, moved in to the rooms on the top floor and Karen who moved in to the basement room opposite me. This has somewhat supported my mental health, as I know I am being surrounded by three other people.

I am extremely ambitious when it comes to striving for the next big thing. I do a hell of a lot of travelling up and down the country to perform my whimsical anecdotes and screen my short films at various exciting festivals. These are the main causes of the stress that I deal with, as well as fatigue and a meagre diet. I do try and moderate the pressure when I'm involved in practical projects but can tend to absorb too much during those times.

When I relapsed back in mid-August 2015, I decided to find out more about my episodes. Bipolar disorder was another condition which I looked into, personally feeling that I could have similar symptoms to this. I didn't experience hallucinations but I had the characteristics of a manic depressive with a split personality. I made an appointment with my doctor in Batley for a bipolar disorder test. Without even assessing my temperamental mood patterns, the doctor immediately confirmed that I did not have this condition. I personally felt at the time, that there were obstacles to diagnosing mental health symptoms, since people do experience a degree of one mental health condition or other. The human mind is a merciless, unrecognisable, fucked up jigsaw.

I am maturing every time when I'm swallowed up by an unwanted episode. I deal with my psychosis better now compared to when I did in my twenties. It is normal to feel completely shit from time to time, there is no shame in that. It is fantastic that mental health awareness is giving people the platform to open up and to say "It's OK not to be OK." Stephen Fry and Denise Welsh are brilliant advocates in leading the path for more people to speak out and accept the demon that lives within themselves. Like I have previously said and shall say again, I am eternally thankful for the brilliant support my family and Marc have provided me with. Without their compassion, I would be completely fucking broken.

My mum still provides me with spiritual healing when I go through an episode. It is a beautiful form of relaxation that provides your whole aura a feeling of warmth and serenity. During this process, I sit on a chair with my mum stood behind me. With my eyes closed, she guides her hands around my outer body. I feel a tingling sense of warmth overcome me as she brings back messages from the spirits. The strength that healing provides you with is remarkable. I have to be in a very oppressed state when I turn to healing.

I cannot find enough words to describe the debilitating impact of intrusive thoughts. Examples of intrusive thoughts can include sexual thoughts, violent thoughts, compulsions and even religion. I have persistent recuring unwanted sexual and violent thoughts, which are completely uncomfortable and abnormal, compared to the caring person I actually am. The physical torture that you have to endure is indescribable. Just imagine feeling completely content with life and then in a split second you are plagued with an unwelcome stranger. It is incredibly frightening how your mind can suddenly trigger a compulsion. You can reassure yourself as much as you want but the monster is still there feeding you with thoughts. Then these thoughts begin to grow bigger at a more alarming and catastrophic levels, when calming rituals are performed. At this rate, I'm thinking that the worst is about to happen.

Speaking from my own personal experience, it does get better. Sometimes, you have to take the plunge before you can rise like a phoenix. I can detect when manic episodes is about to erupt as I know the pattern of an episode. Allow it to happen, learn not to supress it by performing rituals. Acknowledge your thought process and accept it for what it is - just thoughts. Anxiety doesn't care who it crucifies, it can mindfuck anyone on the highest level known but you are only human.

On Monday 28th December 2020, I decided to stop taking sertraline and discarded the tablets which was an aid for me to feel normal again. I know the difference between what is normal and psychological. My delusional thoughts are just psychological. I am the only person who is feeding off this anxiety, nobody else. I do feel apprehensive about ending my prescription and I know there will be future hurdles which I will need to go through in order to come out of the other end with a stronger mentality, but I am willing to bide by this. People react differently when your mind is burgled by a frightening intruder. Some have the courage to fight it off, whereas others need that extra help, to support the chemical balance that portrays the difference between what is fiction and non-fiction. I have spent years suffocating with my preposterous psychosis, trying to reassure myself of the OCD which I fucking bear every time I hit rock bottom. Explicitly demonstrating my perspective of how I deal and cope with my mental health will hopefully allow others to heal, respire and understand the manic significance it has on the vulnerable, like myself. It is a strenuous journey, but you have to confront it as a means to cope with it. Remember to accept it, bide by it, understand the logic and let it go.

Friday 27th November 2020

I completed an extremely intricate sketch this evening. This piece vibrantly illustrated my own mental health experiences. I began the sketch last summer but broke away from it when I encountered my recent episode. However, tonight, I felt enraptured by the resulting sketch. It is titled "A Thing about Something," which shows a side profile of myself, surrounded by precarious lines which represented chronic neurosis. It only took one glance after a good few months of leaving it unfinished and tonight, the whole visual narrative was drawn in an instant.

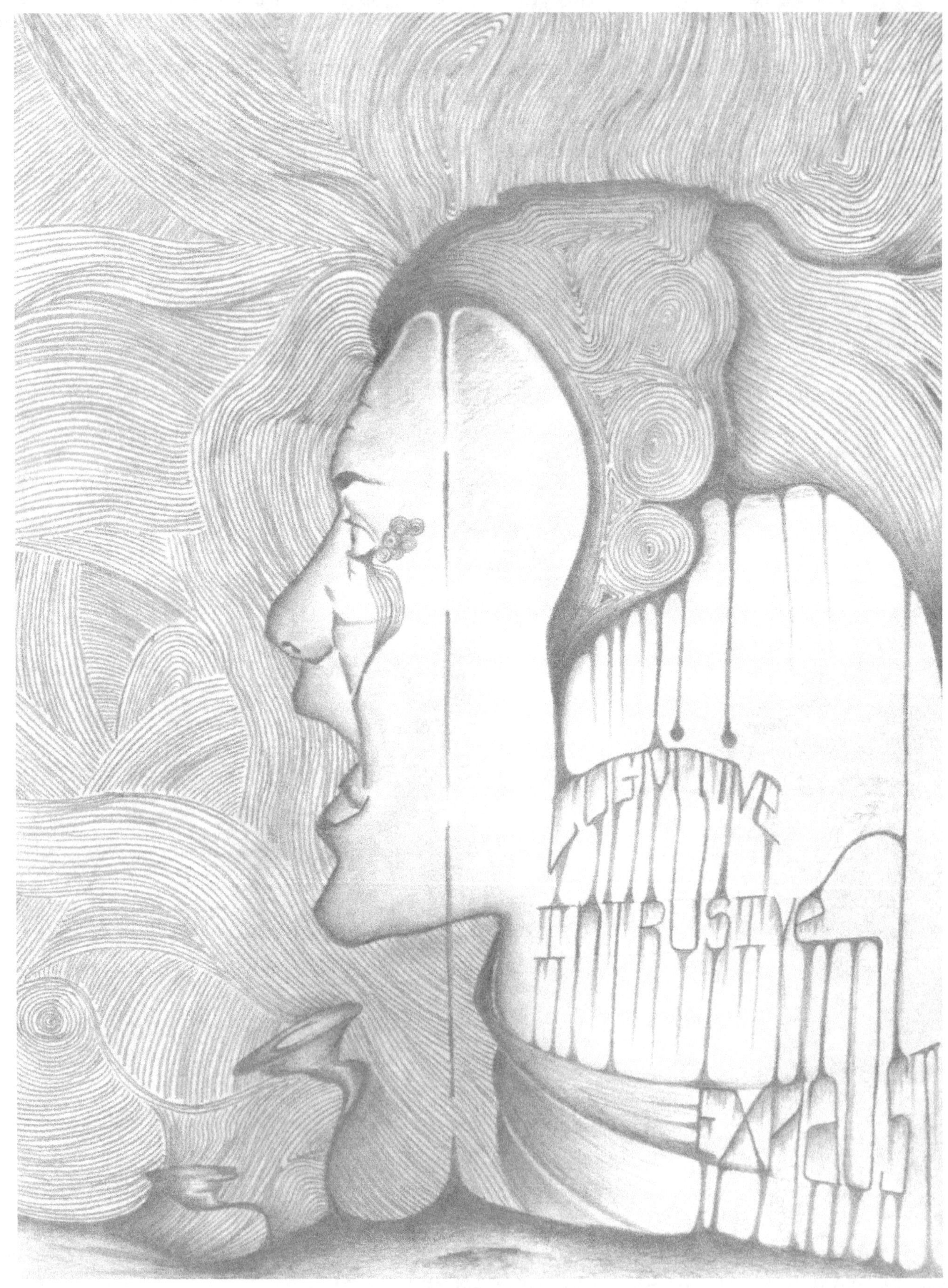

"A Thing About Something"
A4 Pencil sketch

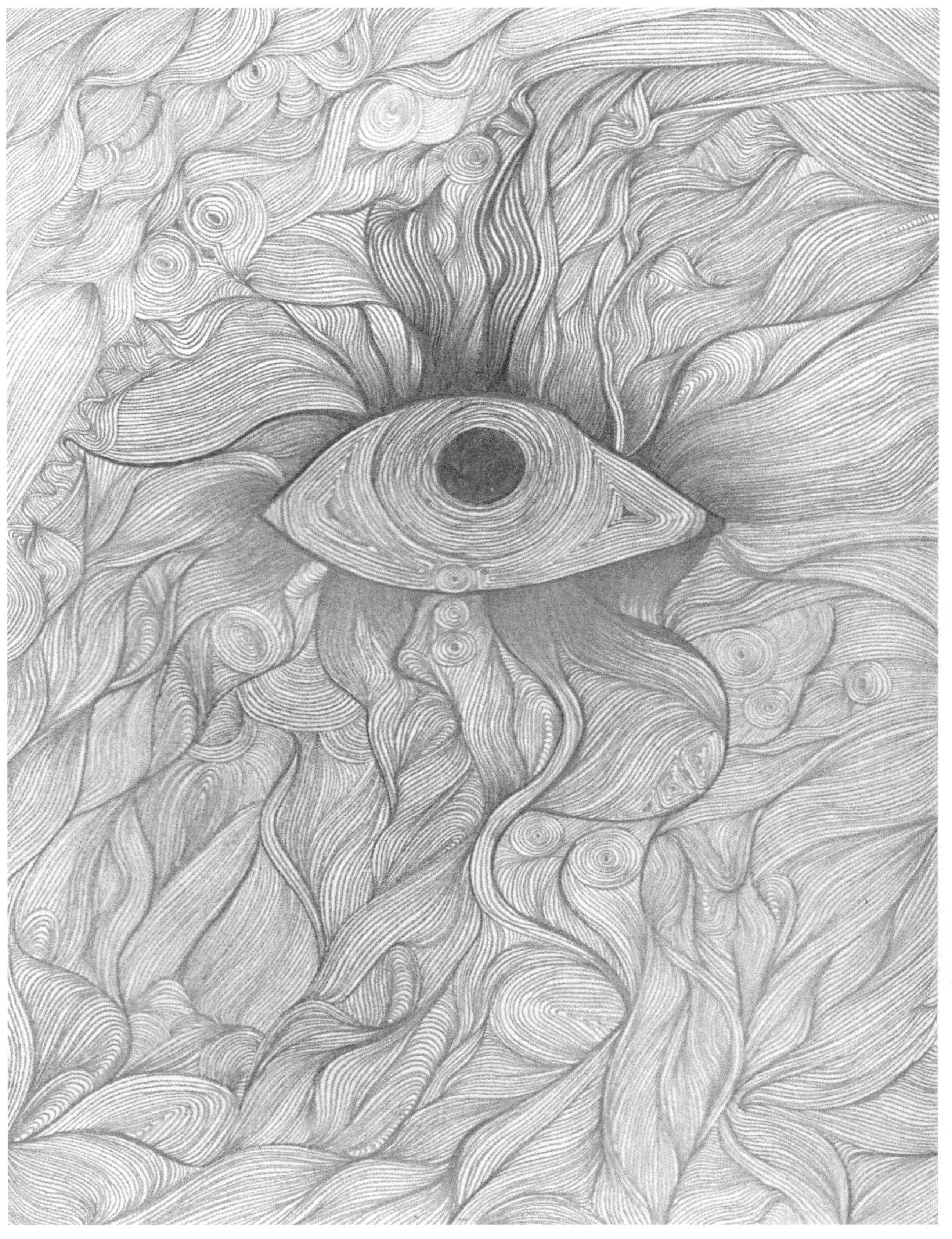

"Tunnel Vision"
A4 Pencil Sketch

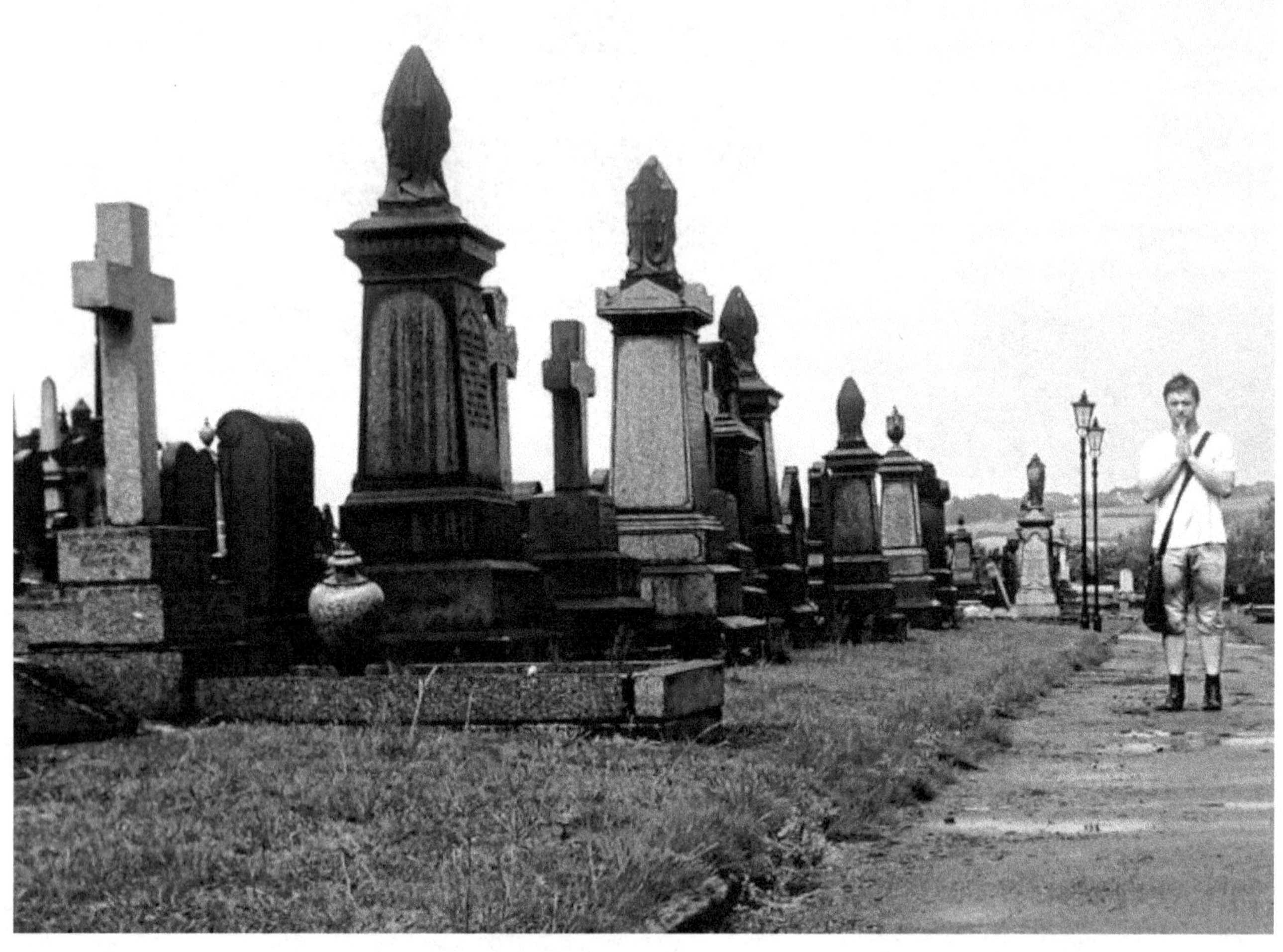

4/8/2011

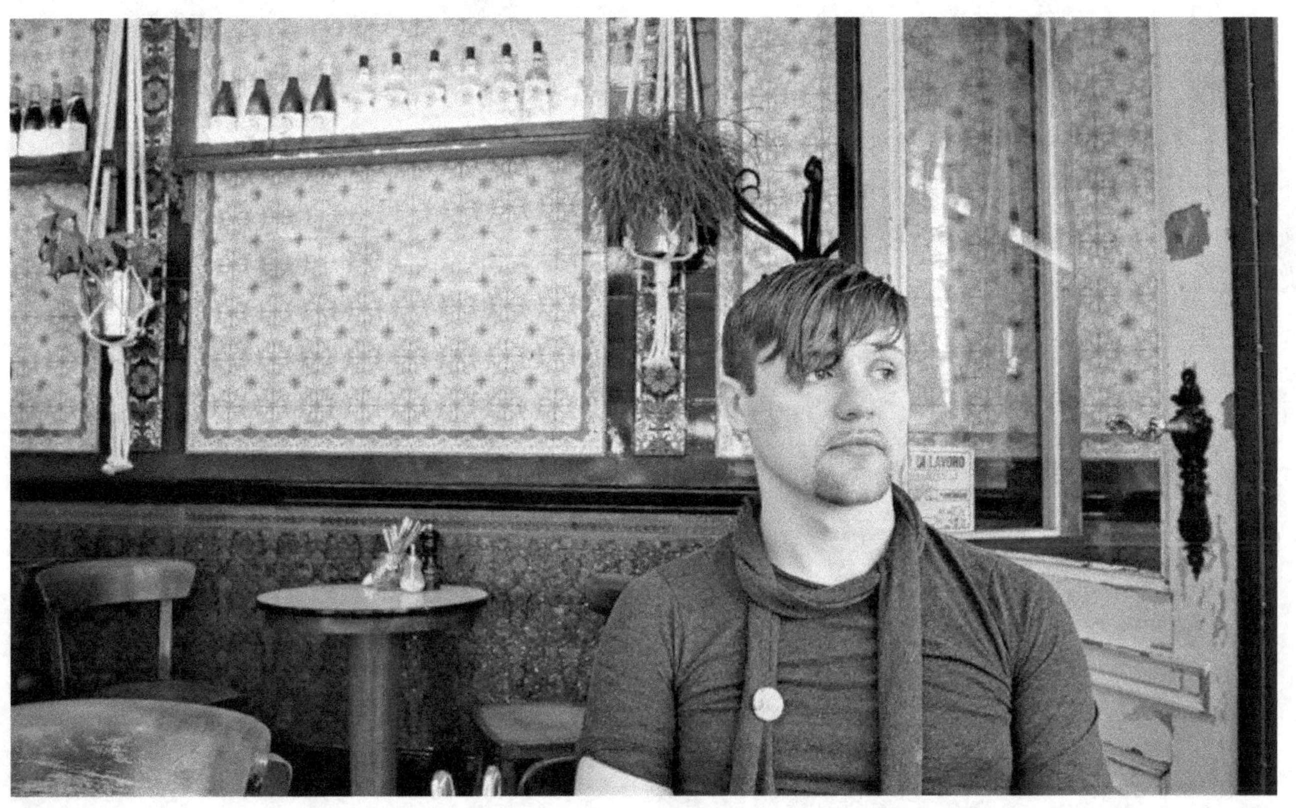

"Berlin"

"Artsy as fuck!"

- Quoted by Louisa Claughton

Photo Courtesy of Louisa Claughton, January 2017

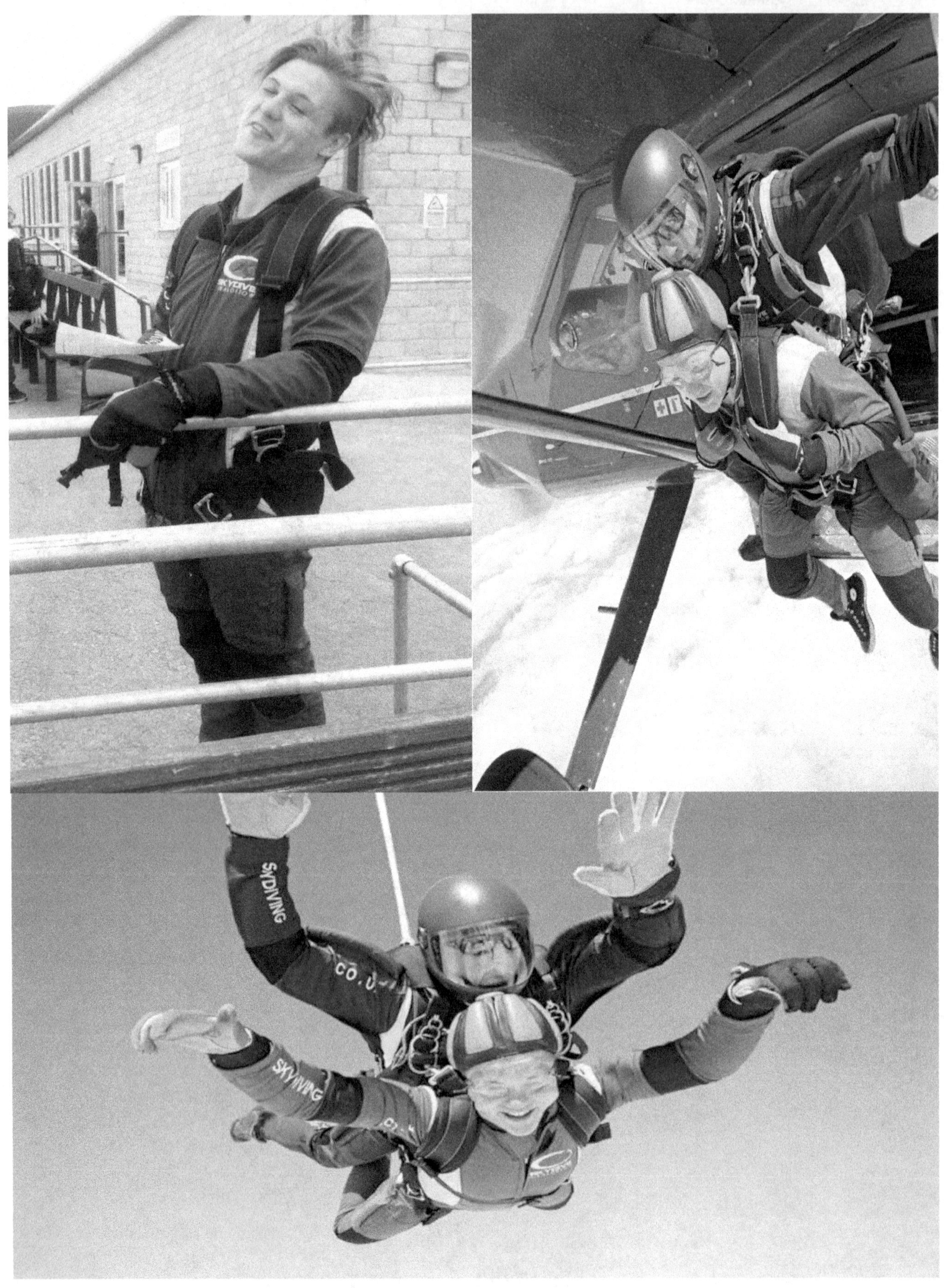

Skydiving - Hibaldstow, Lincolnshire
15,000ft plunge (23/5/2015)

Menopause

All of the hot flushes and all of the night sweats,
The horrific psychosis, how can I forget?
It's part of this existence, it's part of the cause,
It's all of the symptoms of this menopause.

I feel ever so consumed, I feel ever so oppressed,
It's the sign of libido, it's the sign of distress,
When I hit fifty, I wondered what it could be,
But then I discovered this cycle when I visited my GP.

I understand the effects, It's all logical,
Why I am feeling disdain, it's all psychological,
My husband is making me feel embittered, I feel ever so wired,
I feel ever so lethargic, I feel ever so tired,

My heart is beating to the rhythm of palpitations,
SHIT! I think I am going into hibernation,
My conscious is deteriorating, I really do not know what to do,
I am in frequent need to skip to the loo!

I was advised to take a sage tablet, just one a day,
I have heard it takes the hot flushes instantly away,
It works a phenomenon, so splendidly,
It's an invigorating cure and a brilliant remedy.

I am experiencing excruciating migranes and I am losing my brain,
I have obnoxious nausea and abdominal pain,
It's unbearable to heal, it's an irritating twinge,
It's ever so laborious and it's making me cringe.

With all of the spots on my chin and my nose,
I have finally concluded this menstural dose,
If it ever returns, now I know its subsequent cause,
I am free for now, from this morose menopause!

This anecdote, with a serious poignant tone underneath its rhymical layers, is obviously written from a female perspective. A very good female friend of mine asked me to write a verse which describes menopausal women, through my own original style. I know that I am extremely far out of reach to ever experience a menstrual cycle, which causes a hell of a lot of pain for women, but it was an honour to be asked to dedicate a piece specifically to a topic which needs to be widely acknowledged.

Tena Men

Men incontinent?
They are according to Tena,
I have never been exposed to an abnormal product,
which causes our penis a dilemma,
We are cautious of our friend!
We dry in just one shake.
But sometimes there are moments when we have to be cured,
Because we can only take, what we can take!
Maybe I don't have to treat it until I am forty,
Maybe I have got a tight, reliable bladder,
But one big sneeze can conjure a trickle,
and we are spraying directly out of our adder!
These are designed to benefit us,
To supply and comply our pole,
Because you really don't know when we erupt a leak,
and next we are pissing out of control!
Half of the people didn't believe me,
When I told them of such a thing,
It is just like your ordinary product,
It's a pad with its body and wings!
It also consists of various other choices,
It keeps your little fella, comfortably sealed,
With a trusting absorption and an odour defiant,
comfortable, alternative shield!
So, men it is OK to leak,
Everyone has a sufferable dilemma,
Get yourself to Boots and treat your bladder,
To a fabulous ten pack of Tena!

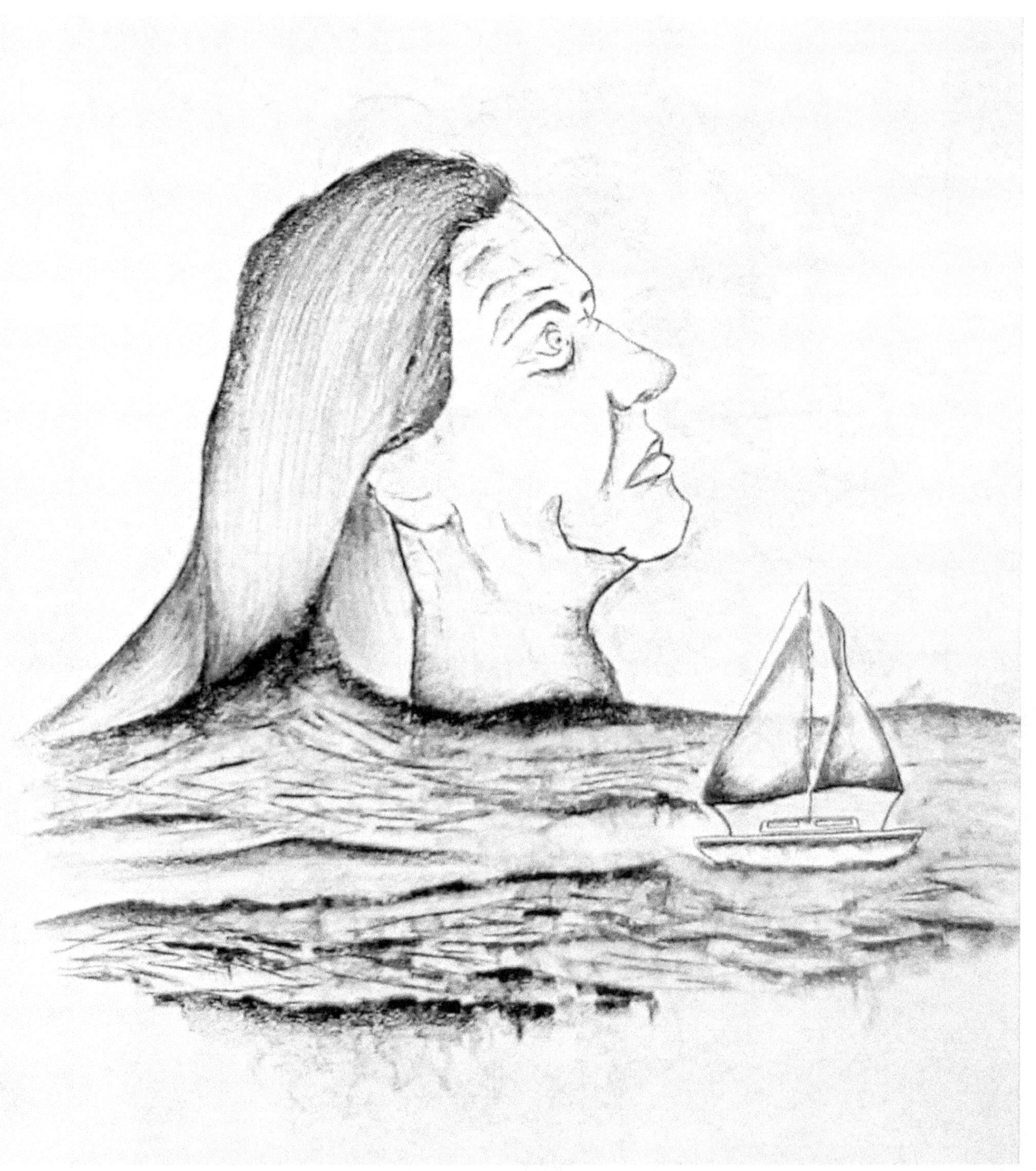

"Drowning"
A4 Pencil sketch
April 2018

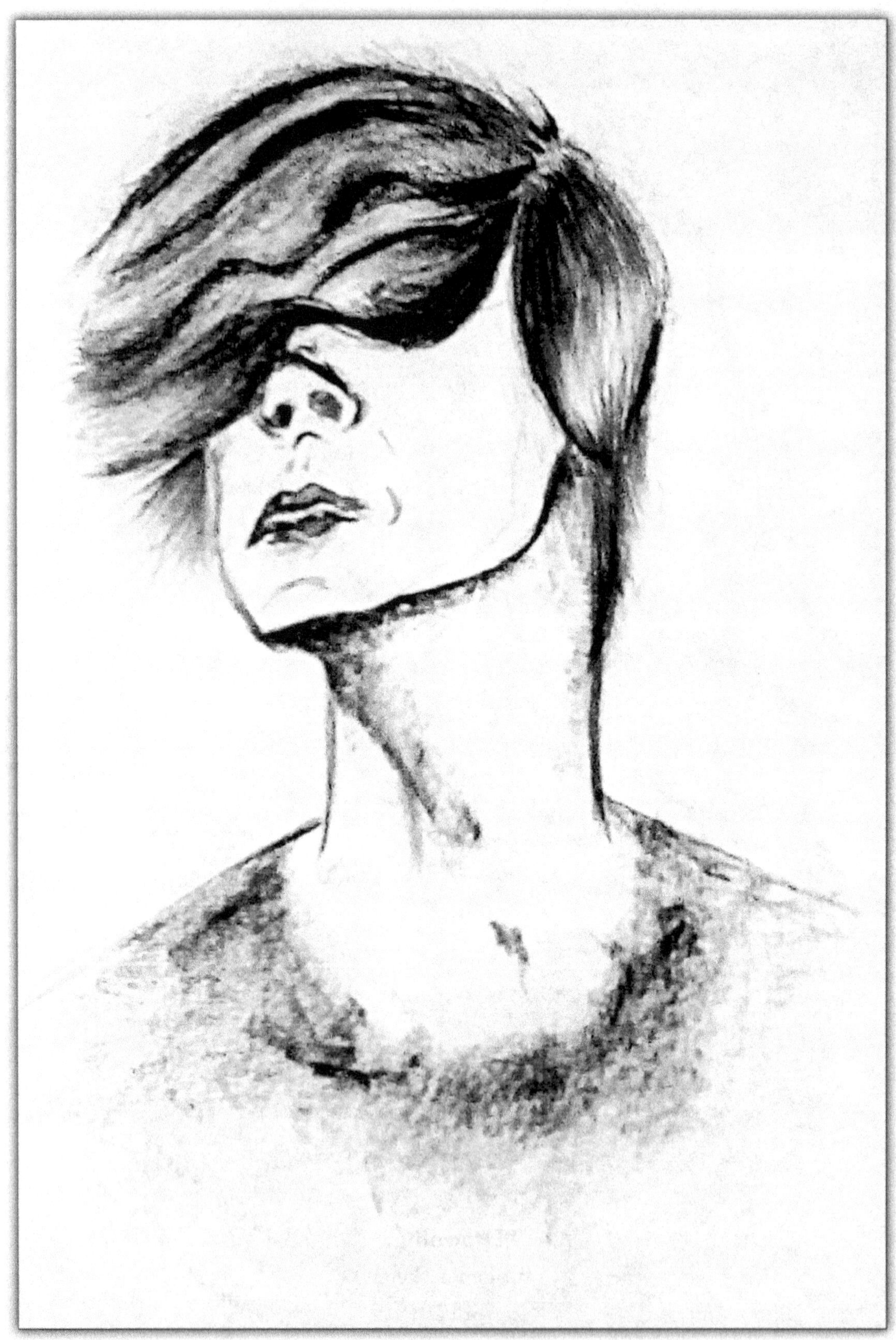

"Self Portrait"
Pencil doodle in Sketchbook - August 2018

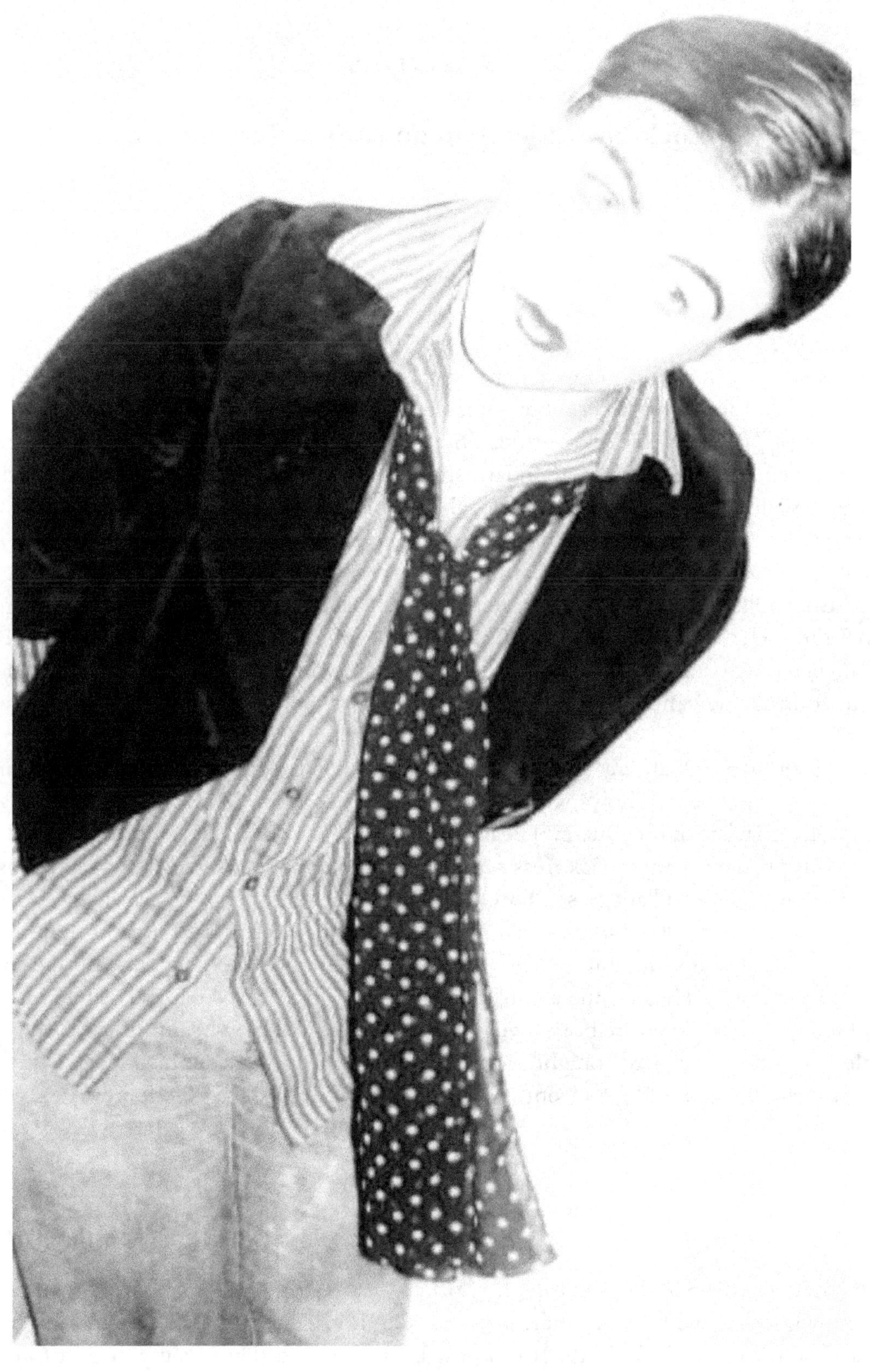

As a Fine Art Student at De Montfort University, Leicester
Summer break - August 2009

COVID-19

Lockdown Living in an Artistic Expression

Monday 16th March 2020

I worked at the box office at the Playhouse between 10am and 6pm, answering phone calls which related to ticket cancellations and queries on whether performances were going ahead as scheduled. At this point in time, the scheduled shows were certainly going ahead.

"Be the Example, Be the Voice," a youth theatre show, was just about to start in The Bramall Rock Void theatre. Twenty minutes into my 6pm attendant shift, two Front of House attendants and the Duty Manager announced that the show had been cancelled. The production of "Missing People," at the Courtyard Theatre was going to host a press night but this was cancelled too.

I stood at the rear entrance to the theatre with another attendant called Unique, letting the very few members of the public aware of the unfortunate cancellation. Two Front of House colleagues, Liam and Sarah, based themselves in the Front Row Cafe, to make the incoming public aware of The Courtyard Theatre's cancelled performance. Of course, the audience members were extremely accepting of the news, due to the uncontrollable pandemic but there was uncertainty about what the following weeks or months would bring.

On Friday 13th March 2020, my shift at the box office was predominantly focussed on responding to phone calls about whether the shows were going ahead. At 6.30pm, I worked as an attendant during the production "Oliver Twist" in the Quarry Theatre. When the show finished, I walked to Leeds train station, to catch the 10:10pm Transpennine Express service to Huddersfield, where Marc would subsequently pick me up at 10:30pm. It was brilliant to see him again and to be able sleep over at his gorgeous cottage for the first time. We gave each other a kiss when I got into his car and travelled the ten-minute journey to his house. He drove me past his old house, which he does miss but he is content with his current place. I had a lovely evening with him. He gave me a couple of beautiful gifts - a scented wax candle burner lamp and a cute small teddy bear, which were both lovely. He complimented how beautiful I was.

A couple of evenings prior to tonight, he messaged me saying that he loved me. I was initially taken aback, as I was getting used to the concept of us potentially becoming a couple. I was excited though!

Tuesday 17th March 2020

I had a shift between 10am and 6pm at the box office. I went for a cuppa and a sausage sandwich in San CoCo to fill my boots up with Lynn. Quite a few coffee shops, even KFC were temporarily closed due to the continued outbreak of COVID-19. It has now been reported that seventy-one Britons had died due to the fatal pandemic. This evening, I was informed that the event I was scheduled to host and perform at called "Bronte's Bards" based at The Otley Labour Club, on Friday 24th April 2020, had now been cancelled. This week's performances at The Playhouse had also been cancelled, so our shift today was centred on answering phone calls, regarding ticket cancellations. There was a shared concern amongst those who were working in the arts, regarding whether this pandemic would affect our incomes.

I had a lovely evening with Marc. He met me at The Playhouse at 5:45pm, when Helen, the box office team leader, allowed me to finish fifteen minutes earlier. He drove me to my flat, from the John Lewis Car Park, spending the majority of the evening with me until 11:45pm. This was the first time that Marc had visited my flat. My flat is a lot different, in comparison to his beautiful homely cottage. I was a little apprehensive to what he may think of my room. I was introduced to his friend named Pat, who was seventy-four years of age. Marc was talking to her on facetime. She was an extremely lively woman who was also deaf. Marc cares for her every Thursday and Friday, here in South Leeds. He told her off jokingly, as she laid down on her chair and pretended to flirt with me by raising her leg up in the air. I genuinely had a lovely evening with Marc. We kissed each other goodnight at my front door, shortly before midnight. I waved him off as he drove down the narrow alleyway to Clarendon Road.

Wednesday 18th March 2020

I haven't done a single thing today, apart from popping out to the shop and isolating myself in my own basement room. I had a couple of hours sleep in the afternoon, due to consistent hypertension in my head and to feeling slightly oppressed by this ongoing global pandemic. But I am staying optimistic, knowing that life will go back to normal. I decided to cancel all the gigs that I had been booked for until at least Autumn.

I haven't got a television in my room, but I am not seduced by the ongoing hype of breaking news announcements. I am aware that schools in the UK, Scotland and Wales will be closed temporary for the foreseeable future from this Friday. Anyone who has symptoms of a cough or a high temperature must self-isolate for fourteen days to prevent the inevitable spread of the virus. Apparently, an experimental lung drug is to be tested in the UK on coronavirus patients. London could go into lockdown, under tougher measures. The capital has the highest confirmed number of cases of the epidemic, rising from 676 to 2,626. Major scheduled global events such as Glastonbury 2020, the Eurovision Song Contest and The Grand National were postponed.

The world is seemingly heading towards a total lockdown. I received an email from Yorkshire Dance confirming that they will be closed until the 20th April 2020. Despite all my shifts being cancelled during the upcoming weeks, I was still going get paid which is a relief. Today, it was also announced that the UK death toll had risen to 104. The youngest victim being a forty-five year old man. The Archibishop of Canterbury described the coronavirus as a nuclear explosion, which will reshape the nations's future in unforeseeble ways.

This COVID-19 literally feels like an uncontrollable predator on the loose. It has completely hijacked the world, with its formidable force. Virtually nothing is in operation now. Even humans are self-isolating. It is a detrimental hollow time.

Thursday 19th March 2020

This afternoon, I received an email from the Theatre Manager, stating that my Front Of House position at the Playhouse had been terminated temporarily. Twenty-three hours of box office shifts which had been cancelled will be paid for so this will give me some income for the time being. I am feeling deflated about how this global pandemic is destroying people's livelihoods. Apparenlty, the death toll has now increased to 128 fatalities within the UK, whereas Northern Ireland has just confirmed their first death victim. Forty London tube stations have now closed to the public in preparation for the capital to go into lockdown. It feels like we are living in completely dystopian society, with everything around braking with a sudden halt.

Italy's death toll has rose to 3,405 fatalities. Boris Johnson has announced that the UK can "turn the tide" to reach some form of normality by the summer, under his strict regimes, which he could have implemented weeks ago.

Liz, the box office manager, phoned me just after 6:30pm this evening which I genuinely appreciated, to essentially discuss the options of either keeping my box office post, receiving minimum income or alternatively cutting my ties with the Playhouse in order to live on government benefits. To cut to the chase with my position at The Playhouse, in July 2020, I made the ultimate decision to leave the theatre for good. I have been ready to leave the organisation for a while but hesitated as it provided me with many opportunities and platforms which helped me to develop as a working artist.

On a more elated note, this evening, in the mock studio of my basement room, I performed two of my whimsical anecdotes of mine on a live Facebook Poetry platform called "Big Poetry Goes Viral," hosted by the marvellous Robert Garnham. The WiFi signal proved to be a little shaky but it was an enjoyable hour of Spoken Word. The online gig commenced at 8pm and ended at 9pm. My slot began at 8:25pm, as I performed "The Fabulous Tom Ford" and "Big Knickers Rule" through the lens of my Samsung mobile phone, which was balanced upright, against the handle of my window. It was an interesting perspective performing live for a virtual audience, as opposed to a real-life crowd. The online gig was designed to help writers keep their creativity going, whilst living in isolation, during the outbreak. A huge congratulations should go to Robert Garnham for curating and making this unique platform happen, which you never know may become an ongoing concept in the long term future.

Boris Johnson ordered a closure of public places from 10pm, on the evening of Friday 20th March 2020, including pubs, nightclubs and restaurants etc. The global statistic for the number of people infected with COVID-19 has now reached a quarter of a million. The total number of deaths recorded in Italy is now at 627. 177 deaths are also confirmed in the UK. The death toll continues to rise across the world.

Saturday 21st March 2020

It is currently 7:45pm and I am sat on the couch in the living room at Marc's cottage. He is preparing supper in the kitchen. I will be spending the weekend here with him providing that the strict UK lockdown doesn't separate us. The country's death toll is now at 233, which is a drastic rise in comparison to yesterday's count.

When I was walking through Leeds just before midday on the way to the train station, I felt apprehensive. Leeds is normally bustling with people and traffic but with the closures imposed on all public gatherings, there was a dreadful sense of dystopia. My anxiety started to swell. Leeds Train Station appeared desolate as I only saw just a few commuters there.

I caught the midday Transpenine Express Service to Huddersfield and arrived at approximately 12:17pm. Twenty minutes later, Marc picked me up in his car and we greeted each other with a kiss. This afternoon, I made our relationship official and gave him a photograph containing a banner which said "Marc, will you be my boyfriend?" I created this banner and embedded it on the photograph, and made it look like I was holding it while I was riding on the back carriage of The Big One at Blackpool Pleasure Beach. My original plan was to ride the rollercoaster today and surprise Marc with with a real-life banner, but this was cancelled due to the lockdown. Marc teared up when I gave him the photograph and accepted the commitment of becoming my boyfriend.

According to news reports, there are currently 5,000 patients infected by the COVID-19 outbreak, including two members of NHS staff.

Monday 23rd March 2020

It is currently just before 11am and I am sitting in the living room whilst Marc is working at home with his male interpreter named Max.

Whilst the outbreak is continuing to wreak havoc on the world, it was confirmed that the youngest person who had died was an 18-year old teenager with underlying health conditions. The government has decided to introduce stricter measures in order to contain the spread, by closing non-essential shops.

Max left at approximately 2:15pm. It was lovely to meet him. He is currently learning Swedish as he has a Swedish girlfriend, just like me learning BSL for Marc.

The death toll within the UK has now risen to 303 in the last 24 hours. Patients were aged between 47 and 103 years old. I arrived home shortly before 7pm this evening, after spending a fantastic few days at Marc's cottage.

As the crisis escalates, Boris has placed more restrictions in place. These being, not to go out, except for an hour's worth of exercise, shopping or work. Any gatherings of even two people, excluding family members are banned. The UK lockdown is not as strenuous as other countries. In Australia, the state of Queensland has announced that it will shut its borders from tomorrow. The UK Government has ordered that now is the time to return back to the country if anyone is travelling abroad. It is predicted that Covid-19 may reach its peak at Easter. This pandemic is completely unbelievable. The outside world appears incredibly lifeless, like its soul had been taken from its heart. It is pretty oppressive to be honest.

Tuesday 24th March 2020

The time is currently 10:05pm and I am relaxing on the couch with Marc, as I record today's journal entry. Marc kindly picked me up from North Lodge House at approximately 7pm with a few of my belongings, including my 8kg Kettlebell and then drove the 16-mile distance back to Huddersfield. This evening, I performed my Whimsical Anecdote "Fleas" via the online Facebook gig "Big Poetry Goes Viral." I positioned myself on a chair, surrounded by soft lighting on the landing of Marc's cottage, as I performed my anecdote. My slot was between 8:15pm and 8:20pm, following a poet called Clive Oseman. Marc sat chilled on the couch, down in the living room, watching my five-minute live showcase on his mobile phone.

In parts of the country, Police have been patrolling the streets, in a bid to keep people isolated indoors, as the UK death toll is now at 422. Penalty fines from £30.00 to £1,000 are going to be issued on Thursday onwards, for those who decide to break the lockdown rules.

Wednesday 25th March 2020

Marc and I spent the day indoors. Marc was working at home with Keren, his interpreter, who stayed at the cottage between 11am and 1:45pm. It was brilliant to see her again. Making her way into the cottage and taking off her coat and shoes at the bottom of the staircase, she mentioned how frighteningly quiet it was outside and that the police were patrolling the streets.

According to news reports, a healthy twenty-one-year-old girl has died of COVID-19. Prince Charles is displaying symptoms of the virus but remains in good spirits. Spain's death toll has now surpassed China's. Apparently, another disease by the name of Hantavirus, which is contracted from rodent's through saliva, urine and faeces is now being discovered, although I don't know if this is as contagious as coronavirus. I hope not.

Thursday 26th March 2020

I went for a forty-minute run, shortly before midday in the dazzling, revitalizing, spring sunshine. At 8pm, the whole nation stepped out onto their front doorsteps and applauded in honour of the NHS for their consistency, courage and determination during the pandemic. Marc and I joined in the applause too. In London, the government is currently converting a huge conference centre into the Nightingale Hospital to accommodate and extra four thousand beds. This is a bleak, oppressive time of grief and uncertainty. I don't know how long I will be based here at Marc's cottage, but he is brilliantly compassionate.

Sunday 29th March 2020

I am beginning to develop intrusive thoughts and feelings of animosity towards loved ones. I am also incredibly irritated by the British government, for not reacting sooner to this escalating pandemic. The government has also inhumanely declared that the nation would have do well if we manage to keep the death toll within twenty thousand. Again, the deceased are categorised as a number and not as an actual human beings. They have no compassion for the people who have lost loved ones. Boris Johnson and the health secretary have been tested positive for coronavirus. Boris previously stated how he shook hands with a vast amount of COVID patients and NHS workers, to learn more about the virus. He is also planning to spend over five million pounds by distributing letters, to every individual nationally, as opposed to investing in more ventilators for the NHS. Again, importance is geared towards the Government, when millions of NHS frontline workers are still waiting to be tested for the virus. It has also been revealed that the lockdown could continue until June with another six months required before the UK can return to back normality. With all of this turmoil consistently unfolding and with Marc and I locked up indoors, my mental health is deteriorating.

In today's news reports, it was confirmed that the NHS consultant, Amged El-Hawrani, aged 55, had died of coronavirus at Leicester Royal Infirmary. The UK death toll has now risen to 1,228. There are now nine cases in Hull and a further thirty-one cases within the region of East Riding. Around half of the UK coronavirus patients are currently in intensive care dying, with at least 1.6 million infected in England.

Tuesday 31st March 2020

It is approximately 1:45pm and I am currently sat in the living room whilst Marc is working from home in the kitchen. I am experiencing physical and mental state of aggravation and antagonism. Often in turbulent situations, the slightest thing can needle me. My psyche has the tendency to operate either conveniently or inconveniently during the most untimely moments. My patience is wearing thin, so times like these can be challenging and overwhelming. I am extremely lucky to have met Marc, pre-COVID, as he has provided me with an affectionate relationship, compassion and support, which is what I need.

Boris Johnson is recovering, though he still has mild symptoms of the virus. The coronavirus has now been declared as a major incident with the death toll including nineteen year old and a thirteen year old boy.

This evening, based upstairs in the front spare bedroom, I performed an online Facebook showcase of my whimsical anecdotes, as I sat in an armchair beside a drawer with a lamp on top shining on the right-hand side of me. My performance was an intimate, unplugged set, which consisted of sixteen poems. These included "Big Knickers Rule," "Thank you Special K," "I've Fallen in Love with Mr Muscle," "Chubby Lollipop Lady." I also recited Carol Ann Duffy's renowned piece called "Havisham," to celebrate the tenth anniversary of a short film I made as part of a university project. This film was called Havisham too.

The gig commenced at 8pm and ended at 9:10pm. This platform gave me the opportunity to sustain and build a virtual audience, whilst a real-life spotlight on stage was just not possible.

Wednesday 1st April 2020

I need an outlet to express the oppressive frustration that I'm mentally and physically feeling at this current moment. It has been announced that apparently, despite the rapid total of today's further 563 fatalities, a 50 percent increase in comparison to yesterday's death toll, Boris Johnson and his diabolical government had only managed to fund thirty ventilators - which is shambolic.

Saturday 4th April 2020

I went for a run. between 1:25pm until 2:25pm. This evening, I performed another Facebook Live gig. This time it was a ten-minute set to raise funding for the commendable NHS frontline staff. The online event was titled "A Night for the NHS," organised by the brilliant Eva Curless.

There were technical issues with the live video facility on Facebook, so the artists pre-recorded their own sets and posted their clips online. Sitting on the landing, on a 1960's style black and white chair, with a lamp beaming in my direction, I performed my anecdotes "Monobrow," "Fleas" and "Big Knickers Rule!" I was honoured to be asked by Eva, to share a portion of my whimsies for such a credulous cause.

The whole country is still in lockdown, meaning that I am having to stay here at Marc's cottage until further notice. My intrusive thoughts have somewhat subsided, which is a relief.

Monday 6th April 2020

I have managed to produce two black and white sketches, which has somewhat preoccupied my spare time. Marc bought me a sketchpad and a small set of graphite pencils on Saturday afternoon in order to keep me sane and also to produce a drawing for him which he can frame and up on his wall. Yesterday, I produced a drawing titled "For Marc." Today I produced a second sketch titled "The Lighthouse." The pencils which I used were - HB, B, 2B, and 4B. I used a piece of tissue to smear with and create a blemished effect in the background. I applied hair spray on the drawings to prevent them from getting smudged.

In today's news reports, it was confirmed that Boris Johnson had been taken to Saint Thomas Hospital in London last night, due to his increasing symptoms. He is now in intensive care. The death toll has grimly increased to 5,413 and 439 people have died within the last 24 hours. A total 51,608 people have been tested positive so far.

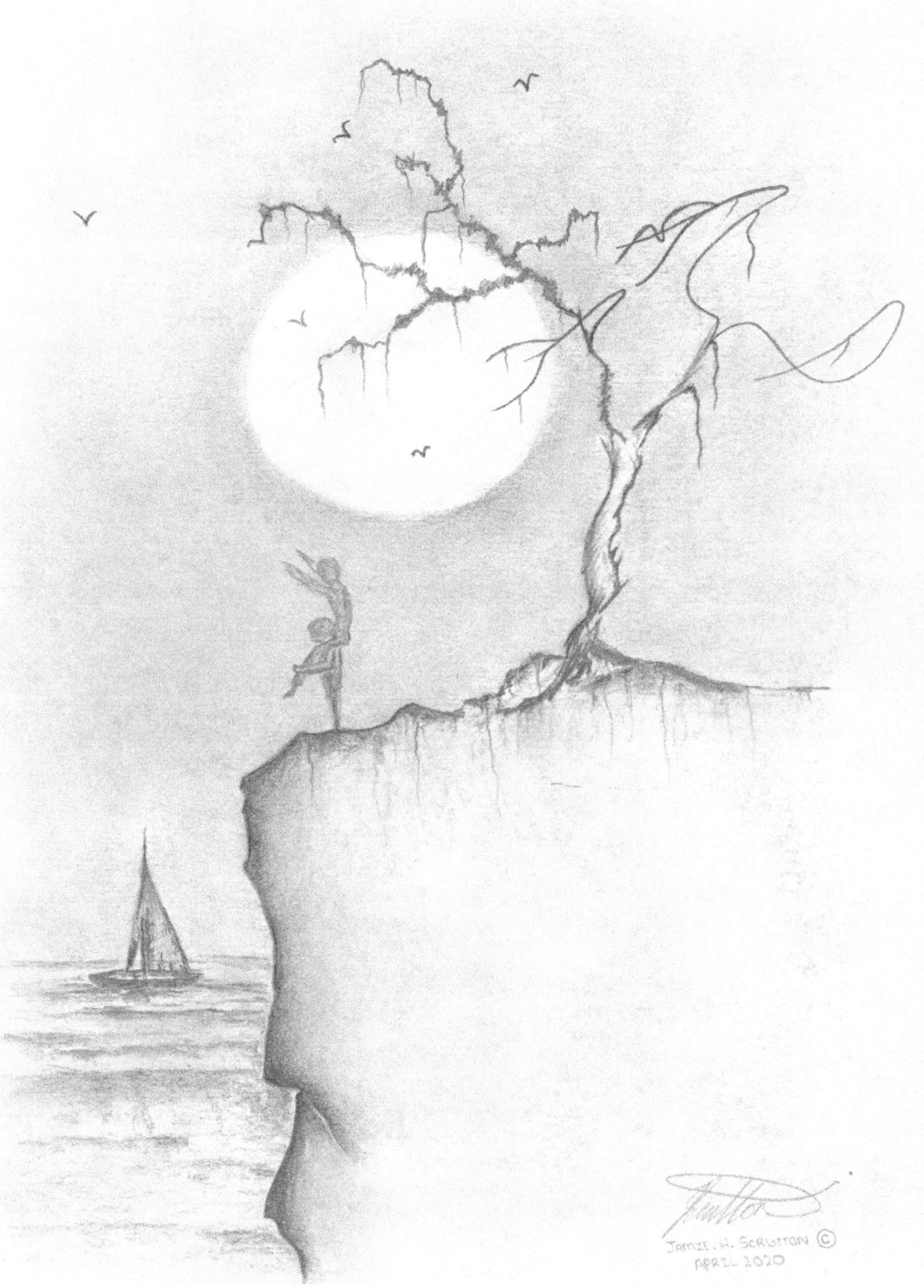

"For Marc"
A4 Pencil sketch

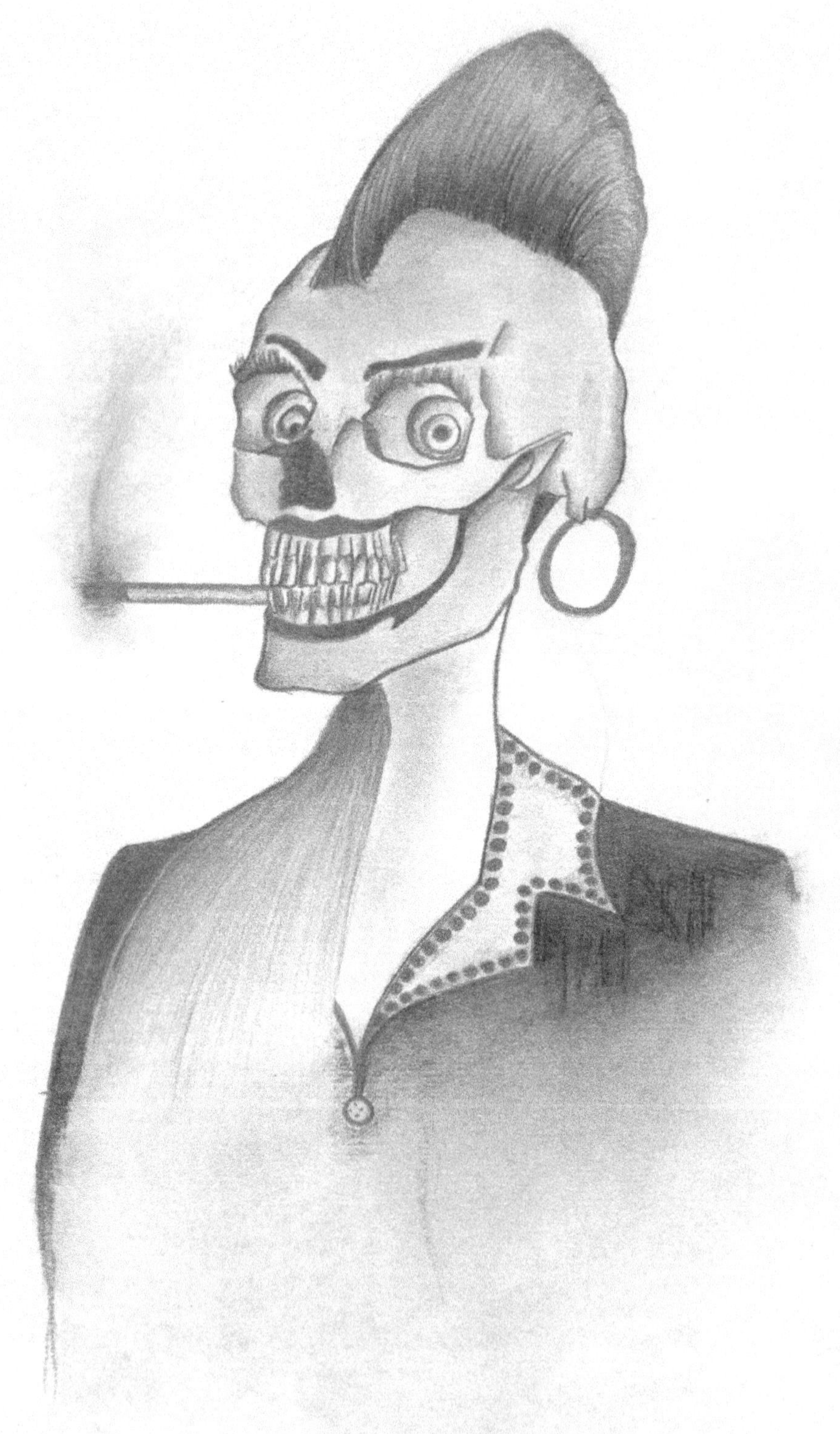

"Skeleton Rocker"
A4 Pencil sketch

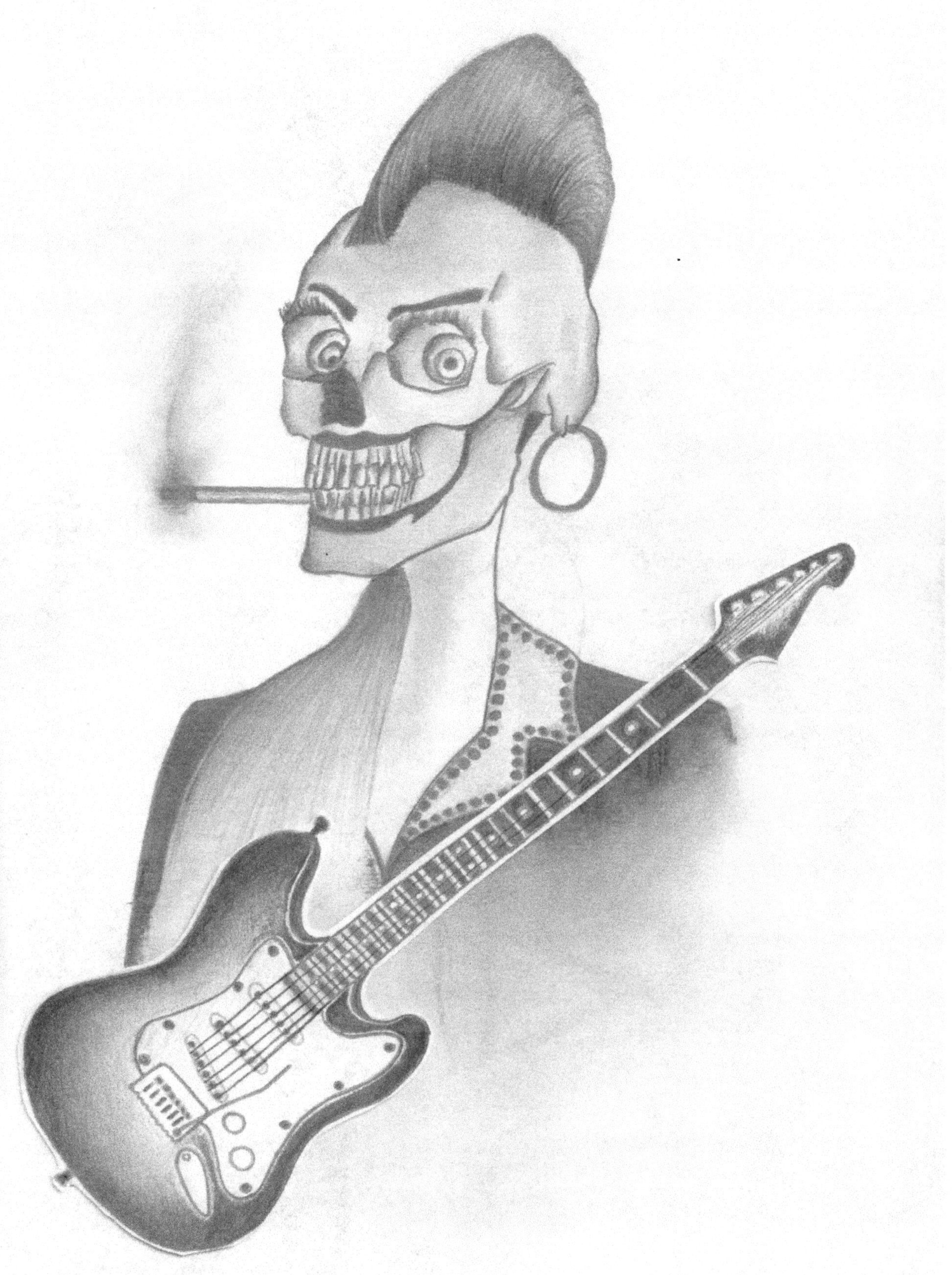

"Skeleton Rocker Air Guitar"
A4 Pencil sketch with Guitar prop

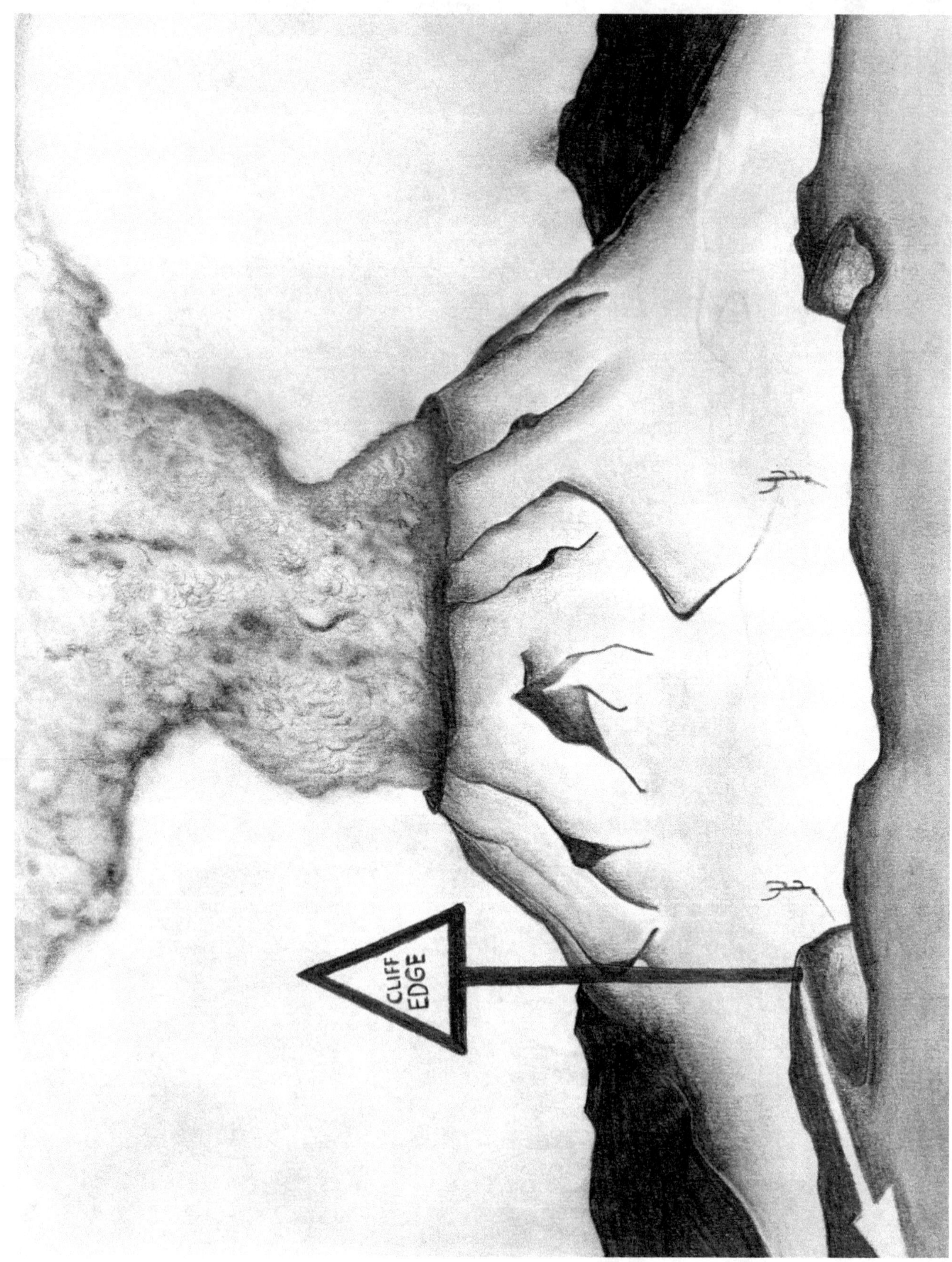

"Volcanic Eruption"
A4 Landscape Pencil Sketch.

Wednesday 8th April 2020

I produced another sketch titled "Volcanic Eruption."

Yesterday, I produced another drawing titled "Skeleton Rocker."

News reports have said that Boris Johnson remains in intensive care and is stable. China has currently lifted their lockdown measures, meaning life returns to some form of normality for them. I am praying that we don't face a second wave. I have been overwhelmed with animosity with the lack off PPE equipment and the boarders still open. Today, my mental health has been stable. My temperament can be extremely unpredictable at uncertain times like these.

Friday 10th April 2020

A further 980 fatalities have been recorded in UK hospitals, during the deadliest day of the pandemic yet. Boris Johnson has regained the ability to walk again, sources say. He is currently trending on Twitter as "Boris the Butcher," for letting this virus spread and for his lack of support for this country. The worrying peak of this pandemic is yet to surface, within the next couple of weeks.

Today, I would complete sketch number five, which I begun late yesterday afternoon. The piece is titled "She Wolf." I am thinking of reproducing prints of my Art work to sell.

Sunday 12th April 2020

This evening, I performed two of my whimsical anecdotes, titled "Big Knickers Rule" and "Monobrow" via an Instagram Live Spoken Word event called "Storytellers." The event is curated by the fabulous Simone Kelly aka Ethereal Truth. The Gig commenced at 7pm with the evening's guest artist, Otis Messiah. I was the eighth Poet to deliver my slot. I was positioned at my wooden desk in my basement room, wearing a pink shirt and a pastel blue tie.

I did a six-lap run, around the perimeter of Woodhouse Moor between 1pm and 2:20pm. It has been an extremely humdrum Sunday apart from having two minor episodes.

News reports have confirmed that the latest death count is now at 10,261, with half of NHS's workers contracting the Virus.

News articles are predicting that the UK could become the most badly affected country in Europe to be struck by COVID-19.

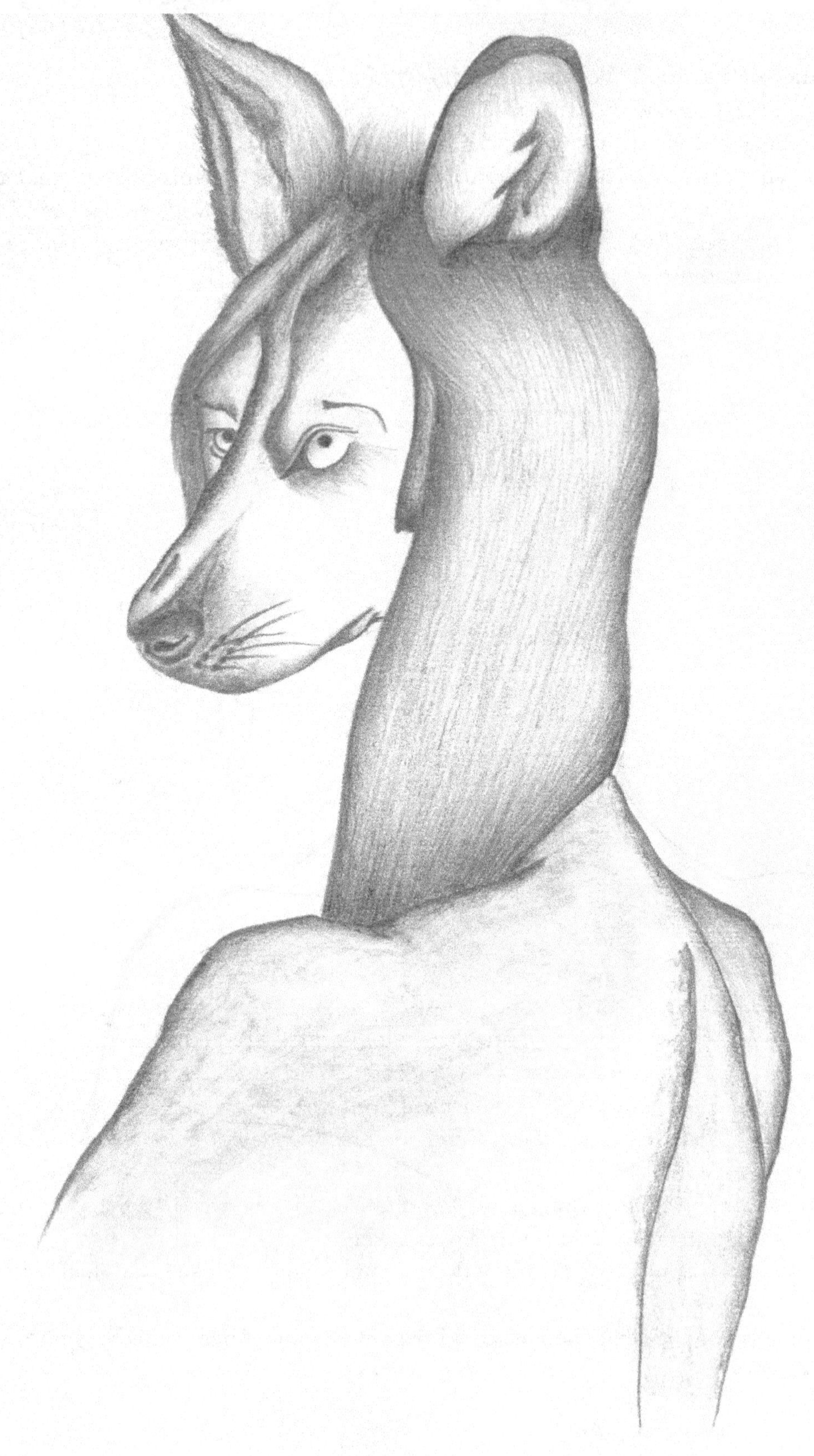

"She Wolf"
A4 Pencil sketch

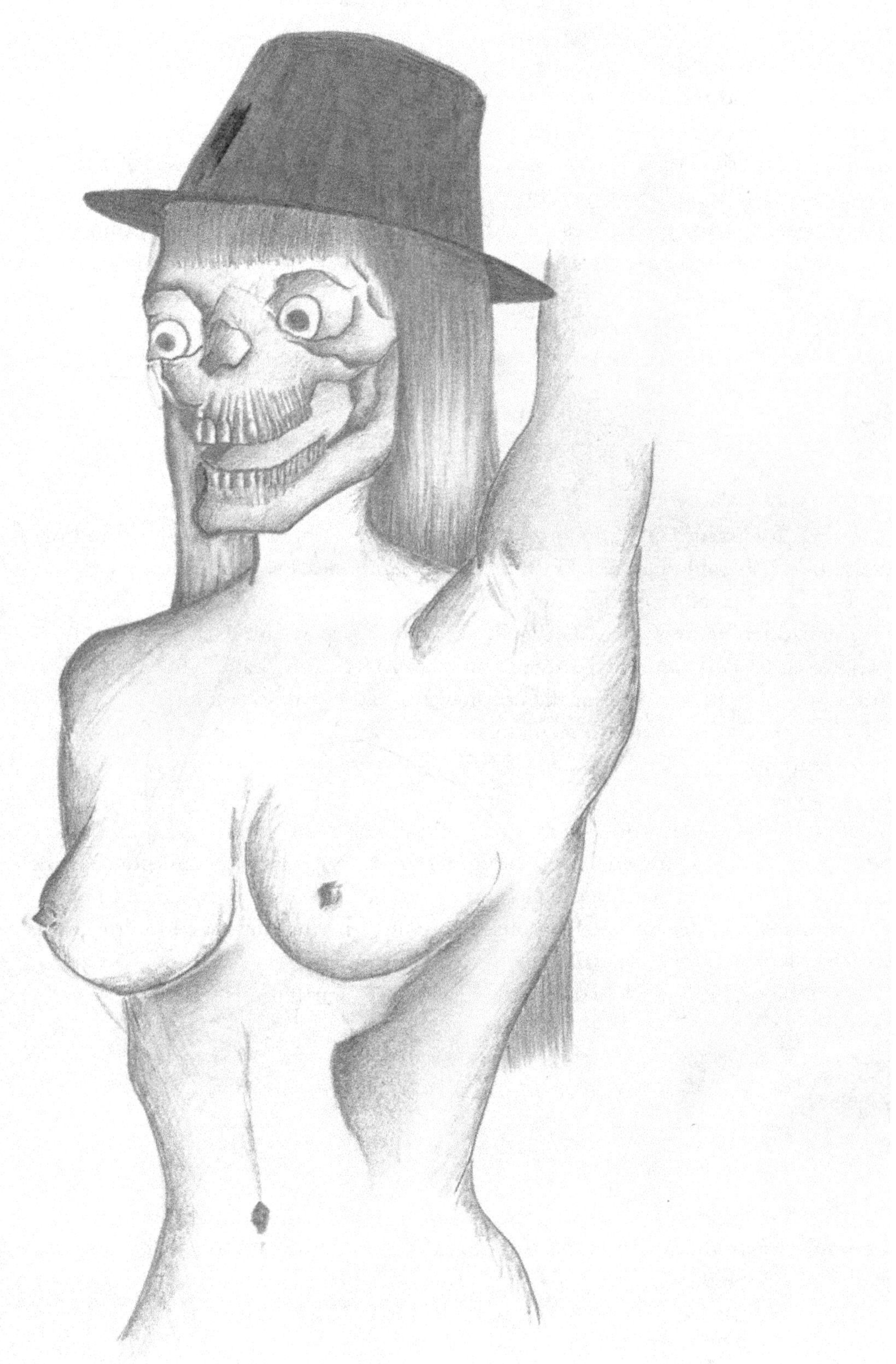

"Femme Fetal"
A4 Pencil Sketch

Tuesday 13th April 2020

The time is currently 8pm. It was a productive afternoon when I returned home from a four lap run around Woodhouse Moor. I firstly attempted to sketch out a suited-up pig, posing in a top hat but this didn't quite work out as expected. I subsequently produced a sketch titled "Pug Prays for World Peace." This sketch took me a good few hours to finish. Anything I do is a valuable distraction during this consistent lockdown and three weeks of no contact with relatives. The only possible way to have direct communication is through a letterbox or a windowpane. Alternatively, there is the luxury of modern day technology, such as social media apps and facetime. Prohibitive social restrictions are still in place which results in work redundancies, the collapse of businesses and the economy losing trillions of pounds. We are still waiting for new ventilators from the government. There is a general sense of hostility towards the ruthless leaders of our country. As soon as Boris was discharged from the ICU, he swanned off to his lavish dwelling at Cheqeurs. It is literally World War three.

Thursday 15th April 2020

The time is currently 5:30pm. Approximately half an hour ago, I completed my isolation sketch number eight, titled "Femme Fatale." This piece had been left aside unfinished on my desk for a several days now, so today I managed to get it completed.

It is saddening to hear about the 28-year old pregnant nurse named Mary Agyeiwaa Agyapong. She had contracted COVID and died after giving birth to a healthy baby. There has been quite a lot of speculation going round in the media that the coronavirus had been developed as part of some conspiracy. Scientists are also speculating, that potential radiation from 5G could be the cause of this deadly disease. Others are suspecting that the virus has been fabricated by someone who wanted to control the global population. Some are even assuming that the virus escaped from a Wuhan laboratory, nearby the Chinese wet market. There is a lot of conflicting information about where the virus originated from.

Going for daily runs and expressing myself through drawing and poetry is helping me to cope during this oppressive time. This weekend, I am spending my time at Marc's cottage in Huddersfield. Normally I wouldn't be allowed to but I can due to having a mental health condition. He is driving me from Leeds, which will be safer than travelling by public transport.

I will be on Furlough leave at Yorkshire Dance, starting this Monday.

Friday 17th April 2020

I completed another sketch at 3:30pm this afternoon, titled "Grotesque." I used the following pencils - 2H, B, 4B, 5B, BB and HB.

News reports have confirmed that the death toll has risen by 847 in the UK, which results in a total of 14,576 fatalities.

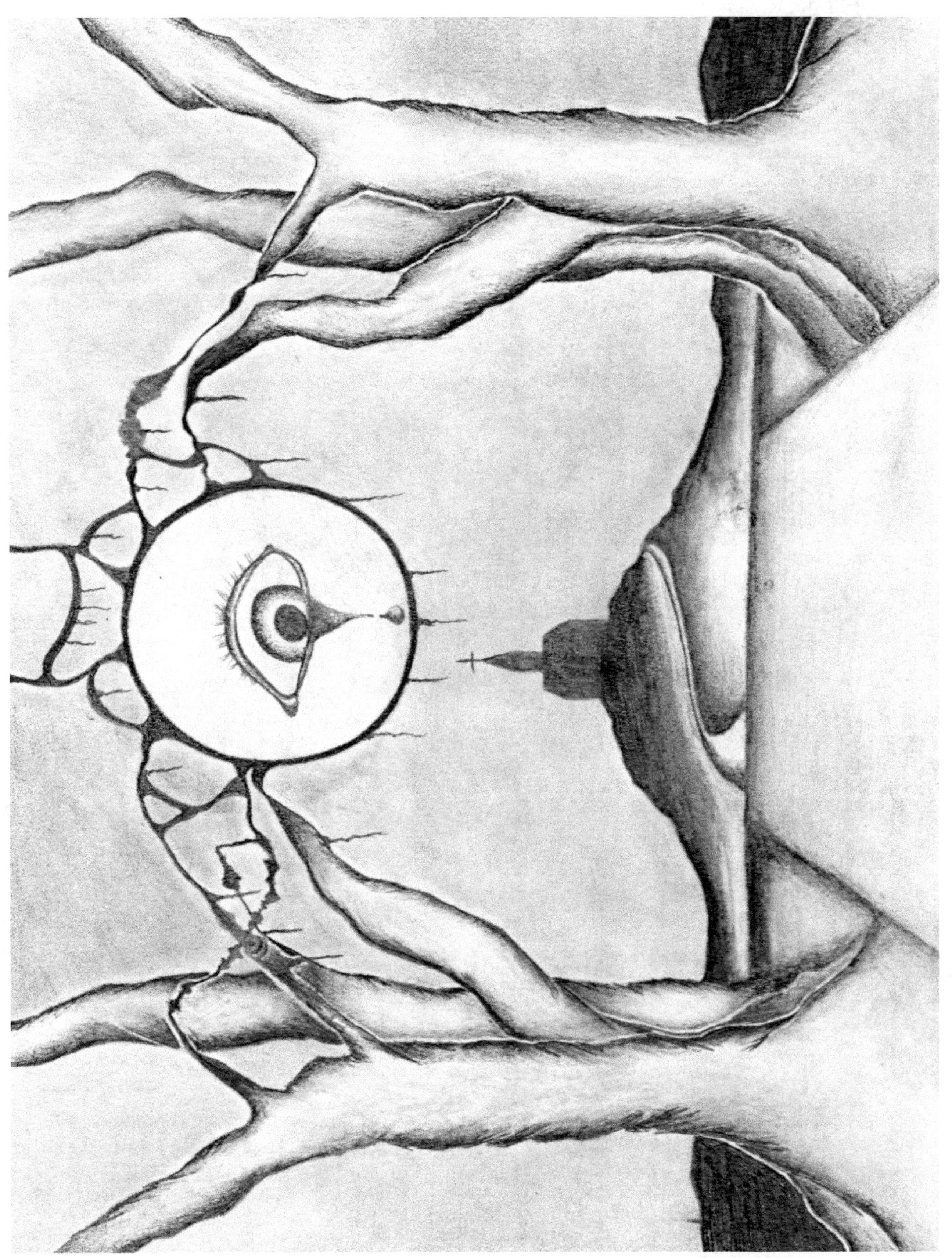

"Grotesque"

A4 Landscape Pencil Sketch

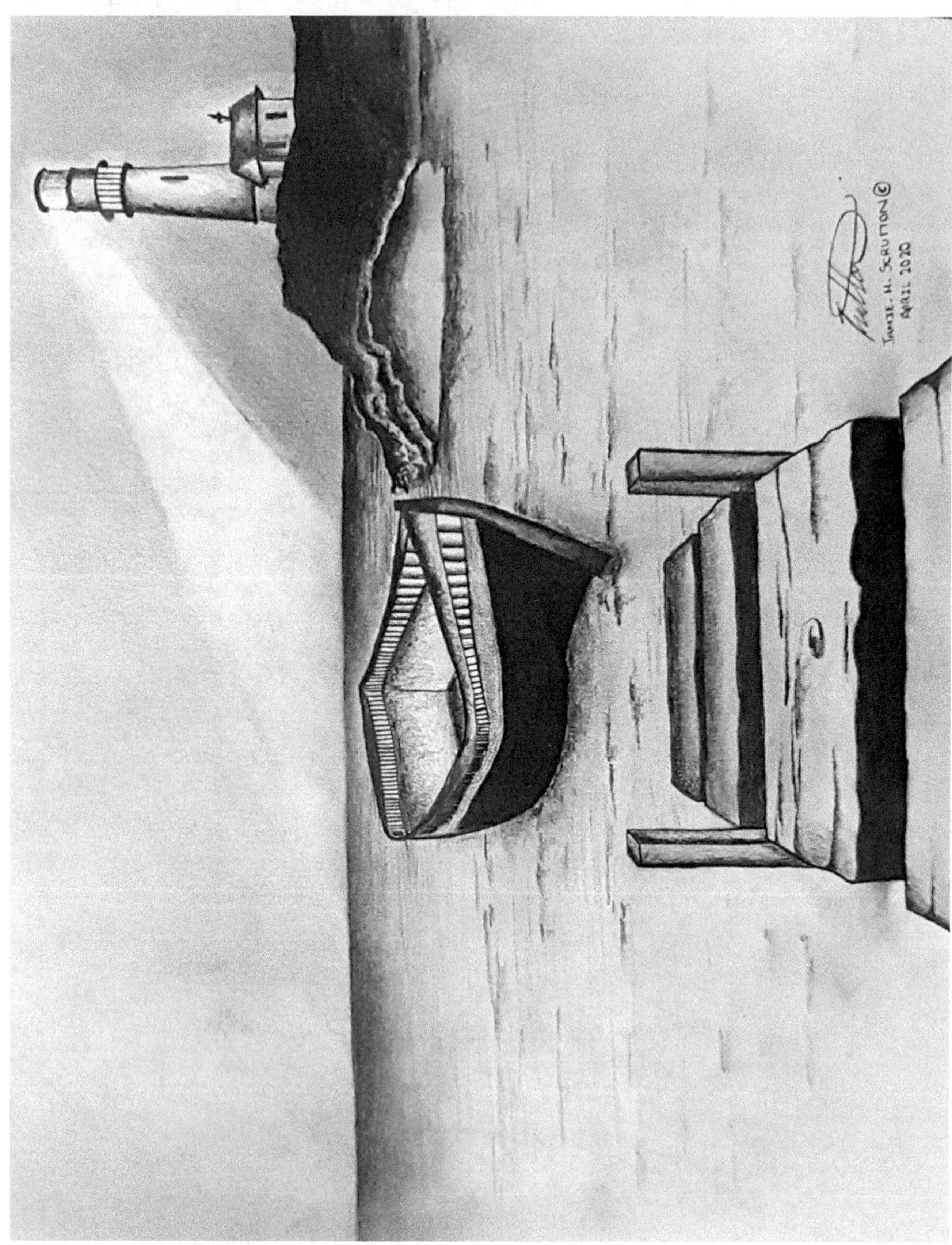

"The Lighthouse"
A4 Landscape Pencil Sketch

Tuesday 21st April 2020

It hasn't been the best of days for my mental wellbeing. My feelings of oppression have really hit hard on me. I am trying to feel upbeat. I have had better days.

Forwarding to mid-October 2020, over three hundred Conservative MP's voted against free school meals for children despite being served with free luxurious banquets, as well as receiving a £3,000 pay rise. They are spitefully letting families starve and letting the NHS disintegrate before our eyes. Fucking disgusting! Thank the lord that the prolific footballer named Marcus Rashford, has campaigned for food vouchers to be made available for the destitute families around the country. He should be highly praised and honoured for his virtue and support to bring survival back in our communities.

The following day, Matt Hancock suggested on the news, that we are one of the best prepared countries, pre and during Covid-19, which clearly we are not. Apparently, the PPE order was only placed last Sunday in Turkey. The government also cannot establish the exact number of fatalities of victims in care homes, let alone the hospital figures.

Wednesday 22nd April 2020

I completed a four lap run around Woodhouse Moor between 1pm and 2pm. It's been another quiet day. My mood has slightly improved compared to yesterday. I also submitted a 500 word short story to an online contest run by Pleasure Beach. The story is titled "The Rollercoaster Enthusiast." This piece is based on my first experience of riding The Big One and how I had bloomed as a rollercoaster enthusiast. The story was produced in third person, spotlighting my twelve-year-old thrill-seeking self, in the name of Jameson. The winner of the Short Story contest will win four wristbands which can be used to enjoy the theme park when it reopens on Saturday 4th July 2020.

Spain has extended their lockdown measures until mid-May. But tourists are still flying in from other countries to Heathrow without an ounce of testing. I mean, what is the whole concept of this fucking lockdown, when testing is not in place? Incompetent!

Thursday 23rd April 2020

This evening, I recordered a non narrative shrilling "Anecdote" titled "An Ode To Lockdown." Basically, I screamed into the video, based down in my basement room and gently said "Thankyou" afterwards.

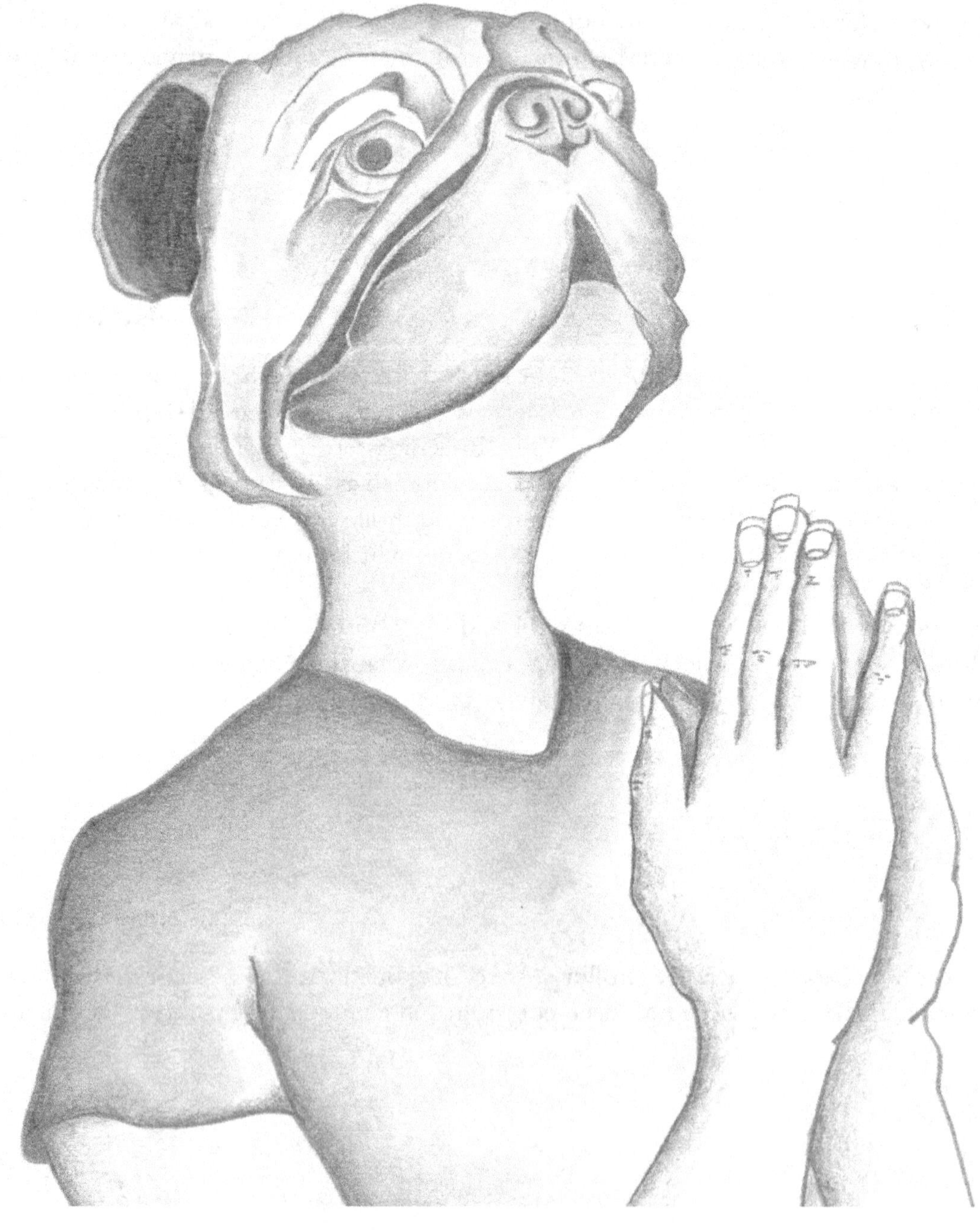

"Pug Prays for World Peace"
A4 Pencil sketch

Friday 24th April 2020

What can I say? The UK is still in lockdown. Non-essential shops are allowed to gradually reopen from May. A beautiful, golden day and the nation is prohibited from setting off for the day.

I did a three-lap run around Woodhouse Moor, between 1:15pm until 2pm.

Monday 22nd June 2020

The lockdown is gradually beginning to ease. The 4th of July aka Super Saturday will be the day when we see the country opening back up again. I have booked to visit Blackpool Pleasure Beach during this weekend, where I can indulge in thrill-seeking after a four-month hiatus. Some people are anxious about the relaxation of the lockdown and are adamant that there is a second wave on the horizon. A number of regions including Wales and Leicester have gone back in lockdown for the second time, due to fresh new cases. The government are allowing theatres to reopen but they are prohibited from staging live performances. What is the fucking point in that?

Marc has been brilliant providing me with compassion, admiration, love and support during this turbulent time. We are completely devoted to each other. He is an incredible soul mate. Compared to my previous partners, they are a miles behind in comparison to how Marc is. Without him, I would have been confined within the four walls of my basement flat at North Lodge house, without anyone to physically communicate with.

As my furlough leave is coming to an end at the Playhouse, I have decided to leave the establishment, to focus on myself as a practicing artist. During the nine years of working at the theatre, I have met some interesting characters of various ages, including one of my best friends named Sandy, who passed away from cancer in September 2020. We both once hid in the cleaner's cupboard whilst on shift at The Playhouse, secretly devouring a salted caramel ice cream, whilst discreetly on the lookout for any passersby. Sandy overheard a couple talking about their financial worries after spending a lot of money on shopping. They were trying to reason why they had spent an extortionate amount of money. Anyhow, they were reading through their receipts.

"Well, the vibrator was forty pounds!" The woman said.

"Did I just hear that right?" Sandy chuckled, telling me about the conversation.

When a rather handsome gent passed us by, we would both look at each other with a flushed expression of excitement. God bless her soul. She will forever be in my heart. Sandy was a beautiful lady. I am honoured to have had her as a friend.

Friday 3rd July 2020

Shortly before midday, I completed an acrylic painting on a piece of A2 wood panelling as a painted take on "The Lighthouse" sketch. I commenced work on the painting at 2pm yesterday in the kitchen. I swept over aspects of the painting with a 4B gradient pencil, to bring in mixed media to the piece.

The painting is named "The Lighthouse Technicolour".

Monday 6th July 2020

I produced an A4 sketch titled "Desree Owl."

Tuesday 7th July 2020

A slow start to the morning. Four cups of coffee. I went to WHSmith to purchase an A3 cartridge pad, to produce additional sketches for my website.

I completed an A3 drawing titled "The Owl and The Pussycat." Pencil mediums used were H, HB, 4B and 5B. The artwork is a surprise for Marc.

Thursday 9th July 2020

I commenced work on an A3 sketch titled "The Lion" at 10:30am, whilst sitting upstairs in the kitchen at North Lodge House.

I then took a break from the piece at 12:30pm, to meet with the lovely Jo at 2pm nearby the Playhouse. I collected my first batch of art prints from the Printworks based on Call Lane, in between leaving our local Wapentake to go to The Duck and Drake pub on the opposite side of the road. It was brilliant to see her again.

Friday 10th July 2020

It has been quite an active day. I resumed work for a short while on "The Lion" sketch, shortly before midday. I then freshened myself up and headed into town, to find a frame to display "The Owl and the Pussycat" for Marc.

He loved the piece when collecting me from North Lodge House at 4:50pm, to take me to meet Pat, a friend of his for thirty years. She resides alone with her black cat in a bungalow. She is a charming character. Pat has an oxygen tank which is attached to a nasal tube to help stabilise her breathing. Because of this she is exempt from going outside due to Covid-19. It was brilliant to meet her.

Marc drove me back to my flat to drop off a wooden desk that Pat kindly gave me. We subsequently arrived at his cottage in Huddersfield at 9pm.

Wednesday 15th July 2020

Using pencil mediums 2H and B with a dab of colour for a rose, I created a Casanova-esque pig, dressed in a shirt, tie and waistcoat. He had a charming appearance with a rose held in his mouth. The A4 piece is titled "Pig Charming."

Thursday 27th August 2020

I had a brilliant evening, performing my whimsical anecdotes "Big Knickers Rule," "The Fabulous Tom Ford" and "Thirty Pence to Have a Piss?!" at an event called Moetry, based at The Lock Up in Leeds. It was refreshing to perform in front of an actual live audience, as opposed to an online event. My material was very well received by the supportive audience, as I stood at the microphone in a dimly lit space, near a silver stand holding candles.

There were a variety of acts who showcased their talents including poets and musicians. It was brilliant to see Tash aka T/MO and Nabeela Ahmed who also performed this evening. Nabeela introduced me to her lovely friend Michelle Bradley who came along to support her. Nabeela performed in the first half and Tash and I performed in the second half. As always, I was the first one to arrive at the venue, which was situated at the end of Butterfly Street, neighbouring Crown Point in Leeds.

I walked the two mile distance from North Lodge House, after Marc dropped me off there before midday en route to Pat's bungalow. I took myself out for a four-lap run around Woodhouse Moor. I also met the new residents in my apartment; Vinnie who is from Brazil and Karen from the North East of England. I briefly met her ex-boyfriend too. I didn't feel as apprehensive when settling in my basement room for the afternoon, although my delusions were present. I am glad that there are other occupants in North Lodge House, as opposed to living alone like I have been for the previous couple of months.

I arrived back at Marc's cottage shortly before midnight, with a lovely couple who gave me a lift after this evening's gig. During the rainy journey down the M62, we talked about our backgrounds in the arts. The man is a male dancer and a fashion designer and the woman is a Social Worker. Both are extremely lovely. I spoke about my practice as an animator and how I adapt my whimsical anecdotes into short animations, which I often perform live alongside. I handed over a business card of mine to them both. They dropped me off outside Huddersfield train station and Marc picked me up from there. Jane is staying with us for a couple of nights. It is always a pleasure to see her.

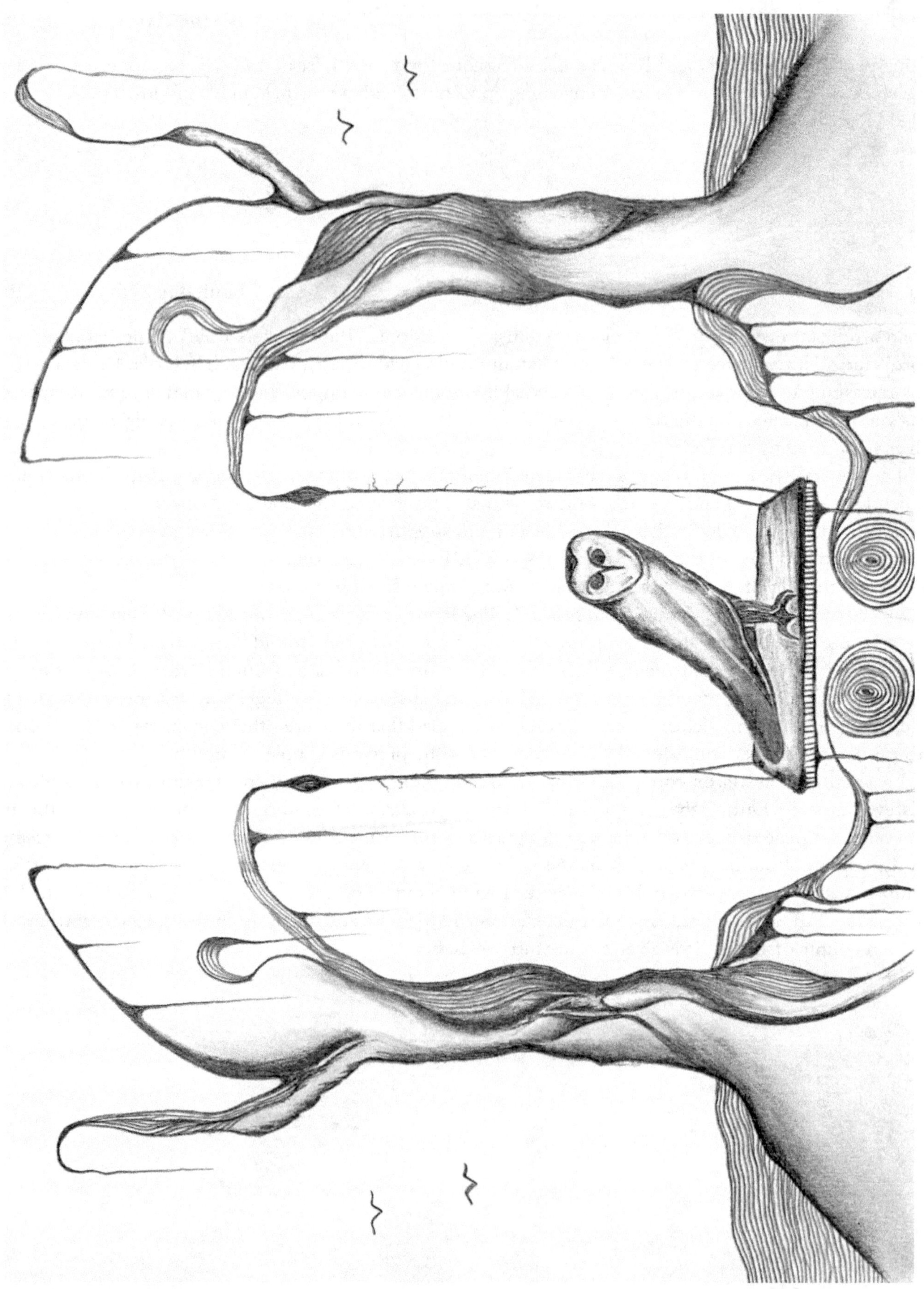

"Desree Owl"
A4 Pencil Sketch

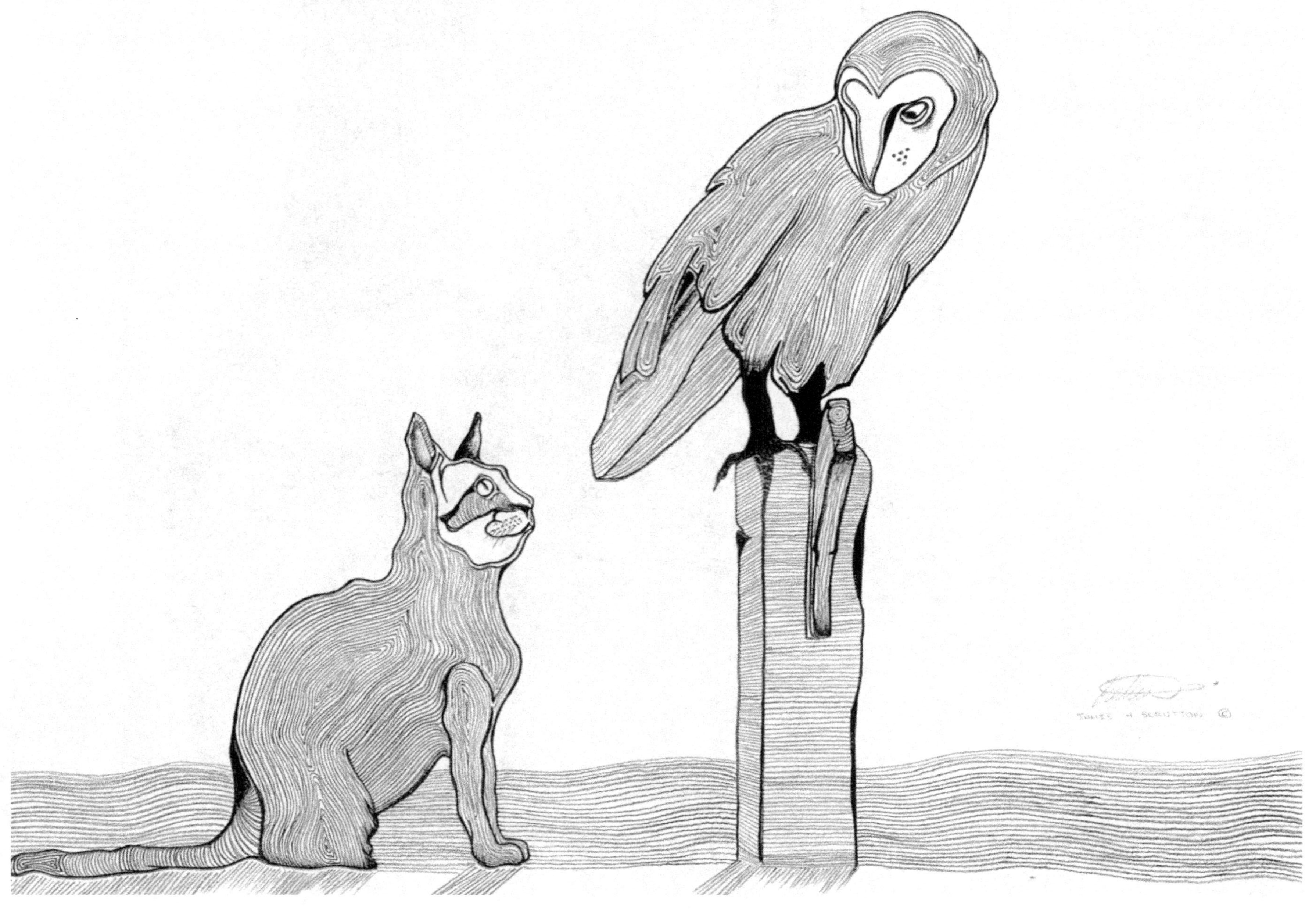

"The Owl and the Pussycat"
Pencil Sketch

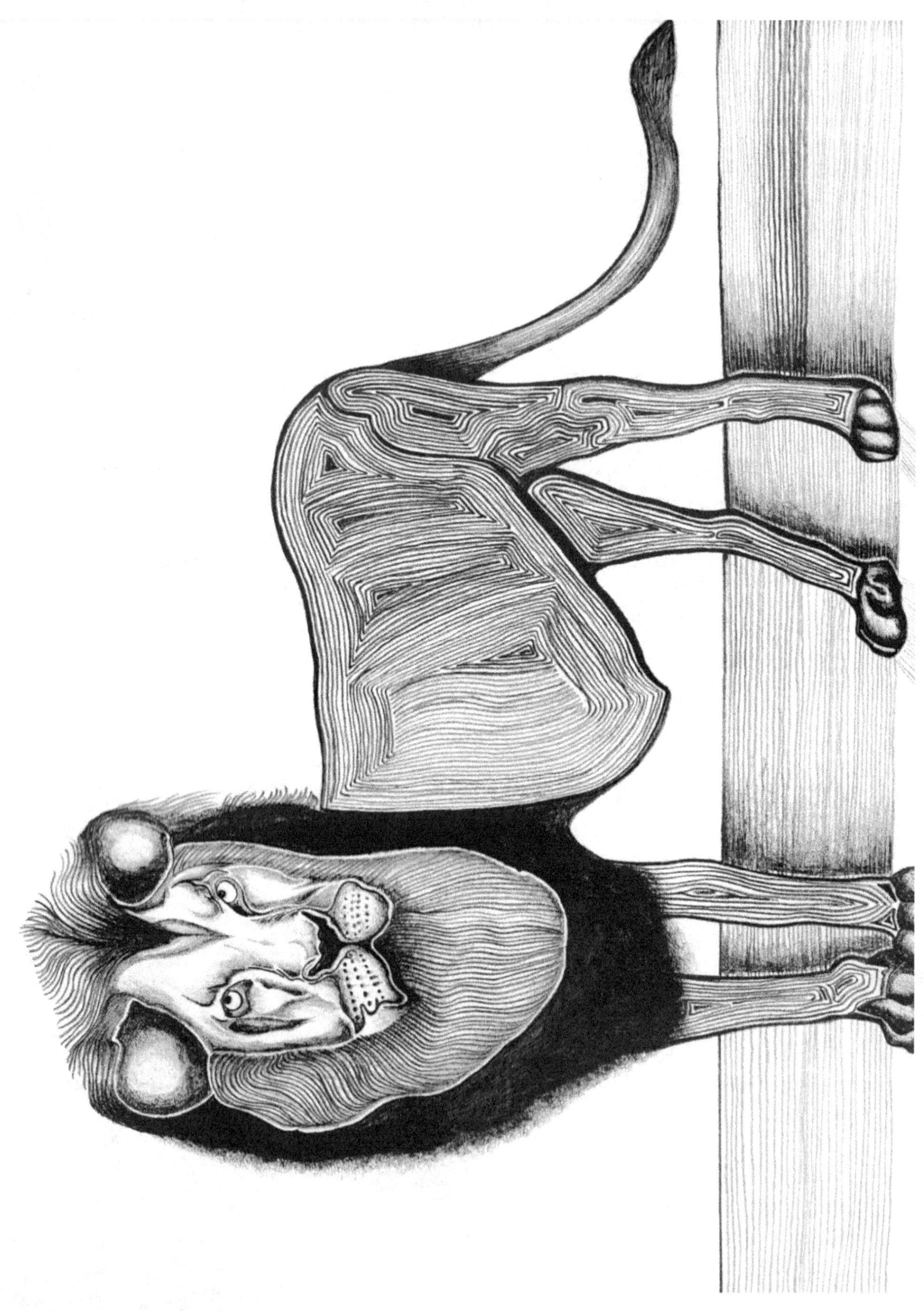

"The Lion"
Pencil Sketch

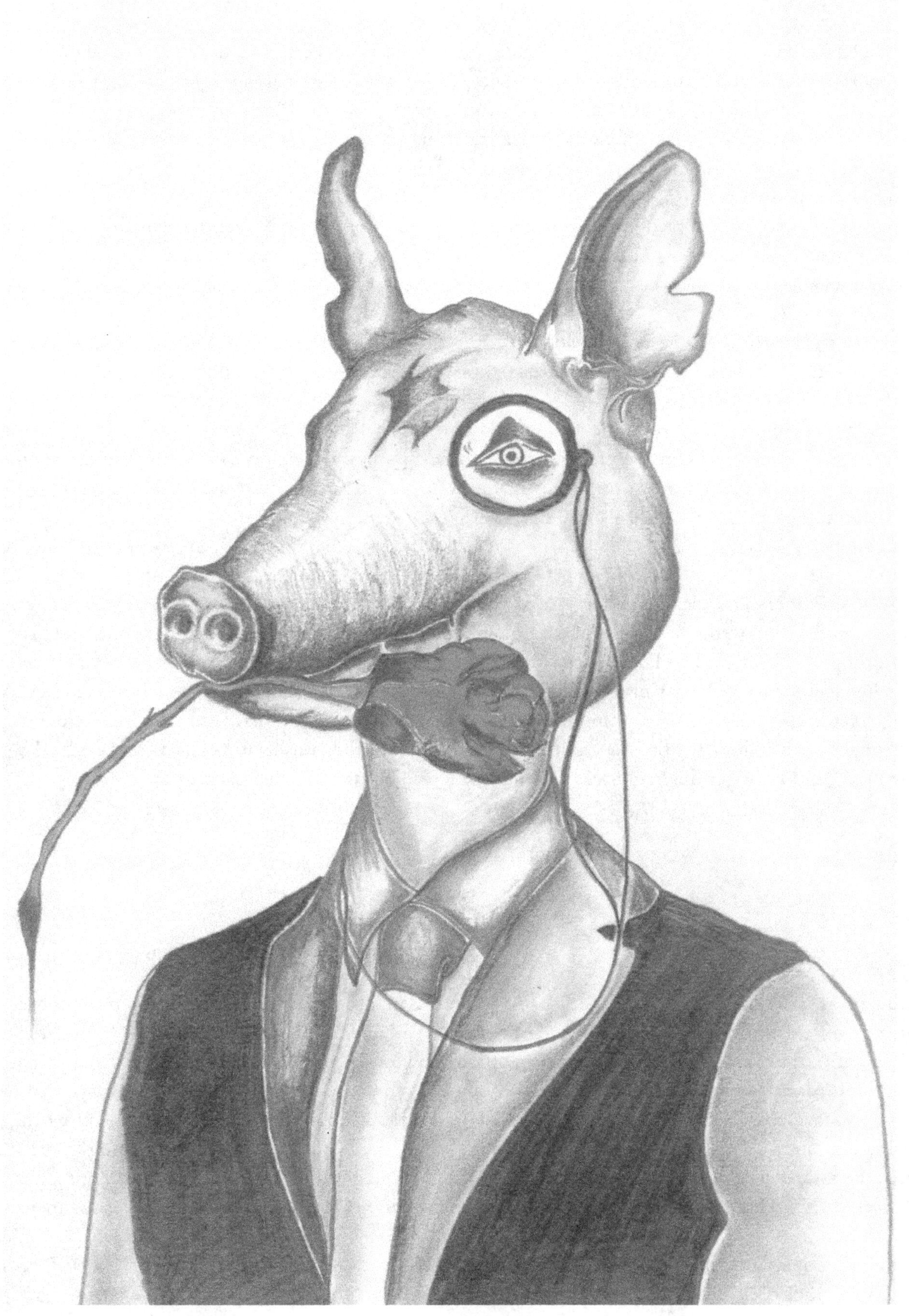

"Pig Charming"
A4 Pencil sketch with Acryllic paint

Wednesday 2nd September 2020

I attended a training session at Yorkshire Dance today. It commenced at 12 noon and finished just before 2pm. Lauren guided us through the newly revised procedures for managing the building, to ensure safety from Covid-19. It was good to see Laura H and Lucy Dyson from the Playhouse and also Samya and Judee. It was good to have some form of normality again. I had a bite to eat and a decaffeinated tea at the San CoCo Cafe, soon after the training session had ended. I returned home at 3:15pm and had a quick sleep between 4:30pm and 6pm.

The country was placed back into lockdown from the beginning of November for three weeks, due to a rise in Covid-19 infections. The new lockdown measures weren't as strenuous as the previous ones, as non-essential shops were allowed to open. Although restaurants, cafes and pubs were only able to operate a takeaway service.

Four days prior to Christmas, the government thought it would be a good idea to do a U turn by scrapping the five-day relaxation for the celebrations altogether, just after people spent an abundance of money. Why they didn't announce this a month ago prior to the 25th December is completely beyond me. On Saturday 19th December 2020, when the announcement was made public at 4pm, London Kings Cross was heaving with thousands of commuters heading home for the festive period despite the capital being placed in tier four. A new strain of the coronavirus has now been discovered with fears that it is seventy percent more transmittable than the previous one.

Subsequently, there was a new spike in cases, reaching a total of 50,000 infections on Tuesday 29th December 2020. As a result, there was no available capacity in our hospitals. Patients had to wait for aid outside in stationary ambulances. There are also talks of a third lockdown and plans for a more stringent lockdown tier system in the new year. The whole of Lancashire has been placed in tier four, with Yorkshire also heading in this direction. These lockdowns are causing major concerns for this country, plunging the hospitality sector into a deeper pit of recession. We don't hear what is being done for mental health. The rate of suicides is at the highest I think it has ever been. Where was the British Sign Language interpreter during the daily briefings for the deaf community? Marc and the rest of my deaf friends, who I worship the ground of, do not get the benefit of knowing where they stand in this pandemic.

Saturday 28th November 2020

I produced another intricate sketch titled "Optical Delusion," this evening while I was sitting in Marc's living room. Marc, Danny and Jane were playing online deaf bingo in the kitchen. Jane won £1,000, drunkenly howling with excitement. I completed the piece the following evening, as I sat in Danny's living room with himself and Marc, after a lovely Sunday roast cooked by the one and only Danny. Jane stayed for dinner but had to leave a few hours ago. The drawing depicts a delusional perspective of a perfect world, when in reality it is on the verge of a climate catastrophe. I didn't have any idea what I was going to draw at the start. I just improvised and developed the portrayal of our planet's destruction. An optic mirror in the illustration, displayed the difference between beauty and ugliness. I felt in the end, that I had achieved what I wanted to portray.

I completed another sketch that I began in July 2020, the week when my anxiety exploded. I rediscovered it on Monday 30th November 2020. The finished sketch is called "Meddlesome Warmonger."

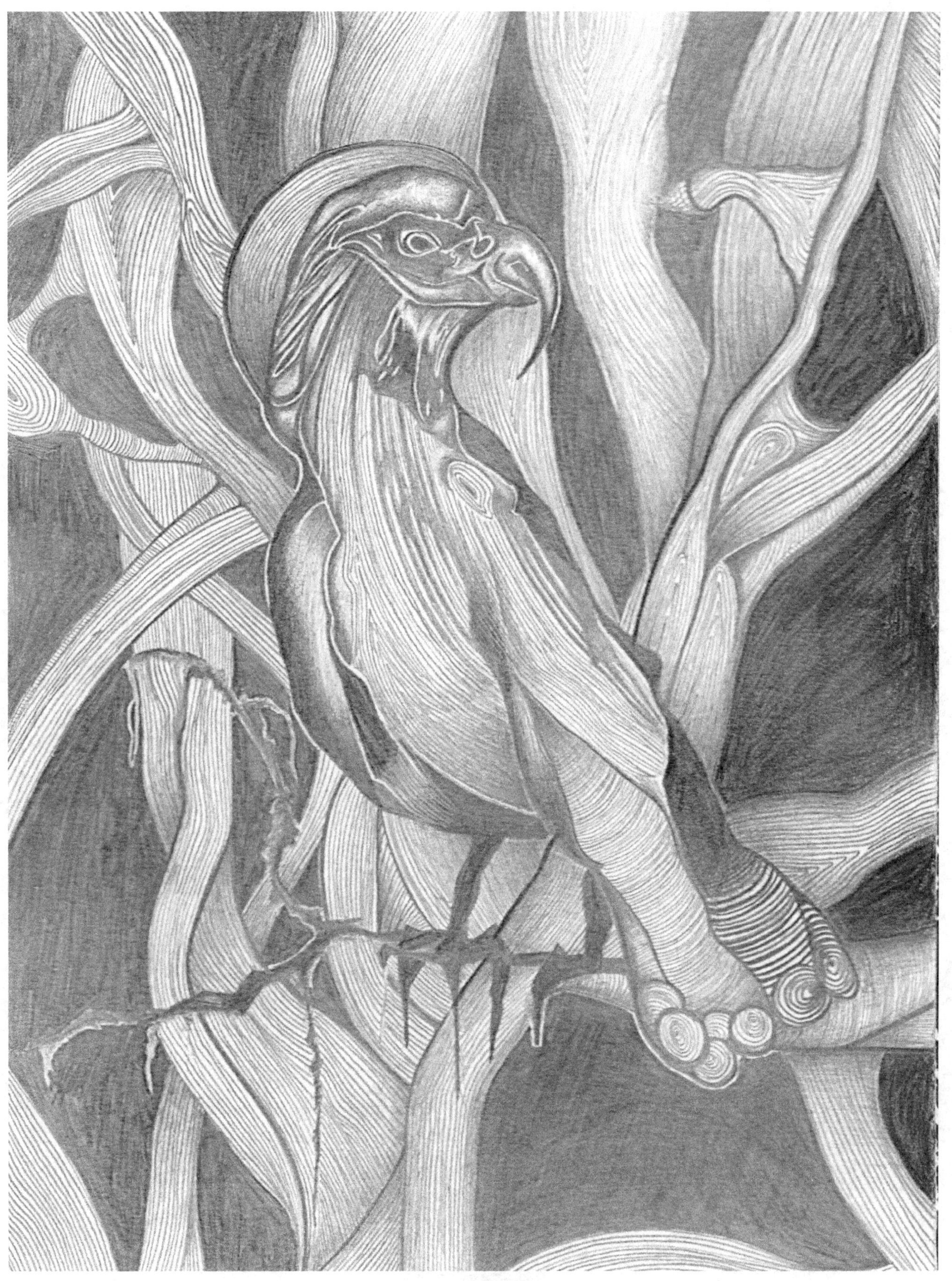

"Meddlesome Wormonger"
A4 Pencil sketch.

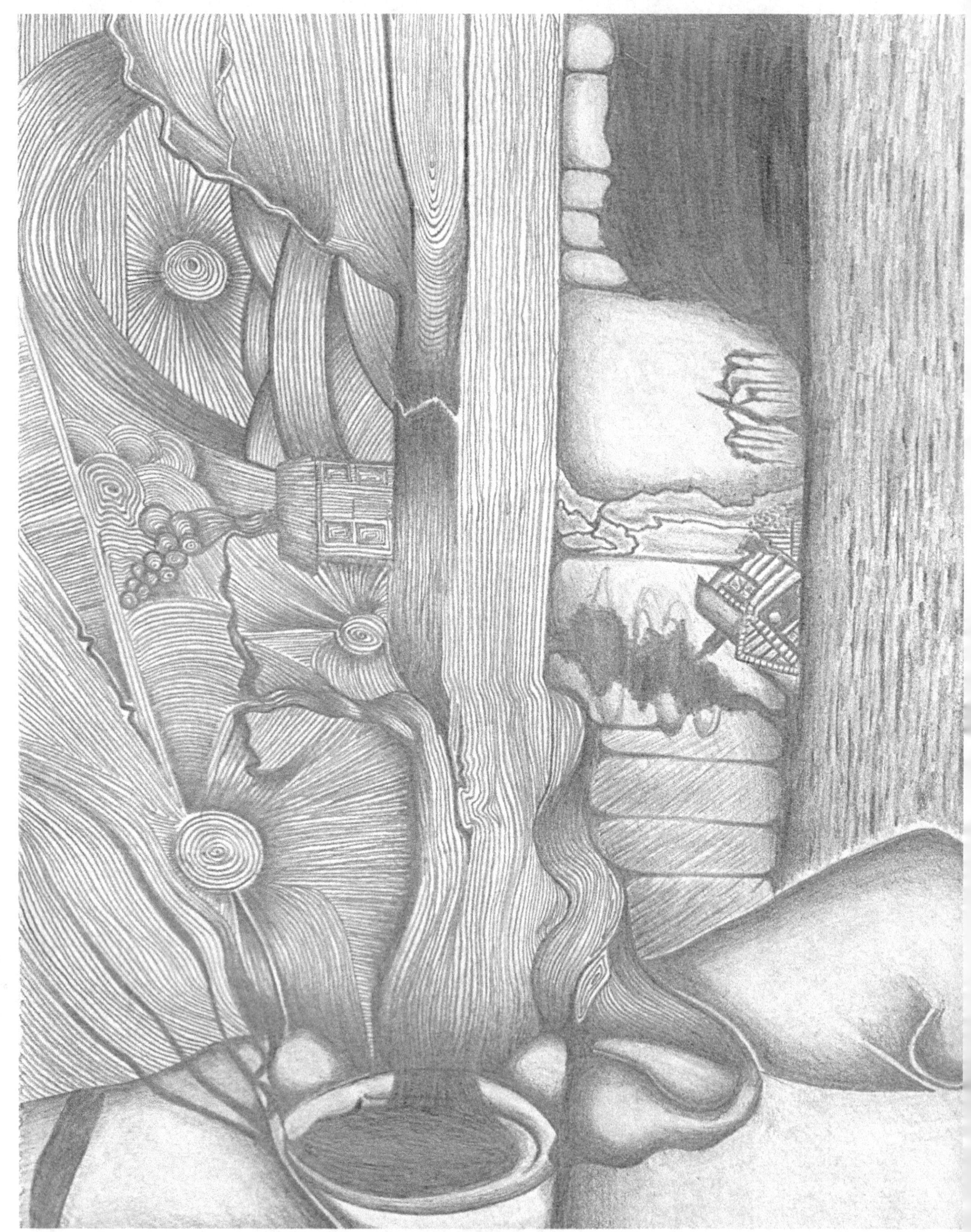

Optical Delusion
A4 Landscape Pencil Sketch

Tuesday 4th January 2021

The hillbilly clown has just addressed to the nation that there will be a third lockdown. Marc was curious to know what the new measures were. Again, no BSL interpreter was present during this evening's briefing.

Marc and I went for a COVID-19 test in Batley at a mobile drive through testing centre, which wasn't as bad as we imagined it to be. I have been experiencing some minor breathing complications and Marc has been getting chest pains. Obviously, I have been worried for Marc but not as much for myself. If the breathing isn't anything to do with Covid -19, maybe I have some form of abnormality in my heart, even though I am physically fit. My biological dad, David, once popped out for a cigarette after picking his children up from school and died of a heart attack. I will never meet him again. I discovered this information on social media, after becoming curious of his whereabouts back in spring 2016.

I remember having this overwhelming feeling of envy, as I read of how he was supposedly brilliant and exceptional as a dad to his children. Nevertheless, he dismissed me as a child and didn't want to have a relationship with me. I once planned to visit Grimsby where he lived, to leave a note on his grave saying how despicable he was as a dad but decided not to.

Marc and I received our COVID test results after forty-eight hours of waiting, and they both came back as negative. My mood has been extremely bipolar today as well as last weekend but this is normal particularly in the new year. The uncertainty of 2021 doesn't help my anxiety.

A new Oxfordshire based vaccine known as AstraZeneca was given to its first patient today. His name being Brian Pinker, aged 82. I just think it is strange how you don't hear of the first vaccine anymore which was released back in December and whether it was effective at all. I cannot see ourselves returning to normal lives any time soon.

On Wednesday 6th January 2021, the UK began its third lockdown. Again, with all shops, pubs and restaurants having to close, except for the ones that sell essential items. Schools have had to shut their doors once again, why they were ever allowed to reopen is completely beyond me. Another matter in news reporters was panic buying! Hasn't anyone learnt throughout the first two lockdowns that if the nation helps each other well and shows courtesy, supplies will still be available to purchase.

On Monday 11th January 2021, a surge of deaths in the UK reaches a devastating total of 81,431, whilst the rising cases of infections are currently at 3.07 million. Leeds infection rates have slightly declined since the third lockdown began but has risen in surrounding areas such as Kirklees.

Sunday 17th January 2021

Jane is currently sat in a motley verdant green chair in Marc's living room and is talking to Marc about life. I am sat next to my art work on the couch which I have been working from time to time. It is currently 4:15pm and the brisk evening is gradually drawing in.

In today's news reports, the government have apparently announced that the current restrictions may be eased by March, adding that every adult will have received the vaccination by September. The NHS are delivering 140 jabs a minute supposedly. Australia is now completely liberated from the pandemic with normal life resuming for the fortuitous citizens down under, although self-isolation remains in places for those who may have symptoms. Whereas in China, apparently, an ice cream tests positive for Coronavirus, whilst the global death toll reaches a devastating two million victims. Since photographs have emerged showing hospital wards looking empty, protesters are rebelling against the government and are suspecting that COVID is a hoax and is part of a conspiracy.

Personally, I really do not know what to believe anymore, as there is so much misleading and conflicting information being spread by journalists. It is difficult to stand next to what is actually the truth.

One year on and life around the world is curiously transformed. Even though the roll out of the vaccine is seemingly successful so far, it was recorded on the morning of Tuesday 19th January 2021, that the UK had the highest death toll in the world and yet we have no idea why. Staggering isn't it? It has been suggested that bars and restaurants should stay shut until at least May, to avoid a disastrous R-rate, whilst government reckons that lockdown may last into the summer. I suspect Covid-19 will be with us inevitably for a long while at least.

The death toll reaches a devastating 100,000 fatalities on Tuesday 26th January 2021.

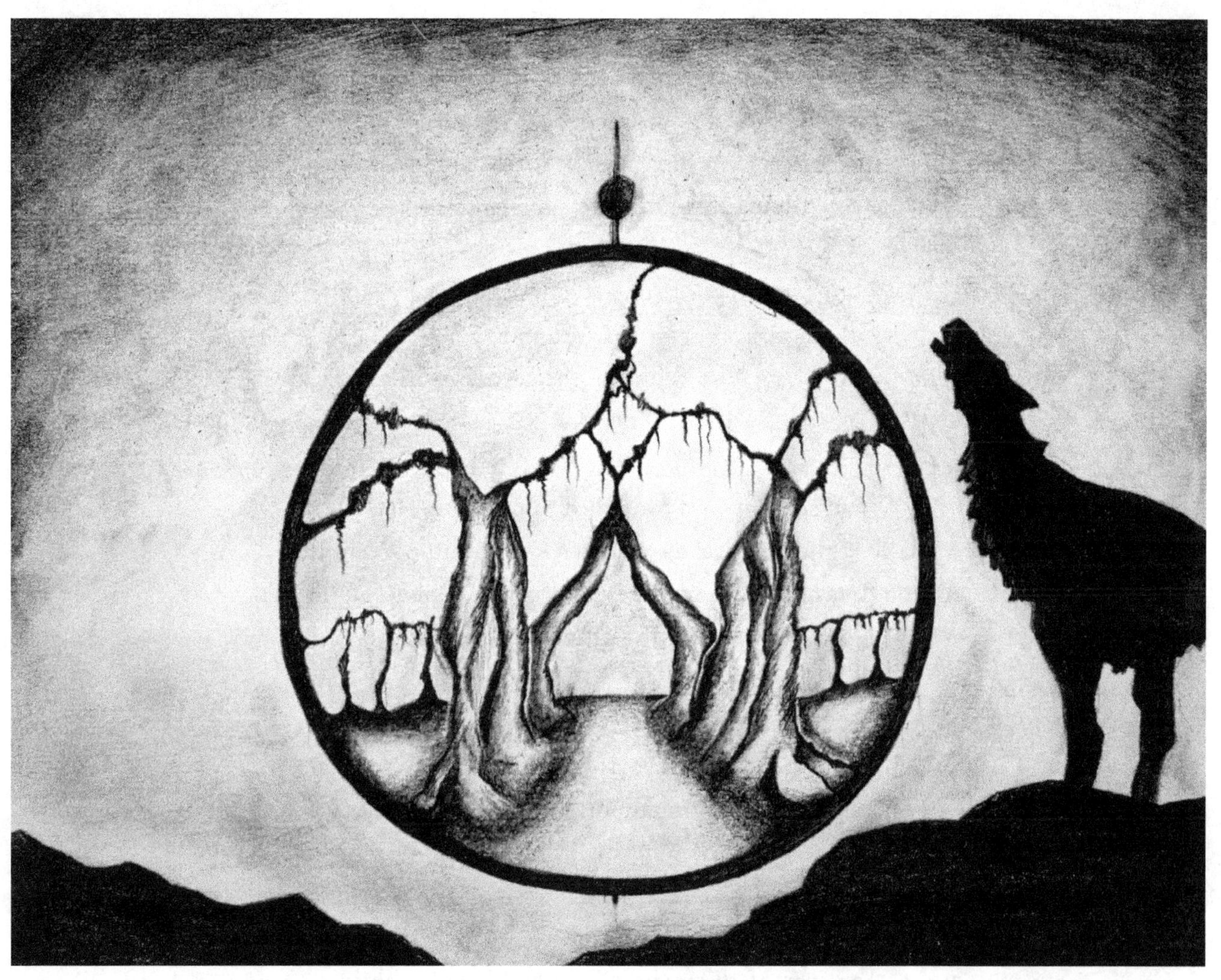

"Midnight Dynasty"
A5 Pencil Sketch

TAX

I'm doing the bastard taxes this morning,
I think I'm going to need a stiff drink,
An abundance of receipts, declaration forms and possibly a corpse,
I have absolutely no time to think!

I am certainly not surprised if I dig up a heap,
Of henionsbecause I am sure they will be plenty,
I think I would have lost count of the carcasses in my back yard,
Especially after 2020!

You see, I would propel of succeeding a task,
Chuck the barbaric clowns in a coffin and off a cliff,
Although taxes I have to annually do, it's the bane of my life,
It's an activity of a bothersome tiff!

Everything is electronic; it is giving me trepidation,
All of this persistent theorising is making me see stars,
I am becoming impatient; I am losing the plot,
It's a pain in the bastard arse!

I should treat accountancy like a replenished new life,
As a way of distraction from the Janaury blues,
But I am beginning to lose my fill with these repetitive duties,
It becoming somewhat of a muse!

I wish my psyche was a wonderous thing,
At the end of today, my brain cells will be destroyed,
I wish I had a robot to fulfil these services,
Which I could simply avoid!

A tedious day of static mathematics,
Another year I can salute "auf wiedersehen" and relax,
I am going to kick off my shoes and indulge into my robe,
and finally say fuck off to the tax!

I've Fallen in Love with Mr Muscle!

The typical, skittish behaviour when your body begins to bustle,
All in the fact that I've fallen in love with the one and only Mr Muscle,
How his passionate vibe shines when cleaning down my decks,
As his toned articulate physique moves, rhythmical with his pecs!

I absolutely idolize his devotedness to cleaning; his pure dedication,
I never knew in a million years that I would fall at the feet of a fictional animation,
Every time he appears on the telly, he sends me into an ultimate lust of dreaming,
of his hard grafting work of solving solutions; the master scientist of cleaning!

Everyone reckons I am CRAZY; When I tell them that someday he will save my fate,
He is the heroic figure who loves the jobs, that I certainly hate,
You can rely on his problematic fixtures; you can abide by his terms,
You can depend on his assurance when he says he can kill your unwanted toilet germs!

He assassinates those horrid spiders; he knows that they drive me insane,
He is the superhero with the professional touch of unclogging my crummy drain,
He knows how to abide in a woman's animosity, when the hygiene repells HELL,
He knows how to achieve the optimism with his magical bathroom gel!

So divorce your apathetic husband sisters; upgrade to a supreme,
A man that can harbour the pressure and contain a vigorous hygiene,
Experience the typical, skittish behaviour when your body begins to bustle,
All in the fact that I've fallen in love with the one and only Mr Muscle!

This was written back in the summer of 2014. I was inspired to write about a current marketing brand, creating my own original character and then merging the two together, to deliver a whimsical anecdote. This poem is narrated from the perspective of a woman, who adores a TV commercial featuring Mr Muscle. This was a prominent piece of mine, which I performed regularly between 2014 - 2016 at various spoken word events. The first performance was at a Verbal Remedies event, based at The Outlaws Yacht Club in Leeds, in November 2014. I performed again after that at Jawdance, based at The Rich Mix Venue, in Bethnal Green, on Wednesday 27th November 2014. It was here where I met the brilliant Hertfordshire based Poet Daren Peary, who I collaborated with to develop an animation piece called "Grenfell," in late 2017. Daren comperes his own spoken word nights, which I have performed at on a couple of occasions, named Tongue and Cheek, at The Jungle Bar in Hertford.

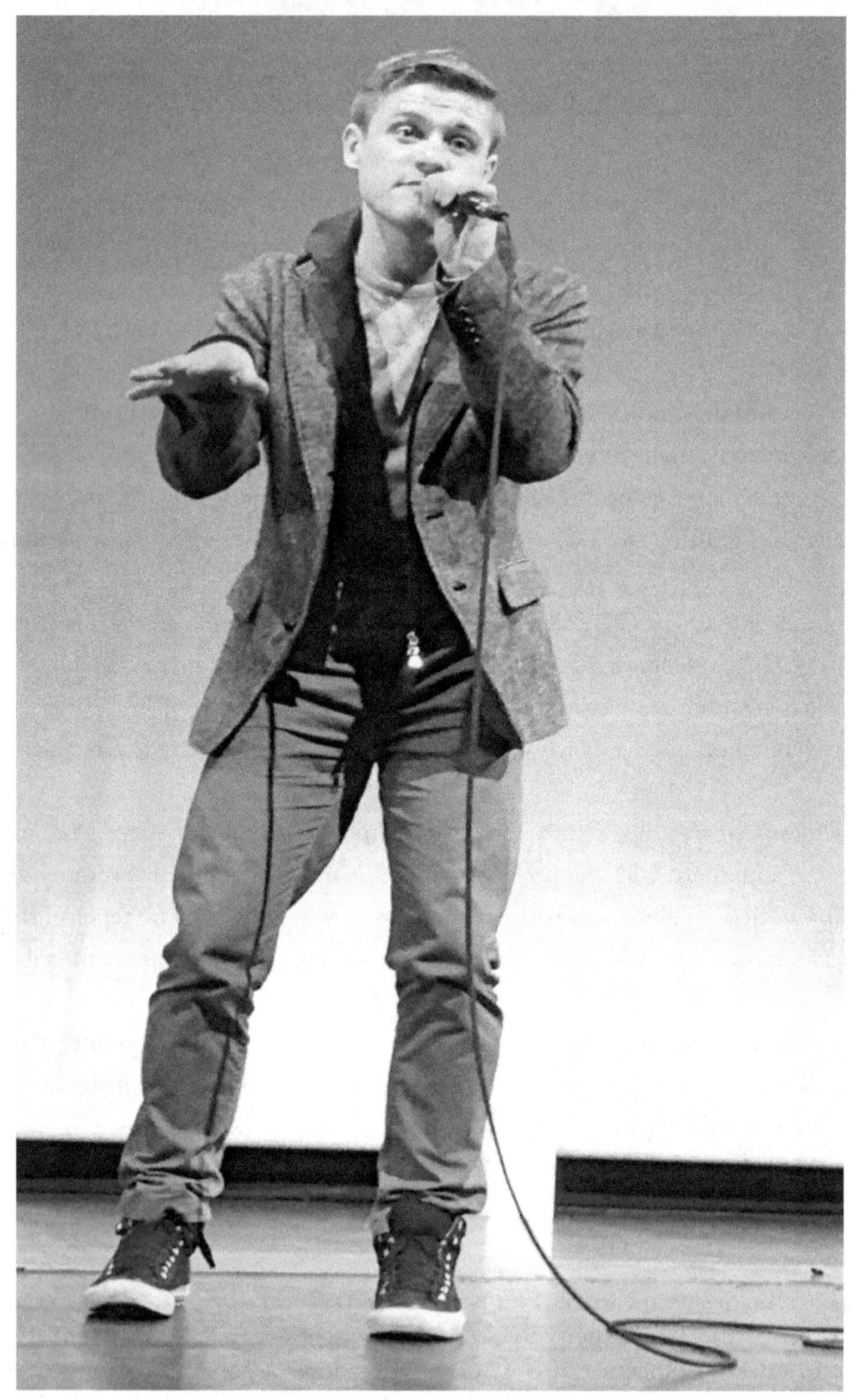

Performing "I've Fallen In Love With Mr Muscle" at Jawdance
Rich Mix, Bethnal Green - 27/11/2014

Thank You Special K

£2.29 for a big box of Special K,
It's the best bloody bargain I have bought today,
There should be more of these stores in this great shopping mall,
Bargains in here and wall to wall.

You can't go wrong with such an unbeatable price,
There'll be no more slimming on that Pilau Rice,
Now I have a fancy, to that sweet almond taste,
My husband will be in his element, with my new sexy waist.

You can't go wrong though, when the shopping money goes up,
Well, it ain't like it is coming out of their pension book,
They can gambling and drink all their money away,
Well, I'm spending my money on this bargain Special K.

You see, it's a woman's luxurious prerogative; Men don't understand,
Of all the hard work involved, to make us girls feel grand,
But they don't seem to complain, when our slim figures slip into bed,
Their hearts palpitating and their eyes bouncing in their heads.

Two months have passed, and I feel a spectacular new bird,
There'll be no more slouching, like a jar of lemon curd,
I wanna bounce to the sky, even if my hair is going grey,
Because I have lost stone stone; YES! THANK YOU SPECIAL K!

Written from the perspective of a middle-aged woman wanting to improve her figure by eating nothing but Kellogg's Special K. This piece inspired me when an elderly lady came into the shop where I was working at, back in 2012 and commented on its marvellous cheap price. My mind was surging with creativity. When I returned home after finishing my shift, I immediately wrote "Thank you Special K." I performed this witty piece at a spoken word night in a tightly packed conservatory at The Exhibition Hotel in York on a spring evening in March 2012. The event was compered by a poet named Rose Drew. It was the first time that I met the brilliant Sarah Beavers, who gave the audience a taste of her fabulous wittiness. She had the support of her lovely daughter Cori, who sat close by in the crowd. I performed "Thank you Special K" at The Wine Bar based in Otley, a week or so later, for a Performance Poet contest. Although I wasn't crowned the champion, I received a £20 voucher directly from the Kellogg's company, after I sent them the video of my performance at this specific event. It was a brilliant response from them, which I did not expect in the slightest, even though I would have much rather preferred the delicious red dress. Another delivery of this anecdote was at an open mic night named "HOWL" which was based down in the basement at The Blue Rooms in Huddersfield, hosted by Luxx, during the spring 2012. I remember mentioning my Kellogg's vouchers post performance. Luxx smiled that I will have to write a poem about Jack Daniels and send them the piece, in the hope that they will send a crate of alcohol. Even though I don't particularly drink it, as all alcoholic beverages taste like sour piss to me and no, I haven't tasted sour piss either! I have submitted some of my brand-based anecdotes to a number of companies but haven't been lucky enough to receive a response for the second time.

I enacted the character (Mrs. Kay) in the spring of 2016, wearing a leather jacket, a short, grey wig, a headscarf, a little bit of lippy. I carried a handbag along with this outfit in my bedroom one April evening that year. I imitated her voice slightly and delivered my anecdote in front of the lens of my camera. This is how I perform the poem vocally now, when live on stage, minus the full costume. I gravitate all that I have, to deliver a distinctive performance. I am extremely animated, when I have a microphone in my hand and the narrative expresses itself.

I take a lot of inspiration from the older generation. Representing an observation or conversation from their perspective, gives me the freedom to tell a humorous story within a poetic medium.

Thanks to Eden Mobility

Do you know, this fantastic Mobility from Eden,
Is the best thing I have ever bought,
I have never known anything so serene and complacent,
Which provides me with the extra support.

It has given me the independence which I need,
And a whole new lease of life,
An excuse to liberate myself from tedious chores,
Especially my winging wife.

I recall my stalwart physicality, when I was a nipper,
A long time ago, back in the day,
But nowadays I cannot seem to stand on my own two feet,
Without my bloody legs giving way.

My wife pities my stability,
And dreams of carting me up the stairs,
But the Eden service, has impeccable choice,
From scooters to recliner chairs.

With fourteen fantastic stores located,
Up and around the region,
It's like walking into Toys 'R Us for us OAPs,
So step in now, to your local Eden.

I want to display, my gratified support,
By giving the service, my credibility,
For my whole new spring in life,
Thanks to Eden Mobility.

On Wednesday 24th September 2014, I went to London by train, to perform at a spoken word night called "Jawdance," based at Rich Mix, in Bethnal Green, with my anecdote "Thanks To Eden Mobility." The narrative was based on an elderly gentlemen's awe, of his fantastic new mobility scooter.

Thirty Pence to Have a Piss?!

Thirty pence to have a piss,
I'm so, so skint as it is,
All I want is a lousy wee,
But you require a 30p.
I've got notes and cheques,
In every range,
But they just want my bastard change.
All I want is a lousy wee,
But you require a 30p,
Thirty pence to have a piss,
I'm so, so skint as it is,
All I want is a lousy wee,
But you require a 30p.
I can't believe that's the law,
Just to pay the urinal whore,
I wonder how much a shit would be?
Just an extra 30p.
Thirty pence to have a piss,
I'm so, so skint as it is,
All I want is a lousy wee,
So goodbye my 30p!

I was sitting down at Kings Cross station desperately needing the toilet. I was mortified at the fact that you had to pay a fee to use the public toilets. I returned to the menacingly cold seats, just before boarding the 11:30pm East Coast service back to Yorkshire and wrote this whimsical anecdote. This piece is renowned on the local poetry circuit, due to the fact that I thoroughly love performing it. Life observations are a primary focus of mine which I record, such as real-life situations, or conversations. I then interpret them as part of my anecdotes. I challenge audiences to look at the everyday taboos with a humour and provide them an optimistic message. Depending on the location of a gig, I have to explain the narrative to the audience, in order for them to grasp the content of what is happening in other areas of the UK. I performed this piece, during my seven-minute set at "Stanza Extravaganza" based in Torquay on Monday 21st December 2015. The petite audience wasn't familiar with the 30p business, so the material was education to them.

A friend of mine, who I am very rarely in contact with, as she is training to be a Nurse, introduced me to an open mic night at a bar named "The Handdrawn Monkey," based on Woodstreet in Huddersfield. My debut performance at the gig, was on Thursday 17th September 2015. There were only a few people attending, but it was a really pleasant evening and the audience was very supportive. The open mic was originally intend to showcase musical performances, but the platform was an open to anyone who wished to share their delights. I began my very short set with "Thirty Pence to Have a Piss?!" and the crowd love it. The bar supervisor, named Anthony, was drawn to this anecdote. He suggested that I should perform it again at the next couple of Thursday sessions. He pulled me aside after my performance to praise my delivery and to say how much of a show man I was. I thanked him for his kind words.

This gig coincided with the time when I began experiencing a relapse in my mental health, during the summer of 2015. Even though I was on sertraline, performing allowed me to supress my oppressive heinous and concentrate on the passions that I love. Everything which crippled me mentally, I discarded when I posed behind the microphone. I consider this poem to be a signature piece of mine.

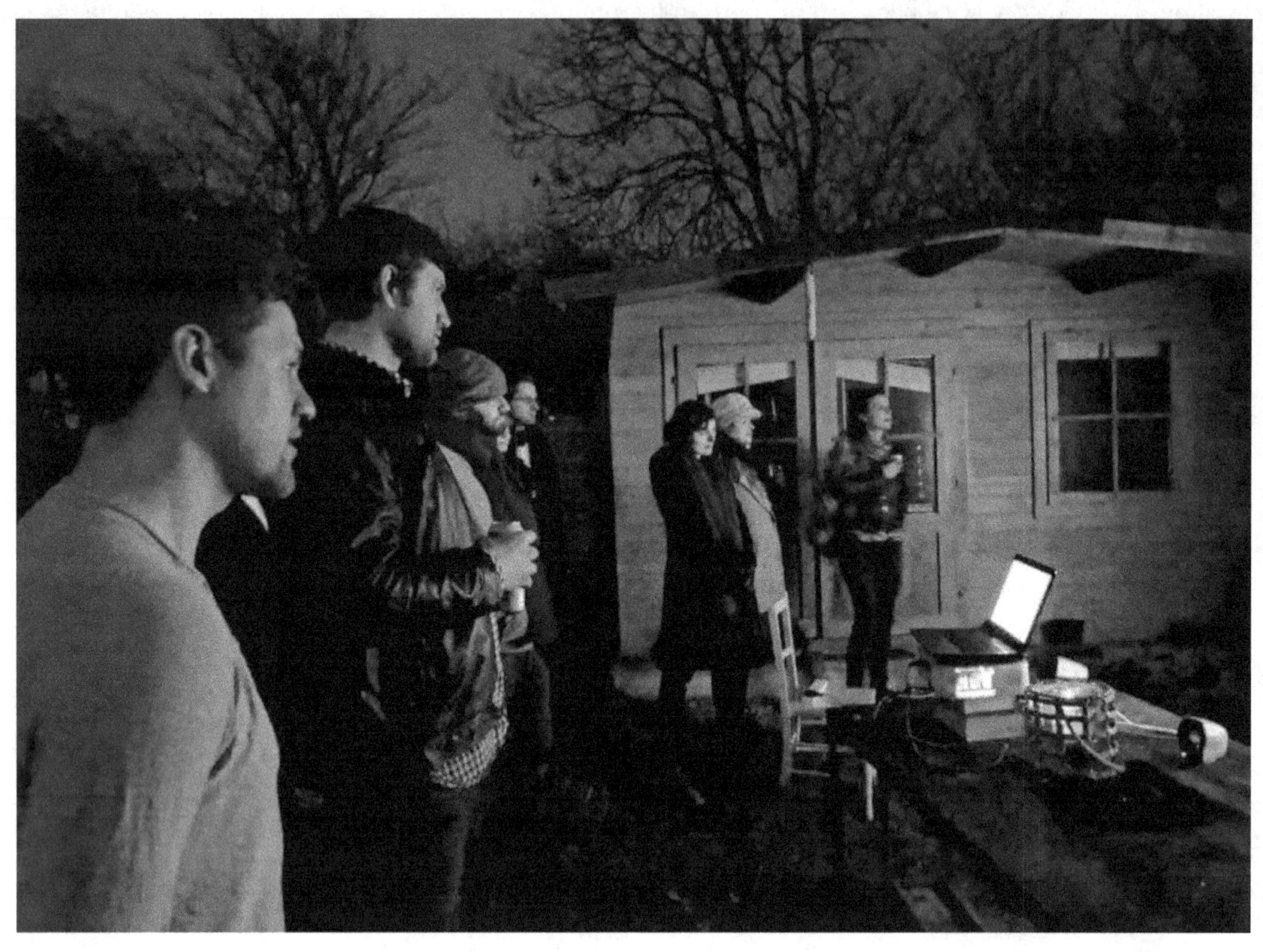

"Sylark"

Screening my Animations in a garden based in Loughton.

Blur The Lines

Monday 4th November 2019

At the Playhouse, myself, Laurence, Nina, Ash and Tahira took part in a brief rehearsal between 6pm and 8:15pm. We were getting ready for an upcoming event called "Blur the Lines." Ash and Tahira rehearsed their original work a good couple of times, as Laurence filmed snippets of their performances for a promotional video which himself and Lisa were compiling. I subsequently rehearsed "Lycra" and then Laurence delivered his piece titled "The Brink." Ash and Tahira had to leave after discussing how they would like to be introduced to the stage. I delivered a second performance of "Thirty Pence to Have a piss" and then "FLEAS!" Laurence wanted me to deliver an impromptu performance after every other act, hence the rehearsal of additional material.

Nina treated Laurence and I to a drink in The Wardrobe Bar. We sat down and shared ideas for our upcoming event. Nina spoke about a having a possible sitcom that she going to write, based on her friend, who is an activist, and the witty stories which emerge from the activist movement. She added that she still wants capture the austere underlying truth of activism, whilst adding a tone of humour to this topic. We also discussed the hymn "Kumbaya my Lord," replacing the original lyrics with "Come By Car, You Fraud." This was the perfect song for the activist sitcom. All the copyright for this goes to Nina Carter-Brown.

Friday 15th November 2019

Wow, what an absolutely immense evening it was for "Blur The Lines," which was staged in The Bramall Rockvoid at The Playhouse. Crafted and directed by the incredible Laurence aka Lence, bringing all of us artists into one performance space, to express ourselves on a creative platform. There were twenty performers in total, including myself, delivering their individual splurges of genius, in front of a full house. The show commenced at 9pm, with Laurence stepping onto the platform, to introduce me as the first performer and host for the evening. Tingling with apprehension and standing behind a curtain, I headed towards to the microphone and performed my anecdote "Lycra." When I finished my one-a-half minute delivery, I began my duty as host and welcomed the first artist to the stage called Sally Anne.

This lively evening flowed with the fusion of multiple performers capturing a diverse range of current societal issues. A couple of comical performers congregated on the platform, including Kevin Flaherty, who performed his rap esq hip hop satirical verse titled "Cloth Cap Rap." Nina performed her parody of Radiohead's 90's original classic "Creep." Her version was titled "Sleep" which is based on sleep deprivation. Nina arrived at The Playhouse at approximately 10pm, after travelling back to Leeds from a stand up gig in York which went extremely well. She positioned herself on The Bramall Rockvoid platform with her acoustic guitar, humorously serenading the audience with her witty melodies.

It was an incredible experience sharing the platform with a bunch of talented artists, who performed their original works in front of the Furnace Festival audience. It was also a privilege to share the stage with my close creative beacon, the one and only, Laurence Inman. He should be incredibly proud with the immense showcase he has staged this evening. It was brilliant to have the support of my mum, grandma and grandad, alongside Sandy in the audience.

When the show ended at 10:30pm, with Tash, the final performer, I returned to the mic to thank the whole creative team for allowing "Blur The Lines" to happen. The nineteen spoken word artists subsequently immersed the stage behind me, and Laurence delivered a second round of thanks. We both embraced each other with open arms. The prolific song by Chumba Wumba titled "I Get Knocked Down" play out in the end, as the audience exited the auditorium.

Nina gave me a lift back home at 11:50pm, soon after we had a drink in the bar with Laurence, Lisa and a few of the audience members, to celebrate this evening's brilliant event.

The following couple of days after the event, I experienced a mental and physical meltdown. It is normal for this to happen to me, post gig or a film screening. It has been quite a busy week, with three gigs and a coach commute to London and back on Saturday 8th November. I had completely dried up all my energy, though I know it's only temporary.

Friday 6th March 2020

Laurence arrived at North Lodge House at approximately 2:05pm, to run through the final preparations for this evening's repeat of "Blur The Lines" at The Holbeck WMC. We subsequently walked to Lisa's flat, before heading to the venue in an Uber cab, arriving at 5:45pm. Phenecia, a female musician, performed in the second half and a DJ friend of Laurence's was already present at The Working Mens Club.

This thriving event commenced at 8:20pm, when a female volunteer from the Leeds Lit Fest, welcomed Laurence onto the stage. I opened the event with my anecdote "The Fabulous Tom Ford." and begin my role as a host, introducing Yvonne Ugarte on the stage. Twenty other spoken word Artists performed their whimsy works and politically charged verbal deliveries, in front of good-sized audience. Nina delivered her own parody of "Hallelujah," originally composed by Leonard Cohen, during the first half. Kevin Flaherty performed his signature piece "The Cloth Cap Rap" during the second half. I then went on to perform "Thirty Pence To Have A Piss?!" between acts in the first half and opened up the second half with a third anecdote of mine, titled "Big Knickers Rule." Laurence delivered a brilliant performance and so did Lisa. Everyone deserved to have their artistry recognised on stage, thanks to Laurence Inman. He is tremendously brilliant. It was fabulous to see Talie again, as we excitedly hugged each other backstage, behind the red velvet curtain. She performed her spoken word piece "Angry Black Girl." It was a fantastic showcase of dedicated artists. The event ended at 10:45pm. Marc came along to give his support and it was also an excuse to spend an evening with me, when I wasn't needed on or behind the stage. Laurence and I gave Marc a list of the poets performing that night and their introductions so that he could follow what was happening, as I couldn't directly BSL interpret for him. I think he appreciated the event and it was brilliant to see him again. Marc drove me back to North Lodge House, after stopping for a post-show drink with Lisa, Laurence and Laurence's cousin Ben. Marc pulled up near the iron gates at North Lodge House just before midnight and we gave each other a prolonged kiss goodnight. He then drove back home to Huddersfield.

On Monday 2nd March, after I finished my shift at the Playhouse at 6pm, I went for a drink with Marc at Costa Coffee, near the Pasta Romanga Restaurant in Leeds. We spent a good hour or so together, before bidding each other goodbye with a kiss in the city centre.

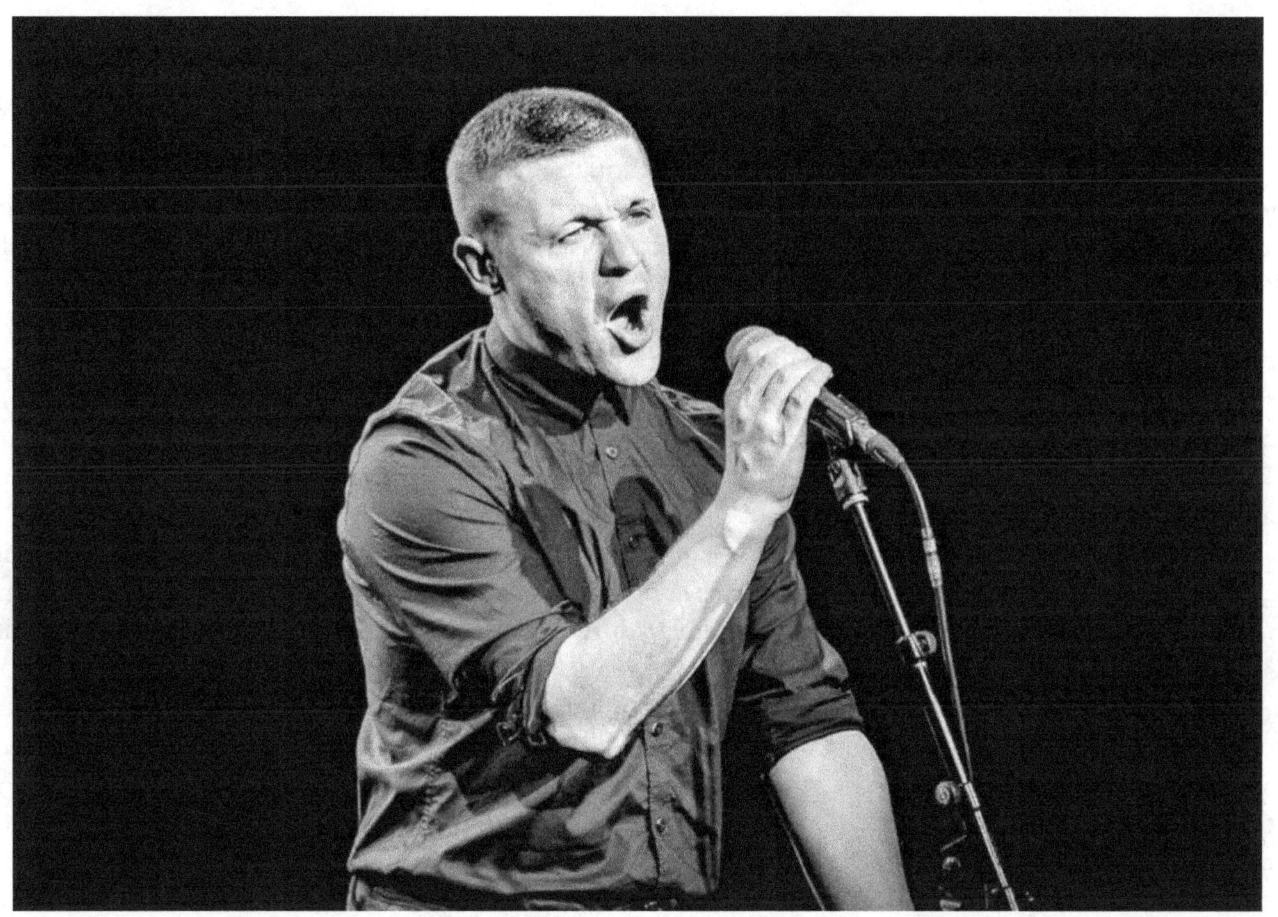

Performing and Hosting Blur The Lines
Leeds Playhouse - November 2019
Photo courtesy of Anthony Robling

Lence Loved *and*
Ring Around the Rosie

Tuesday 19th May 2020

A couple of weeks ago, Laurence asked me to collaborate with him as part of a music video of of his. He sent me three tracks, which I listened to, when I sat at the end of my bed. "Loved" would be the track which stood out for me as his next release. This track is about being detached from his sister and the strength of connection that they had for each other.

Between 12 noon and 6:30pm, I spent this time creating a twenty second animated clip which involved producing an intricate sketch of a human heart. Laurence admired it at first but later decided it was too gruesome for his video. I followed a suggested artist brief, which Laurence had emailed to me. I used the human heart drawing as directed for the second chorus. The lyrics repeated rhythmically - "I love you." The heart appeared and disappeared in sepia tones. This very short clip ended with a rotoscope visual of Laurence performing in another music video of his titled "Rock By The River."

I sent the clip through to Laurence. He thought it was brilliant but a little too dark. His response triggered my tendency to overthink. It made me feel dejected and a sceptical about my artistic abilities. I immediately attempted to create something completely different but it wasn't successful. I am meeting with Laurence tomorrow at 2pm, to create some footage for me to make a rotoscope of him. In all respect, it is his project and I am extremely honoured that this is our second collaborative project. I had a brilliant time creating his first animated music video during November 2018, for a track titled "Heard." The video consisted of a montage of all the twelve animations that I had made in the past. Extracts were selected to fit with the meaning of the lyrics. "Lence - Heard" (the animation title) had its debut screening at Kino London, based at The Candid Arts Trust, on Thursday 8th January 2018.

On another note, on Friday 15th May 2020, I submitted my animation "Fleas" to "The Walthamstow International Film Festival" and "Wigan and Leigh Film Festival" to be screened in October 2020.

Friday 22nd May 2020

It is currently 11:45pm and I have called it a day with the eventful activity of rotoscoping, for "Lence - Loved." I have spent the previous couple of days attempting to animate the footage I made of Laurence. Socially distancing, we shot the live action footage in Saint George's Park, which is only a couple of minutes walk from North Lodge House. It is a beautiful part of Leeds which I didn't know about, until Laurence introduced me to the tranquill cemetery. Laurence wants his music video to portray a lot of movement and to capture the meaning of the lyrics. A heap of video footage was captured with a good couple of hours on the afternoon of Wednesday 20th May 2020. Footage consisted of high jumps and of him sitting on a wooden bench with his head in his hands. We completed filming with him lip syncing parts of the "Loved" track.

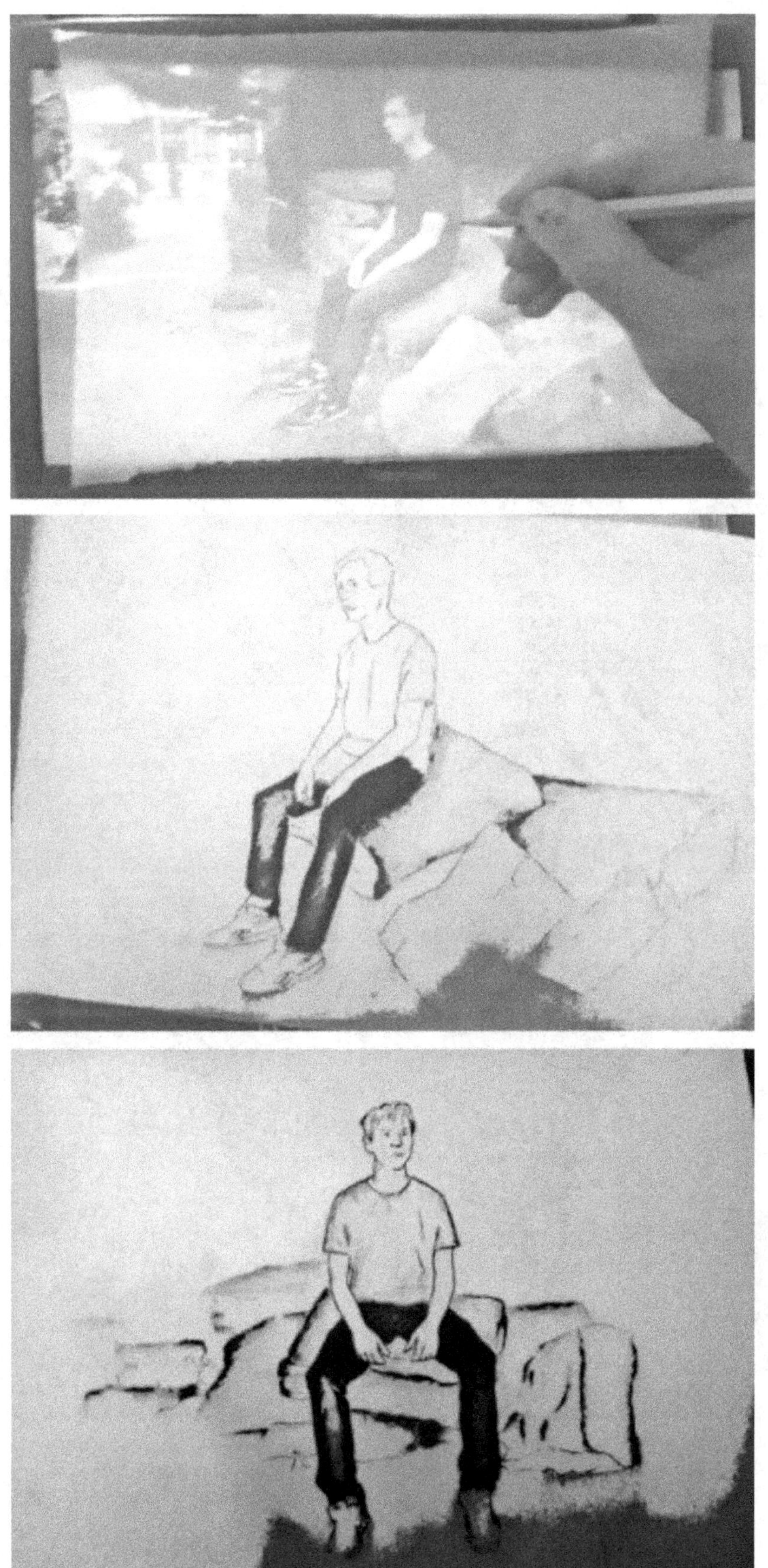

Rotoscoping the opening of the Animation.

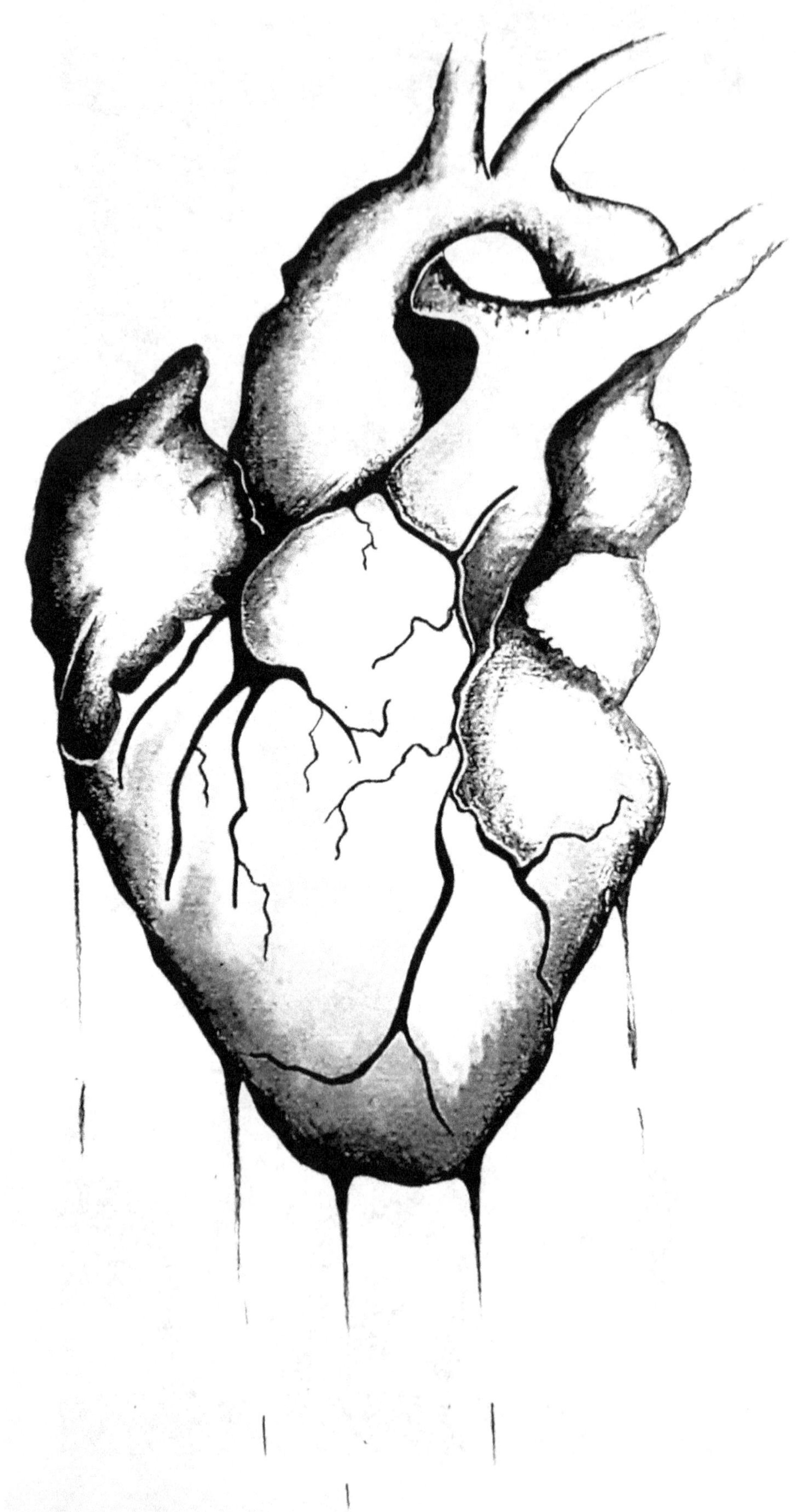

We returned to the park again, for a good couple of hours on the afternoon of Thursday 21st May 2020. I captured him sitting on the edge of a rock near my flat. This portrayed Laurence feeling defeated by his sense of detachment to his sister. I subsequently rotoscoped his twiggy anatomy using tracing paper on a laptop screen, as well as producing a sequence which would rotate around his head.

Sunday 24th May 2020

It is 4:20pm and I am sitting on a wall in the yard of North Lodge House, with a warm weak cup of tea, flavoured with seven sweeteners. Whenever I am overwhelmed by any immediate pressure, or any negativity perplexing my imagination, I take myself out for a run and a quick circuit walk around Woodhouse Moor.

I have forced myself to have a break away from the "Loved" animation which I have been tirelessly working on in the past few days. Yesterday, I worked a solid six hours on the project, in an attempt to achieve a descriptive visual that Laurence was looking for. I managed to rotoscope photographs of him strolling away from the camera, stopping then glancing back at the lens. The eye of the camera represented his sister watching Laurence. I also had an attempt of rotoscoping a close up of his feet. I also made a start with the snake depictions, which would transition from his so called friends. I produced these drawings free hand. I am bouncing backwards and forwards whilst developing this music video. I finished work for the day at approximately 6:15pm.

Monday 25th May 2020

Between noon and 3:20pm, I concentrated on drawing free hand, as opposed to rotoscoping. For the first hour, I sat down in the kitchen, sketching out a representation of what would be Laurence's sister. I then returned to my basement room, to photograph a close-up of this sketch and I made seven to eight frames. Her eyes began to blink repeatedly, now that I have placed oval black cut outs as closed eyelids over the eyes. As a scene, this represented motion. With the appearances of Laurence and his sister moving back and forth within the scene, as a metaphor of loss and disconnection.

Later, I sat outside in the yard, on a little wooden chair and decided to experiment, by free hand sketching out three venomous hooded snakes, which represented Laurence's so-called companions. I then worked out how the "snakes" would eventually move within the animation. This section was created by freehand.

I later rotoscoped a sketch of Laurence, looking contemplative and very stern. I then cut it out and placed it onto a plain piece of paper, so that I could make this move from the left-hand side of the screen to the right in the animation. To achieve this, I placed the camera back onto the tripod and manually moved the image by hand, an inch at a time. If I did this by moving the camera on the tripod, the visual would go off spectrum during playback. I e mailed the camera shots via WeTransfer, so that I could create a cartoon look to the photographs using Pics Art software. I then transferred the frames onto my laptop to form an animation sequence on MovieMaker. The final and professional edit was completed in MovAvi. I finished for the night at 10:40pm.

Tuesday 26th May 2020

At 12 noon, I resumed work on the current animation project and spent the day rotoscoping Laurence posing in a messiah-prophet-esque stance. I later added a pastel gradient to the shots using Pics Art on my mobile phone. I then sent the final edits through to my laptop and put them together in a sequence.

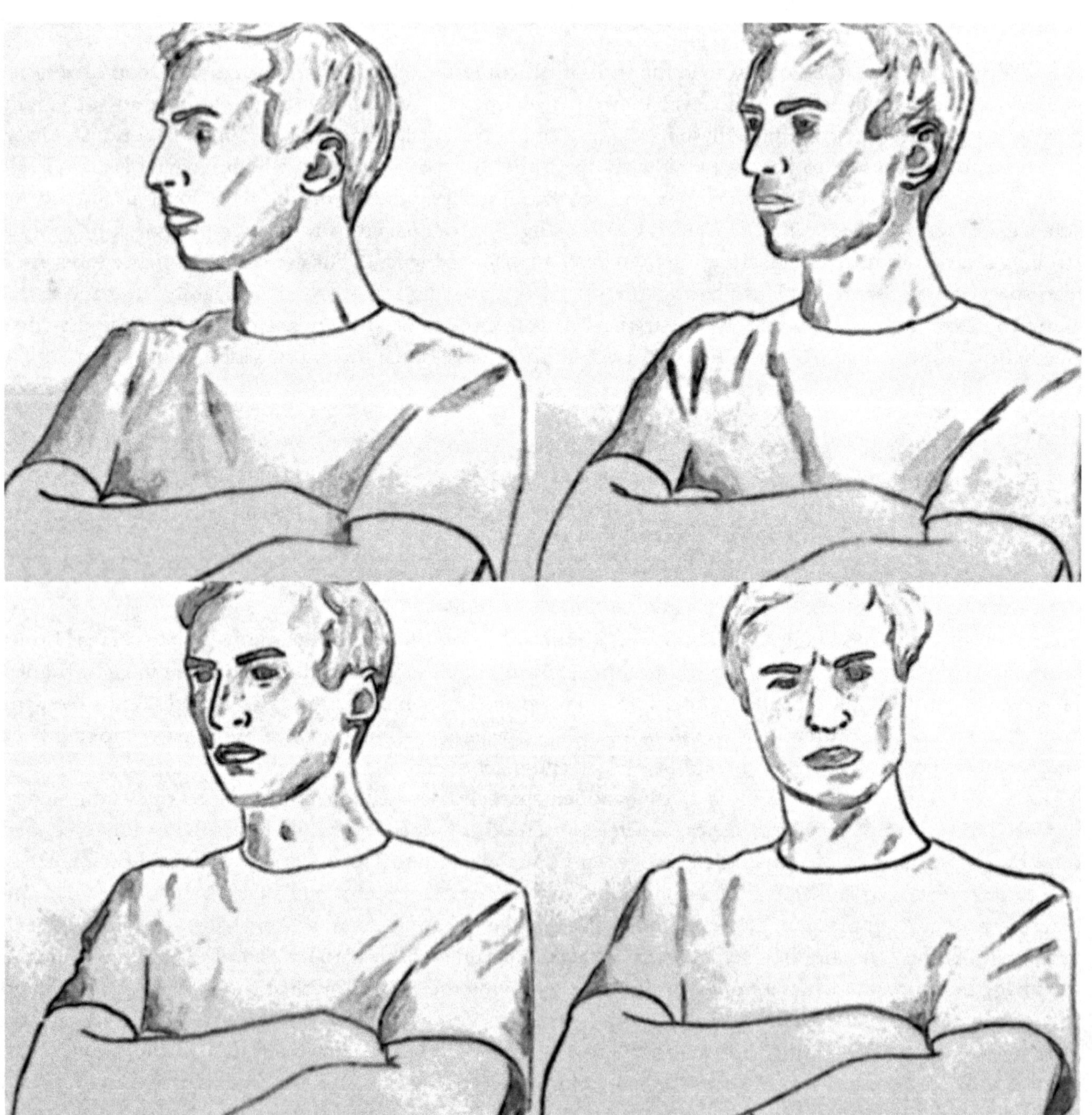

(Above) **Sequence taken from the first bridge in the video**

From 8pm until midnight, excluding an hour break in between, I rotoscoped Laurence lip syncing, using the footage that I made in Saint George's Park. This would be used before the final chorous.

Wednesday 27th May 2020

I produced a free hand sketch of three of Laurence's menacing friends, this would be used as a template for the animation. I then sent a partial edit of the video to Laurence for his consideration. He seems to like it, even though I was a little bit sceptical that he was going to feel the opposite. I finished for the day at 7pm, and sat outside on the wall with a cup of tea.

Saturday 1st June 2020

I awoke at approximately 10:30am. I spent the weekend at Marc's cottage. He picked me up outside the rustic gates of North Lodge House at 6pm on Friday 29th May 2020. On the Saturday, I met Marc's friend John, who is also deaf. We went to Danny's house to have a little barbecue gathering and a walk in the fields. It was a lovely day.

I had a coffee or two before briefly resuming work on the "Loved" animation. I produced thirty frames of lip syncing. I then went onto producing a further 15 frames of Laurence running towards the camera. I worked between 11am and 5:30pm and finished as soon as I ran out of tracing paper.

Marc drove me back home in Leeds at 9:40pm. We kissed each other goodnight in the car and I waved him off as he drove back up the stony driveway and to Huddersfield.

Tuesday 2nd June 2020

I resumed work on the current animation, shortly before midday. I stayed upstairs in the kitchen, continuing to rotoscope Laurence running towards the camera. Thirty sketches were produced to create this scene. In the evening, I sequenced the frames together, and the overall result looked very effective. I then completed the visual of his friends manifesting themselves into snakes. I have been putting the snake sequence off for a while now, due to the repetitively challenging difficulty of making this clip. Using my very own magic animation process, I placed the snake template beneath the visual of the three friends and gradually fused the images together, by slightly erasing aspects of the human shapes and until the snakes appear. This process involved erasing lines, adding new ones and taking photographs. In the end I had made sixty shots. When the three snakes were fully in view, I made cut outs of their heads and placed onto the end of their necks, so that I could make them appear to extend and sliter in the animation. This scene was developed from 5:15pm and was completed at 7:30pm.

Later on in the evening, I edited the lip syncing scene, which I produced yesterday. I then stopped and looked about on my laptop, as I sat in my comfortable, cotton white chair in my basement room. I discovered some of my past animation footage, which I never managed to complete.

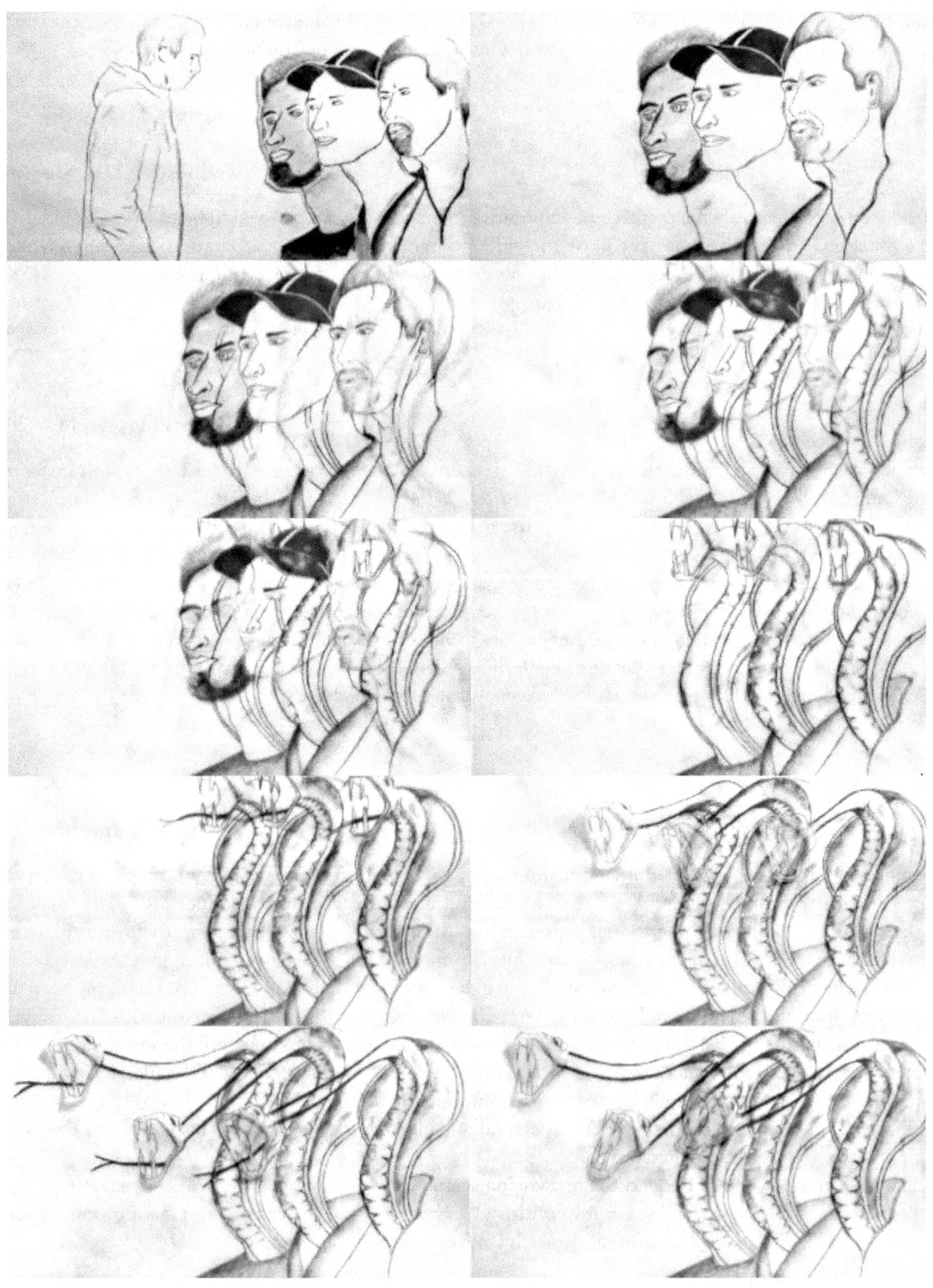

The animated snake sequence

Between midnight and 2:30am, I commenced work on an experimental animation titled "Ring around the Rosie." This was a sinister take on the prolific nursery rhyme. I found a short clip of an animated forest which I worked on back in February 2019 but never finished. I had just moved to Leeds at the time, so I was distracted by the vibrant hustle and bustle of what this northern city provided. I was also performing my whimsical anecdotes at local spoken word gigs, particularly at The LS6 Cafe.

Going back to these unfinished pieces which I'm using to create experimental animation with, I also stumbled across a sketch of a porcelain doll, which I made in the summer of 2018. It was originally in a sketchbook which I had misplaced during my house move from Batley to Leeds. The porcelain doll was never used in any animation projects, so it became a fantastic subject to include in my latest gothic animation. I copied the porcelain doll and made a photograph of it, then created a forty-three second experimental animation of it. I selected vocal soundtrack of the nursery rhyme, Ring Around the Rosie, and distorted it to make it sound extremely creepy. I then embedded this on the animation clip.

On Wednesday 3rd June 2020, I resumed work on "Ring Around the Rosie," as I sat upstairs at the kitchen table. I made an intricate drawing of an American style haunted house. This would go in the scene, where a crow flies and lands on the spike on the rooftop. I'm not sure whether I will use this animation for anything. I may submit it to experimental film festivals. It is more of an exercise for me as an artist.

Thursday 4th June 2020

Laurence came to North Lodge House, shortly after 1:30pm. We returned to Saint George's Park to shoot some extra footage. We shot scenes of him jumping up onto a wall which I later included in the animation. I made the wall transition into a stage, where a microphone would appear in view as well as an audience. A spotlight projected onto him from the top righthand side of the screen. Another piece of footage we made, was of him walking away from the camera. I wanted to use this to show him walking away from his venomous friends in the animation. Any ideas we had, we captured to create additional clips for the animation.

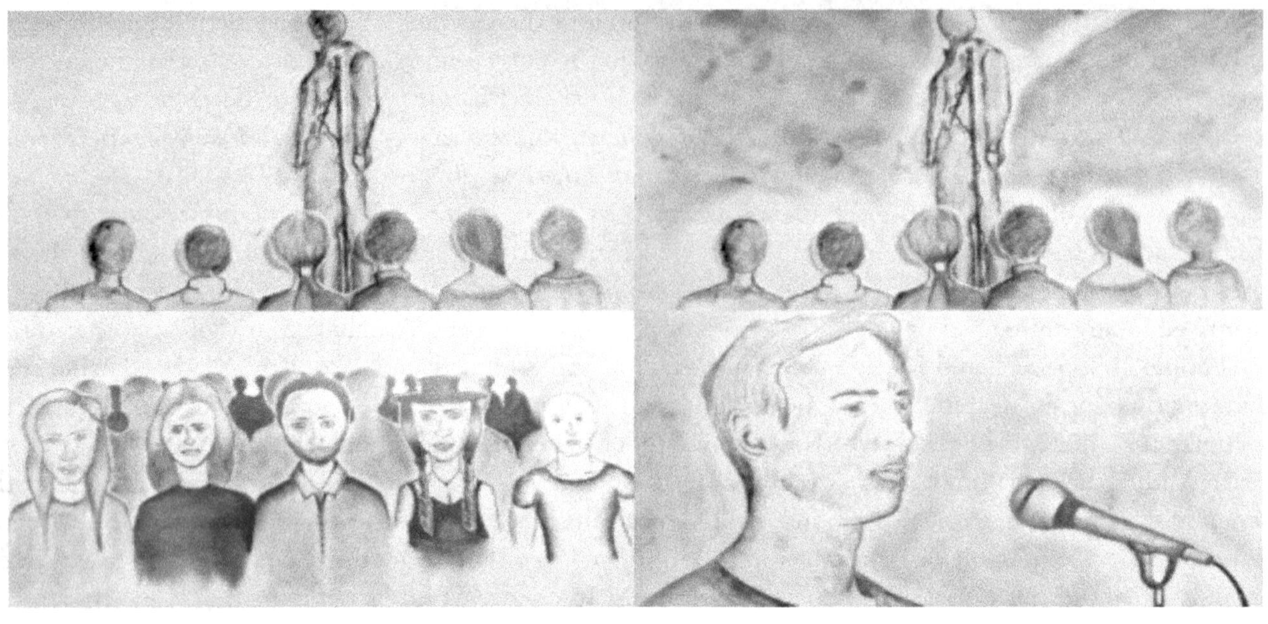

The wall to stage transition.

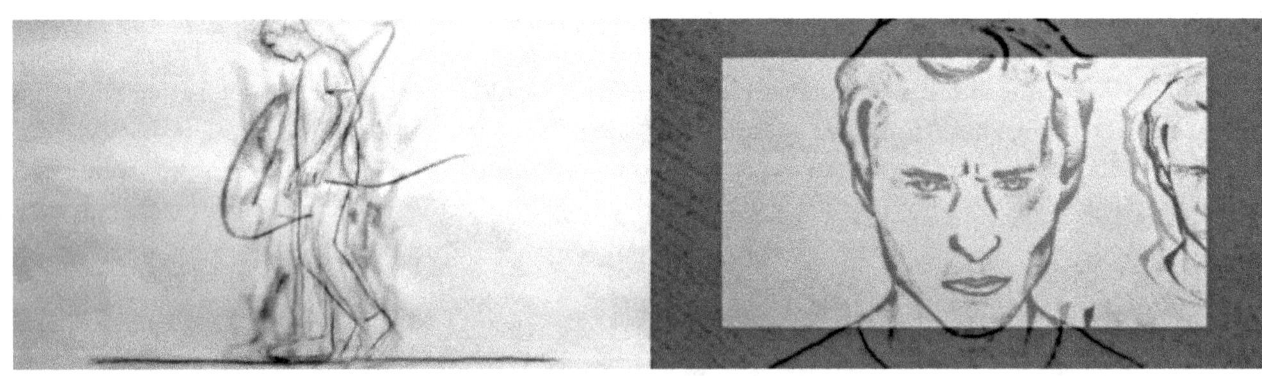

I returned home at 3pm and resumed my work on "Ring Around the Rosie." There has been some slight progress. I was deciphering what I could add. Later on in the evening, I produced a sketch of a plague doctor. I cut out this drawing, placing the illustration onto a plain piece of white paper. I then cut the beak in half so that I could make the mouth move, as if singing the opening line of "Ring around the Roses" I also created paper chain of five girls holding hands in a ring. I then placed them onto my firesafe on my desk, moving them an inch of a time, capturing each step using my camera.

I completed the "Ring Around the Rosie" Animation, just before midnight. I then posted the clip on my social media pages. Lyrics appeared as if written in calligraphy and in red ink on the screen throughout the clip, which gave an ominous feel to the animation.

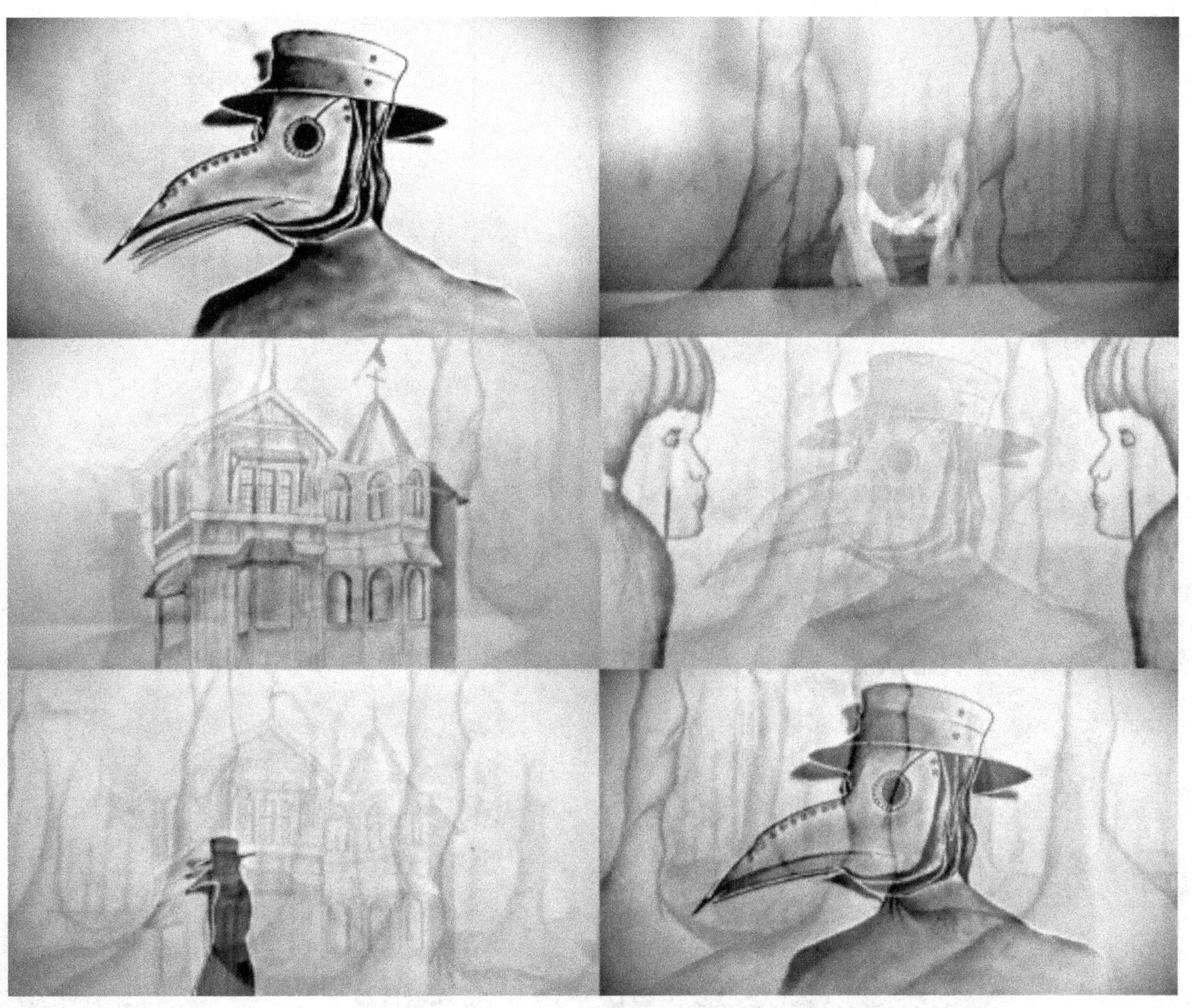

"Ring Around The Rosie"
Animation stills.
Duration: 01:58

Friday 5th June 2020

I resumed work on the "Loved" animation, sitting upstairs at the wooden table in the kitchen. The lyric, "I don't draw the line when I used to-," was the line I focused on. I rotoscoped a 360-degree rotation of Laurence, pointing his right hand out. Whilst photographing thirty different movements, I added a thick line at his fingertip, which represented movement. I subsequently broke off from the animation at 4:30pm, to have a walk around Woodhouse Moor.

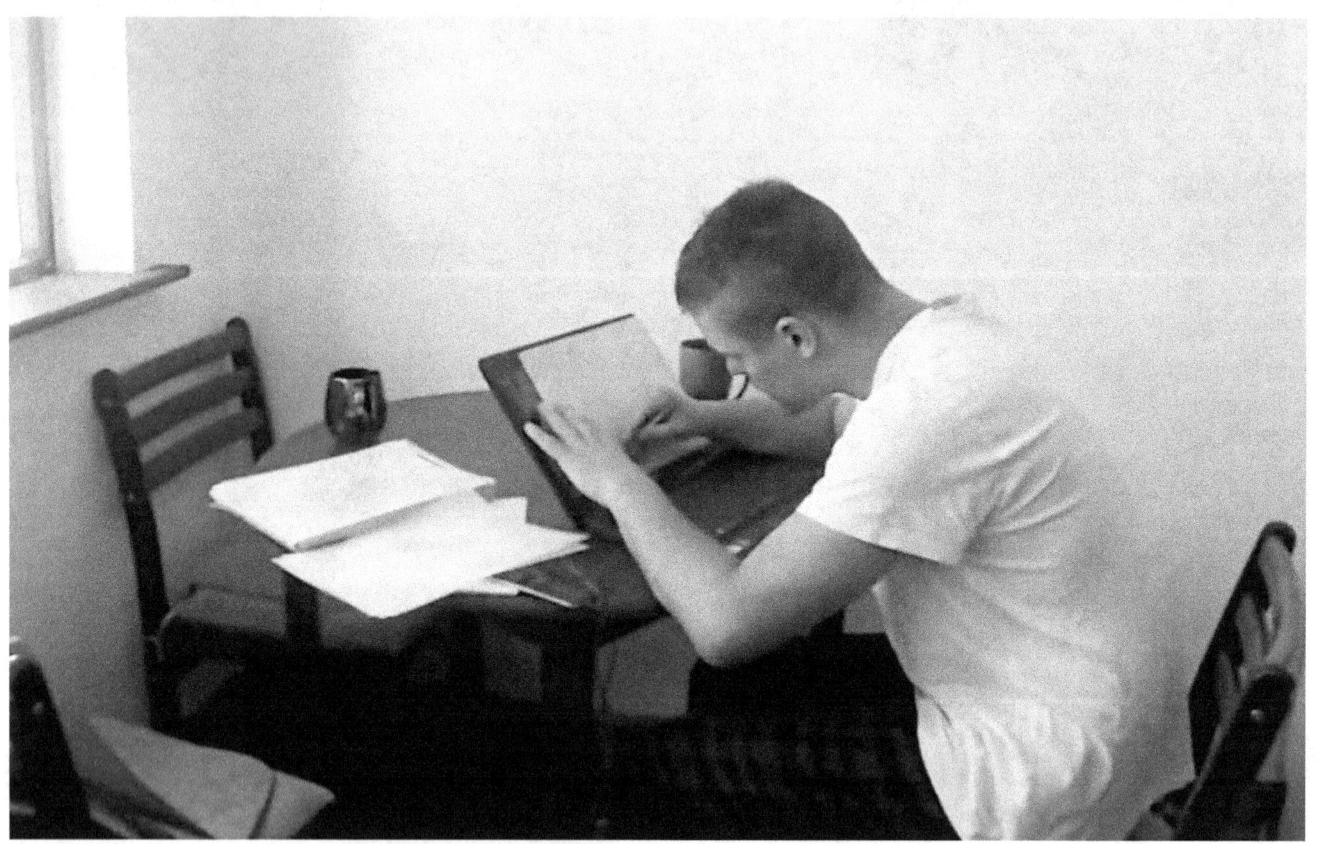

Based up in the kitchen at North Lodge House, Leeds.
Rotoscoping a scene for the "Loved" Animated Music Video.

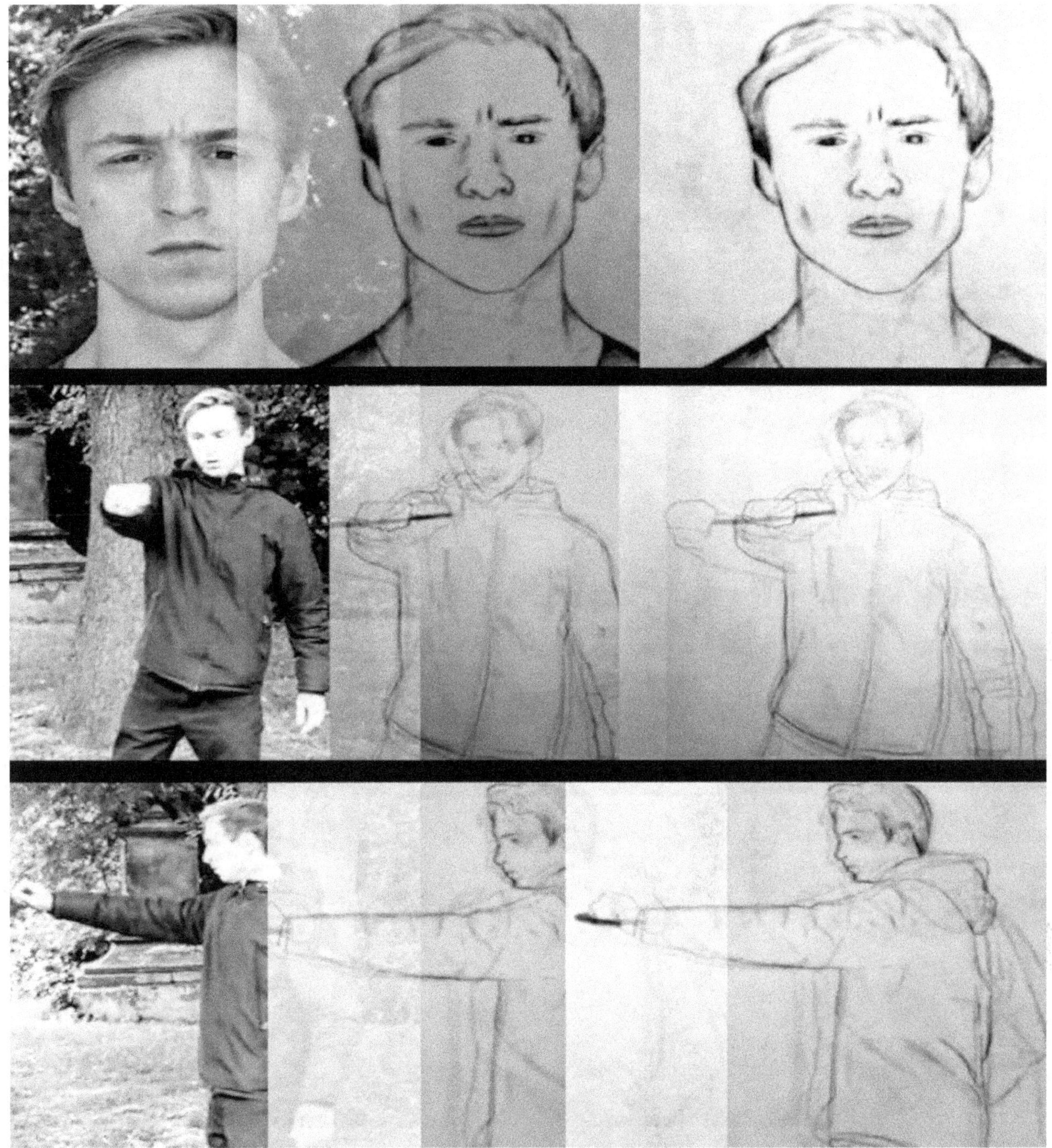

I have spent seven and a half hours working on this animation today. I am feeling extremely lethargic and infuriated as it involves intense concentration and constant rotoscoping.

On the Monday evening, at approximately 7:30pm, I began rotoscoping live footage of Laurence taking off his coat and throwing it into the next scene. It took me four days, to eventually complete the rotoscope technique, which consisted of 67 sketches, to produce a three second clip. The intense process has completely wound me up.

From Thursday evening until Friday teatime, I produced another rotoscope sequence, of Laurence laying down on his back and ascending upright from the ground. He was wearing his coat in this scene. I then created a clip of him and his sister growing up holding hands. The silhouettes would crumble and dissolve into a heap of ash. This crumbling effect was successfully achieved by smudging the drawings.

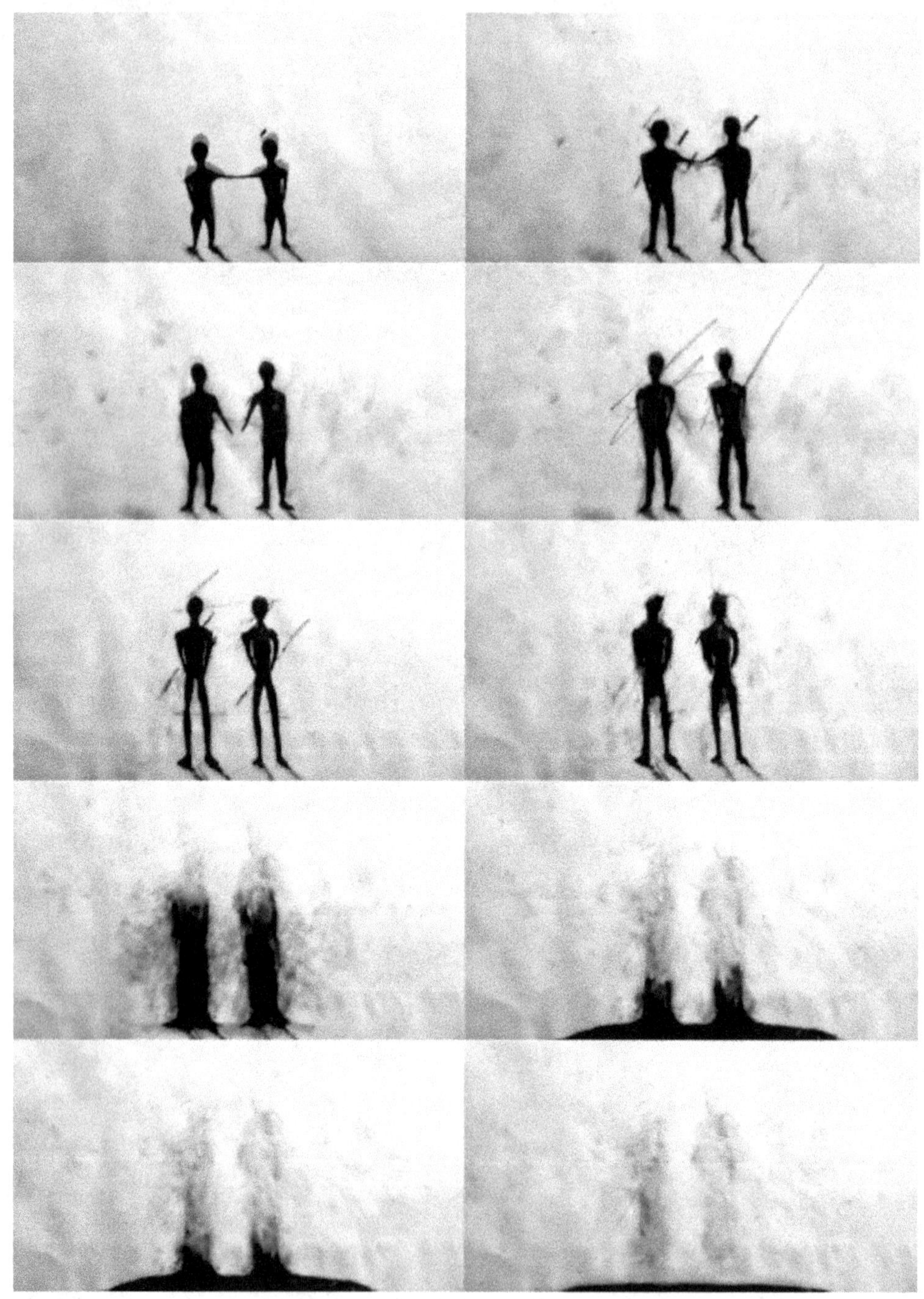

Laurence and his sister growing older and departing.

With every frame, I used a rubber to erase the silhouettes. This is one of my favourite techniques, which allows me to create the effect of something disappearing and evolving into a different image. I like to think of this effect as a trademark of my work.

I completed the animation at 8:45pm on the evening of Wednesday 17th June 2020. Even though this process has been emotionally challenging, I have fell in love with it when I played it back and breathed a huge sigh of relief. I sent the final edit to Laurence via WeTransfer at 9pm. He phoned me up, a good seven minutes afterwards, stating that this piece was phenomenal. I could hear his excitement in his voice and it was brilliant to hear him say that the quality of my work has been taken to the "next level."

There are two versions of this animated Music Video. Laurence went away and reworked the edit I had finished. The official version had an urban feel to it, with animation mixed with real footage, provided by Lisa Boardman. We met up one afternoon in July 2020, for a drink in The Library Pub, to talk about the official edit. I thought this juxtaposition of animation and footage worked well with the song. The second version was the original black and white edit of mine, which I use to show as part of my portfolio and to demonstrate an example of working collaboratively with other artists.

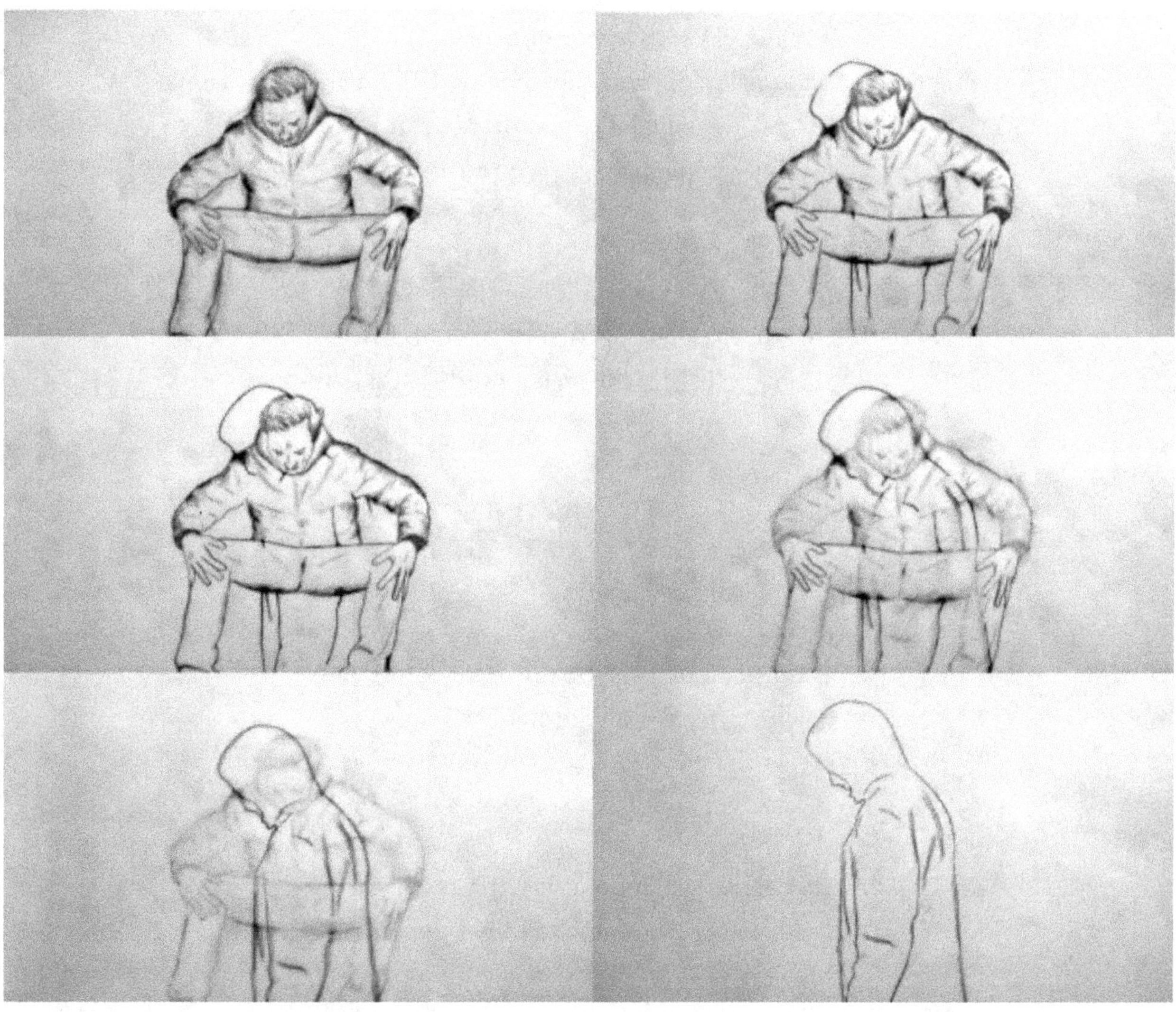

The opening sequences transitioning into each other.

Sanitize the Bride

The church bells merrily perform,
Drowning out this perpetual, monotonous year,
Though PPE is the appropriate dress code for the blessing,
The bride still appears sincere.

This is her moment to confide her tenderness,
To her groom who is looking affectionately serene,
Nothing is going to destruct their big day,
Not even Covid-19.

She glides down the aisle blissfully,
The minimal capacity of bridesmaids follows behind at a distance,
Whoever could imagine the grandest day of your life,
To be implemented with resistance.

Fourteen guests unquestionably pose the current trend,
Latex gloves and face mask galore,
A pocket full of sanitizer, as opposed to an abundance of confetti,
As the globe battles through a third World War!

As the bride approaches the groom with lust,
Obliterating the reality of this pandemic objector,
The vows commence from the gaiety masked vicar,
Looking like Hannibal Lecter!

The muffled exchange of the word of honour,
The exchange of the sterilised rings,
Whoever could imagine a wedding to be so particularly beautiful,
Whoever could imagine such a thing?

Physical contact is temporarily a tribute of the past,
To witness from the minimal clump,
No urges to embrace or endear your prince,
But an opportunity for an elbow pump!

As she eloquently ascends her veil,
And the groom hungrily gleams at her with pride,
The vicar beholds a serene tranquil candle and announces,
"Now you may sterilize the bride!"

This Whimsical Anecdote was written on the evening of Thursday 15th October 2020, between 11:30pm and midnight, as I sit upstairs in the kitchen of North Lodge House on the leather couch. The title was inspired by a very good friend of mine named David Archer, as he joked about "sanitising the bride," as opposed to "kissing the bride." I was immediatcly inspircd by this jocular line that I knew I had to word it within in some form of anecdote. This is dedicated to the lovely David Archer.

I filmed myself performing this anecdote, sitting on a bench in Saint George's Park, on the afternoon of Friday 16th October 2020.

The Fixodent Story

The Oxjam Music Festival - Sowerby Bridge

So, I had to adapt when I moved to Leicester for three years, to start my new adventures as a Fine Art Student, bearing in mind that I was a little introverted when living in Batley. I used to hibernate in my bedroom and expressing myself creating abstract paintings. I had a fear of going anywhere on my own. Anyhow, I leaned over my bedroom sink in Waterway Gardens Student Accommodation, discovering I had run out of toothpaste. A bastard when you want to brush your teeth! I popped out to the shops and came across this brand, of what I thought was toothpaste. I picked this unusual looking tube up and thought "Oh, I feel like a posh bird with this new brand."

Returning home, I immediately started to brush my teeth with this product. I began to feel an unusual, sour, gritty taste in my mouth and teeth started to glue together. I looked at the instruction manual, tucked away in the rectangular container and saw a diagram of a toothless gum. To my disbelief, I only went and brushed my teeth with Fixodent! I immediately spat out the paste and rinsed my mouth with cold water, in the hope I will still have my bloody teeth left by the end of the ordeal. Fortunately, I did. This was the one lesson on my radar which taught me to look at brands more carefully, instead of just purchasing something because of its sophisticated name, but you live, you learn.

Saturday 24th October 2020

I arrived in Sowerby Bridge on train from Huddersfield at approximately 3:05pm. I made the 1.4 mile ascent by foot up the hill to Woodfield House, based on Berry Moor Road. This was the venue for this year's Oxjam Music Festival which will be held in the garden. A temporary performance stage has been erected for the online Facebook Live platform. Gatherings of more than six people is still prohibited due to the government's pandemic rules. I made my way to the stage, to prepare for my seventeen minute set, wearing a long brown fur coat, provided to me by Toupon, who performed earlier a female vocalist.

I had such a fabulous time delivering my whimsies to the online audience. I commenced with "I Ran Off with the Local Vicar," mentioning to the audience that I hadn't performed this piece since 2018. "Just As I Sat Down" was the second poem to follow. I also told "The Fixodent Story," and completed the set with an anecdote, which I wrote back in January 2011, titled "Fetch Us Up Another Beer." "Big Knickers Rule," "Man Bun" and "Fleas" were also on the bill.

Marc picked me up from Huddersfield train station at 8:15pm. We picked up a take away curry, settling in for the evening at his cottage. The bedlington whippet dogs, Rosie and Daisy, are with us this weekend as Danny is based in Leyburn for a couple of days.

On the afternoon of Sunday 18th October 2020, a week prior to The Oxjam Music Festival, I filmed a few anecdotes of mine, as promotional purposes and uploaded them on my YouTube channel. I travelled to Sowerby Bridge by train from Huddersfield and met the event organisers of The Oxjam Music Festival - Ben, Mel who shared a few of her humorous provocative stories with us upstairs at The Blind Pig, where the session took place. They filmed me performing "Big Knickers Rule," "Just As I Sat Down," "Mr Kipling" and "30 Pence to Have a Piss?!" It was an enjoyable opportunity to perform in an actual Venue, as opposed to an online session. I had an hilarious time with the technical team too.

Varicose Veins

It's just nice to get away from the pandemonium of life,
Slip off my sandals and have a paddle in the sea,
But I don't feel entirely complacent with one segment of my body,
It doesn't sit right with me.
I have always been in a predicament with my feet,
It's bumps and lumps of grains,
I can't bear to look at my lower half anymore,
Because of my varicose veins!
I am extremely appreciative of what god gave me,
The existence of compassion and zest,
But it's my feet that I can't bear to see,
It's the one thing I detest!
It wouldn't surprise me if I crucify the life,
That live deep down in the sea,
It wouldn't be a sight for the poor innocent souls,
It certainly isn't a sight for me!
My feet are like the road map of Britain,
The veins pop right through my skin,
I don't like how they are present in my view,
I don't like how they impale within.
But the beach is the only place I feel content,
It's the only place where I can feel free,
These varicose veins are the bane of my life,
They'll never sit right with me!

To be recited from a elderly lady's perspective.

Monobrow!!

How can I break it to my dear old husband?
I need to break the silence but I don't know how,
That every time I go to kiss him, I'm invited,
To his sprouting bushy monobrow!!
He takes great pride in his appearance,
And he is everything that I want him to be,
But I don't want *that* affecting our relationship,
And growing out of proportion at me!
I try to fix the dilemma when he is asleep,
But I don't seem to have no luck,
And every time he is awaken by the sound of my tweezers,
When I lean over him and start to pluck!
He always reminds me that he is a man,
And that "Men ain't meant to groom!"
But I wish he would do something about it,
Than just let it sit with us in the room!
But how can I break it once again to my husband? Does anyone please know how?
I am wanting to invite myself up for a kiss,
But I can't because of the monobrow!!

Married to Albert Trotter

I miss his sleek complexion and that retired express tenderness,
Day after day I am becoming a mystery plotter,
I'm planning to get out the hedge trimmers because I am sick of feeling,
like I am married to Albert Trotter!

It's like kissing Father Christmas after a glass of sherry,
I pray that one day he will get it sheared,
I am tired of waking up next to the honey monster,
With his thick, grey, gangly beard!

He stands gracefully stalwart and poses into the mirror,
I mean, what form of attraction does it bring?
More and more men are levitating the trend,
Please tell me why is it suddenly becoming a thing?

I often discover last night's supper in his woolly fibres,
Everytime he kisses me, I somewhat flinch,
I dread each week when it develops in breadth,
And descends to his feet, inch by inch!

I do religiously pray for the Mediterranean heat to come around,
When I prefer him as a clean, genial, amiable otter,
There is nothing more frightful than seeing the resemblance,
Like I am married to Albert Trotter!

How to Deal with a Snoring Spouse?!

It is the first time in weeks,
I have slept serene in the other bed,
I had to escape from my husband's snoring,
It was drilling right through my head!

Earplugs do not do a thing,
They do not aid his persistent shroud
I cannot even protect my ears with a pillow,
Because he snores so bloody loud!

I am beginning to reach the end of my tether,
I don't know how much more of this I can take,
All I want to do is to have a cuddle at night,
But the bastard keeps on keeping me awake!

Last night my sleep felt tranquil,
It was a blissfully needed occasion,
It was amiable to sleep without the persistent effects,
Of his incommodious, aggravating vibration!

So please Lord have mercy,
Before I kick him out of the house,
Advise me on how to obliterate this dilemma,
How to deal with a snoring spouse?!

He Belongs in a Zoo!

He picks and chips away at his toenails,
Then he leaves them on the floor,
My exasperation and vexation is boiling,
To the point that it is melting me to the core.
He sits back and chills out watching the television,
Making himself at home on the settee,
He wonders why I am always on the edge,
Because he leaves the house chores to me!
I have honestly had enough of his laziness,
I really cannot think what to do,
My spouse doesn't deserve to live in my home,
He belongs in the zoo!
I am up every day at 6am,
Whilst he indulges in more time in bed,
The way I keep on tending to the house myself,
One day I may drop down dead!
He has a nerve to complain about the sound of the vacuum,
And the stale stench of the kitchen's bleach,
No wonder I go on and on at him,
Every day as I consistently preach!
I am aggravated by his nasty habits,
Lord have mercy, what shall I do?
My spouse doesn't belong in this elegant house,
He belongs in the zoo!
He takes off his shoes and socks,
And then places them down at the side of the chair,
The number of times that I stress about this matter,
I am surprised that I still have my hair!
He is completely aimless when he hovers over the toilet,
He pisses all over the lid,
Can you imagine the state of the house if I passed away tomorrow?
I wouldn't want to think, heaven forbid!
I have had enough of messy bastards in my life,
The one thing which I really must do,
Is to pack up his belongings and ship him out,
Because my spouse belongs in the zoo!

I'd Rather be a Nun

A woman doesn't go swimming without ogling at men in their swimming trunks,
I'm here for the Rocky and the Gladiators, the muscular hairy hunks,
It's the only action I get for a woman at the age of seventy-two,
It's an enthralling experience and definitely a magnificent view!

I thought I would have a peek in the male showers, hoping for a wink,
Men's penises nowadays seem to shrivel and shrink,
The men were wrinkly distorted and incredibly old,
Diminished features, petulant characteristics and so horrifically bald!

I don't know what they shove down there, it isn't to impress, definitely not for a speedo,
Once they drop their kecks, it's that bloody small, it's just like finding Nemo,
It's not gonna be much of a thrill, it's not gonna be much fun,
It's put me right off sex has that! I'd rather be a nun!

It's a very peculiar shape, it's like a 1920's bowler hat,
It's so round, podgy and miserable, I can't be doing with that!
It wouldn't be of any use, it wouldn't do its thing,
It's like a turtle in hibernation, it doesn't hang nor swing!

I thought I was in for a chance, dressed in my florescent, floral bikini,
But there isn't anything much to offer with a stump, two-inch size weenie,
The talent has evaporated, these men are too frail to function,
Their grey, tweedy pubes, are like an unbearable congestion on the Spaghetti Junction!

I now our engines seize up and shut down, the moment we retire,
But by god the exhibition of talentless men are too premature to admire,
My Friday swimming isn't of any use to me anymore, my fanatasies here are done,
I've excluded men from my memory! I'd rather be a nun!

This Anecdote was inspired by two female friends of mine when speaking about the function of a physical relationship, back in 2017. One of them was describing man with a strunk penis and that he was unable to perform when reaching a certain age. She also mentioned that she would rather be a nun, than attempt to help arouse a man with her flattering ways. I was instantly grabbed by that particular line. I arrived home from work one evening, sat myself down with a cuppa and immediately wrote this poem. I performed this anecdote for the first time at the LUU Spoken Word Society which was a student run poetry event, based at The Brundenell WMC in Leeds, on Thursday 13th February 2018.

Men Are Like a Bowl of Soup

Men are like a bowl of soup,
They can be smoothly lukewarm, or downright thick,
They can be a warm blessing when coming home,
Or they can either get on your wick!

Men can be the inviting flavour of tomato,
They can be the perfect ingredient,
But they can be as tasteless as vegetable soup,
Not the best but moderately obedient.

They can lay their passion in the blend,
They can give romance when dunked with bread,
They can appreciate your passion when you swallow,
But it can be a different story when getting into bed!

That is when the sour taste of Chicken Soup appears,
When you spit it out, it is like wanting to go to sleep,
But when they cuddle you and kiss you goodnight,
It is like a favourite can of soup that you want to keep.

When the arctic, bleak weather arrives,
They microwave their cuddles like troupes,
They come in a variety of favourable choices,
Men are like a bowl of soup!

My Husband Has Booked Our Funeral

My Husband has taken me to book our funeral,
One of the perks of being wed,
I know we are in our sixties and it is good to be cautious,
But I don't want to think when I might drop down dead!

"We may have twenty years left," he says,
"Tomorrow we may pop our socks
Mary, we need to be safe than sorry," he says,
As I sit pondering about laying in that box.

The oak wood, varnished casket which I chose,
The time it'll become my homeward bound
Except that it won't be very pretty, when I am six feet under,
And buried with rats in the ground.

The measurements and fixtures and approximates,
My anatomy becoming an entangeled warps
There is no use of feeling great at appointments like these,
Because I come out feeling like a corpse.

Well, at least I know what my new habitat will be like,
Right now, I have no more strive,
Today has knocked me for six and I feel so drained,
And I feel so buried alive.

So now I am going to wrap up this anecdote,
As I prepare for reincarnation,
This poem is for you and I hope you can make it to the wake,
With this personal invitation.

Tuesday 14th November 2017

This evening, I wrote a whimsical anecdote on my laptop, titled "My Husband has Booked Our Funeral," which is inspired by my grandma and grandad. They went to book and pay for their funeral at 1pm, so that there were no hassle when it came to their time. Grandma wasn't really bothered about going. I asked grandad if he had to select a particular type of coffin.

"Yes." He said.

"What, we see our coffin? I don't wanna see what I'm going to be buried in," grandma said, sharpening her eyebrows and piercing her eyes expressively.

Grandad mentioned that you don't physically see the coffin, you just select the material of the casket.

"Oh, I'll send you in," grandma said to grandad.

"No Jean, we both have to be there," grandad said, sat on a chair, at The Masserella's Coffee Bar in Batley.

This whimsical anecdote is inspired by them. I haven't written a poem since March 2017, so it is good to be creating new material again.

Tuesday 2nd January 2018

I arrived up at my grandma's house at approximately 10:15am, as we were going to the Mill Village for a coffee. Grandad was coming along too. He sat dressed on the couch in the living room, still niggled with the cold bug which is swarming about. It's the irritable cough that he cannot get rid of. They were both back to their witty ways with each other as I sat on the armchair, noticing something white in Grandma's hair. I reached over and got the piece of white flake out.

Grandad shimmied away from grandma a little, looking at her with bewilderment, murmuring "I don't like owt like that."

"Like what?" grandma asked with a scowl. "It's a bit of fluff. I haven't got owt crawling about in my hair!"

I just laughed at this Comedy duo, sat opposite me. You see, grandad knows how to amuse me, attempting to wind Grandma up but she dusted it off by saying "He's only doing it because you're here love!"

Grandad has been retired for nearly three months now. They are both coping well, meaning they haven't killed each other yet! On the 31st December 2020, grandad video called me to wish me a happy new year. We spoke about various subjects including the ongoing predicament of Covid-19. Then he passed the phone to grandma so I could wish her happy new year too. The next thing I saw was a glass of sherry being given to her at 10:30am.

"Have you seen what your grandad is giving me? A glass of bloody sherry when it is still morning," Grandma frowned, with a glimpse of a smile.

"Well, we can get merry and go to bed for a bit of delight tonight," Grandad responded, knowing that I was on the receiving end of the phone which would make me cackle.

"Oh shut up Richard! No wonder your beard keeps on growing, you mucky old bugger!" Grandma scolded him, holding the glass of sherry in her right hand and the phone in the other.

A stimulation of creativity manifested within me, this late afternoon, as I commenced work on a new animation. I am beginning to re-experience the sense of being sceptical and pessimistic about my work. I worry about people having a negative aversion towards my work. I have to learn to abide by how I feel, bite the bullet and continue. My new animation is an adaptation from my whimsical anecdote "My Husband Has Booked Our Funeral." I began the project, after de-cluttering my bedroom, to make room for an artist studio. I was practically earning a pittance whilst working at The Playhouse, so renting out an actual studio out for my practice is out of the question for me but I don't mind it. The only thing I care about is being able to create which is exactly what I am doing.

After heading out to Dewsbury to buy the essential supplies that I needed, I began animating.

The opening of the animation showed a couple sat in a taxi on their way to a funeral parlour. At the end of the 10 seconds, I produced an A3 Sketch, using tracing paper to show three buildings appearing - "Bob's Butchers and Son," "Mrs Tart's Bakery" and "Sugar Coated Sweeties." These buildings would pass by as the couple are riding in their vehicle. I placed my camera onto the tripod in a stable spot to capture the images. I also used the vibrant torch light of my mobile phone, to experiment with tone, and to create a sense of movement, which interestingly worked. The intricate structural drawings of the three shops, reminded me of the terraced houses on Coronation Street, for some reason, especially the top part of The Rovers Return Inn. My initial aim was to have the taxi, being a cutout of a vehicle and mounted on a black foamboard, so I did this. After making sixty photo shots, I captured the vehicle moving at least a couple of inches at a time. The camera was set to a ratio of 16:9. The photo set to black and white and set on a "Fine" mode, which allowed the stills to appear a lot more linear. I edited the photographs on the MovAvi Editor. The animation clip lasted approximately ten seconds.

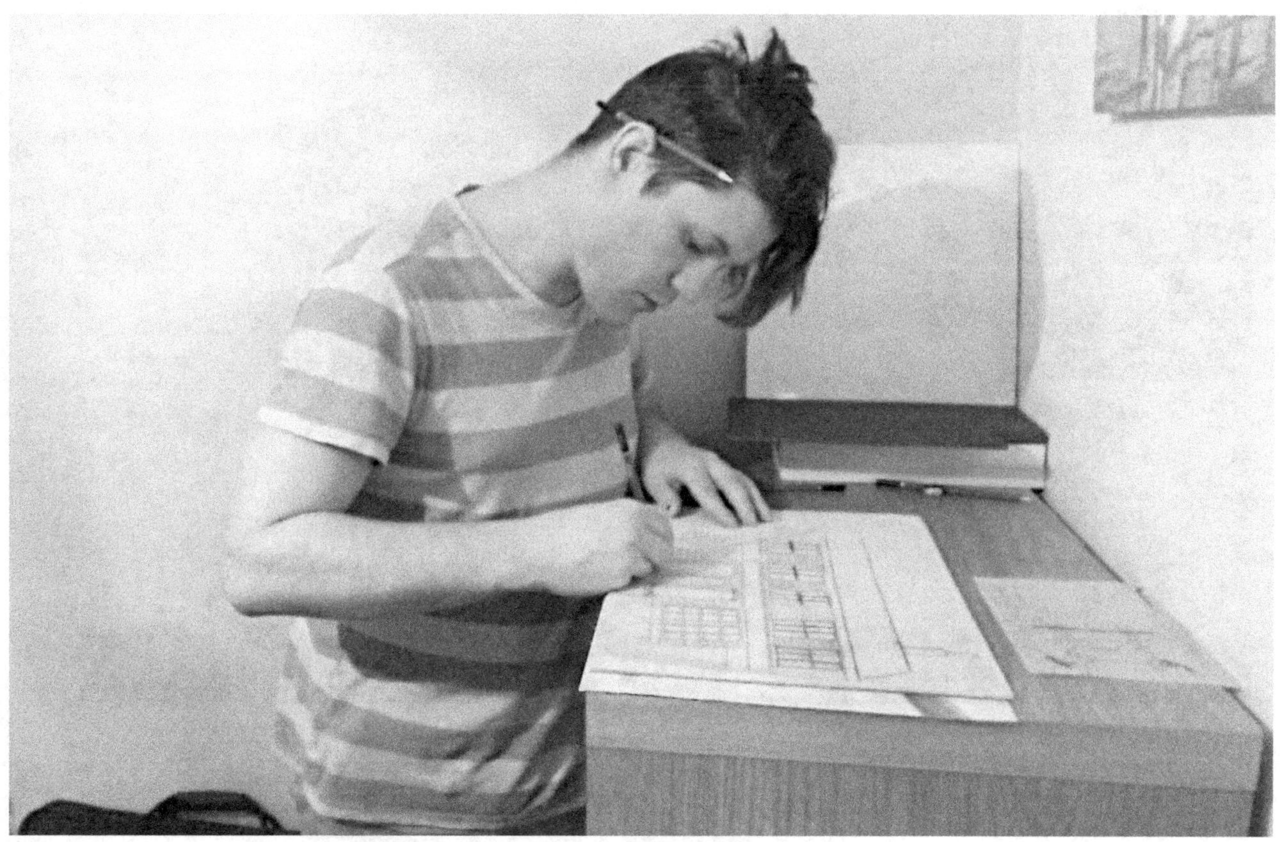

Working on the street sequence.
- January 2018

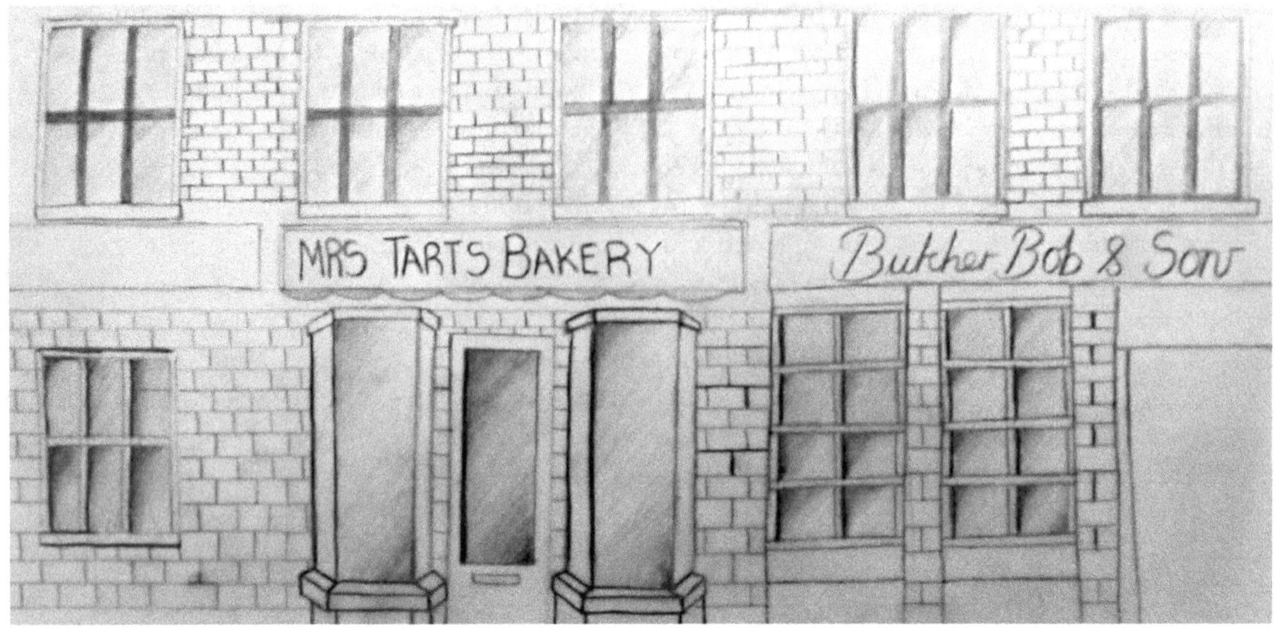

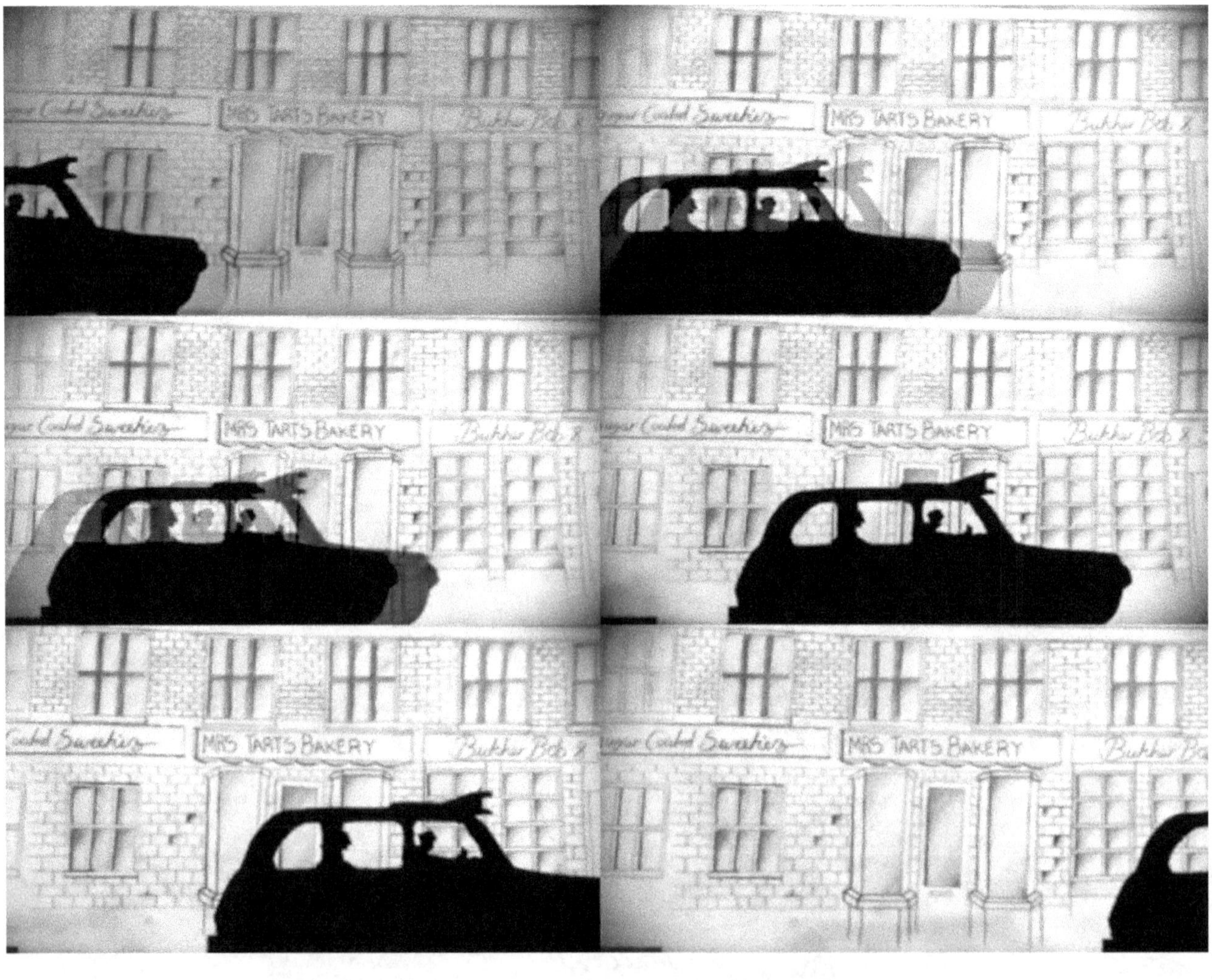

The opening animated street sequence.

Wednesday 3rd January 2018

I began to experiment with small maquettes, to include them in the animation. I made a petite table, as well as the front visage of the funeral parlour, where the taxi pulls up outside. I felt I was getting carried away with using 2D prototypes so for now, I scrapped the Maquette concept.

It is currently 5:35pm and I am sitting up in my bedroom on the wooden chair, feeling drained and pessimistic with how this project is going. I have come to a halt as a result of experiencing an artist's block. Absolutely no sense of progression or ideas is channelling through me. It is normal for me to sense some kind of apprehension about my work, particularly at the beginning of a project. My mind has become paralyzed and exhausted, by the constant thinking of various concepts and working out how I feel the finished animation should look. I really like the opening of the animation, it's just thinking of which direction to take from here.

This evening, I made a few alterations to the opening of the film. I have decided to sequence the introduction credits together before I go further with the animation. I recorded me reciting the anecdote, a good couple of times, which I then edited on the visual timeline. I added a high pitched audio effect to the narration, to grasp the sound of a senior lady's voice. It is currently 10:30pm and I'm still struggling with my sense of creativity. This is something of an artist's horror, becoming mentally imprisoned inside a box. A good night's sleep and a couple of day's absent from the project, allowed time for me to breathe and feel refreshed.

Saturday 6th January 2018

I resumed work on the current animation project at approximately 2:30pm and finished at 7:15pm, with an hour or so break in between. I managed to get motivated again, even though the artist block is still present. I am feeling a little apprehensive about my work, because I do not want it to be a project that I just push aside. Inspiration will eventually rekindle itself and turn into a crazy, spiral of energy and I will have this endless stream of sketches materialising from the lead in my pencil.

Anyhow, this afternoon, I completed a seven second sequence of the character "Mary," selecting her "oak wood, varnished casket." I had the concept of the casket opening with a skeleton jumping up out at her and with Mary scuttling away in surprise as the skeleton lays back down in the coffin. I mounted the casket sketch onto a piece of foamboard, to give the piece a subtle 2D look, as opposed to a flat looking pencil drawing. The lid on the Casket, was a cutout placed onto a piece of black foamboard, which would be able to open it and capture this in the sequence. Mary would then run out of the wake room, startled by the living skeleton. The rise of the skeleton was created using six photocopies of its contour. This saved me the precious time of redrawing it. When the skeleton was in movement, I had to cut around the casket edges, to make sure that the skeleton fitted into the coffin perfectly.

"The oak wood, varnished casket which I chose,

The time it'll become my homeward bound,

Except that it won't be very pretty, when I'm six feet under,

And buried with rats in the ground!"

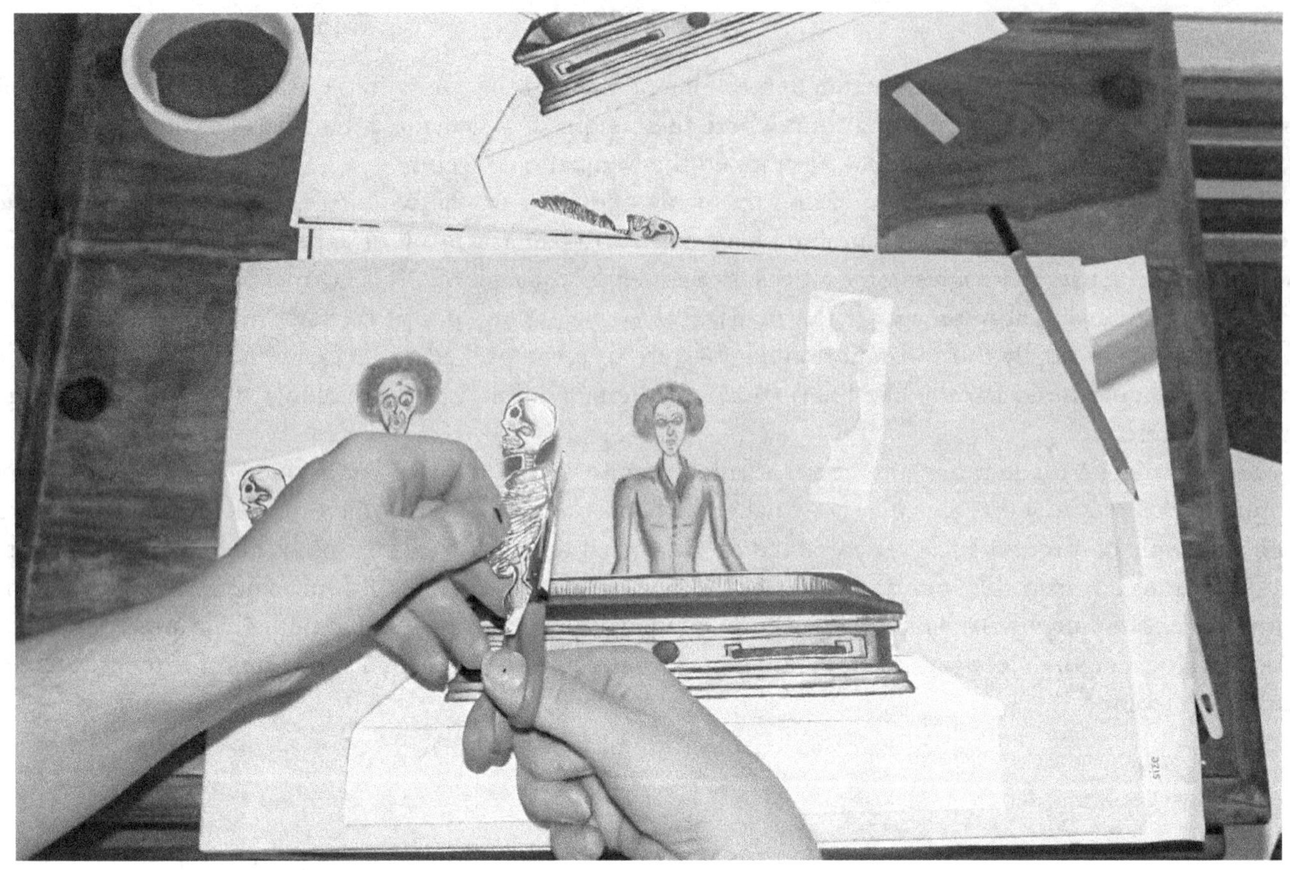

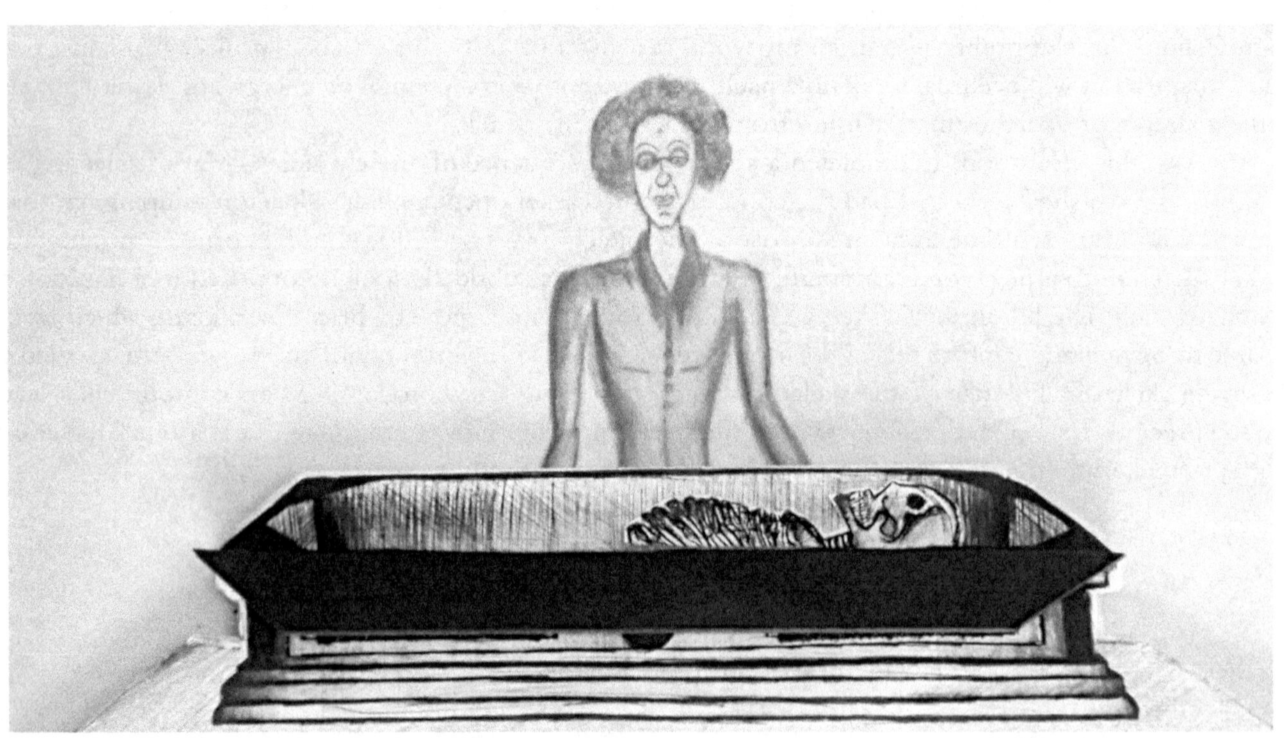

"The oakwood varnished casket which I chose"

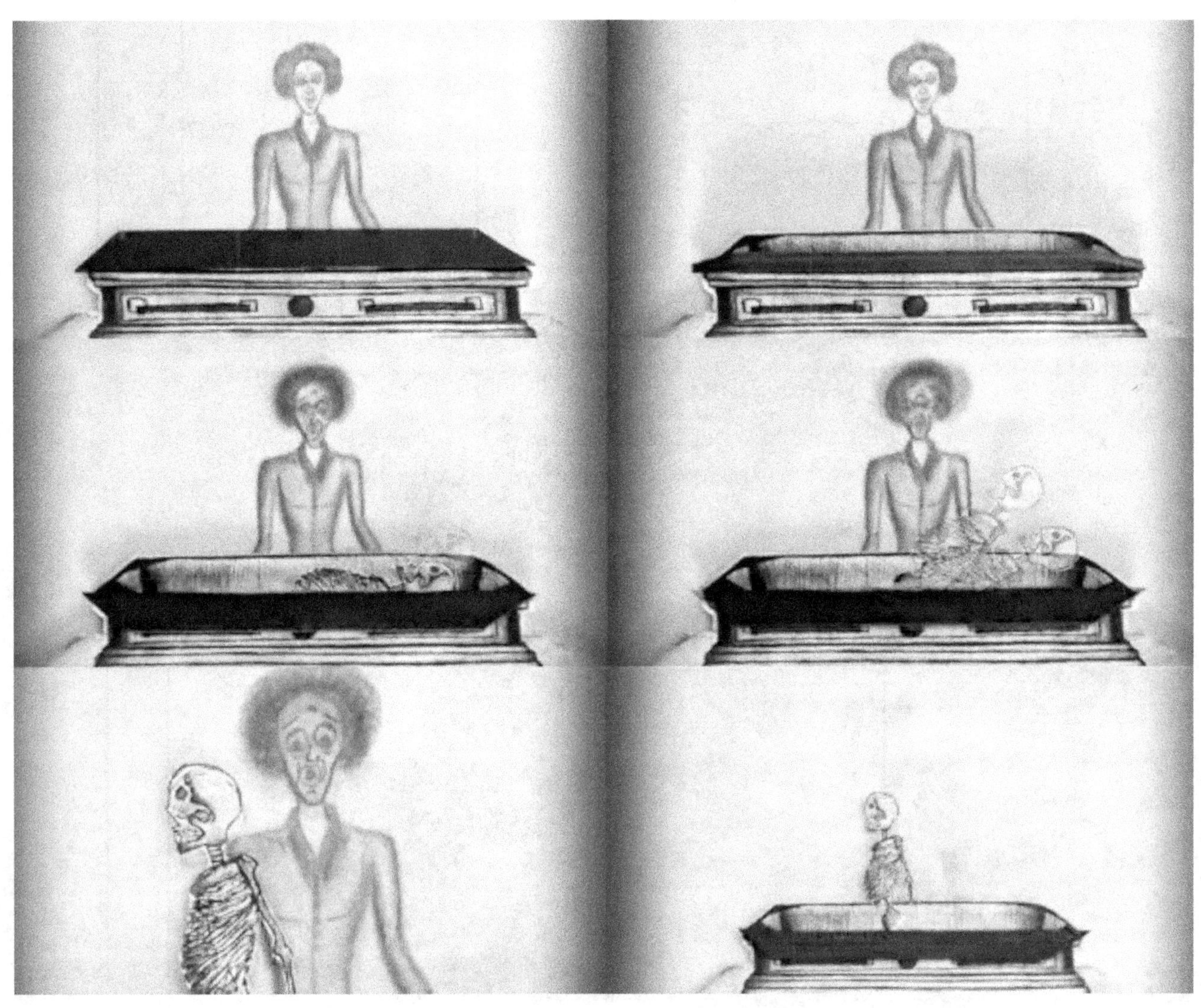

(Above) *The Animated coffin scene.*

Mary would then become entangled with a reel of a measuring tape, during this verse-

"The measurements and fixtures and approximates,
My anatomy becoming an entangled warp,
It's hard to feel great at appointments like these,
Because I come out feeling like a corpse!"

After the entanglement with the tape measure, the spinning motion of Mary would transition her into a zombie. As I keep on mentioning, I have this artist block. My vision seems transparent. Meaning that I can visually imagine how the sequences play out, but when I attempt to produce the sketches that I need, it feels seemingly impossible. I never believe of "giving up." Persistence always has a way of getting the creative juices going again. A good several years ago, I used to "give up." But through maturity and resilience, I nurtured this my negative thoughts, by turning them into a force of power. There is always an outcome to everything, no matter how big or small and I am speaking with regards to my own mental health experiences too. I drew a quick sketch of the skeleton in the casket, whilst I was on a shift at The Playhouse and managed to incorporate this as part of a sequence.

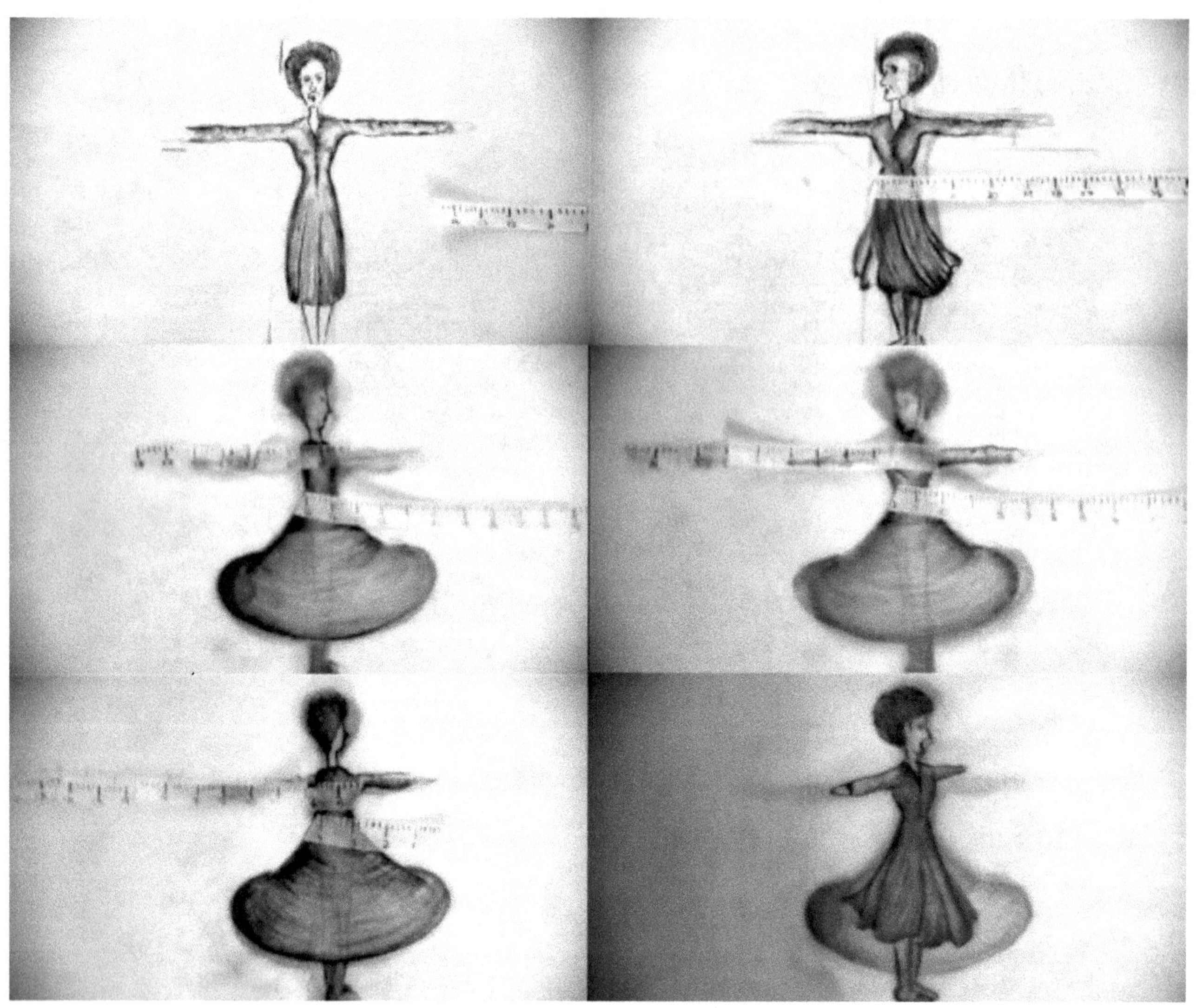

(Above) *"The measurements, fixtures and approximates"*

Monday 8th January 2018

I resumed work on my animation at approximately 11.30am and focused on it for the majority of the day. A flare of optimism spiralled through me a little. I developed the scene for the verse, which referred to Mary being measured up for her casket. I drew Mary, twirling, using my wooden mannequin to imitate her movement. The measuring tape was created separately with a very thin, lengthy piece of tracing paper. From the right-hand side of the screen, merging to the left, the tape wrapped itself around Mary's hip. To achieve this, I cut a piece at a time, whilst key framing the shots, to make the tape appear like it was enveloping her. Wriggling around and back out onto her chest, the tape left the scene, spinning Mary in an erratic fashion. I have yet to work out how to end this scene. I was thinking of having Mary transitioning into a demonic zombie, approaching her husband and pecking him on the cheek whilst giving him a fright; his hat whipping off from his head, maybe?

Subsequently I drew a side profile of Mary, laid peacefully in her casket, with six cut outs of small rats, scuttling up and down and around her body. To allow for this motion to happen, I moved each rat sketch, a couple of inches and captured them frame. Following this, I made the rats appear to scuttle off to the left hand side of the screen. These rodents would hurrying past, during the following narration:

"The measurements and fixtures and approximates."

I made Mary appear to stand upright, with her arms extended in front of her as she was being measured up. This project is sailing along nicely and I am eventually the conquering the oppressive feelings of doubt that I had throughout the previous week.

It is currently 11:40pm and I am sitting on the flamboyant, ribena purple couch in the living room. I spent the past half an hour sketching out an original template of Mary transitioning into this mellow looking zombie, with her arms outstretched, and her ripped sleeves draping. I have added alot of tonal values, to capture any present lighting, as they would be in reality.I then sketched out Mary's husband, posed in a chair. This was visual template to work from when animating the scene.

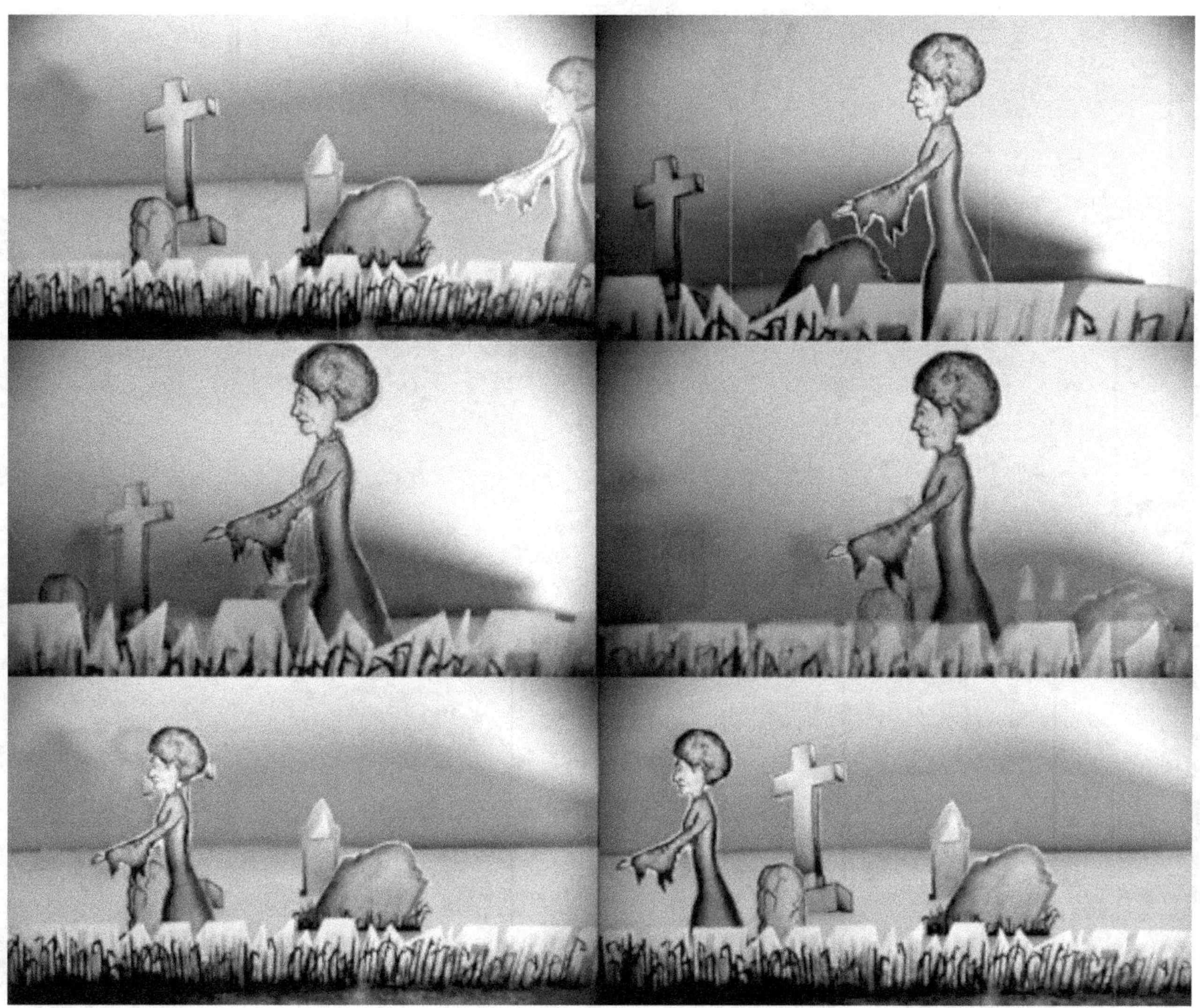

"It's hard to feel great at appointments like these,
Because I come out feeling like a corpse!"

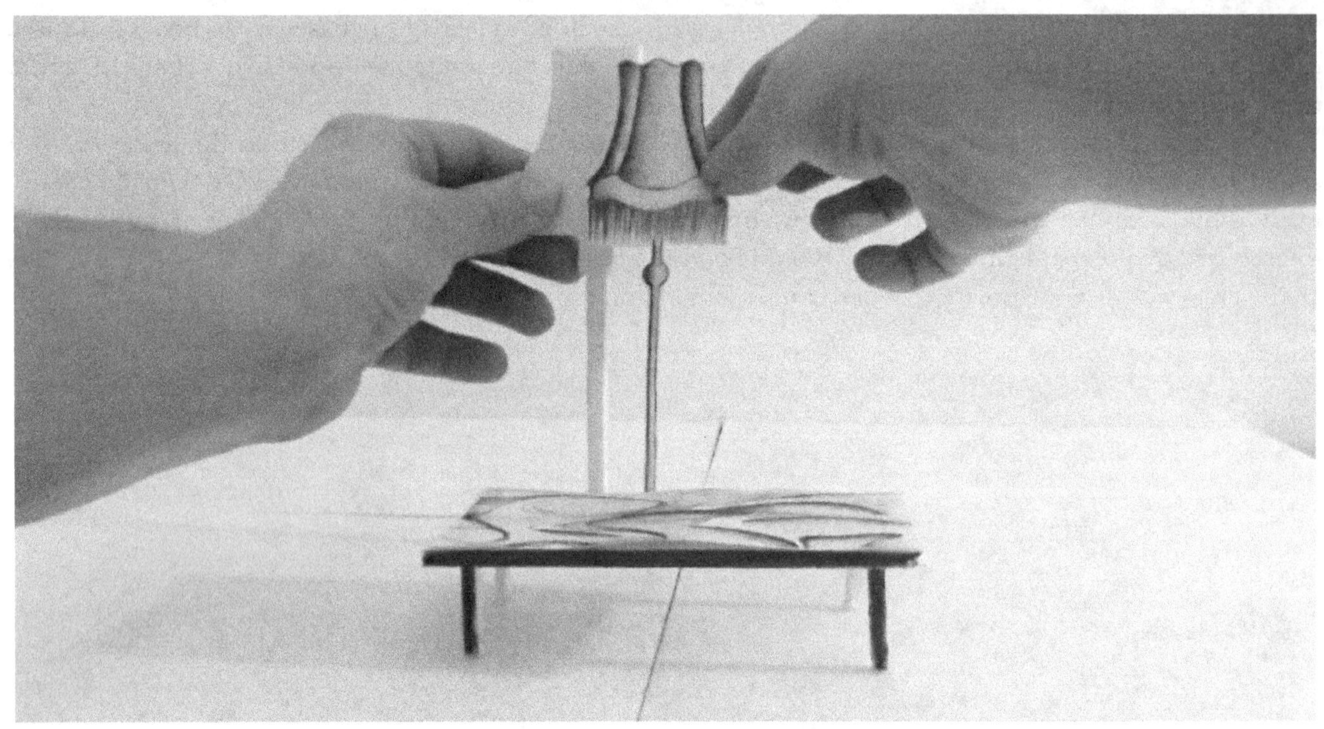

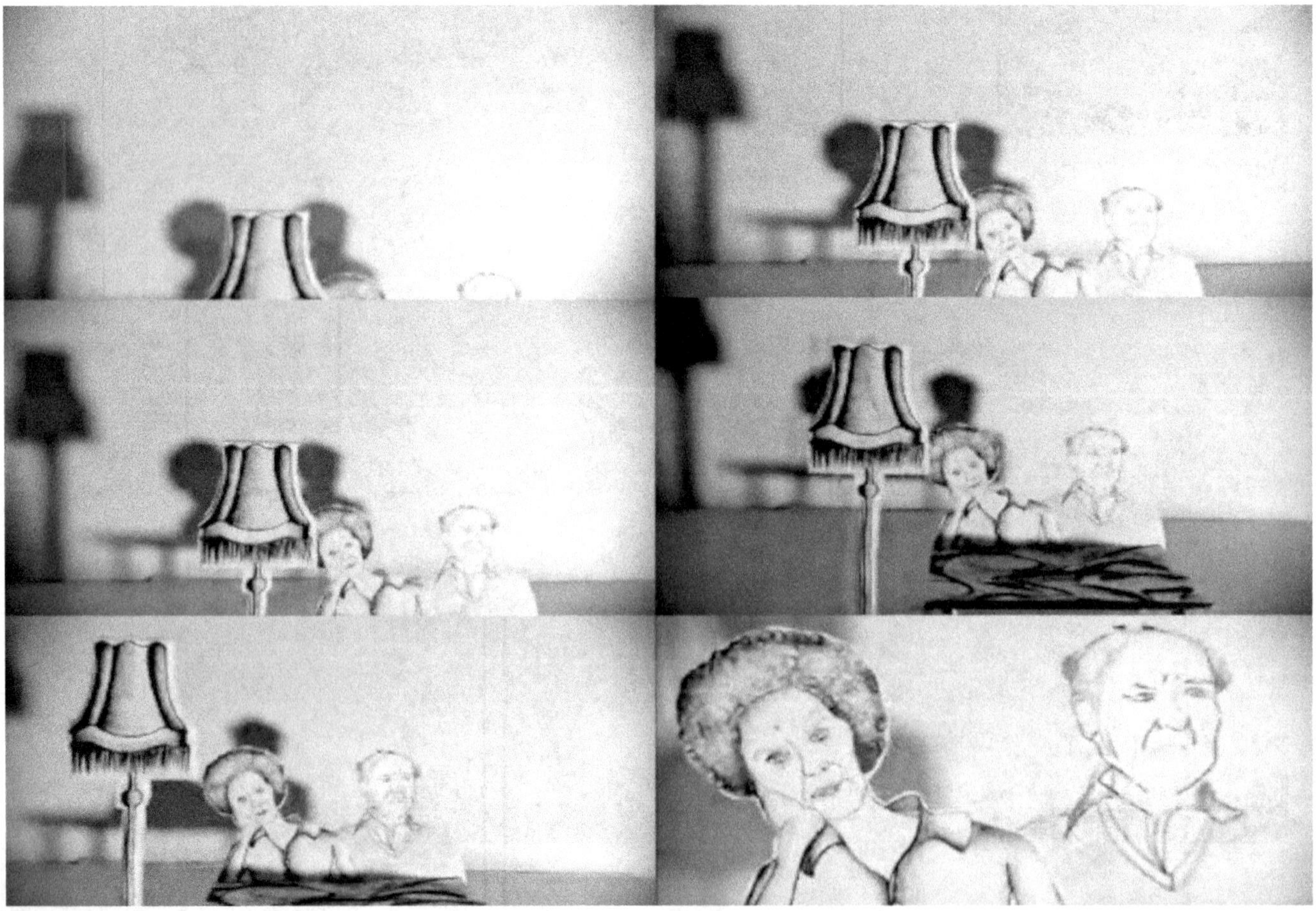

"We may have twenty years left' he says"

Saturday 13th January 2018

I focused on the 2D cut outs today to create the scene of Mary and her husband sat waiting impatiently to view their casket options. I wanted to keep the idea of using a 2D effect through some parts of the animation and not just during the opening scene. The cut outs consisted of a miniature tall lamp with a victorious looking lampshade, a table with an oak wood effect, which I made using pencil mediums "H" and "B." I made another cut out of the elderly couple which I positioned behind the table. After making numerous photograph stills, I composed the scene featuring the couple which will play out during the narration of the second verse. I experimented with lighting using my lamp, to draw a silhouette of my petite maquette, reflecting onto the wall. The materials which I used for this setting was Foamboard and paper sketches to mount on their appropriate prop's. I have developed this animation bit by bit once a day throughout this week, either sketching, doing photography or editing. It feels like the animation is coming on well. I re-recorded a recital of my anecdote, "My Husband Has Booked Our Funeral," to keep the audio clean and crisp, whilst using the original very high pitch vocal tool, to make it sound like Mary is narrating the piece.

Sunday 14th January 2018

It is shortly before midnight and I have just retired to bed. There is a treacherous storm brewing, with the beating rain. I am feeling quite knackered after another productive day on the current project. I made a sequence with a number of shots and edited it to show Mary wandering through the eerie graveyard. Then I focussed predominantly on the final verse, working out how I felt it should conclude. The line being -

> "So I am going to wrap up this anecdote
> As I prepare for my reincarnation -"

For this, I decided to draw a side profile of Mary, glancing to the right. I produced a second sketch of this but this time her expression slightly windswept, with her hair dancing to the rhythm of the breeze coming from a hairdryer and a selection of pampering products on display. All of these items were also made in two-dimensional sketches, gradually ascending closer to her face. These would then decorate Mary's face, during the narrative - "As I prepare for my reincarnation." The scene would follow on with Mary being whisked off to her funeral, plonked contently in a hammock, gripped firmly by a bird's beak. I made two cut out drawings to represent the bird flying. One resembled its wings lifting and the other was identical but with its wings moving downwards. This is the same technique which I have used in previous animations. The process of making the bird appear to fly, involved embedding the images onto a piece of foamboard, which I then moved an inch at a time during motion capture. This led to Mary being dropped into her open casket as part of the penultimate verse -

> "Well, at least I know what my new habitat will be like,
> Right now, I have no more strive,
> Today has knocked me off for six and I feel so drained,
> And I feel so buried alive."

I decided to include Mary's homely cottage enveloped by trees in the animation. The tweedy you mean skeletal? trees were made out of cut outs. During the animation, the camera gradually zoomed in on the cottage, as a black bird is seen at the top right hand side of the scene, before fluttering out from the trees.

This evening, I sketched out two trees, for the scenic foreground of the final graveyard scene, using pencil mediums F, 4, 5, and 6B. Scenery together with a few tombstones were captured on my camera and my animation was complete at approximately 2am on Thursday 18th January 2018. Another visual, after the credits, showed the couple giving each other one last kiss, in the form of skeletons lying in their coffins. I used a quote to summarise the whole subject of "death", as part of this closing visual -

"Dying is a very dull, dreary affair and my advice to you is to have nothing whatever to do with it!"

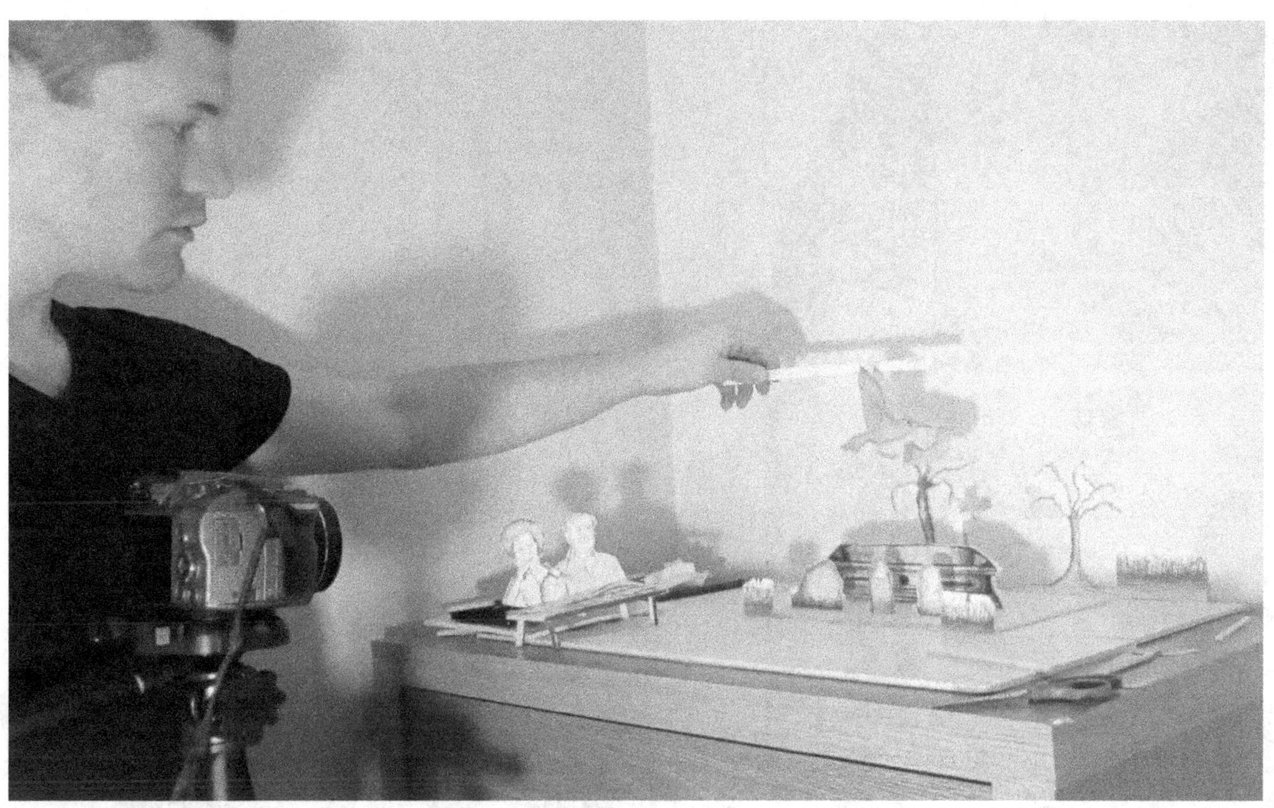

(Above) *Filming the concluding scene, in the graveyard model.*
(Below) *The concluding animated scene.*

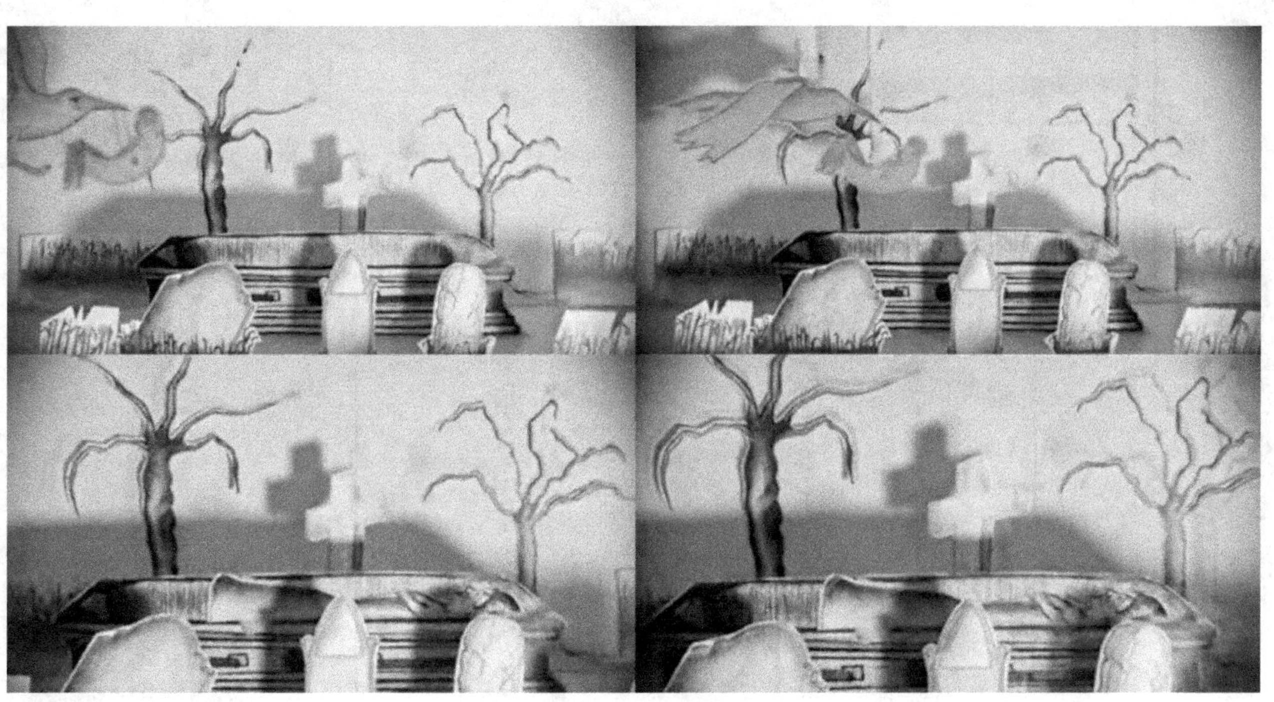

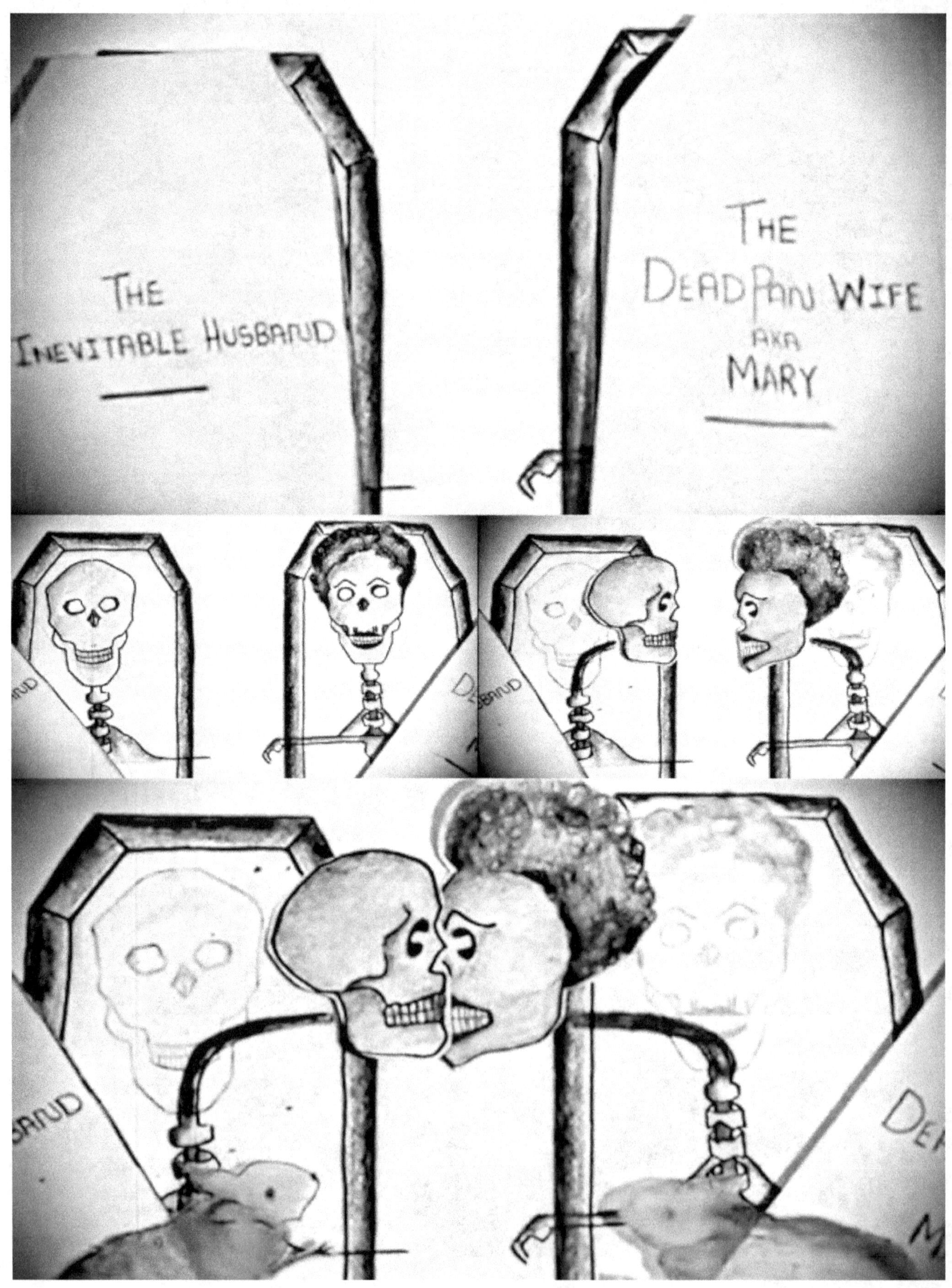

The final Animation scene.

Saturday 27th January 2018

I previewed a screening of my new animation "My Husband Has Booked Our Funeral" this afternoon, at event called "Jackanory," based at The Westgate Studios in Wakefield, organised by the brilliant Halima Mayat. It was an opportunity to seeing the resulting animation projected in front of a petite live audience for the first time. It was the final piece to be played during this afternoon's programme, after a bunch of Spoken Word artists stood up and did their thing. The only minor technical issue was the music, overpowering the narrative in parts of the film. Even though I know what Mary is saying, it is strenuous for the audience to follow. I rectified this matter when I returned home at approximately 6:05pm. Visually, I think the audience enjoyed the screening.

The other writers who performed pieces or excerpts of their original material was a talented young Ahmer Bashir. He recited a chapter from his forthcoming book titled "The Diary Of An Halal Kid," which is sexual orientation, coming out and acceptance within a Muslim community. A Derbyshire based poet by the name of Dwane Reads gave us a little insight into his beautiful work. Bard Medal and a poet named Nick Toczek, plus a few other open mic performers also shared their words. It was brilliant to see Halima Mayat again and of course Ashley Redcan and his lovely mum.

Tuesday 30th January 2018

I checked in at The Elmwood Hotel on Argyle Street in London at approximately 2pm, which is situated opposite the King's Cross train station. I chilled out in the hotel until 6:10pm, and then walked to Angel, for this evening's "Kino 94" event at The Candid Arts Trust. I met Molly and Brandon upstairs in the café. They were lounging on the sofa in the back room, where candle lights beamed with a welcoming vibe. They both welcomed me to join them, as I took off my mustard toned, knee length coat, resting it beside me on the couch. Molly witfully referred me to a "stranger" as she noticed that I wasn't dressed in my signature dungarees like I usually do.

"I don't know this person," Molly added to her wisecrack. It was brilliant to see them both again. Molly was telling me how well her screening went at "The Horror-On-Sea Film Festival" based in Southend, where she received promising feedback from the audience. A woman also approached her with an invitation to appear in a slasher film she is making. Molly agreed.

It was that time again, 7pm, to make our way down to the basement for this evening's screening, which surprisingly only consisted of eight short films. It was busy but not as usual. Molly commented that pretty much the majority of the audience was new and that there were not really any regulars in attendance.

My animation "My Husband Has Booked Our Funeral" was the third short film to be screened during the first half. In traditional Kino fashion, each filmmaker stood in front of the audience, to formally introduce their films. I did this myself and my film was presented, ending with an applause from the audience. A London-based Asian student named Wemble approached me to say that he really enjoyed the animation. I spoke to him for a good ten minutes or so, before Mark Bowsher introduced himself to me. I had already met him at the Kino 93 Edition, back in November 2017. He screened a short sitcom during the second half, depicting a young male producer who secures a job attending an interview to work in a film company. Molly Brown's fantastic short animation titled "The Double Life of Hannah Schnee" was screened after my film. It was a fantastic piece, collated with archived historic footage, in order to create a clever narrative.

The evening was good, despite finishing slightly earlier at 9:30pm. Molly and Brandon had to dash off for their tube journeys, after mingling with filmmakers. I hung around for the subsequent 20 minutes, speaking with a female set designer, who created installations for prolific films. Her name is Jayne Proctor. She is currently based in Brighton but had previously worked in Leeds for four years. Mark Bowsher joined in on our conversation.

I returned to The Elmwood Hotel at approximately 10:20pm, after walking from Angel, down Pentonville Road in the dreary drizzle. The next day I caught the 10:35am Virgin East Coast train back to Leeds and then a second train to Batley, where I visited my family to celebrate my birthday. It was like the reprise of 'The Waltons' all over again.

I screened another animation of mine titled "A Visit to the Dentist" during the second half of a "Roots To Shoot" film night on Wednesday 11th March 2018. I stayed overnight at The Highcroft Guest House Hotel, hosted by two incredibly accommodating elderly Indian women, who I wholly respect.

Thursday 15th March 2018

"Hello?" I politely called out at the foot of the pantry door to check out of The Highcroft Guest House Hotel at approximately 9:45pm. They were two considerate senior Indian ladies. One I met last night. The other lady, I presumed was her sister.

"You are very kind. Very handsome." The sister smiled, gently clenching her hands together.

"Thankyou." I smiled. "I don't feel quite handsome with my hair all over the place." I added.

"You are a girl." Smiled the other lady.

"Thank you, I'll take that as a compliment." I laughed.

I thanked them for their hospitality as I left the accommodation. A good two and a half hours later, I arrived at London Victoria coach station at 1:30pm, catching the tube to King's Cross. I then checked into The European Hotel situated on Argyle Square.

At 5:30pm, I arrived in Loughton. I had a fabulous time at Sam Hacking's home for this evening's edition of "Skylark," formerly known as "The Shag." I highly recommend this intimate event. This evening's edition consisted of a screening of two music videos by Sam Holloway with the first Video being shot in Sam Hacking's cabin, where both Sam's collaborated together. The second music video was titled "Thunder, Lightning, Dance," which featured a choreographed physical dance piece. Molly screened a couple of her distinctive animations. Kayleigh "Magpie" Cassidy read out an ode to her Irish man, standing before us with her laptop. The story captured her mother celebrating the moment Kayleigh became a victorious woman by having her first period. It was a brilliantly humorous tale with a fantastic delivery by the one and only Kayleigh herself. An artist named Nathania Hartley gave us a delivery of her spoken word piece. We then stepped outside in the back garden, on this chilly spring night, to watch Gerald perform a mystical piece about burning and cleansing away your sanity, as he was dressed like an eerie looking music hall performer. He knelt down hovering over a flickering candle and cremated small slips of paper. Then it was my turn to project four of my stop motion animations onto the white brick garden wall. I screened "My Husband Has Booked Our Funeral," "Nose Job," "Director's Cut" and "A Visit to the Dentist." I received some positive feedback from the group. Sam Hacking was extremely impressed with the treacherous surge of the crashing sea scene in "Director's Cut."

"If you had to choose one animation as your favourite out of all the four, which one would be your favourite? " Sam Hacking asked.

"Erm, I kinda like them all but I am self-critical about my own work," I answered.

"Every Artist is self-critical about their own work, but if you were to choose that very one which stood out the most, which would it be?"

"Director's Cut" was my answer, as it links to various people's experiences of mental health, as well as my own and it has an extremely important role, enabling us to speak out about our inner gremlins which we battle with constantly. Also, it is a topic that needs to be amplified, to create a better understanding of how to alternatively deal with this condition. It was an honour to adapt Eva's compelling narrative, into an animation form, to express depression through a different medium.

We headed back into the house and settled in the living room, where the final artist named Chris Blewitt gave us a reading of his poetry, sitting-crossed legged in front of his laptop. Camilla gave us a couple of minutes of her time to promote an exhibition of hers, which will be showcased this spring. She presented a very small piece of slate to the group, which displayed a beautiful concoction of radiant, pastel pigments that she produced herself. It was a brilliant evening of distinctive creations, presented within a very small group of artists. A light feast of vegetarian pizzas, crisps, pastry, wine and a variation of teas were made available as part of this chill out showcase. Sam Hacking accompanied us during three stops to Loughton tube station and kindly dropped us off. Sam Holloway and myself were the last people to head out to the station, keeping each other company, until we reached our destinations. He was tiddled after drinking wine. We hugged each other goodbye until the next time, as he got off at Miles Green. I arrived back at The European Hotel, just after midnight.

After two evenings of publicly screening my animations to a live audience, I returned to Leeds at 12:15pm, catching the train from London King's Cross and then caught a bus back to Batley on Thursday 16th March 2018.

Saturday 23rd June 2018

I arrived at London King's Cross station at 9am. The sun was blazing its tropical presence on the capital. I took a long walk along Euston Road, passing a good half hour or so, reaching as far as Regent's Park. I subsequently arrived at Walthamstow Central at 11:30am. Becoming a little puzzled in which direction to head in for The Vestry House Museum, I eventually arrived at the venue, after asking an estate agent for directions. Then an old lady with her shopping trolley walked me 100 yards to the museum. She seemed isolated, even though you could sense this, she had a sense of humour. I very much appreciated her help. I am here "The Walthamstow International Film Festival," where my animation "My Husband Has Booked Our Funeral" has been selected for this Matinee's schedule.

"Is this where the film festival is?" I asked a young woman, wearing spectacles and shoulder length hair. She was hanging up a yellow poster advertising the festival on the black railings outside.

"It is, yes. I'm just hanging the posters up now." She smiled.

I waited outside in the communal garden. Another man named Jason Britski, also a filmmaker, who has two of his films selected to be shown at the Festival. He was sitting down on a wooden bench in the gardens of the venue. I made my way into the huge garden, where Liz Fletcher, one of the founders of the festival, welcomed me back with a firm handshake.

"Your animations are really exciting." Liz complimented, as I thanked her for her praise.

The film festival was held inside an air ventilated room. Before we were allowed in, Paul Fletcher had to rectify a technical hitch. He had to dash home for a memory stick containing all the films that were due to be projected. The short film showcase commenced at 12:30pm. My animation, "My Husband Has Booked Our Funeral," was the third film to be screened. I stood up in front of the intimate audience, and briefly spoke about my animation. I sat back down, and the film was screened. A man perched in front of me during the rolling credits turned around towards me and praised the film. He then asked me how long it took me to make it.

"About 3 months." I answered.

There was an eclectic range of seventy four films included in the full programme, even spoof advertise-ments produced by Fletcher Fletcher Films.

Liz hugged me and kissed me on both sides of my cheeks as I thanked her for screening my animation. She advised me to keep my animations going.

Tuesday 11th September 2018

It is currently 4:45pm and I am perched at a petite oak wood table with a cup of English breakfast tea, in a contemporary café called Fluence, based in Ladbroke Grove, London. It is the evening of the low budget sci fi and horror category at The Portobello Film Festival, which will be taking place at The Westbank Gallery on Thorpe Street, just around the corner. Two of my animations which have been chosen to be screened in this category, are "My Husband Has Booked Our Funeral" and "A Peculiar Imagination."

I arrived at the studio bar above the Westbank Studio, with a couple who I met downstairs by the names of Suranne and Laurence, husband and wife. Suranne also had a short film screening this evening titled "Lavender Blue." Molly arrived afterwards, as she perched with us on the middle leather couch at the front. The audience size was impressive but it started to decrease as the evening went on. An eclectic varied stream of deliriously surreal but humorous short films was shown throughout the hefty marathon showcase which commenced at 6pm. It finished at around 10:30pm. Molly and I had to dash at 9:30pm, after her friend's film titled "Protein" was shown. Filmmakers in attendance were invited to the projection platform to introduce their work. Both of my animations were the sixth and seventh projects to be screened. I took the opportunity to briefly introduce the films and concluded my speech with "Here I present to you "My Husband Has Booked Our Funeral" and "A Peculiar Imagination." Then they were screened. I had a few Filmmakers approach me a little later on in the evening, to congratulate me on my animations, which I very much appreciated.

As previously mentioned, Molly and I made our way to the tube station at 9:30pm to travel from Ladbroke Grove to London Victoria, via Hammersmith. I headed back to Leeds on the 11:30pm National Express coach.

Sunday 13th January 2019

I am currently sat on the London Kings Cross train in Leeds, leaving at 10:45am, to reach Southend Central via London Frenchchurch Street. My animation "My Husband Has Booked Our Funeral" will be screened at 10:30pm, before the final main feature of the day, titled "House Shark" at The Horror On Sea Film Festival based at The Park Inn Radisson Palace Hotel, where I will also be staying this evening.

I arrived in Southend at approximately just after 5pm. I walked my way through the high street to the sea front, stopping off at McDonalds for tea as dusk fell. My hotel was directly opposite Adventure Island on the sea front so it was easy enough to find. I checked in at reception. A man directed me up to Room 307, where I will be staying for the evening, after asking a senior gentlemen to take a photograph of me, posing in front of festival banner, pinned onto an iron railing outside the hotel. Room 307 was lovely and spacious, with a king size bed. I slept on it for an hour before making my way downstairs to collect my festival pass.

I met Molly very briefly, who happened to be leaving the bar at 8pm for the screening of "Six Headed Shark" based in the function room. I decided to join her too. She introduced me to the other film enthusiasts who were accompanying her. A couple of short Fflms titled "Delicacy" and "Zombie Time" were pre-screened before the main ninety-minute feature, which were interesting. It was good to see Micheal Fausti again with his wife Lou, whom I met at The Portobello Film Festival 2018. The screening event this evening wasn't as busy as the previous ones that took place during this weekend but at least there was some form of audience. My animation "My Husband Has Booked Our Funeral" was the short film to be screened before the final feature of the weekend titled "House Shark." I really didn't know what to make of "House Shark," other than it was alright and seemed cheaply produced. One hour and fifty-one minutes the feature lasted and, my didn't it feel like it! I was invited to step onto the stage and briefly introduce my animation which I did and then it was screened. 10:30pm, the final film was screened afterwards and it ended at 12:30am. A middle-aged couple, who Molly introduced me to, had to leave at 9:30pm. They managed to get enjoy a preview of my animation when the projection man was testing it, prior to the screening.

I headed back to my hotel room on level 3, soon after the screenings. Molly went to the casino for a quick drink with the festival team. She mentioned, the next morning, that she was there until 2:30am. I had an interesting time at the festival, even though I wasn't there for the whole experience and it was more of a flying visit.

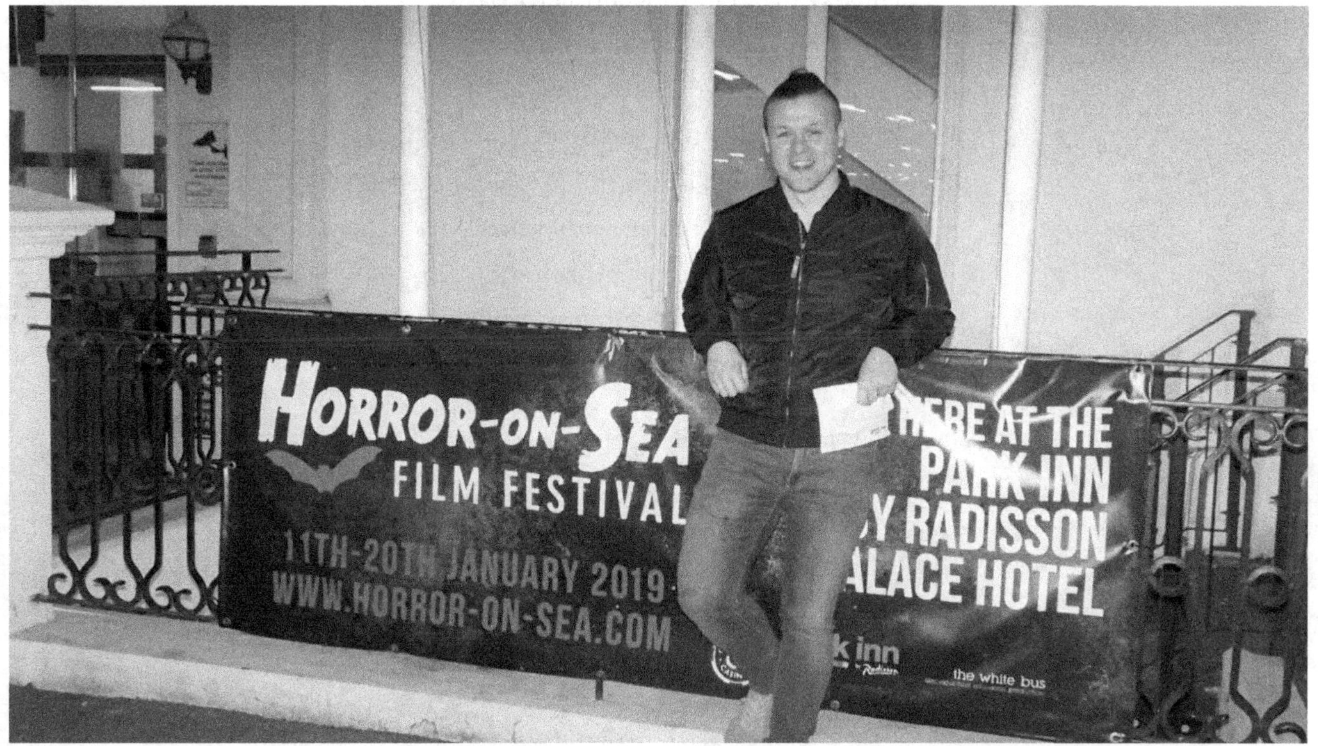

"Horror - on - Sea Film Festival"
"My Husband Has Booked Our Funeral" screening.
The Park Inn Raddison Palace Hotel, Southend on Sea - January 2019

The Day My Gran Rode a Rollercoaster

The day my gran rode a rollerocoaster,
She nearly lost her teeth,
As she climbed a hundred feet to the top of the pullup,
And looked down at the drop beneath.
The train plummeted down the turbulent tracks,
Gran pierced the air with a shrill,
As she closed her eyes and held on tight,
Not grasping the fun nor thrill.
I have never laughed with so much wit,
As her pride was on the seat bequeath,
The day my Gran rode a rollercoaster,
She nearly lost her teeth!

With my adoration for rollercoasters and the pump of adrenaline that they bring, I intentionally wrote this whimsical anecdote, to be adapted into a stop motion animation. The project was more about exploring motion with 2D cut out templates of fairground rides and experimentation. On the evening of Friday 18th November 2016, I completed the animation.

The animation was premiered at "Showroom Shorts" based at The Showroom Cinema in Sheffield on 17th Janauary 2017. I was championed with "The Audience Choice Award" based at The Winter Gardens Film Festival" based in Blackpool on Sunday 5th February 2017, which was completely unexpected. The Short Film was shortlisted at "The Walthamstow International Film Festival" based at Walthamstow's Empire Cinema.

Saturday 3rd June 2017

I caught the 5:30am train service from Leeds to London Kings Cross, arriving at the capital at 7:50am. I am currently sat at a petite circular table in Starbucks based on Pentonville Road. A couple of hours later, I was stood in The Empire Cinema complex in Walthamstow, waiting for the festival to begin at 11am. It was a very good event with a positive reception too. It was nice to see my animation, "The Day My Gran Rode a Rollercoaster," alongside the commendable talents of other artists. My short film didn't win the animation category, but I am just thrilled that the piece was even chosen to be part of the film festival. Liz Fletcher, one of the organisers, asked all of the shortlisted filmmakers to stand before the audience and tell them a little bit about their submitted films. The animation category prize went to Fin McMorran, for her film "Garden." The documentary category prize went to Mustafa Koray Polat for "The Wall." The drama category winner was Francis Albarones for "What If." The Experimental Category Winner was Ryan Powell for "Mud, Sea, Sky." The silent category Winner was Neil Needleman for "Two Landscapes" and the young person's category winner was The Leyton Six Form College for "No Exit."

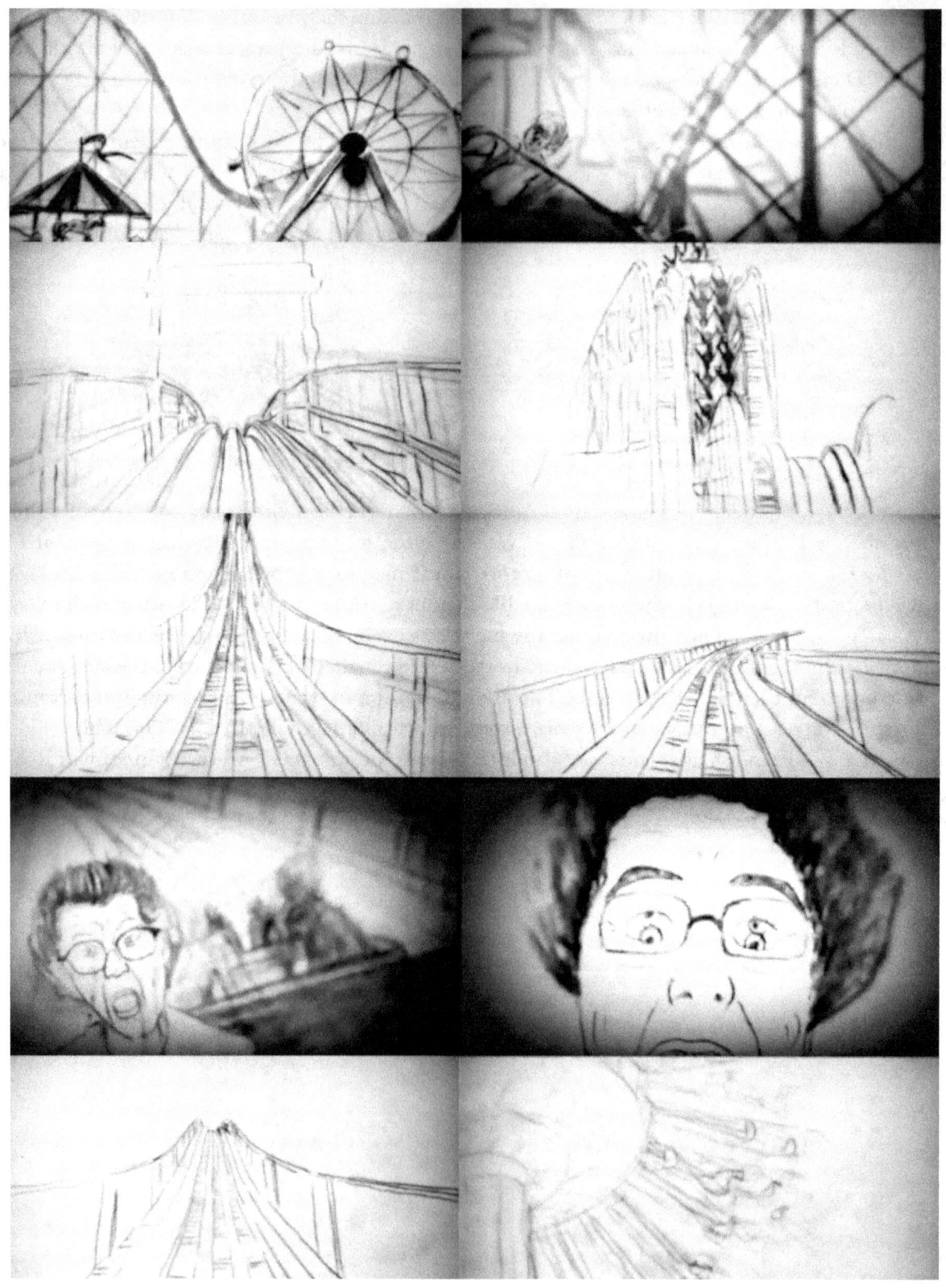

"The Day My Gran Rode A Rollercoaster"

Film stills - November 2016

A huge congratulations should go to them all. Thoroughly deserved. It has been an honour to have the opportunity to showcase my work to a new audience. A male filmmaker, aged in his sixties, said that he loved my short film, whilst a woman approached me and mentioned that she voted for my piece. I thanked them both. The festival will be giving another screening throughout tomorrow, based at The Vestry House, also here in Walthamstow.

I headed back to Walthamstow tube station in the penetrating, blistering heat and the radiant sun. An instrumental Jazz group, made up of four men, performed a quirky number during the tube ride back to King's Cross, jumping between carriages, at each stop as they were busking. I stopped off at Costa Coffee, which was neighbouring King's Cross Station, before I headed back to Yorkshire on the 2:34pm train service.

At approximately 11pm, whilst lounging on the couch, I discovered that there had recently been a terrorist attack on London Bridge. A white rental van ploughed along the bridge, deliberately mowing down several people. individuals then descended from the vehicle to violently stab the helpless victims on the ground. The terrorists then raided bars and restaurants, to horrifically prey on their targets, by shooting and wounding them. I was feeling a little freaked out, when this atrocity unfolded before me on the television, because I was only there, not so long ago. I originally planned to stop overnight in London, but I didn't due to travelling to Blackpool the following day. I could have easily been a target today if I was still there. I know that I was in Walthamstow and not anywhere near the London Bridge, but this could have happened particularly on the tubes or at The Empire Cinema. I am very lucky. Seven victims were confirmed dead at the scene, whilst three suspects were shot dead by the police. My heart goes out to the victims and their families.

I sent my animation through to three film festivals - "The London Short Film Festival 2018" and "The Manchester Animation Film Festival." I didn't have any luck with being selected. However, on Monday 17th July 2017, it was screened at "The Drunken Film Festival" based at a venue called Home Brewed, in Bradford, organised by the brilliant Jax Griffin.

Arbitrary Journal Excerpts

Monday 10th November 2008

Working on two university projects was stressing me out, so I decided to take a break and go out for a walk along the canal with Aishling. It was absolutely freezing as we set off on our journey. It was fairly light when we started to walk but the winter night gradually settled in. It was a bitter feeling to stroll along the canal without a single light in sight. The only captivation we got was the beam of the lamp posts shining above us on the roadside but eventually they disappeared. We passed three strangers, dressed in black, sitting on a bench. They seemed unusual. Everything was appearing to look darker, but we were too terrified to turn back due to these three strangers. We wanted to know where the rowing club was, as we were told it was based along the canal. They was no sign of it anywhere, and we wondered if we took a wrong turn. The walk gradually led us into an abundance of long sweeping grass, passing dark ginnels. Just in case you don't live in the north, a "ginnel" is a term for "alleyway" and this is what my fellow students had learnt of when they move here in Leicester. Aishling thought I was referring to a guinea pig as "ginnel" sounded like "guinea." We passed derelict mills with their lights on, the further we went. There was a thudding noise coming from one of the buildings. It sounded like someone playing on a drum set. Aishling described this journey as something out of The Saw films. There was no light at this point. We didn't know whether to take a left or right turn. I suggested that we should take the right turn because I noticed a shine of light in the distance. Ahead of us was a man and his dog. He had a vibrant stench of tobacco. We cautiously passed by him then quickened our paces. The man and dog went walking in the woods. All we could hear was the dog's collar jingling and this was when we got our mobile phones out ready to dial 999 because they seemed to keep stopping in the tracks. Aishling kept on getting visions of us of both on the front of the national newspapers with the headline "TWO MISSING!" Luckily, we discovered an extremely busy causeway which was based at the end of a quiet street. We decided to head in this direction. It is better to be safe than sorry, I suppose. We were so shook up that we laughed hysterically about the situation. We found our own way home in the end. Jean, a fellow student and friend, told us that the police had cordoned off parts of the local area as they had discovered a dead body in the canal. Our walk wasn't that much of a frantic ordeal because I guess, if you was at my age, a young student, you would envision this whole experience as a thrilling adventure. Although I will admit that I shitted myself during that walk!

I immediately told my family about the walk. My grandma told me about an experience she had when she was at my Uncle Rodney's house based in Manchester. She decided to take a walk with my great grandma Gertrude, who was her mum. The stroll gradually descended into darkness. Pitch black. Just like mine and Aishling's experience, my grandma saw a man smoking a cigarette in the distance. She was absolutely shitting herself, but she had to pass him as this was the only direction back home. They arrived back at my Uncle Rodney's safely, mind. I did express our walk as part of a painting project during the time.

Friday 4th December 2015

I performed as a guest poet at Jolene Rae Walshe's event "Let's Get Real" based at The Huddersfield Hat Festival, in a unique, quirky shop in The Byram Arcade. I performed "30 Pence To Have A Piss?!" "Monobrow!!" and "He'll Be Carrying a Suitcase." The first guest poet was the brilliant Marina Poppa.

Saturday 12th December 2015

I performed a twenty-minute set of my anecdotes at a scratch type event called "Verbal." The event was based at The Banks Art Centre in Sheffield and was curated by Hayley Alessi. She has an artist residency at the premises. I performed my verses such as "Monobrow!!" "30 Pence To Have A Piss?!" "Mr Quakers, My Man," "Thankyou Special K" and a few more. I met with the other artists who were performing that night and they were very talented indeed. I was congratulated on my delivery and rhythmical style by a husband and wife called Paul and Sue Casson. The two also performed a rehearsed reading of a script, composed by a writer, which is still in progress. Paul was part of an ensemble in the Tim Piggott Smith's adaptation of "Richard III" at The Playhouse. Another poet named Dan Horrigan, also admired my material. Hayley mentioned to me that she wanted me to perform at a London event which she curates, although she didn't say anything about it. Hayley loved my set and has asked me to come back to a future verbal event which I will definitely accept.

I caught the 10:20pm fast train back to Leeds and then a second train from Leeds to Batley.

Thursday 28th January 2016

I had a little tour around London for a good couple of hours and then returned back to The Elmwood Hotel to freshen up for tonight. I am going to be performing at "Bang Said The Gun" based at The Bloomsbury Theatre. I performed "30 Pence To Have A Piss?!" to an enthusiastic audience. I didn't win the Golden Gun Award, mind. Laurie Bolger was the evenings compere. I returned back to the hotel after a Burger King meal. I returned back to Yorkshire the next day on the 10:11am train service from London Kings Cross.

Thursday 28th April 2016

I performed my anecdotes "The Egotistical Jeremy Kyle" and "Monobrow!!" at "The LUU Spoken Word Society", based at The Fenton in Leeds.

Saturday 21st May 2016

At 2:05pm, I caught the train to London, as I will be performing a twelve-minute set of my whimsical anecdotes in Covent Garden, based at a posh venue called "The Library". The event is called "The Shag." I performed verses such as "I've Falllen in Love with Mr Muscle!" "30 Pence To Have A Piss?!" and "He'll Be Carrying a Suitcase." I stayed at The Central Station, which is a gay bar and hotel, not far from Kings Cross station. On Sunday 22nd May 2016, I headed back home on the 11:05am train service to Leeds then hopped onto the 229 bus service back to Batley. I decided on having a break from gigging and screening my short films throughout the remainder of the summer. I have fresh new material which I will be publicly sharing when I feel ready to present them. I subsequently submerged back into depression, cowing under a foreboding cloud. I've had the feelings of worthlessness and oppressiveness and also wanted to attack my bedroom using violence, though I never went through with it. I didn't frankly give a shit, to be perfectly honest with you.

Saturday 8th July 2017

I caught the long tedious train journey to Newton Abbot from Leeds, on the 6am service. The journey took approximately five hours. Arriving at Newton Abbot, I jumped into a taxi to Fairfield Farm in Denbury, a 3.2 mile journey costing an astonishing £10.00 taxi fare. Robert Garnham asked if I wanted to perform at "The Glas-Denbury Festival" with the Stanza Extravaganza set, a good few months ago. I feel greatly honoured to be asked and I agreed. I felt extremely surreal and borderline anxious whilst travelling here on the train. This was triggered by pre-performance fears and nerves. The adrenaline was quite overwhelming. I have noticed that my anxiety has triggered a little and I am experiencing the minor effects of hallucinations. I wasn't physically hallucinating but I had the mental impact of it. I've been intensely working on my forthcoming stop motion animation titled "Nose Job" which is the possible source of my developing anxiety. I'm feeling lethargic and a little nauseous with the juxtaposition of emotions that I'm experiencing.

I arrived at Fairfield Farm at approximately 11:30am. I made my way to the Pucker Poets stage where I subsequently performed a ten-minute set of my whimsical anecdotes. The stage was based in a quirky, petite marquee with satin draped around the one foot high stage. I opened up my intimate set with "Nose Job" which was a debut live performance. "I've Sold My Wife on Ebay," "MANBUN," and "OCD" were the anecdotes which followed. The other poets who performed within our group were Robert Garnham, Melanie Barton and the whizz of adrenaline, Tim Vosper. The blistering sun radiantly beamed down, barbecuing the region with its Mediterranean bliss. It was your typical traditional festival with various activities and artistry. Sean Hughes, a famous panellist on "Never Mind The Buzzcocks" performed also on the Pucker Poets stage from 2pm until 3:15pm. Obviously he drew in quite a large crowd. Glas-Denbury was an enjoyable experience.

I have spent the last two hours sitting on the platform at Newton Abbot train station. A carnival march pierced its way through the streets, whilst I watched on from a distance. I caught the 7:04pm train service to Leeds and then a taxi from Leeds to Batley. I eventually arrived home at 1am.

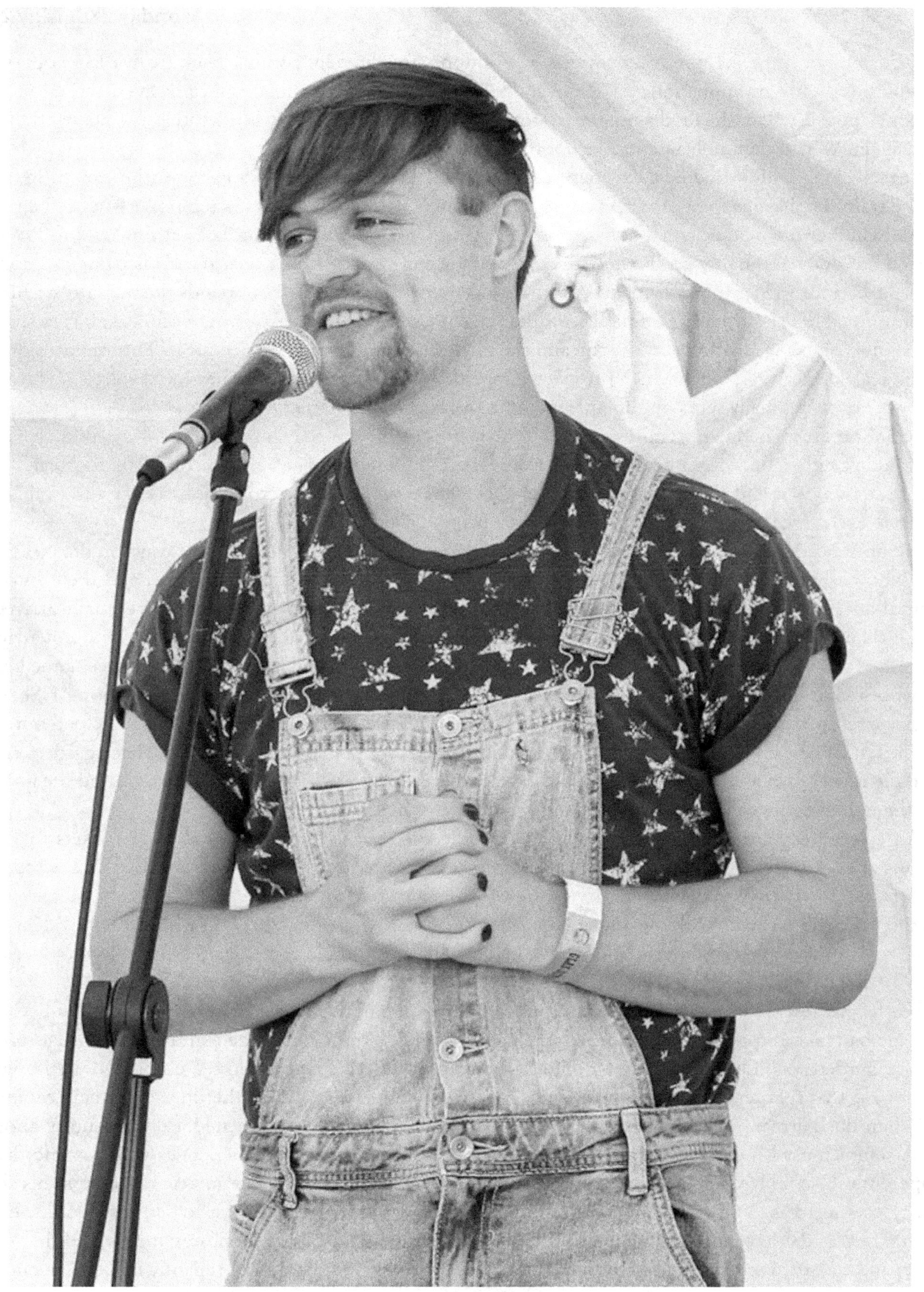

Performing my anecdotes at "Glas-Denbury"
- July 2017

Monday 28th May 2018

I am currently on the 2:15pm train service to London, after literally coming back from Blackpool. I am screening my current animation, "A Peculiar Imagination," at the intimate Skylark event based at Sam Hackings house, where she kindly put me up for the evening. The intensely hot weather is cracking the flags once again. Well, it definitely was in Blackpool. It's a little overcast here.

I'm speaking with a middle-aged man wearing a shirt and waistcoat, sitting opposite me at the table on the train. He has his ipad on display watching a film. The food bar on was temporarily closed and the debate whether it would open or not was on the agenda. He was initially booked on the York to London service but due to a fatality on the line, they were diverting services to York. I think his name is Thomas. He is a freelance trainer in performance, attitude and social being. He said he spends the majority of his life dashing for trains. Fourteen years he has worked in his practice. We spoke about various subjects such as my passion of being an adrenaline junkie and the thrills that stimulate the strive for it. Thomas lives on top of the Dalek apartment block which provides him with a fantastic panoramic view of Leeds city centre and beyond. He occasionally rents out his apartment to producers and film companies as a location setting for a video shoot. He loaned the premises out to a female musician, where she used the flat for her music video. He couldn't remember the name of the musician. He also rented his flat out to a couple of footballers. He made the two hour and fifteen-minute journey feel like a sweeping sail across the sea. The time vanished. We have exchanged contacts, in hope that we can keep in touch.

We both headed down to Kings Cross tube station, where we parted our separate ways on the Northern line. Thomas went southbound and I went northbound. Changing at Liverpool Street and then onto the Central line, I made it into Loughton, fifty minutes later at approximately 5:45pm. I eventually arrived at Sam Hacking's address after getting a little lost on foot to Bloomsbury Road. I had a shower upon arriving to freshen up when I knocked on the door and was greeted by Sam and also her Italian fiance named Marco, who was in the kitchen cooking up a feast of vegetarian delights for this evening's edition of Skylark. He is currently working as a chef at a restaurant based on Brick Lane. His best friend also helped out with the buffet, which was presented beautifully, outside on a wooden table in the decorative back garden. A fire candidly flickered in a chiminea. A couple of shielded candles were lit in various places around the garden, creating an intimate, welcoming vibe for the evening.

An eclectic assortment of staged performance filled the garden, ranging from acoustic sets to visual readings and film screenings, which were projected onto the garden wall beside the cabin. We waited for dusk to fall for the screenings. Natalia was the first artist to perform to the intimate crowd of about ten people, with her beautiful mellow, Italian vocals. One of her songs included "The Moon Song." Kayleigh loved this number and often performed the song herself on her ukulele. Natalia did invite her to duet with her, but she didn't.

Kayleigh presented an array of collages which contained mindfulness writing combined with visuals that she had pieced together, using ripped up pages of various magazines. She exhibited the visuals on the outside garden wall. Dimitri also performed a beautiful but powerful acoustic set, combined with original cover songs. Sam H read out a beautiful fantasy story, as we all huddled together in the candlelit cabin.

When dusk arrived, the film screenings commenced. Sam Holloway screened a documentary about a black senior musician called Clive, who spoke openly about his personal experiences with sex and drugs. Apparently, his family was bewildered about the fact that he collects stray cats and stores them in his shed. Thirty cats in total. As a musician, his audience compared him to Seal. I have to say, his vocals weren't strong, but he did have interesting husky, rippling tones in his voice. Sam Holloway mentioned that Clive wrote and recorded ten songs in a day, which is a fully loaded album. It was a brilliantly intricate documentary.

Daniella was the next artist to screen her short comedy film about a zookeeper educating a class of two, on a pet weasel. The film was shot in a classroom. Daniella mentioned that she initially she had twenty students present in the classroom but one by one, they all dropped out. The comedy was made more amusing, since a very optimistic schoolteacher was saying at the beginning, "Well, are we all excited about today's zookeeping class?" The remaining two students were perched at the table with deadpan expressions. This is what the comedy needed, the disappointment of not winning round a full class of animal enthusiasts. Daniella, the zookeeper, was a good friend of Kayleigh. They both recently performed collaboratively in a live comedy show together titled "The Jerry Hall Show," which was staged in Brighton. I said to Daniella that they both should tour their show in Leeds at the Leeds Playhouse or The Live Art Bistro. She said they would definitely think about it.

Last, but not least, it was time for me to screen my experimental animation, "A Peculiar Imagination," which received positive feedback. I spoke a little bit about the process of creating the piece as a developing montage of illustrations that lived in my sketchbook. I also mentioned that I wanted to merge live footage with animation, to add more diversity to my work. As an artist I feel it is massively important to experiment with individual concepts, in order to create something fresh and original. Sam H asked if I thought about working with colour, which I have done in previous projects. I added that having my work specifically produced in black and white, gave the animation that classic, vintage noir characteristic. I have always been fascinated by simple shades, which can produce a vibrant result.

We all gathered together in the candlelit cabin for a group photo to complete this evening's edition of Skylark. Natalie and Dimitri commended me for my animations. We exchanged contact details because they were keen to see more of my work. Likewise. It was such a brilliant evening. Congratulations to each and every one those who showcased or attended. Sam H let me sleep over for the night, to save me splashing out on a hotel in London. I slept in the front bedroom. I wrote in my journal for a good ten minutes and then retired to sleep.

Tuesday 12th March 2019

I headed to The Verve Bar in Leeds this evening to watch and support the delightful Nina at the comedy open mic night. I arrived at the dimly lit quiet venue at approximately 7:45pm, based on Merrion Street, grabbed myself a cola and sat at the bar waiting for Nina and her stocky black male friend to arrive. They did, a subsequent five or so minutes later. I had a brief chat with a middle-aged comedienne who came from Hull, for this evening's comedy night. Her name is Ann. She was the first comedian to grace the intimate funky basement stage. Apparently, Ann has been temporarily absent from the comedy scene although I don't know the reason why. We were briefly chatting at the bar and that is when Nina and Ramone arrived. Nina was the second act to take the mic and she was brilliant. She opened up her set with a few Brexit jokes and then continued to explain how she applied for the television show "Gladiators" but wasn't physically fit at the time. I thoroughly enjoyed her ten-minute delivery and had no doubt about it. She is a natural comic anyway. I have asked Nina if she would be interested in being a support act for my "Live and Animated" show (which you will later read about in this book.) She instantly agreed. This evening's comedy event was hosted by a rather handsome impersonator, I am struggling to remember his name - I am wanting to say Charlie Connors or Chris Connors but I have no idea. If I find someone physically attractive, I immediately look up their names on all social media platforms.

JOURNAL PAUSE: Although I do not do this now. I am happily spoken for!

He was extremely talented. Any renowned individual that the audience would call out, he would imminently impersonate someone with the most incredible resemblance. I bid farewell to Nina and Ramone at 10:30pm, heading back home in the blustery, showery weather. It was the longest walk home I had ever undertaken since moving to Leeds.

Thursday 16th May 2019

I performed two of my whimsical anecdotes "Monobrow!!" and "Mr Kipling" on the open mic section at the event, Outspoken, this evening, based at The LS6 Cafe. I was the second performer to grace the microphone, soon after the interval ended. As a typical artist, I was forever undecided on which anecdotes to perform. It was brilliant to see my friend, Annie, arrive as a supportive members of the audience. We hugged. It was good to meet Bernadette O' Horro. She performed a rap about hard guys cavorting their ill-mannered ways with their hands down their pants. When she was leaving the venue, I told her how fresh out of prison guys with their hands down their pants aroused me. It was a type of fetish I had although I wouldn't choose them as part of a committed relationship.

"I'll think of you Jamie, whenever I perform it again," She laughed, as she left the cafe with her friend Simon Pickles.

Simon performed a deep, personal poem based on alcoholism and drug addiction, which was profoundly written and delivered from the heart. It was a treat to see Kevin perform his "Cloth Cap Rap" poem again. Laurence arrived at the event penultimately after finishing work. He concluded the event with a live delivery of his artistry.

Prior to the open mic section, there were three poets who delivered a fifteen-minute set each. These being Roz Weaver, Jonathan Eyre, who I previously know from Wicked Words based at The Seven Art Centre in Chapel Allerton, and the delicately formed Laura Potts. Outspoken began at 7:30pm, concluding at 9:40pm, based upstairs in the terrace.

Annie, Laurence and I stayed for a quick drink post show, before leaving Annie to walk Laurence to the bus stop. We hugged each other goodbye as I headed back home by foot.

Monday 27th May 2019

I performed four of my whimsical anecdotes just before 1pm at a twelve-Hour charity open mic event based at The Cuckoo Bar on Calls Lane in Leeds. The anecdotes which I delivered to a fairly petite audience were "Thank you Special K," "The Granny Zimmer frame Race," "Man Bun" and "Thirty Pence to Have a Piss?!" It was lovely to have Nina support me in the audience. I was really appreciative of her cycling into the city from Armley in the drizzly weather. I arrived at the venue at approximately 11:40am with Nina arriving fifty or so minutes later and leaving at 1:30pm. Two female Kate Nash-esque personalities performed their ten-minute humorous acoustic sets. They were the comperes for the subsequent two hours. It was good to see poets Yvonne Ugarte and Phil Pearce again. The Cuckoo Bar is a quirky spacious venue. Audience members would come and leave whenever they felt the need to throughout the day.

Monday 3rd Febraury 2020

When I finished a 10am 'til 6pm shift at the box office, Laurence and I headed over to Lisa's flat at 6:30pm. At approximately 7pm, we headed to Seven Arts based in Chapel Allerton in a cab, for this evening's edition of "Are You Vocal?" which was based in the cafe foyer. The evening was hosted by the one and only Jack Collins, commencing at 8:15pm and concluding at approximately 9:40pm. Another poet by the name of Bethany Rose, joined our company, as we perched at a table about ten yards from the microphone. Jack opened the event with a boisterous, lyrical piece of his, subsequently welcoming twelve open mic performers for the evening. Laurence and Lisa performed their lyrical compositions during the first half. Bethany recited a few of her poems, based primarily on mental health. I opened up the second half performing two of my whimsical anecdotes titled "Big Knickers Rule" and "Man Bun." It was a really interesting evening. A young Hull based poet called Luke Cable closed the event with his larger than life personality and stage presence. He was extremely entertaining.

We headed back into Leeds in a cab when the event finished, dropping me off outside House 2020. Laurence and Lisa kindly walked me to the end of Regent Street, before bidding each other goodnight. I returned home at 10:30pm, testing the projector which I hired out from the Playhouse this afternoon, in preparation for tomorrow evening's performance at Platform 1, based in Manchester. I very briefly rehearsed the animations "Fleas" and "Man Bun."

Tuesday 4th February 2020

I worked a 10am until 2pm shift at the box office with Laurence, Nina, Lynn and Terri. I then quickly ventured upstairs to iron my cotton, cream shirt in the wardrobe department, in preparation for my 3pm interview, based at Yorkshire Dance, which I felt went very well. The visit lasted for about thirty-five minutes, beginning with a short tour of the building with Lauren Clarke, concluding with an interview with herself and Laura Homer.

I then headed to Leeds train station with a projector in my bag and a laptop, to catch the twenty minute delayed 4:17pm Northern Service to Manchester Victoria. I arrived in the city at 6:10pm. I then made the 1.2-mile radius walk to The Electrik Box, where I was going to perform alongside my animations, as a special guest, at an event called Platform 1. The event is based upstairs, in a lukewarm dim lit space. The venue is part of a very hipster but small scaled Covent Garden style commune called Hatch, very close to Manchester Oxford Train Station. It was full house this evening, predominantly made up of music students. The compere, John Darwin, opened up the first half with an open mic. There were poets I had previously met including Anna Percy, Mark Jackson, John Calvert and a load of others, who were going to perform or recite their original material. After a ten-minute intermission, at approximately 9pm, John Darwin introduced me to the mic. All prepared for my eighteen-minute set, I performed on a small wooden chair, where my animations were projected on to a pale white wall. I also performed an impromptu delivery of "Thirty Pence to Have a Piss?!" I concluded my set with my experimental animation "A Peculiar Imagination." I received a contribution of £40.00 for appearing at Platform 1. The event concluded at 9:45pm.

The following day, on Wednesday 5th February 2020, I ventured down to Coventry, to perform two of my anecdotes "Man Bun" and "The Day My Gran Rode a Rollercoaster" at "Fire and Dust" during the second half of the event, based at The Big Comfy Bookshop. I introduced the second poem, by asking if they were any daredevil grandmas in the audience. A tall middle-aged woman raised her hand at the back of the room. Unfortunately, she wasn't a fan of the crazy thrill machines, but it is an ode to them anyway. It was brilliant to see Scott Healey aka Dangermouse this evening, who read a couple of poems from his phone and array of other poets too. Dave Pitt based in Wolverhampton, was this evening's headliner.

A gentleman named Laurence G. Tilley, aged in his sixties, approached me when the event concluded at 10pm. He mentioned that materially and physically my witty style reminded him of the Music Hall era. He asked me if I had ever heard of a whimsy piece titled "Old Sam's Christmas Pudding" by Stanley Holloway. I hadn't heard of it at the time, but I do now. Laurence smiled that my work had some artistic similarities to Stanley Holloway's. I did mention that my great-grandad Schofield was a musical hall performer, whether the credible spirit is being channelled through me.

It was nice to be returning to The Highcroft Guest House Hotel this evening, as opposed to commuting back to Leeds via coach, come midnight. I returned to Leeds the next day on Thursday 6th February 2020, on the 12:40pm National Express service, changing coaches in Birmingham.

Sunday 23rd February 2020

At approximately 5:30pm, I ventured out to the Valentines Fun Fair for the third time this week. It was based opposite Woodhouse Moor, a five-minute walk from North Lodge House. Afterwards, I quickly returned home to change my coat and trousers for this evening's edition of "Spoken Word and Other Stuff" based at The Hyde Park Book Club. I had to refuel myself with much needed adrenaline, so thrill seeking, being my favourite activity, was the best course of action for this.

I arrived at the pretty heaving Hyde Park Book Club at 6:40pm. I purchased a cup of tea and sat down at a table. I subsequently met Trevor Wainwright and Nicky J. Rae, who is trying to inspire a hugging revolution, where individuals would embrace for 20 seconds, to prevent any affliction of mental health. Nicky is a beautiful soul. It was brilliant to see the compere again, Jack Collins, who had a major flashback when he remembered seeing me perform at an open mic event back in October 2015, based downstairs at The LS6 Cafe. The second anecdote I performed this evening was my signature piece "Thirty Pence to Have a Piss?!" It was my delivery of this which spellbound him five years ago. I opened up my five-minute set with my anecdote "Fleas!" During the first interval, I had a poet by the name of Zavar Ahmed honouring me with his compliments on my delivery as a performance poet. He suggested that I should begin to capture my gig experience as a vlogger. This is an interesting concept which I will consider for the near future but recording my experiences on a piece of hand crafted perforated paper is what I think I do best. I bid farewell to everyone during the second interval at 10pm.

My animation, "A Peculiar Imagination," was screened at an event called "Squat Betty Avant Garde Film Night" based in Bethnal Green in London this evening. Obviously, I didn't attend as I was performing my whimsies here in Leeds.

Saturday 17th October 2020

Marc and I arrived at Tatton Park, Cheshire at approximately 11:10am where I planned to experience a three-hundred-foot bungee jump shortly after midday. We parked close by the activity site, where a three-hundred-foot crane towered over a tranquil lake. It was an extremely autumnal, chilly day. I was experiencing an abundance of emotions; exhilaration, married with a slight tingle of nerves but collectively, this channelled a surge of adrenaline, which was the perfect mood for me. After completing the final registration, being weighed on the scales and then harnessed up with the appropriate equipment, I was roped onto the blue cage, where Joe, my instructor, introduced himself to me as we gradually ascended into the sky. Marc witnessed my fuelled adrenaline experience from the ground, as he filmed for my vlog. I slowly made my way to the edge of the cage, as Joe directed me to do so, after recapping the safety guidelines once again. I held both of my arms out, focusing on the vision of the distant horizon.

"You have got this," Joe mentioned, subsequently counting me down from three to one. With immediate effect and without hesitation, I dived out of the cage, plunging into the three-hundred feet drop towards the lake below and projected a deep, vehement scream. The fall was incredibly immense, as I dropped with weightless velocity. It felt like my whole anatomy had detached itself from the safety harness. There is something satisfying about this adventure. I admire how your body feels out of control and in the sudden grasp of gravity. Even though I have experienced an incredible fifteen-thousand-foot skydive in Hibaldstow, Lincolnshire, back in May 2015, today's bungee Jump was crowned the best junkie activity I have ever done. It was simply incredible. Also, with Marc actually being there today support me, I was forever appreciative of his company.

A week passed by and on Sunday 25th October 2020, I had my second bungee jump from a slightly lower height of 160 feet at Salford Quays. Marc came along to support me. I completed a registration form and was then harnessed up securely by the brilliant UK Bungee Club team, before ascending into the autumnal skyline. Marc filmed from the ground, to capture the experience for a miniature vlog, and a second camera was mounted on the upper rail of the cage. After the famous four words "3, 2, 1, BUNGEEEEEEEE!" I made the 160-foot drop towards the rippling river below, and I projected a vehement masculine scream. The physical ethereal, sensation of plunging at speed is an extremely, satisfying fulfilment. Today's bungee jump was approximately at 2:40pm. When I had completed the plunge, Marc and I drove to The Beaumont Arms pub based in Huddersfield, for a three course meal, in an outdoor tee pee. We returned to his cottage shortly before 6pm.

I am extremely excited to be participating in further bungee jumps in spring 2021. These will be a 160-foot plunge off the Middlesbrough Transporter Bridge and a 400-foot plunge over a serene quarry, based at The National Diving and Activity Centre in Cheptstow.

Thursday 29th October 2020

I sat upstairs in Wapentake this afternoon, after meeting Lynn and her grandson at San CoCo. I later saw Jo with her friends, Ian, Martin and Alan. I have met Ian before but not the other two. It was a lovely surprise to see her. And also of course, the elderly, scraggly looking man who perches on the leather couch with his sewn-up trousers and his bag full of books, newspapers and a hidden bottle of Vodka. He comes to Wapentake every Thursday and sits in that exact same place. Jo and I first saw him a good couple of months ago, when he was bizarrely drying out his newspaper on the radiator and his cloth cap which rested on the breezy window ledge. Jo had the urge to knock his cloth cap out of the window, although she didn't. We have decided to name him Boggle Troth, due to his somewhat lack of appearance.

"Oh yes, he looks like a Boggle Troth," Jo sniggered, with her pint of Stroganoff. We always have a comedic name for everyone, including Gypsy Horse Woman, whom we met during a Playhouse community tour of "Around the World in Eighty Days" back in the spring of 2019. The name being because she supposedly had an Irish traveller heritage, even though she is multi-national. She once rescued a herd of apprehensive horses from a maggot farm, which was unfortunately flooded by a river in Yorkshire. This woman was originally named Emma Mellor, but she subsequently changed it to Sapphire Hunter. From what she was telling Jo and I at the time of us meeting her, she had such a horrifically abusive life, which I will not go into because it isn't my place to share. I mean some of the things she was telling us were extreme, so we didn't know what was actually true.

"Then a week after," Jo laughed as I did too. "He (being me) saw Gypsy Horse Woman rolling around the floor in Leeds in just her knickers!" She was also wearing a t shirt but that doesn't even justify the bottom half. It was brilliant as always to see Jo and meet with her friends. Boggle Troth kept on glancing over at our table with a frown.

"He keeps looking at me," Jo discreetly murmured, pulling a face at him when he looked down at the newspaper. I then kept on suggesting that he is provocatively licking his lips for her.

"Stop it!" Jo responded. She had a shift at The Playhouse from 6:15pm.

Friday 6th November 2020

The time is currently 9:10pm and I am perched in the armchair at Marc's cottage. We returned from Meghan and Andre's house based on Edgeware Road in Leeds, where we sat and ate chicken soup beside a crackling fire with John, Kate (both who I only met this afternoon) and Meghan. I met a foreign man by the name of CoCo, who mostly stayed in the house whilst Andre served up the food. Marc only arrived at approximately 5:30pm, after coming from Pat's bungalow. It was a lovely afternoon. Kate resides in Saltaire and she is a former student from Oxford University. She was born and raised in Japan until she was 12 years of age. She immigrated to Surrey, where she continues to live in the UK. She also keeps a consistent journal. She once burnt an entry which expressed her jealousy and apprehension. It was a way to disintegrate negative feelings and produce free spirited energy. My journals, however, are my sacred sanctuary. They are a reflective self-portrait for me to understand who I am through lapses of time. John, I would say, is in his late fifties, a very philosophical gentlemen, with a profound interest in body movement. He works with Meghan as a masseur or something along this wavelength. It was brilliant to see Meghan and Andre again, as I arrived at their terraced house at 2:30pm. Prior to this, I met Nina in town to hand over "The Lighthouse" Art print which she purchased from me. It was displayed in a black frame with a light cream mount. She is honoured to own a piece of original artwork that is made by me and I am extremely appreciative of her support.

Saturday 9th January 2021

Marc, myself, Danny, Jane and Dean ventured out for a bitterly, bracing hike from midday with the dogs. We went through the rolling farmland and country lanes in the areas of Rawthorpe and Kirkheaton, Huddersfield. Jane carried a bottle of prosecco in her backpack, though I stuck to coffee. I recordered myself performing my anecdote "The Granny Zimmerframe Race" whilst on the stroll. Snow began to fall when we reached Kirkheaton.

Saturday 16th January 2021

After several attempts I managed to accomplish Spike Milligan's tongue twisting rhyme, "On The Ning Nang Nong," and performed the piece perched on a dinky 1960's chair, on Marc's homely landing. I have always been fond of this classic verse, hoping that someday, I'll be able to deliver my own rendition to a live audience.

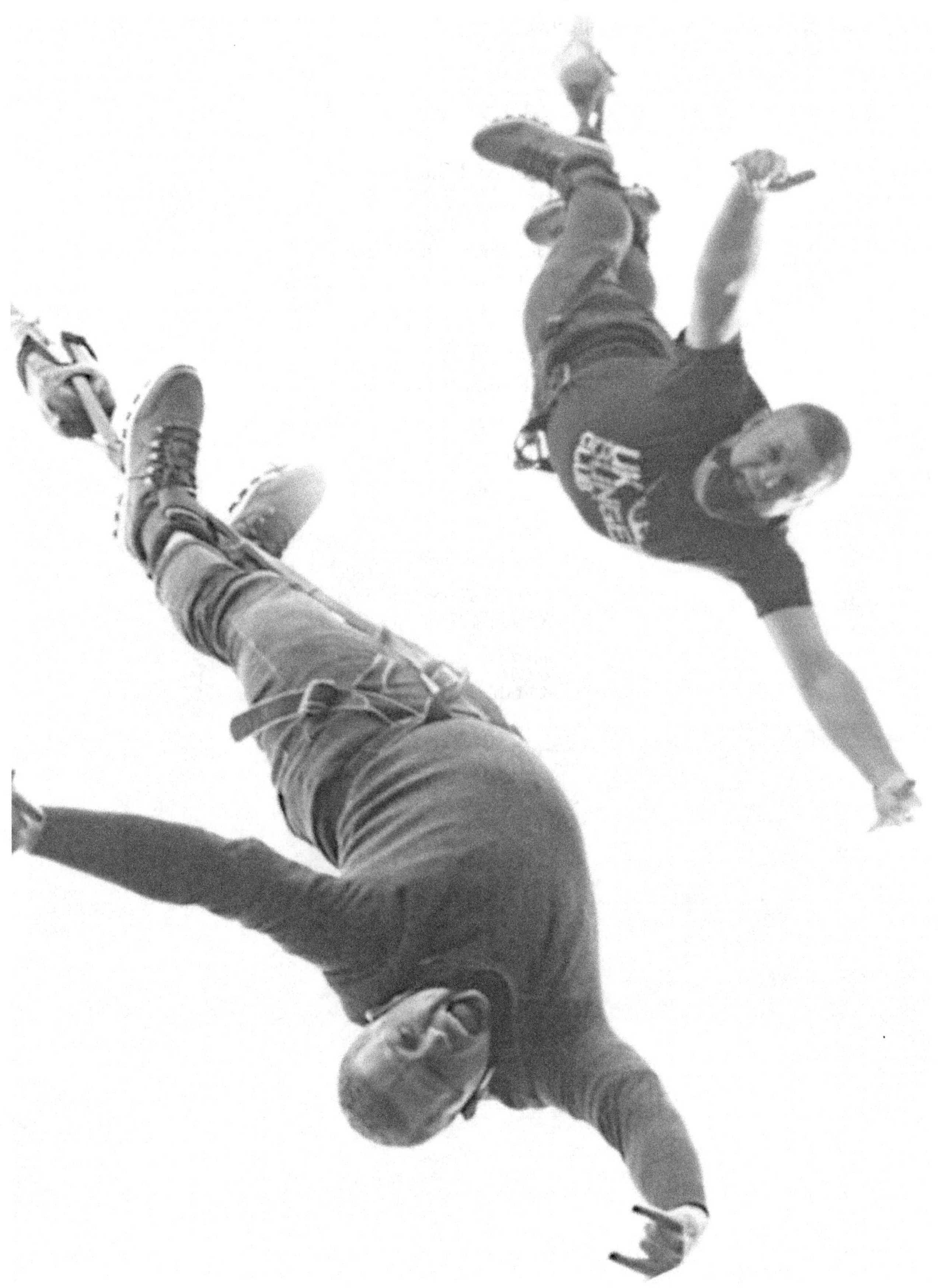

(Left) *300ft Bungee Jump - Tatton Park, Cheshire.*
(Right Top) *160ft Bungee Jump - Salford Quays.*

This following poem is from the perspective of an elderly wife, who is fed up of her husband's idleness.

Just As I Sat Down

He's feeding the ducks,
He's left the house a mess,
I'll surely guarantee,
He will try his best,
To come walking in,
With a grin on his face,
Helping to everything,
And taking my place!
He came walking in,
As I took a nap,
He sniggered a grin,
As he took off his cap,
He offered me a walk,
On the Pennine Hills,
Just as I sat down,
Well, he wants me,
On my heels!
He'll make it all alright,
And leave it all to me,
And come by tomorrow,
I'll be back on my feet!

Chubby Lollipop Lady

Oh, our dear Lollipop Lady,
She is chubby and minute,
Well, if you can call her a lady,
The way she bollocks car queues.
"'Ere, get back you bastard,
The Lights are on red!
Have I got chubby woman dead,
Written all over my sweaty head?"
"Ey up, where's your legs love?"
A driver laughed out loud,
Her wrinkly face melted,
And she never made a sound.
"GIVE ME BACK MY LOLLIPOP!"
She scuttled down the road,
Hop along hop,
Just piss off you stew and dumplin' toad!

Over the last thirteen years, I have had the fabulous opportunity of performing my whimsical anecdotes at many prestigious spoken word events throughout the United Kingdom. My debut gig was on Wednesday 11th June 2008, at a spin off local event called "Batley's Got Talent" based at the then Frontier Nightclub in Batley. I nearly bottled out at first because my nerves were overwhelming me. All my family met me at The Frontier, including my aunty Jenny, grandma, mum, dad, sister, Chloe and two brothers, Joshua and Liam. I checked in at the foyer and waited at the right-hand side of the stage. There were approximately 160 people in the audience. When waiting backstage, I was given a microphone, as I prepared to brace myself to face the local audience. My name was called, I took a deep breath and led myself to the edge of the raised platform and delivered my material. I commenced my five-minute set with an original anecdote of mine titled "Larry Ain't Amused," a rendition of Alan Ahlberg's poem "Please Mrs Butler." The second and final anecdote of mine was titled "Our Grandma and Grandad." My performance was complimented by the judges, who sailed me through to the finals, at the end of the following week. My experience on this stage gave me confidence to do more. This allowed me to take my original writings to the poetry circuit and it allowed me to meet and befriend some fantastic creatives alike along the journey. The gigs of my early days following Batley's Got Talent included "Red Shed Readings" held in literally a red wooden shed in Wakefield on Thursday 2nd April 2009. Whilst the elderly audience members were reciting their own poetry about how lavish flowers are, I performed my anecdote, "Just As I Sat Down" and a second piece about a "Chubby Lollipop Lady," in a rather animated fashion. I participated in another open mic event called "Letterbomb" based at The Milo Bar in Leeds, on Wednesday 15th April 2009. I also travelled to Birmingham from Leicester, with three of my female friends at the end of my first year at university in May 2009. This was for an event named "Autentertainment" at The Red Lounge Bar.

Wednesday 1st April 2009

I was discovered by *Autentertainment* in Birmingham. They were apparently impressed with my talent in creating and performing comic poetry performances and I was invited to perform at their venue. I phoned up the compere and recited to him, "Larry Ain't Amused" whilst I was in my student accommodation at Waterway Gardens. He then booked me in to perform live on the 3rd May. I was ecstatic with this invitation.

Sunday 3rd May 2009

I had a performance tonight, at Autentertainment, based at The Red Lounge Bar. It was hilarious getting there. We, myself and three female friends, phoned a taxi because we had to get to Leicester train station within ten minutes. We all piled into the back of the car. When we reached the train station, we threw our fare at the driver and went colliding with each other as we clambered out of the car. I was sitting next to the door, so I was nearly pushed out onto the pavement, whilst the rest were pushing themselves out. We galloped to get our tickets and managed to catch our train in time.

My performance went extremely well, although we thought we were at the wrong venue, as it appeared to be so posh. On our way out of the venue, an Irish lady came up to me and told me how much she admired my performance and my comical poems. She invited me to perform my work at Glee Radio Station, which is connected to the event. I think it is based here, in Birmingham.

I recall phoning Elaine, which was her name, in the summer of 2009. I had a really long, pleasant chat, whilst settled in the living room in Batley, mentioning that I was still interested in delivering my anecdotes on Glee Radio. She explained that the radio show was on a slight break but had my name in mind in case the show was ever recommenced. I never heard from her again.

On the evening of Thursday 13th May 2010, I performed my whimscial anecdotes "He'll Be Carrying Suitcase," "Larry Ain't Amused" and Alan Ahlberg's "Please Mrs Butler" at a table candlelit scratch event called "Emergency" based at The Y Theatre in Leicester. The evnt concluded with a Q&A session with the audience. A woman commented that I seem slightly angry in the way that my deliver. I did perform a poem about an ex-boyfriend of mine, so the my vexation was definitely there but I was extremely juvenile and I did develop bad habits of of the various artists that I aspired to be. Shortly before commencing my third year at university, I performed at The Pheonix Arts Centre based in Leicester on Tuesday 7th September 2010.

BADLY BEHAVED BABY

Me' mam and dad, hand in hand, walking out of the front door,
I'm perched dribbling on the nappy filled floor,
Me' gran strolls in sipping on her treacle tea,
"What have we got here, Nanny McPhee?"

She picks me up and fastens me in the pram,
Cackling like Dracula "Who's a big man?"
I ain't a man, I'm merely a kid,
Your own four-legged crawling bothersome squid!

I'm sat in the highchair at our local caf',
I try and get giddy and make me' gran laugh,
Half o' the time I'm cranky when she breaks out in song,
That's when I tell her to go and "GET ON!"

Well, I don't want a dose of her ancient witchery shriek,
Her dentures are deteriorating; She's badly boned cheeks,
When she doesn't give me my yummy, tummy food,
I spit out my dummy and "YELL" in a mood!

I'm on my best behaviour, in my manic bouncy chair,
But I seem to bounce higher when my gran ain't there,
Zipping back and forth like a plastic bemused yoyo,
Whilst nibbling on the ear on my toy teddy JoJo!

Well, I know when it is time to go up to bed,
I seem to sit awake and then flip back my head,
My grandma will waste all of her breath narrating The Wind in the Willows,
And the next thing she knows; I'm sick on the pillows!

Tuesday 7th September 2010

I have a comic poetry performance tonight at The Pheonix Arts Centre as part of an event called "Word!" I'm going to perform my new comic poem titled "Badly Behaved Baby." I hope to god it will go well. Well, it can't be get worse than badly burned garlic bread …!

To cut a long story short, my cooking never got better, even at the age of 31 when I attempted to make a corn beef pie for Marc in his kitchen. The expression on his bewildered face was absolutely priceless. He had no choice but to eat the "literal" recipe for disaster. Anyhow, reverting back to the garlic bread incident, I more or less was a fraction of a disaster away from burning the house down, on Noble Street in Leicester and this is from only heating up garlic bread. It was Jess who discovered the cremated serving and threw it into the sink. A couple of hours later, I was on stage, which as I can recall, went extremely well with the audience. I remember dedicating "Badly Behaved Baby" to my (then) baby cousin, Lucas.

I didn't deliver any more live performances of my whimsical anecdotes at any spoken word events for the remainder of my time at university. Although I did create odd video recordings which I roughly produced in the living rooms or bedrooms of the student houses which I resided in. I rehearsed and recorded a reading of my own anecdote at the time titled "Fetch Us Up Another Beer," in January 2011, based in my bedroom, when I came back at home in Batley for Christmas. The piece was written from the perspective of a bored housewife, who attempts to liven up their physical relationship with a little roleplay.

Fetch Us Up Another Beer

So, I wait for you to come to bed,
In my tiny, tight Thong,
Glamour up the mood,
With Tom Jones' Sex Bomb.
Nothing seems to appear,
After ten minutes or so,
Because you are still in front of the telly,
Watching that bloody Ronnie Corbett Show!
So, I call your name in hope,
You would be somewhat here,
No, you are fixing up the shelves that we got from Ikea!
So, I call a second time,
Hoping you would jump at the chance,
No, you are bopping out the beats,
To MTV bloody Dance!
So, I come into the room,
I'd hope you would notice your wife,
One look at my body,
You would be in for the dive,
I was all pumped and ready,
Up to the top of the bloody gear,
But all that you said was -
"'Ey up love, fetch us up another beer!"

Strange Mystique Performance

On Monday 9th November 2009, our sculpture group was given a second brief. Four days prior, we had a critique session, based in the sculpture studio, which concluded in a new brief for our second year. I had just completed a project titled "Shadow Characteristics," which veered towards theatrical set design, capturing my early depression through photography. My final piece, included two pieces of MDF cut jaggedly at the top, positioned together to form a corner, with a white net made of entangled string veiling the facade. A male student commented how this representation reminded him of Miss Havisham's dressing room. The final project of the second year of my studies was predominantly centred on Miss Havisham.

When completing the project "Shadow Characteristics," my tutor wanted me to delve into the exploration of performance and film. This was a medium which I haven't necessarily considered, particularly in film, so it was an exciting avenue to look into.

Monday 9th November 2009

We were briefed our next project today, in the sculpture session. Our tutor got us all in groups to discuss what we were taking on for our space projects. I showed everyone a photograph of an event, known as "Strange Fruit Performance," based in Melbourne and they tour the World, with their brilliantly artistic showcases. They are truly phenomenal. Anyway, Leila was looking up at a student's twelve-foot pole, as she remarked to me in a serious manner - "I can see you clamped to the top of that pole."

I first discovered Strange Fruit Performance, whilst researching international performance companies. They are truly spellbinding. I am sure they staged a festival in Bradford, a few years back or something similar. I had a crazy vision of re-enacting their work but it would have been impossible. I began by imitating an appearance that came from the 1920's, by combing my hair back with gel, wearing an eccentric costume. I posed in front of the camera and immensely wanted to perform on the towering poles, swinging from side to side, but this would have been too much of a risk.

Alternatively, I created an installation, which consisted of paper lampshades suspended from the ceiling, dressed in white netting.

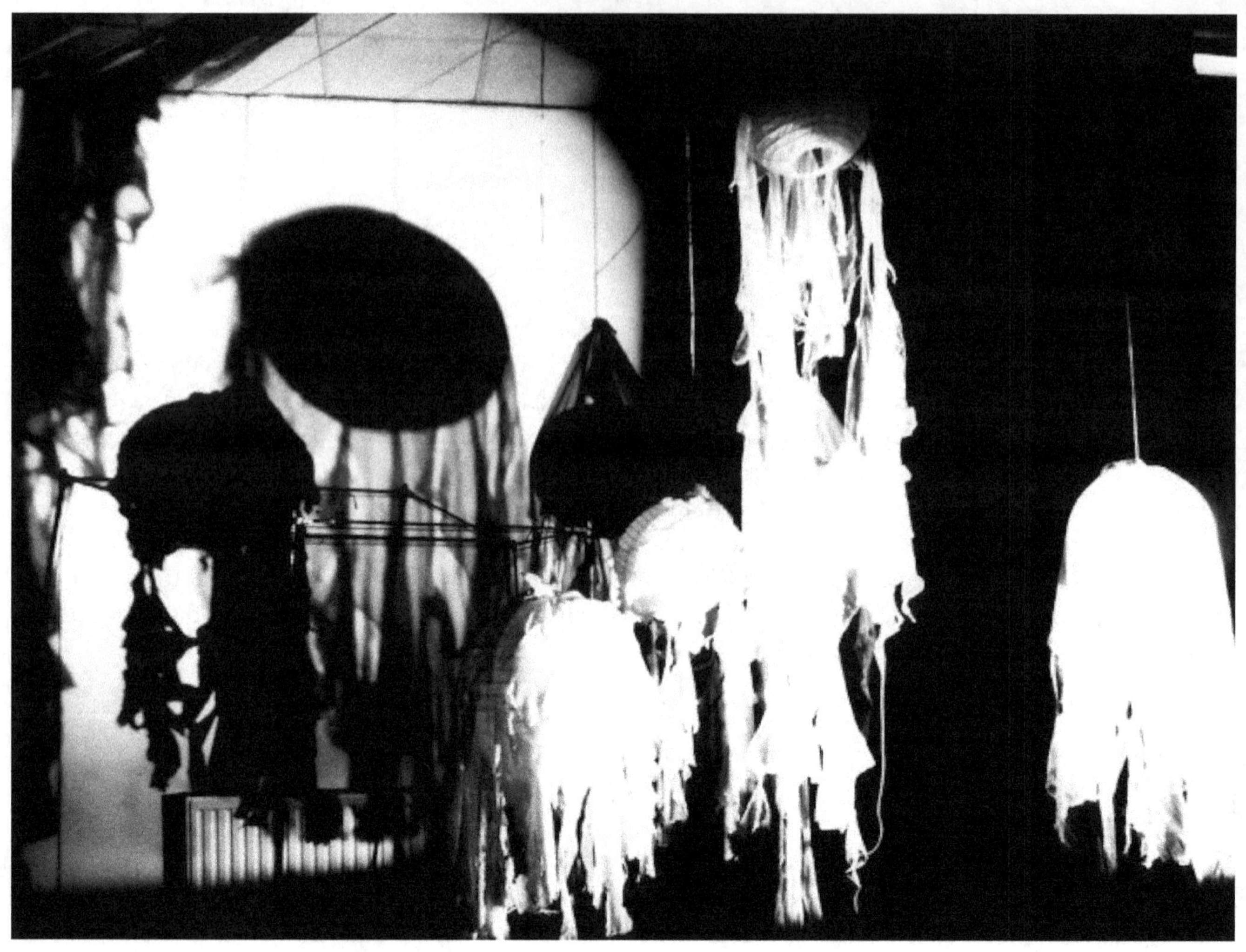

"Strange Mystique Performance" Installation

On the evening of Tuesday 24th November 2009, I shot my debut experimental short film titled "Strange Mystique Performance." I had my friend Chloe Marsh, a student filmmaker, capture the non-narative 12 minute performance, which was edited down to a 1 and a half minute video, the following day. I improvised various movements of struggle, as the wind howled through an open window, erratically blowing the installation, creating a feeling of destruction. I showed the silent film to the sculture group, during a crit session, on Monday 13th December 2009.

Thursday 14th January 2010

I had my "Strange Mystique Performance" assessment today with another tutor named Andy Price. I successfully received a B grade for the video. He compared me to Charlie Chaplin, Laurel and Hardy and the prolific filmmaker Steve McQueen. He screened the film in a CPS (Contextual Professional Studies) session, a couple of weeks later. I provided Andy, with the proposal of my self-directed project, which will be "Havisham." Andy commented that he can't wait to see what the "Dickens" I shall have for this final performance of my second year. He added that he admirers my work because it all connects together all the "shadow" studies that I done up to the final project. We ended up talking about Charles Dickens and his humorous literature. Andy congratulated me and advised me to develop the new project straightaway.

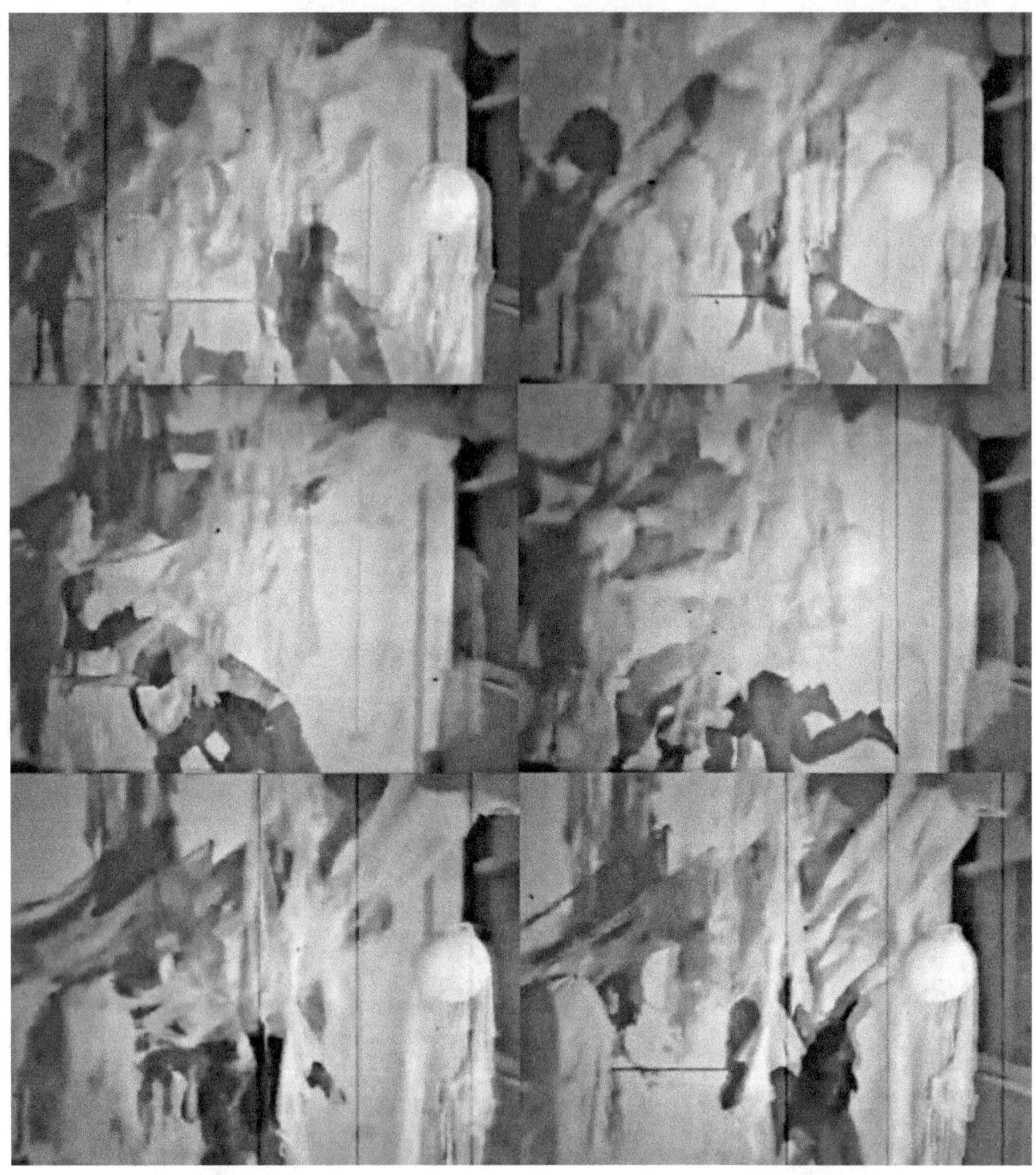

"Strange Mystique Performance"
Duration: 01:30
Filmed by Chloe Marsh

HAVISHAM

Charles Dickens has been one of my main influences since childhood. I remember being introduced to his prolific novel "Great Expectations" when I was around seven years of age. Miss Havisham became one of my favourite heroines in literature. Her unique ambience and sense of fearlessness captivated my attention. I admired Dickens creation of a skeletal bride, waiting for her lover to return to her decrepit mansion, whilst having the tendancy to adopt a little girl to rear in love and to break mens hearts. Her mental health resonates with what many people experience too. The wounds of sexual gratification, rejection and the obsession of secluding herself away from reality, forms this perfect depiction of extreme mania. I can certainly relate to all of these characteristics and I believe, from childhood, these became a prominent part of my life. I based the final project of my second year of University, predominantly on this wicked character.

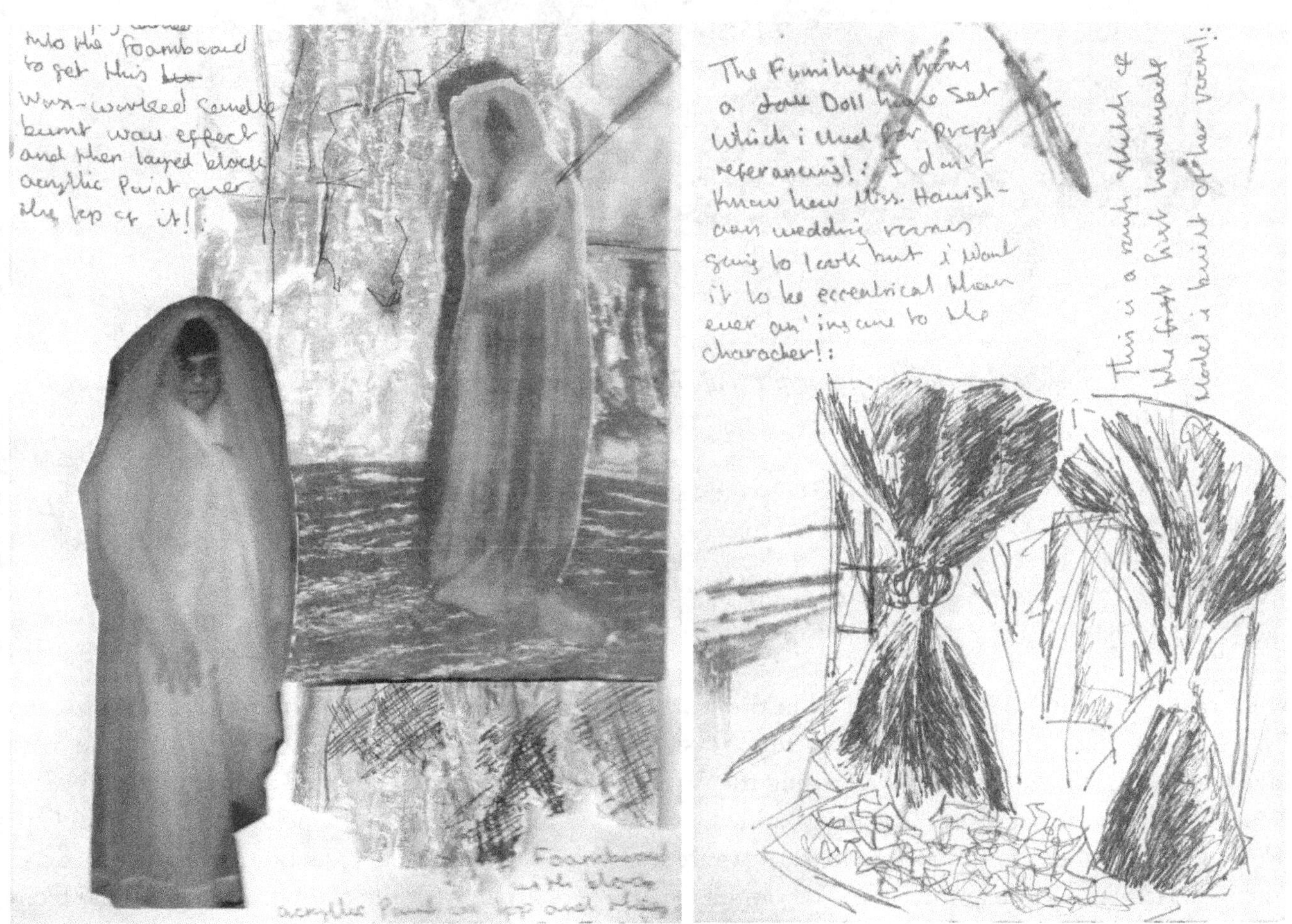

Sketchbook concepts to how the character would fit into her decaying interior.

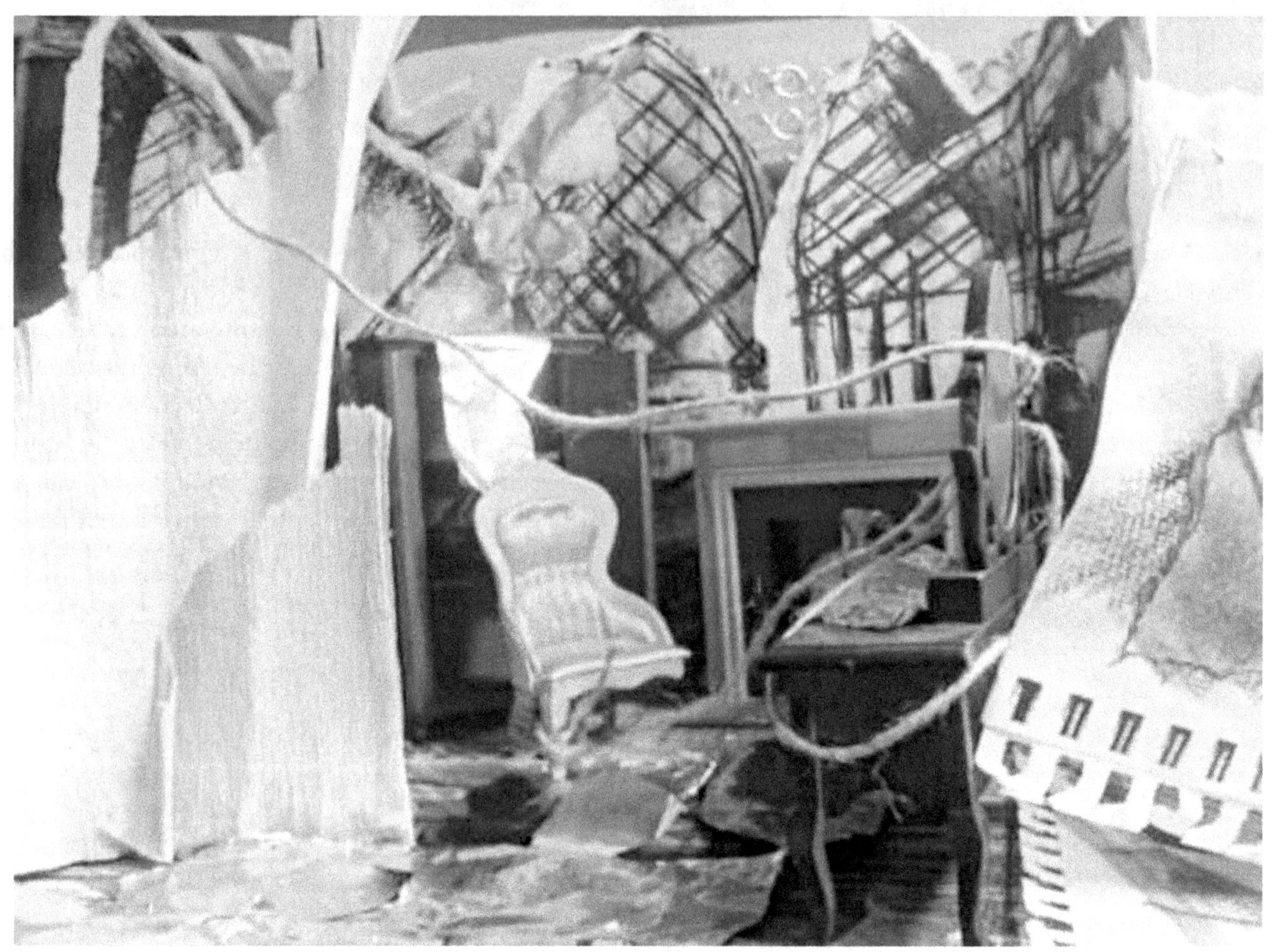

A small scale model of my impression to how I would like the set design to look like.

Friday 15th January 2010

I went into University today and worked in the workshop all day. I made a long and narrow table for the Miss Havisham set. The scale of the furniture wasn't immense, due to the limited capacity of the corner space within the sculpture studio. I am using the two MDF boards which were used for the final showcase of the "Shadow Characteristics" project. I added a window shutter to room in which Miss Havisham kept locked. I left the shutters to dry overnight. I wanted the room to appear as foreboding and eccentric as possible. Placing the table in the room, I drooped a white net curtain over the exterior. The good old techno man in the workshop was a miracle.

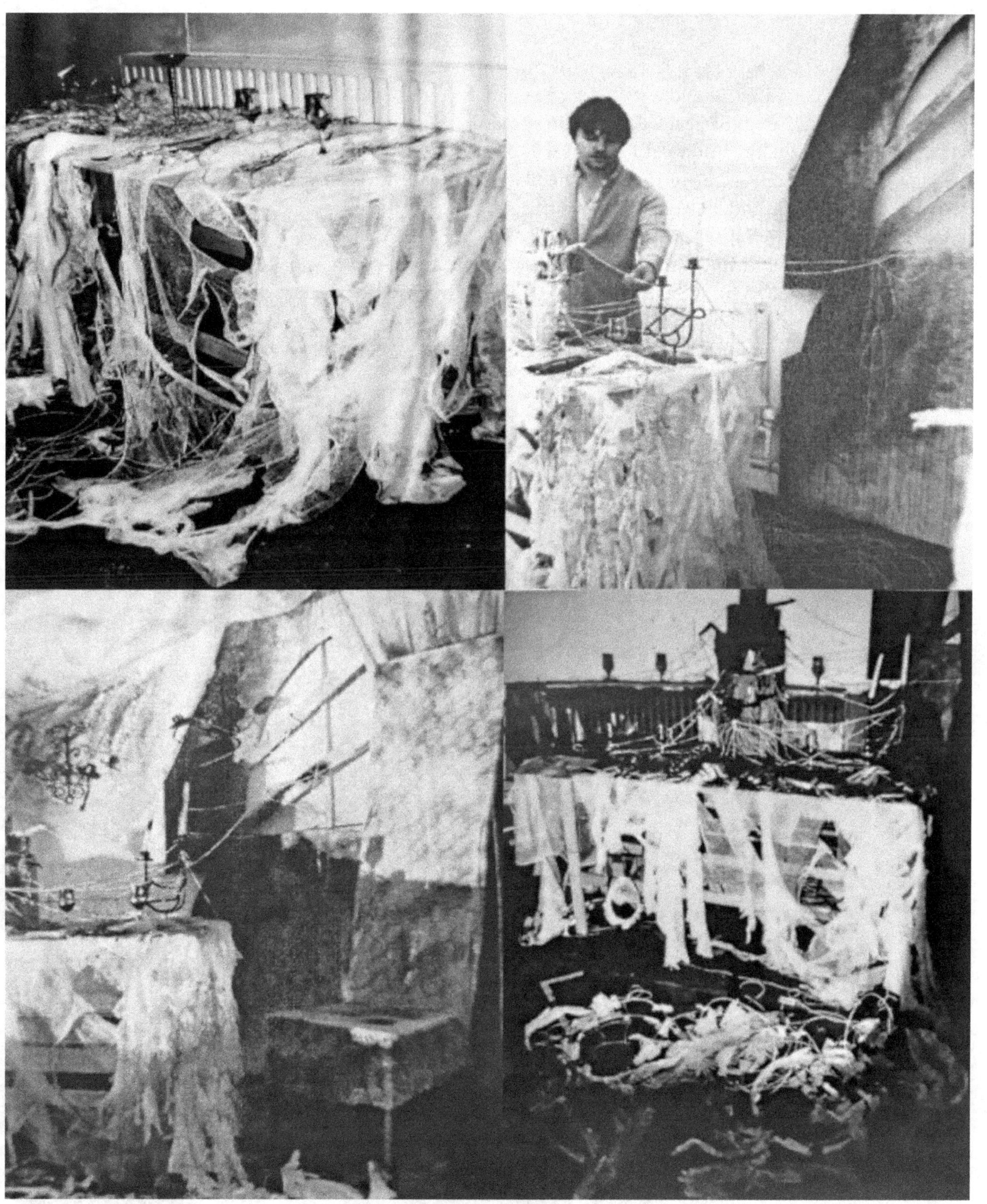

The interior dressing of Miss Havisham's wedding room.
- January 2010

Saturday 16th January 2010

I went to Leicester today to shop for props for my set. It was a bargain when I purchased four wine glasses at a charity Shop for £1.75, a candle stick for 75p and a further seven candles at Wilkinson for £2.00. Those items were only half of what I need, I couldn't find the rest anywhere in Leicester. So hopefully when I return to Batley in a couple of weeks time, I will be able to find everything, which would be ideal for the dressing table that I am making. I definitely need a double sided candle stick to put on the decaying, mice gnawed, wedding table and a piece of coffee stained fabric for the interior. To create the decayed effect of the dressing table, I used black acryllic Paint and PVA Glue andthen made a cut out of a cake using cardboard, also dripped with this paint to represent demoralization. I was originally going to use a real cake I had to rethink this due to health and safety regulations. Further stark curtains were hung up, and became a feature in Miss Havisham's room, which complimented her smouldering wedding dress.

Monday 18th January 2010

I placed the props onto the wedding table. I used white string to represent cobwebs nesting amongst the feast. I christened my area of the studio, to make sure I could erect a good enough set design. I brought in the two boards, from the workshop. I later purchased a wall hanging candle holder in Leicester, which I mounted on the MDF boards.

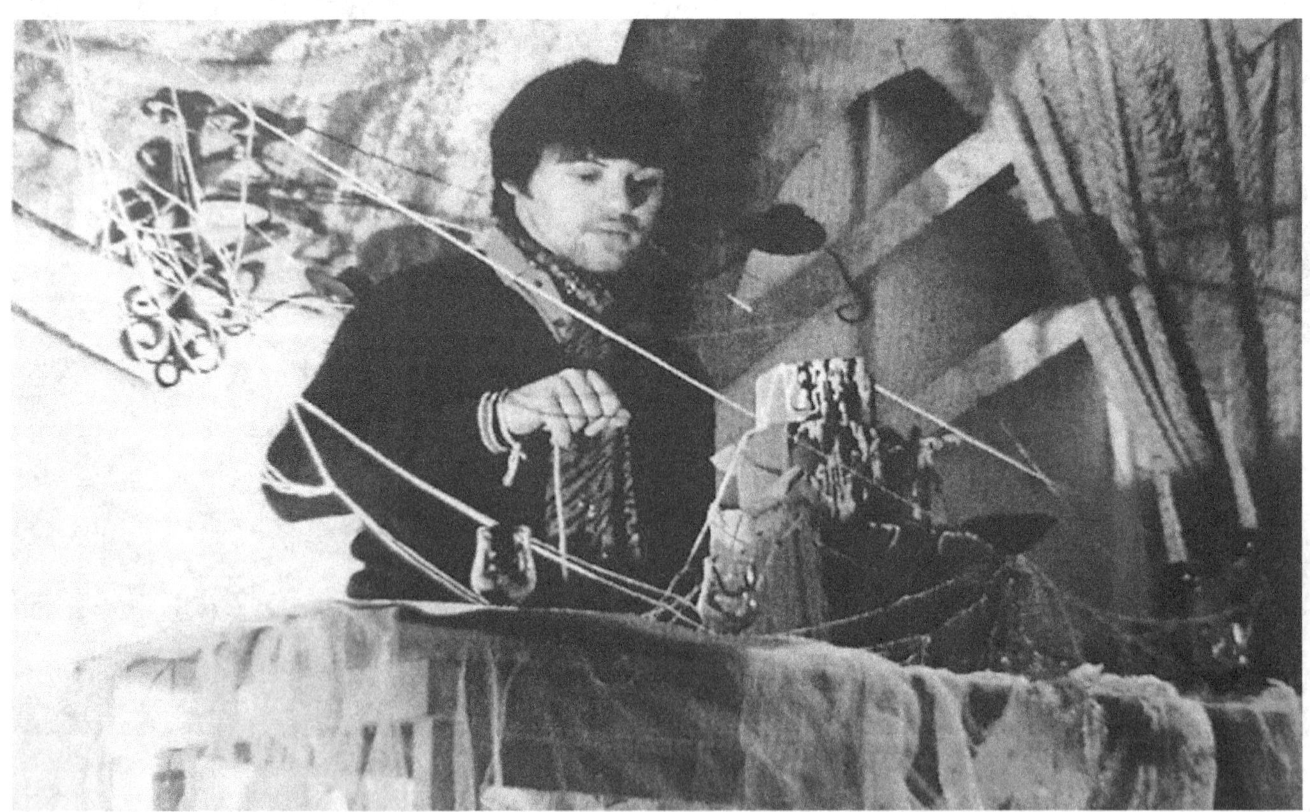

Rehearsing on set for "Havisham" short film
- February 2010.

On Tuesday 19th January 2010, I dressed the wedding room, with sepia toned fabric, which I purchased from the market at a reasonable price. The vibrant shine of an overhead projector light, burdened her room with her oppression, as I captured the mood on camera, later that evening.

I remember a humorous moment, when my friend Jess urged me to try on some ridiculously cheap wedding dresses, in Oxfam charity shop. The shop was pretty busy, with eager bargain hunters, as we both trawled our way through a rail of garments. The wedding dress which I selected, was extremely smoke stained. I had it resting in Jess's room for a number of weeks, prior to the performance, stinking to high heaven. She reckoned that some poor soul had sadly died wearing it, smoking a cigarette.

After a further month of decorating Miss Havisham's dystopian wedding room, I commenced filming on the evening of Wednesday 17th February 2010, which took place over two separate occasions. The short film was shot by Chloe Marsh and her partner Jake, as I portrayed the character of the jilted bride. I included references from Carol Ann Duffy's poem, "Havisham," within my own script. Still keeping incredibly true to the Charles Dicken's novel, Great Expectations, I closely analysed the contempt of the wax skeleton, who slumped at the table in her great throne. Miss Havisham was portrayed by myself, Pip was played by Jess Fury and Estella was portrayed by Melonie King. The scenes with all characters congregated together was filmed on the evening of Tuesday 2nd March. During the morning of the same day, I met a former fine art student named Sophia Braham in the painting studio at the university. She asked me to portray a psychiatrist in her short film adaptation of Stephen King's "No." James Lullaby, her friend, played the character who suffers with debilitating OCD. The short film was filmed in her flat which overlooked Leicester's All Saints graveyard.

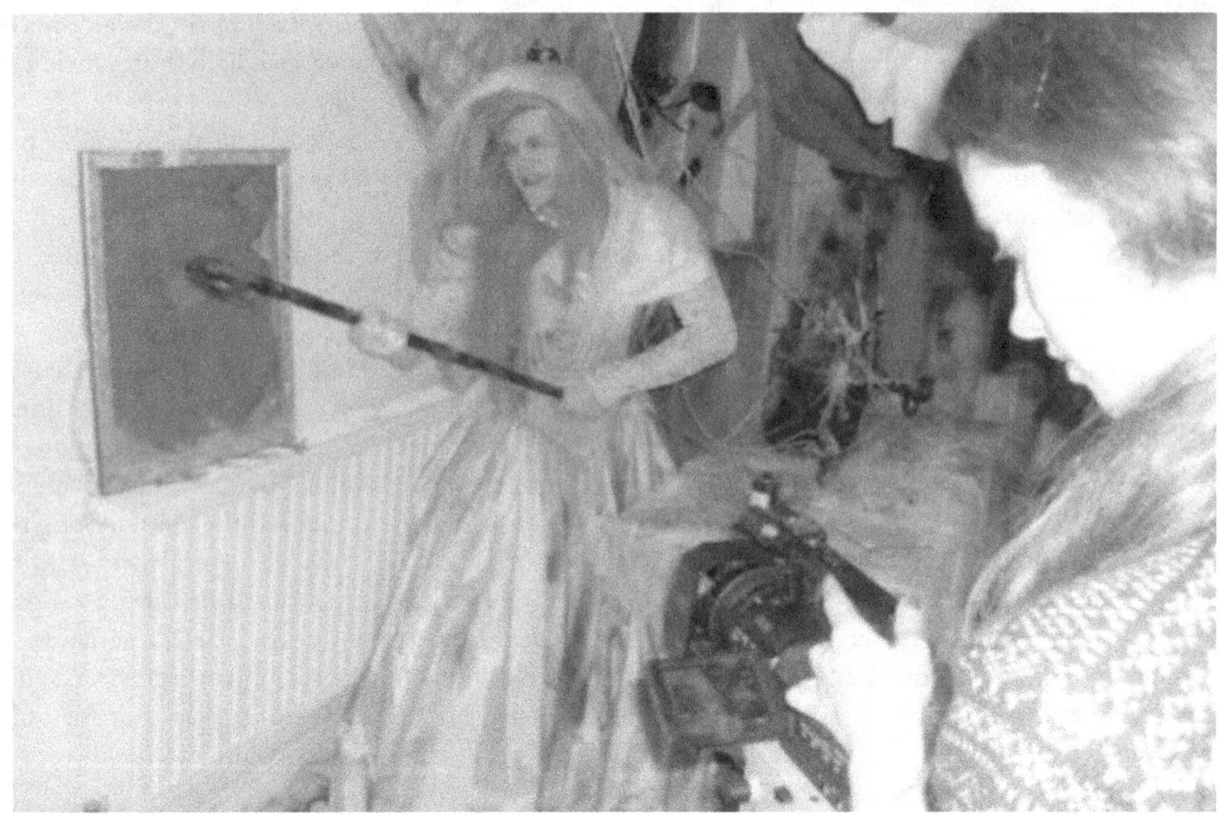

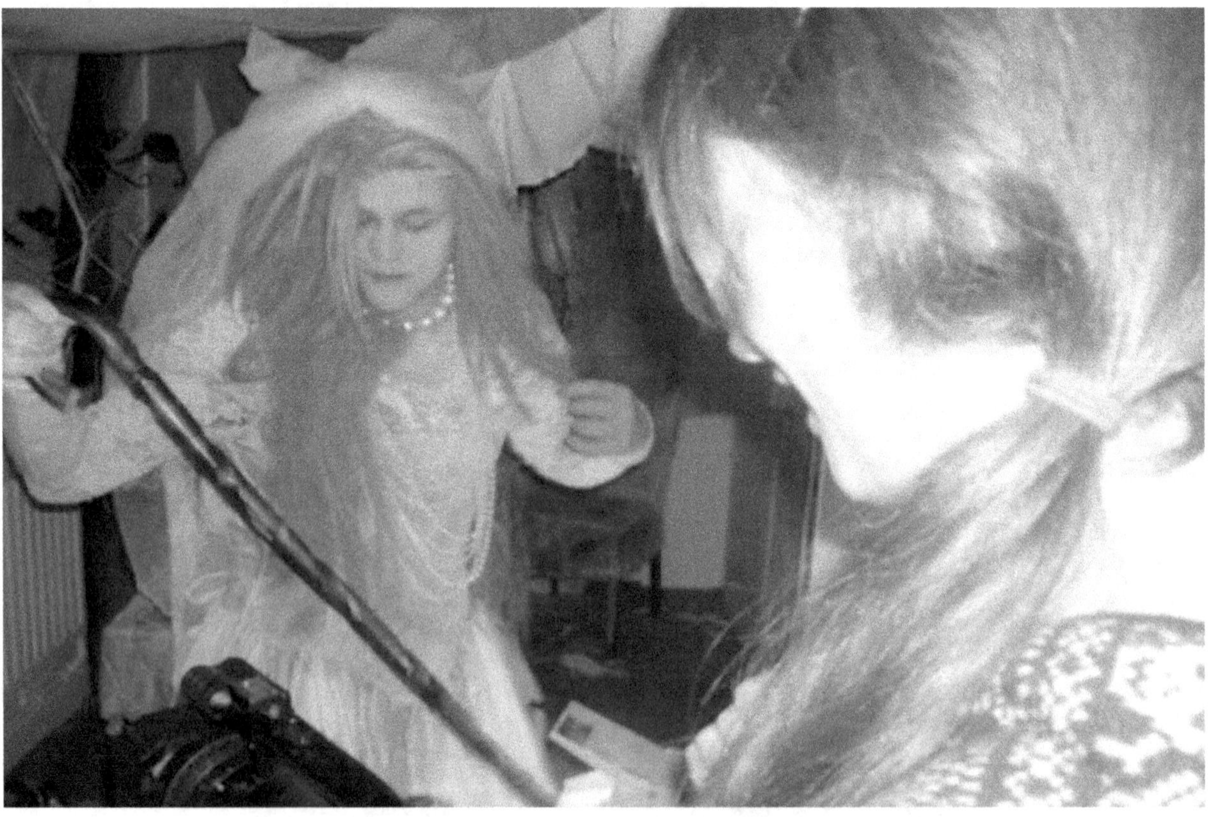

Filming the opening scene to "Havisham"
- February 2010

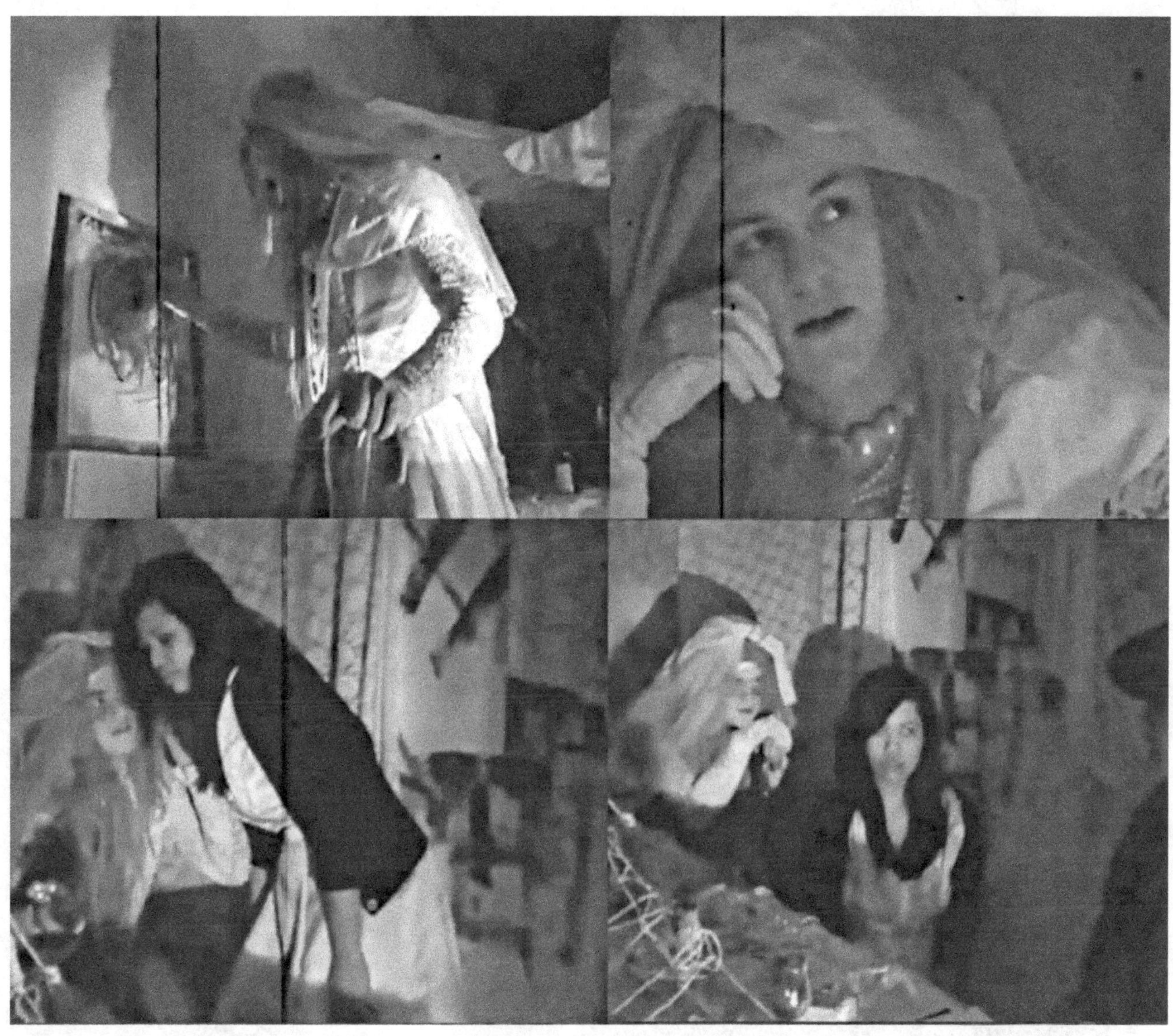

Filming "Havisham" in the sculpture studio, De Montfort University, Leicester
- March 2010

The filming and editing process was simply well established and straightforward. The film began with a visual of Miss Havisham standing, clutching on to her stick, sombrely rolling her fingers down a dusty mirror, reciting the opening stanza of Carol Ann Duffy's poem. After speaking about her "beloved sweetheart bastard," Miss Havisham struck the mirror with her stick. This only took one take to film. Then the 8:48 second piece would evolve using the Dickens narrative. I did use more brief references from the poem into wherever it was relevant. In order to show Miss Havisham's dress catching fire from a candle, I had Jake rapidly flash the OHP light, to create the effect of flames, whilst Miss Haversham clutched onto her stick, vehemently shrieking, before collapsing to the ground. This clip was filmed twice. Throughout the next couple of months, I edited the "Havisham" short film in the Portland editing suite opposite the University.

I absolutely loved the working processes of the "Havisham" project and the journey of interpreting a narrative which I have admired since childhood. This project achieved a first distinction for the 2nd year of my degree.

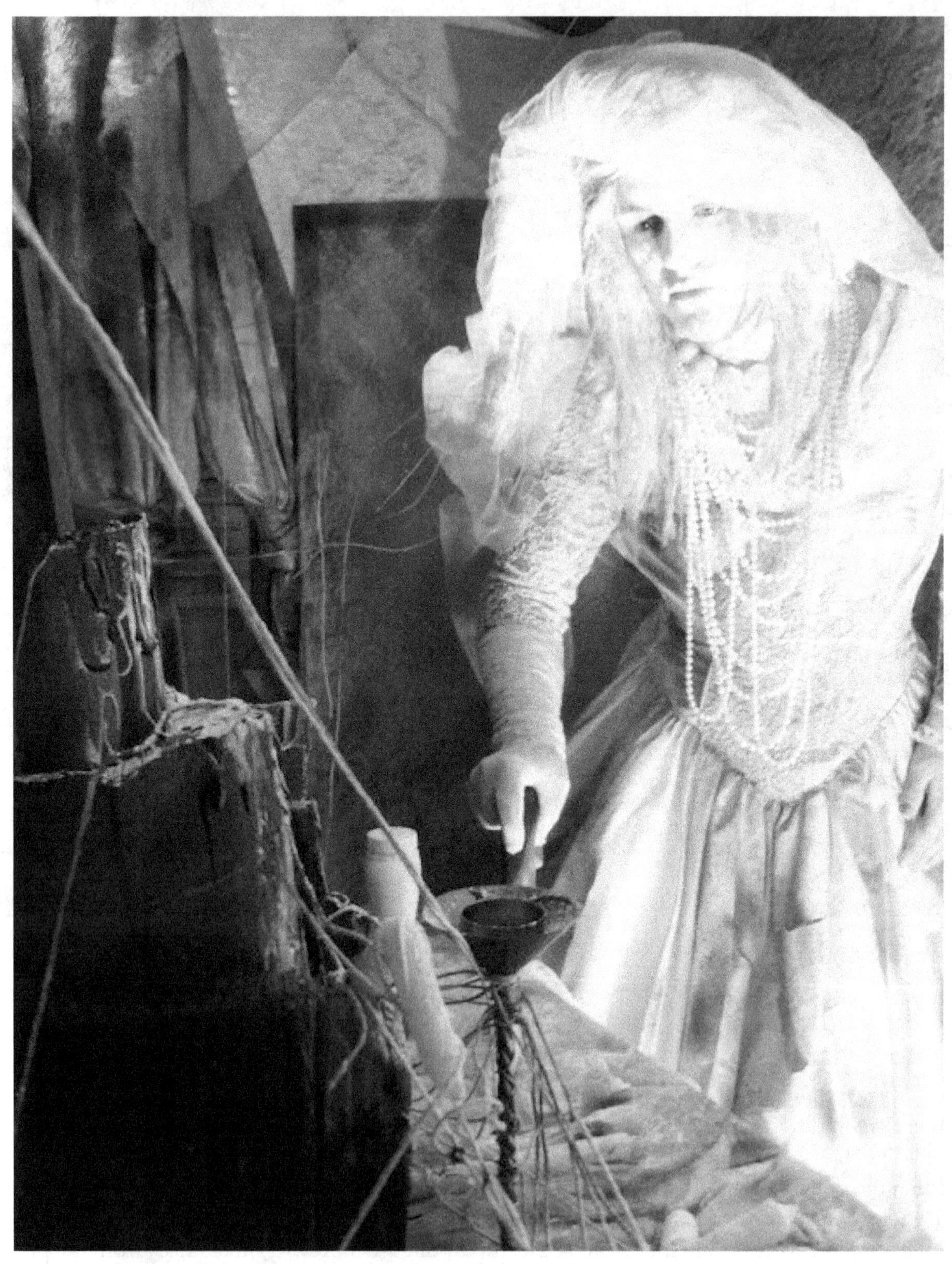

"Beloved sweetheart bastard"

- Quoted Carol Ann Duffy

Me portraying Miss Havisham - February 2010

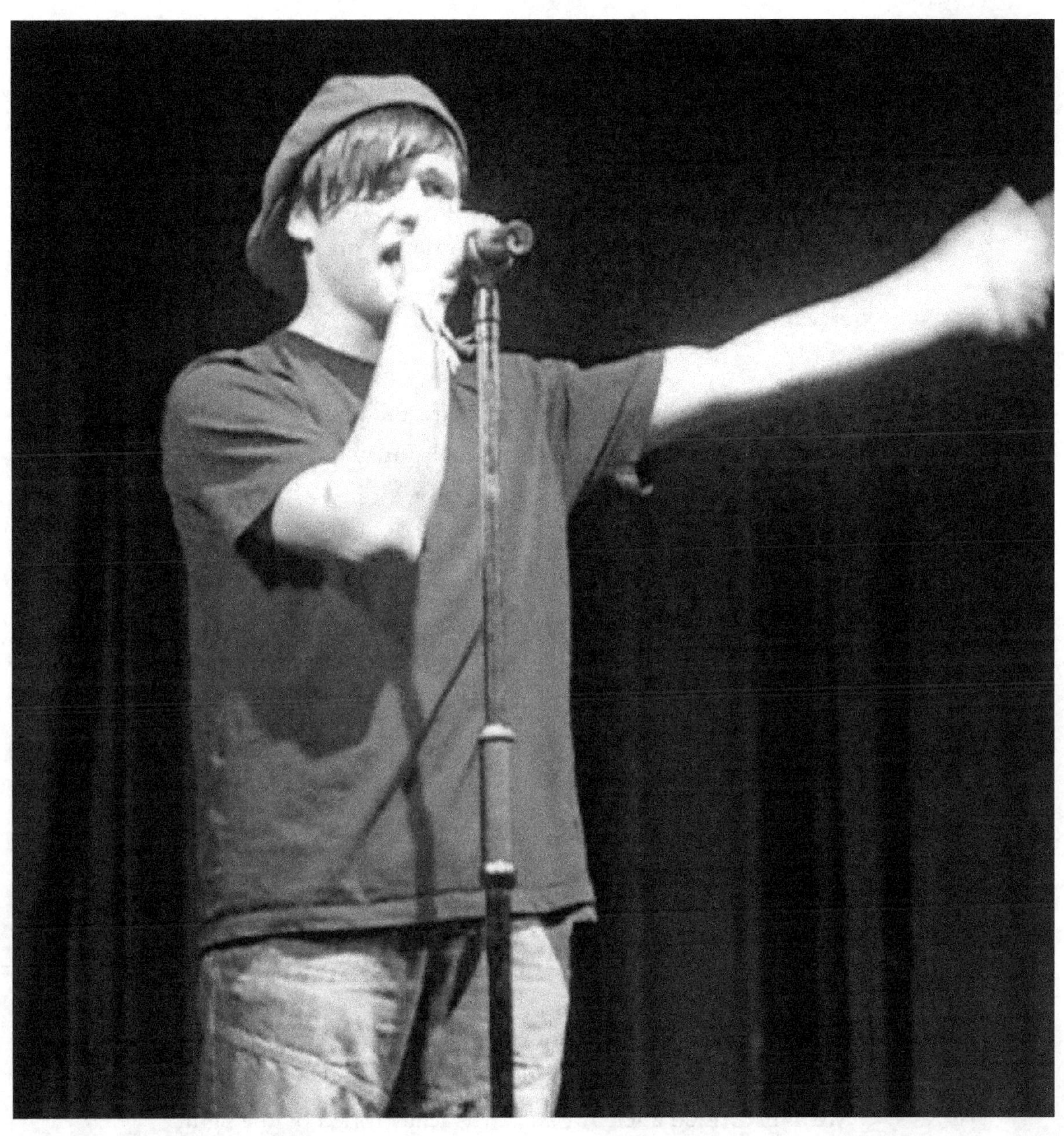

"Emergency" - The Y Theatre, Leicester
Performing my anecdotes at a scratch event - 15/5/2010

Life Model

I have always indulged in the concept,
It has been my one aspiring desire,
I can now achieve my ambitions fearlessly,
Upon the day until I soon retire.

I have decided to head board the plunge,
I have still got it, even though I may toddle,
I am going to fulfil my daring, wildest dreams,
I am going to become a life model!

I have shared this delight with acquaintances,
Though they feel that the idea is rather sour,
Why look down your nose, when you can easily strip all bare,
For £25.00 an hour?

Nothing will dilute this ambition,
Nothing else I could propel would be bigger,
I have been pumping my little booty down at the gym,
To transform into a delectable figure!

The day had eventually arrived,
As I posed delicately and graciously bare,
My transformed ancient torso, artistically toned by the light,
And my unmentionables disguised by a pear!

The students portrayed me gracefully,
This longing aspiration has allowed me to feel alive,
It just goes to show that you can be whatever you want to be,
Even as a man at sixty-five!

This is the most prosperous moment of my life,
I feel that I have "literally" got it in the sack,
Now I am a professional ageing life model,
My Lord, I am never looking back!

His Haunted Laughter

Veering into the final year of my fine art degree, I knew that my artistic forte would be film for the remainder of my forthcoming projects. I commenced work on what would be an experimental short film titled "His Haunted Laughter." The sculpture of the laughing man based at Blackpool Pleasure Beach, gave me the inspiration to make a symbolic piece of history come alive and shock the world in its wickedly wonderful way. The concept of a man expressing his fun and hysteria inside a transparent pavilion, led me to start by replicating this box, which I created and built in the wood workshop on Thursday 14th October 2010.

Thursday 14th October 2010

I felt ready to start building my own version of the laughing man's pavilion in the workshop. The techno man and I decided on making a square shaped box, as a Hexagon-shaped pavilion would have been too ambitious to build, plus there wasn't enough wood to make it. I am sure it will look good. I measured out the lengths for the pavilion and begun cutting out the pieces of wood. It is going to be seven foot tall and five foot wide, which will provide enough space for me to sit inside. I placed a chair inside the structure and it fitted well. The techno man helped me on building most of the pavilion but when it came to gluing and screwing it together, I did this part all by myself. I eventually got most of it done but had to leave it until tomorrow, due to inductions.

Monday 18th October 2010

Back in the wood workshop today. Hopefully, I am going to be putting together the actual Pavilion frame. I have cut out all the parts and now it is time to put it together. It was absolutely massive when I stood the box upright. Jess came down to the workshop to help me carry it to the third year sculpture studio. The journey to the studio was such a struggle, but I did manage to put the Pavilion into the spot to where I wanted it to be. I have a very small space in the upstairs studio, but I feel more at ease with this studio space.

Wendesday 20th October 2010

Andy and Fiona, who are third year sculpture tutors, loved my pavilion. I began to dress the structure with lavish material. I started to feel a connection to the project as an artist. All the creative effort and devotion that had I put into it made it how I wanted it to be. I am fascinated by what the end result will be. A student compared my style of design to Laurence Llewelyn-Bowen's. At this minute, the pavilion is starving for more material. I must have left the university at 5:30pm, as I have been here since the early morning. It's very long and tiresome day.

Thursday 21st October 2010

I went into the workshop today to start work on my wooden rocking chair. The techno man had already got a spare chair which he was offered to give to me. I reprofiled the chair and then sanded it down after attending two meetings this morning. The first meeting was about starting our own business after our studies and the second meeting was about an ex fine art student and how life had dramatically altered for her, after graduating. It was an interesting talk.

Later on, I continued developing the design of the chair by adding extra pieces to it and completed it the following afternoon. I attended my crit session with Max in the third year sculpture studio on Tuesday 26th October 2010. He was impressed by my project. I explained the historic story about the majestic clown and how his laughter is known to haunt the fairground. The clown was founded by Pleasure Beach and it became a prominent feature at the entrance of a fun house which was built in 1935, but later destroyed by a fire in 1991. Only his head survived the blaze. It was discovered at a landfill site and was taken back to a Blackpool based manufacturer to be restored and rehomed at the prestigious park.

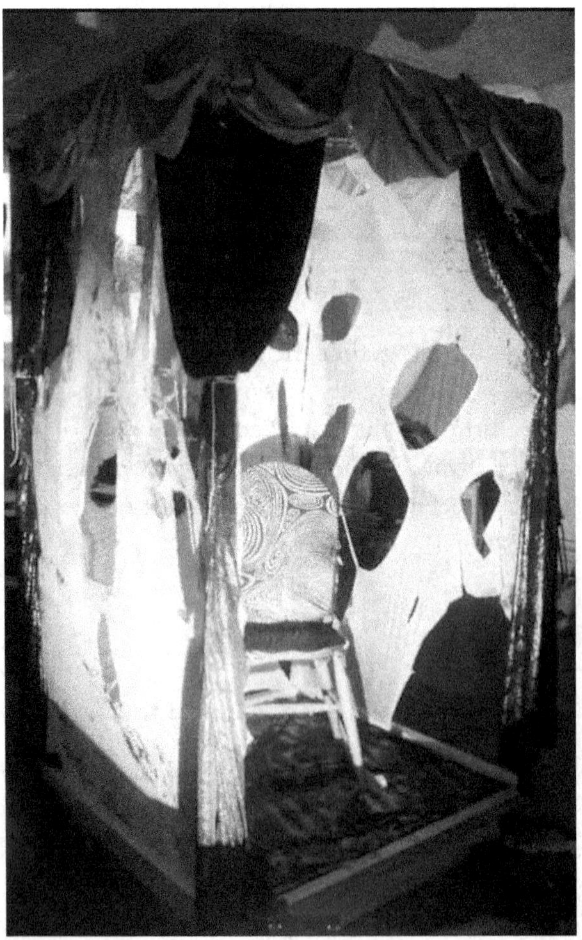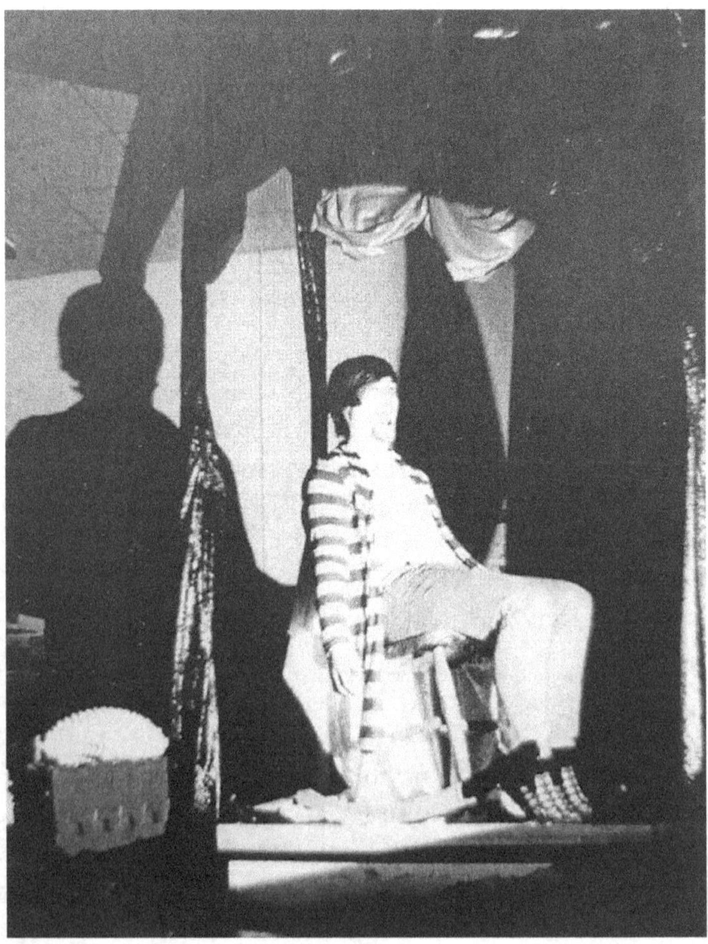

The original Pavilion concept, to perform as a live laughing man.

As part of my project, I will be portraying the clown through my own live performance, I placed myself on the rocking chair inside the pavilion and consistently rocked back and forth, projecting a persistent deep laugh, as Max watched on in fascination. Max had a vision of me either, portraying the clown in this manner as part of a full day performance exhibition, or by having this as a live performance accompanied by projections. Both concepts intrigued me, but I personally felt that the project wasn't developing as I hoped it would be. I hit the peak of losing all my creative instincts. My psyche wasn't functioning as it did throughout my first two years of this degree. I think I was feeling under pressure to making something, which would be better than my previous work. I was only introduced to film in November 2009 and my work through this medium was a steep learning curve for me. So, to retain my energy and motivation was draining for me. I think when an artist is working on something so challenging and expansive, that alone can affect your ability to function. This is what was happening to me as a student, but I had the guidance of my tutors. Now, when I produce work, the only guidance I have is my myself, except if I am collaborating on a project with someone else. Even collaboration can be an ominous task because everyone has their own perception of needs to be achieved. Collaboration or not, expression can be a daunting thing sometimes.

Andy and Fiona had an idea of taking my character to an open location, so that I could produce a film which allowed me to explore the environment and surroundings. I mentally took a deep inhale, I then exhaled and on the evening of Wednesday 24th November 2010, I dressed myself up as a 1920's style French noir clown and took my first of two visits to Saint Mary De Castro Graveyard in Leicester. At the beginning, I simply filmed the trees, the gravestones and everything else which captured my attention there. I then went into performer mode and captured myself stumbling in a wooden manner around the ghostly grounds. With my eccentric looking face and outlandish appearance, I was conscious of being caught by anyone who may be curiously watching on. I then developed the scenery, of the clown visiting various locations as a referance of him of attempting to find normality in the real world but fails to do so.

I returned home in Batley on Saturday 4th December 2010, to surprise my grandma for her 60th birthday. The entire country had been blanketed in snow but this was perfect for the setting I needed, to film what would be the opening to "His Haunted Laughter." I used the Howley Ruins in Batley, as a setting, which conveyed the ambience of an old Russian Film, despite the presence electrical pylons that protruded in my view. I had a camcorder on a tripod filming me I staggered erratically in the snow. I wanted the clown to appear as if he was walking on uneven ground, so I positioned the camera at different angles. The Howley scene was shot, also on the following day, where my grandma came and witnessed the performance. I remember having a harmless little dog chase me down a hill, probably overwhelmed by my unusual appearance. I made my final visit to Howley on Monday 6th December 2010. I filmed the clown as if he was entering a dreary looking cellar. But the cellar scene was filmed in the basement of my third year student house based on Noble Street. The final edit was ready for release and for assessment when I returned from my Christmas break on Wednesday 19th January 2011.

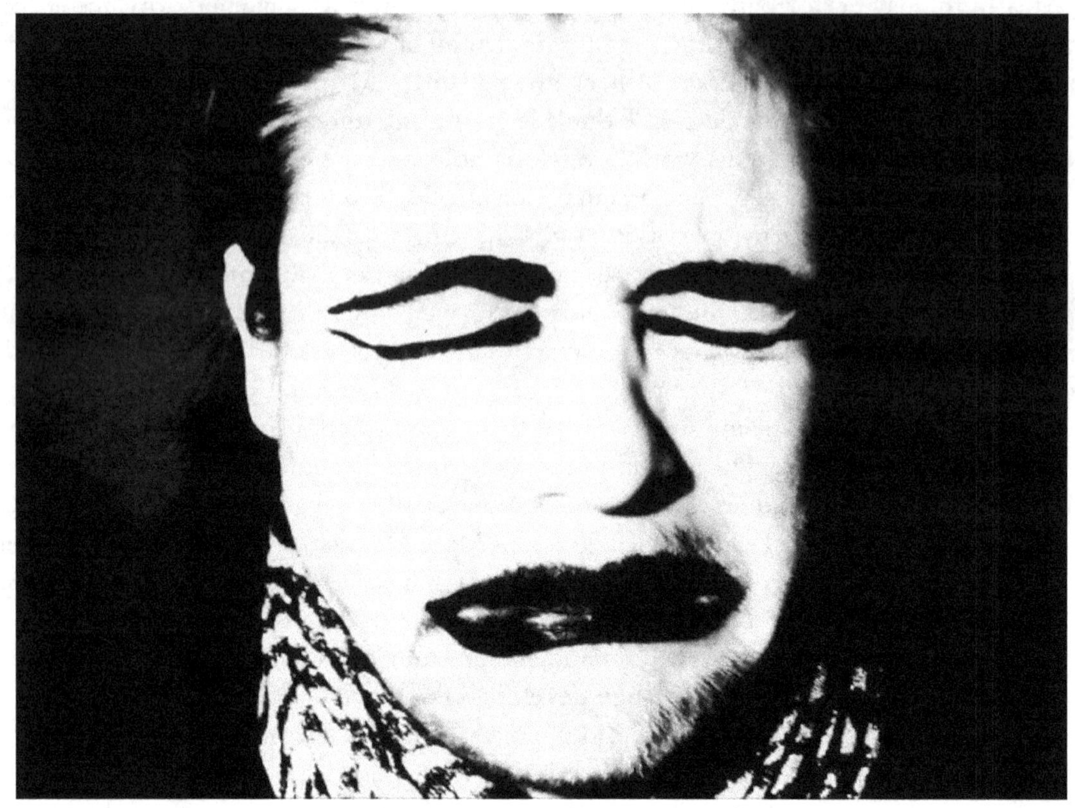

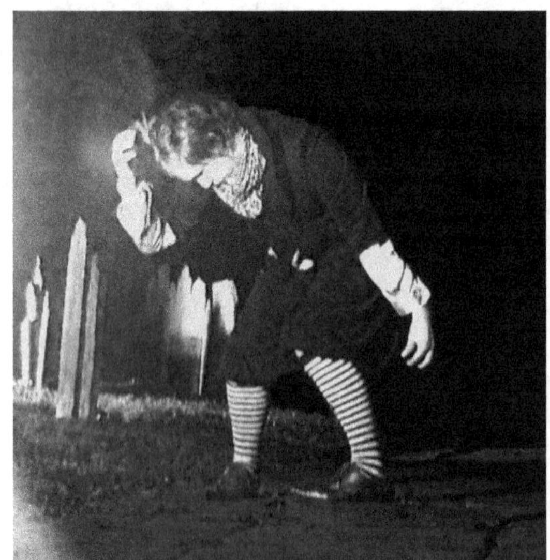

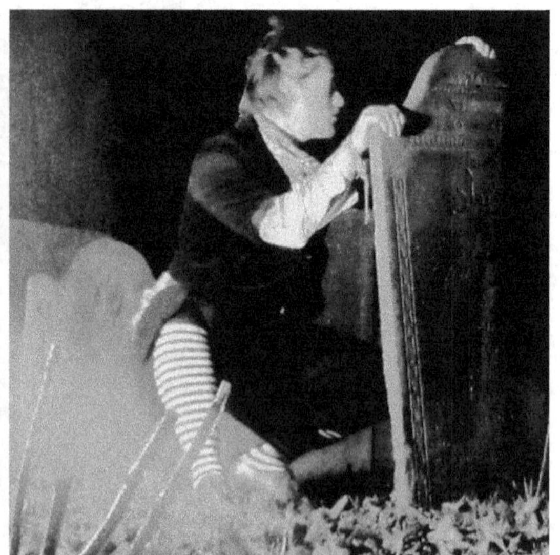

Saint Mary De Castro Graveyard, Leicester

Filming on an extremely bitter evening in November 2010.

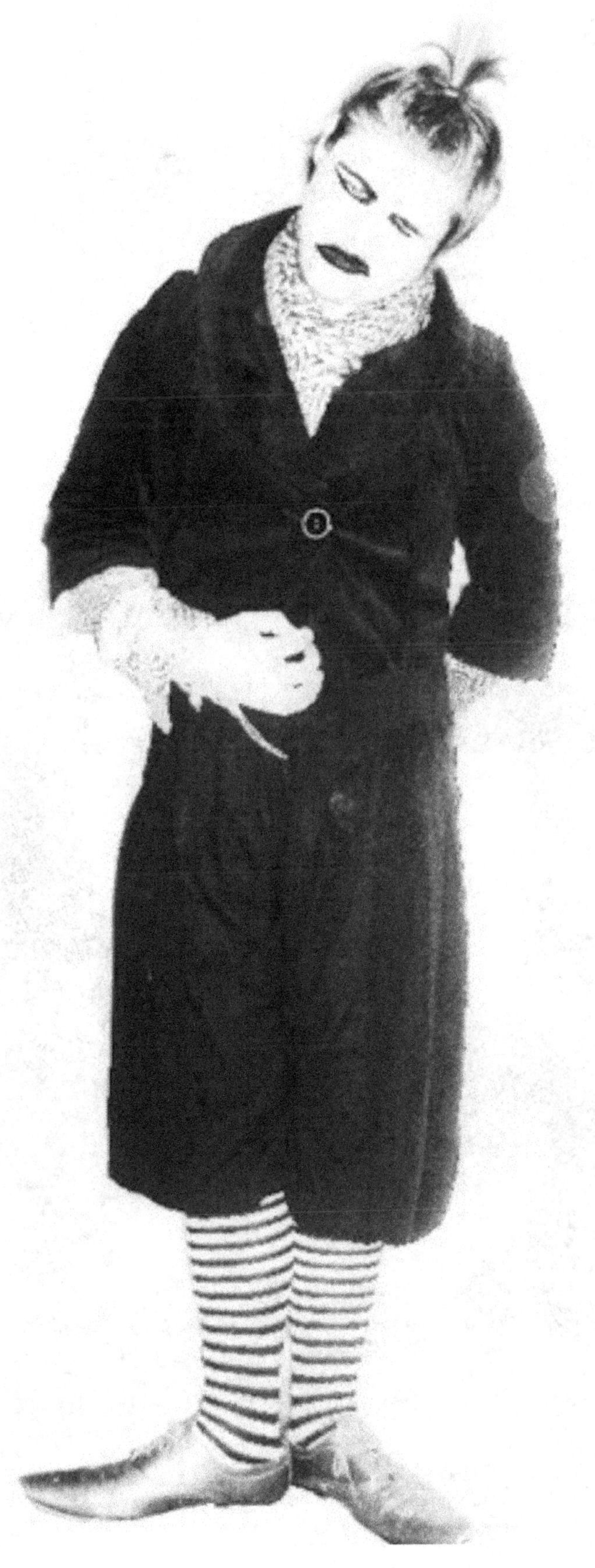

Me portraying the French psychotic clown in the Short Film.
- November 2010.

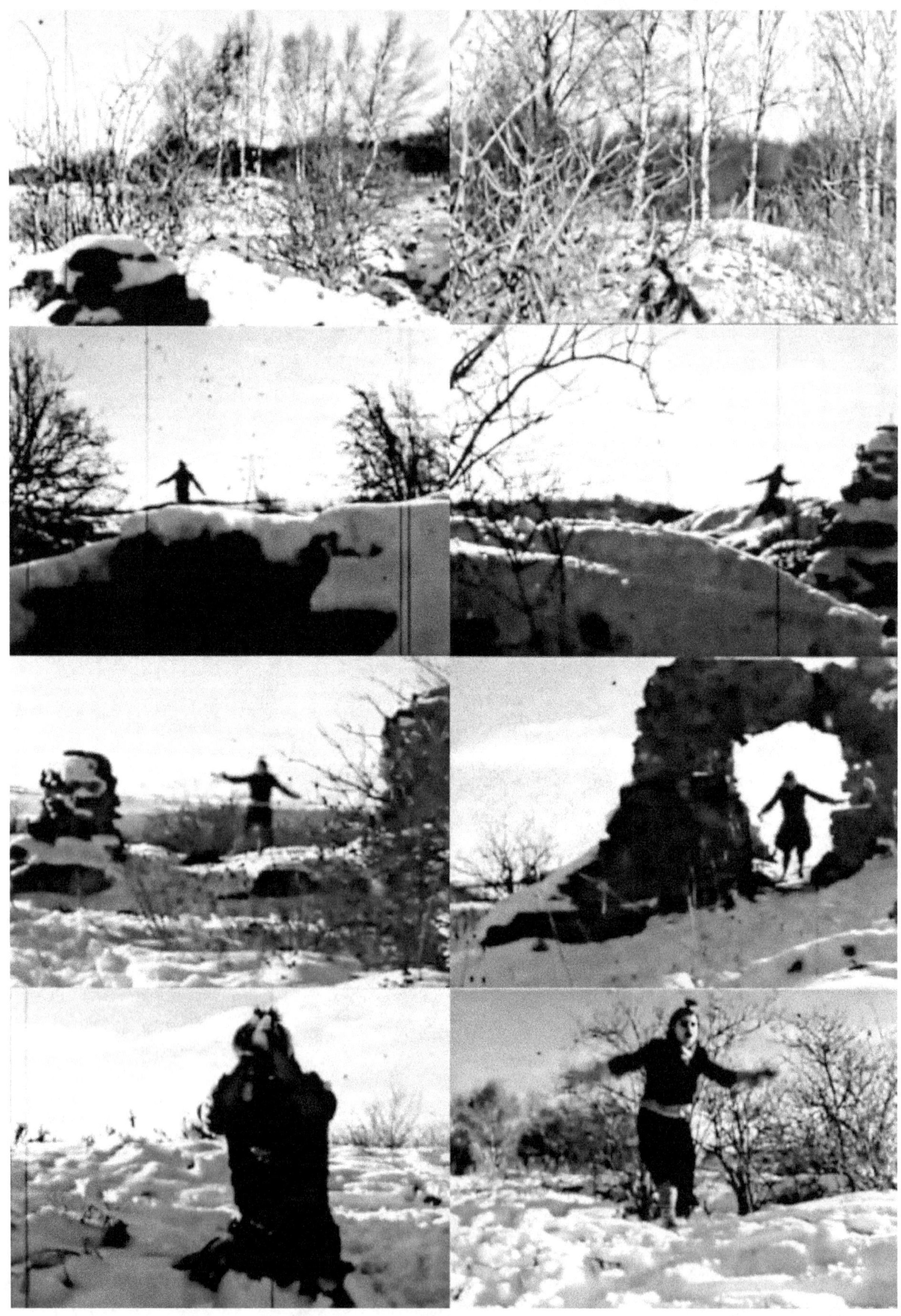

"His Haunted Laughter (Reversed Version)"

Film stills of the opening scene - Howley, Batley - December 2010

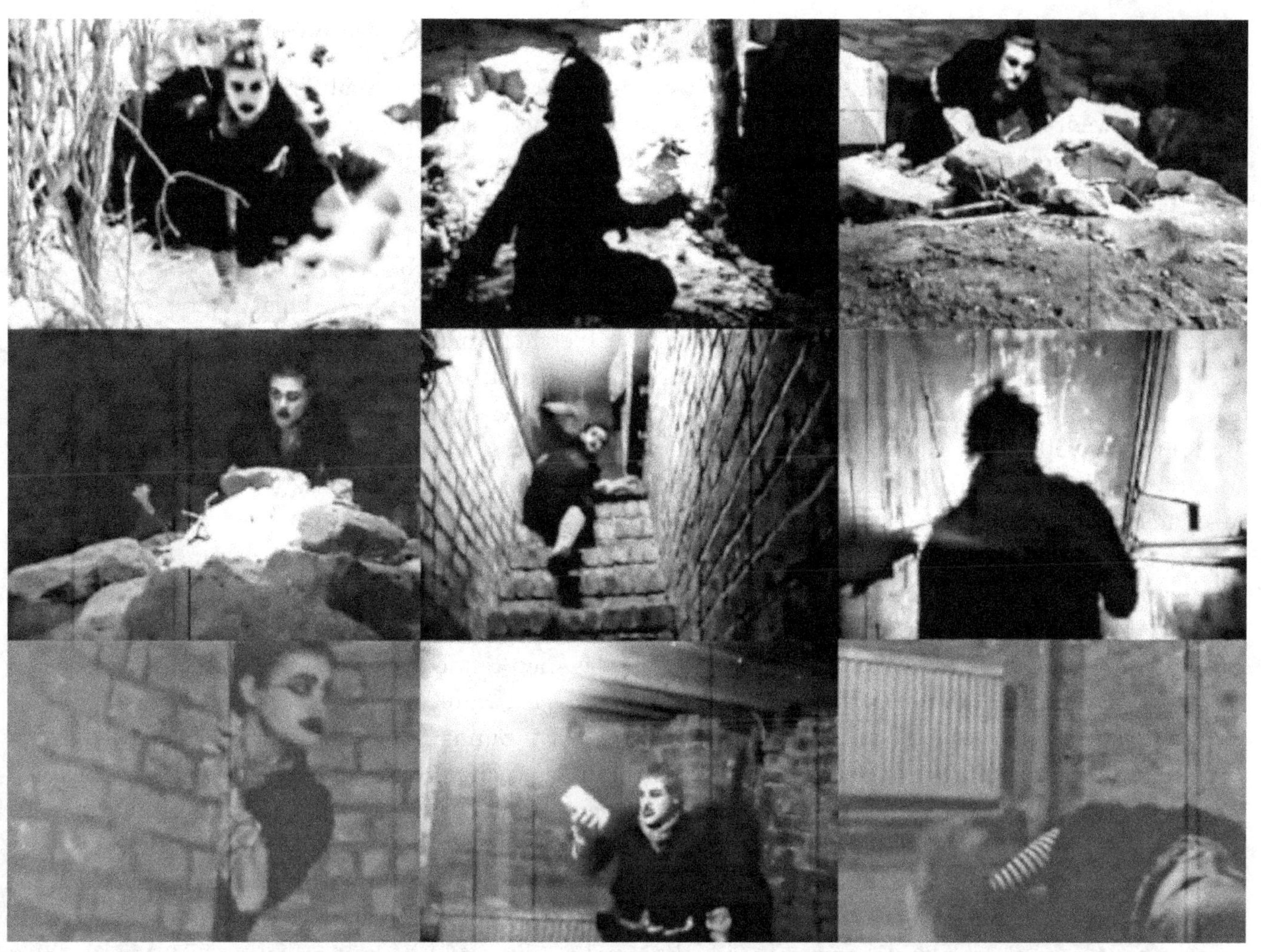

"His Haunted Laughter (Reversed Version)"
Film stills of the opening scene - (Top) Howley, Batley - December 2010
- Noble Street House - Cellar, Leicester - December 2010

Wednesday 19th January 2011

I got up early this morning, because I have an assessment for my experimental film, "His Haunted Laughter." I first went into the Portland editing suite, upon deciding to enhance an eerie soundtrack to my film. As the original sound, is ridiculously crackly, I decided to add an extreme wind sound effect. So, with the help of the sound technician, he helped me to place "Scream of the Wind" from a YouTube video, on the opening to the film, where the clown is marching over the snowy peaks of the Howley Ruins. I was absolutely chuffed with this effect because it effectively gave the view the sense of feeling psychologically overwhelmed. The technician had to save the sound file on the Apple Mac PC. This was then placed onto the edit timeline. I made my way over to the university's Fletcher Building and into the 1.3 studio, to mount the black and white photographs for the project, in preparation for my assessment. With the help of a passing tutor, I played "His Haunted Laughter" on a large screen and he was extremely impressed with it. I returned at 3:30pm and waited outside the studio for the assessment. Andy and Fiona arrived, taking me into the studio to go through the feedback form. I brilliantly achieved a B grade for the film. They both absolutely admired my Film.

I re-edited "His Haunted Laughter" to remaster the piece, to make it appear more slapstick. I added a black and white film noir effect, as opposed to a sepia tone and I completely reversed the whole of the first half, for the Film to conclude at the beginning. The footage would play in reverse, with the clown collapsing on the cold ground and going in the cellar. The film was then retitled "His Haunted Laughter (Reversed Version.)" Being fairly juvenile and pretty much thinking that I would instantly become a renowned filmmaker, I was inspired to enter this ambitious avenue, by distributing my experimental film, as well as my final film during my fine art studies titled "The Trickster" to many prolific organisations. These included Channel 4, Sky Arts and an attempted submission to Danny Cohen at United Agents who produced a live performance of Frankenstein based at Kirkstall Abbey in spring 2011. I received a reply back from United Agents stating that I had written to the incorrect Danny Cohen and the other two agents were either not interested or was not accepting unsolicited material without the prior agreement. I did however, stumble upon a couple of short film programmes, which were broadcast at 10:30pm on Sumo TV, one of them being "ShortCutters." I submitted my films to the production company in early 2012 but unfortunately, they were on a hiatus at the time.

Just before graduating from university, I had the urge to try and accomplish my newly found artistic niche in Film. I had moved back to Batley on Saturday 25th June 2011, after bidding a teary goodbye to Jess and Nick and Leicester, in the living room of our third year student house. I was prompted with a yearning to develop a career in the film industry and do hope to achieve this ambition.

Wednesday 29th June 2011

I jumped on the train to Leeds this morning to visit Screen Yorkshire. I took my portfolio and a copy of my films "His Haunted Laughter (Reversed Version)" and "The Trickster." I arrived in Leeds, unsure where the organisation was based. But I finally found it by asking for directions from passers-by. I inquired at the reception and they guided me to the second floor. There were offices in every direction, so I was unsure where to go. Luckily, this woman in the office ahead of me invited me in and sat me down in the corner. I explained that I was going to graduating in two weeks' time with a fine art degree, adding that I produced short films with using installations. I am wanting to continue with this area of work and was curious if she was able to help me. Apparently, the funding here at Screen Yorkshire has been cut and they are not looking for new talent. However, she did put me in contact with the northern filmmaking network site and a male director named Rob Speranza, who runs the South Filmmaker network in Sheffield. She didn't watch my films, but she was extremely helpful with linking me to different contacts. I had the urge to visit other film companies within the Leeds area, so I paid a visit to the Information Centre. The receptionist found a couple more film companies with one being "Atom Film Company" but was another train ride away to Headingley. I was tempted to jump on the next train and visit but I didn't. I am glad I didn't as they were more of a film service provider, rather than a producing film company. I emailed both "The Northern Filmmaking Network" site and Rob Speranza. I explained my financial struggle of investing in a camera and tripod to continue my filmmaking ambitions. I have loads of ideas waiting to explode in my imagination. Rob Speranza mentioned that he would give my films a watch when he returns to England.

On the evening of Friday 5th August 2011, I travelled down to London with Adele, who I befriended in the final year of my degree course. We went to witness my film being accompanied with live music on stage, performed by the brilliant Making Tracks ensemble. This was curated by The Whirlygig Cinema based at Rich Mix in Bethnal Green. The event was a brilliant experience. This was my very first screening prior many more that I had enjoyed throughout subsequent years. Hearing the live band harmonize "His Haunted Laughter (Reversed Version) with a comedic melody really brought the project to life and added character to it.

On Sunday 9th October 2011, mum, dad and myself went to Hull by car to see the film screened at "The Glimmer International Film Festival," which was shortlisted in The Yorkshire Category, although it didn't win. I can't remember the actual name of the venue but I do recall the screening being held in a cathedral, where the was a good sized audience. The event happened a couple of weeks after my 2011 manic episode. I somewhat healed myself through my own willpower, although a state of irrational thinking occupied my mind, whilst travelling to Hull, but it disappeared later on that night.

I attended further events to see "His Haunted Laughter (Reversed Version)" being screened, including "Kino" based at The Vibe Bar, on Brick Lane in London, on the evening of Thursday 5th January 2012. Also "Moviebar" based at The Caroline of Brunswick," based in Brighton, in June of the same year, where a Q&A session was held after each filmmaker presented their pieces. I remember it being a beautiful radiant day, with the marine parade crammed with tourists and it was my first time in Brighton too. It was quite fitting to show my film during this specific year, as it seemed that the bygone era of silent film was becoming more of a popular style in mainstream cinema, with the 2011 black and white release of the Micheal Hazanacicius film, "The Artist," based on Peppy Miller, who falls in love with the silent film star George Valentin.

Further screenings of "His Haunted Laughter (Reversed Version)" included "The Gingerbread House Presents" based at The Marsden British Legion. Another screening took place at an event formerly known as "ArtFix" based in Covent Garden, during the evening of Friday 28th February 2014. This was more an open exhibition event, as opposed to a mainstream Film Festival. I met a few pleasant people at this event, including a tall eloquent lady by the name of Hilary, who very much reminded me of Miss Doubtfire. I initially thought that she was rather stern but I immediately warmed to her. Shortly after the event, I briefly dined out at Cafe Rouge during the evening, just off Oxford Street with Hilary and her male companion who was also an artist. The artist believed in my film, providing me with the opportunity to hook up with another experimental filmmaker and to screen my work at a festival based in Vienna. Due to not having a passport and low income at the time, I had to decline his offer. It was brilliant to be introduced to these people, although I have lost contact with them. On the evening prior to this showcase, I performed at "Bang Said the Gun" which was compered by the renowned poet, Laurie Bolger, based at The Roebuck Pub on Dover Street in South London.

"His Haunted Laughter (Reversed Version)" had a second musical rescore by a Manchester alternative, psychedelic band named The Yossarions, in May 2014, as part of an event called "Sounds In The City" based in Bexley Square, Salford. I stood inside a marquee with a friend of mine, on a bustling bank holiday Sunday. It was a privilege to witness the film being performed with a live composition again. The music performed was instrumental with an Indie, hippy style, accompanied by a male yodelling vocal.

Thursday 1st May 2014

I'm in a miserable, rainy London. I got off the train about half an hour ago, at London Kings Cross, purchased my ticket to Forest Hill and walked half a mile to a Cafe Nero as it continued to piss it down. I am having my film, "His Haunted Laughter "Reversed Version,)" screened at The Vortex Cinema Club with a live introduction by me. I headed back to Kings Cross station and jumped onto the underground and then overground to Forest Hill, arriving at 6:20pm. I asked a kind woman for directions to Dartmount Hill, when leaving the station. The event was based in a quirky, small shop gallery, at a venue called Doopo Doopo. I walked through the door, finding four people gathered around on chairs, in the space that the screening will be taking place.

"Is this the cinema club?" I politely asked at the door.

"It is," they answered. I was welcomed by them all.

There were two women and two men. One of the women was Polish and tall with blonde short hair propped up in a bun. The other woman was a bit shorter. The short woman is based in Forest Hill, studying fashion and illustration at The Royal College of Fashion in London. I was talking to her for a good twenty minutes, whilst I set up my camera and tripod to film the screening. I met a few people, including a tall and very well-spoken man. He was a professional photographer. I think he was here with his wife and I also meet an interesting elderly woman, who was stood between us. My film was the second last to be screened.

"Would you like to introduce your film, Jamie?" An oldish man with frizzy hair asked with a smile.

I got up and walked over to the side of a mannequin to introduce my film as follows:

"'His Haunted Laughter' is a film that I created during my third year at university. It portrays a French clown who tries to find normality in the real world but fails to do so. I have found that audiences have their own perspectives on this piece. So, here is "His Haunted Laughter".

I sat back down in my seat, whilst the short film was being screened. I think the audience grasped the concept of it and enjoyed it. The male photographer and his wife approached me to congratulate me on my film, but want to share their mixed reactions of it. The man picked up on the fact that he noticed the pylons in the distance in one of the scenes, although he did mention that the actor in the film was good. I told him that the actor was me. It was an absolute privilege to meet the small crowd this evening. I headed back to Kings Cross to meet my then friend Christine. We both stopped over in London this evening, at The Queens Hotel, based in Finsbury Park, returning back to Yorkshire on the evening of Friday 2nd May 2014, after watching "The Testament Of Mary," performed by Fiona Shaw, at The Barbican Theatre.

Monday 9th June 2014

After a two-hour journey on a Northern Rail train, I eventually arrived in Nottingham at approximately 2pm. Having walked two minutes up the road from the station, I found The Hopkinson Gallery. Two of my short films, "Strange Mystique Performance" and "His Haunted Laughter (Reversed Version,)" will be exhibited as part of "The Uncurated Show" at the venue. The Gallery was an antique shop with a window display of furnishings. Downstairs, there was a welcoming café and the upper floors were accessed by a wooden staircase. Each space was characterized by immaculate historical features. It was just like a scene from a Charles Dickens novel; The Old Curiousity Shop, maybe? This is the only Dickens novel which I have not yet read. "The Uncurated Show" was based upsatirs, where an array of artists exhibited their work on the plain white walls. My short films were presented on a small silver television playing on a loop, displayed on top of a plinth with headphones provided. The exhibition was on for a week, completing its run on Monday 16th June. I headed back to Leeds via train.

"His Haunted Laughter (Reversed Version)" was screened as part of a 10th anniversary celebration within an online event run by Kino London on Thursday 19th November 2020. It was broadcasted on YouTube, including my own a pre-recorded introduction, briefly talking about the film, as I perched leg crossed in front of a radiant crackling fire in Danny's living room.

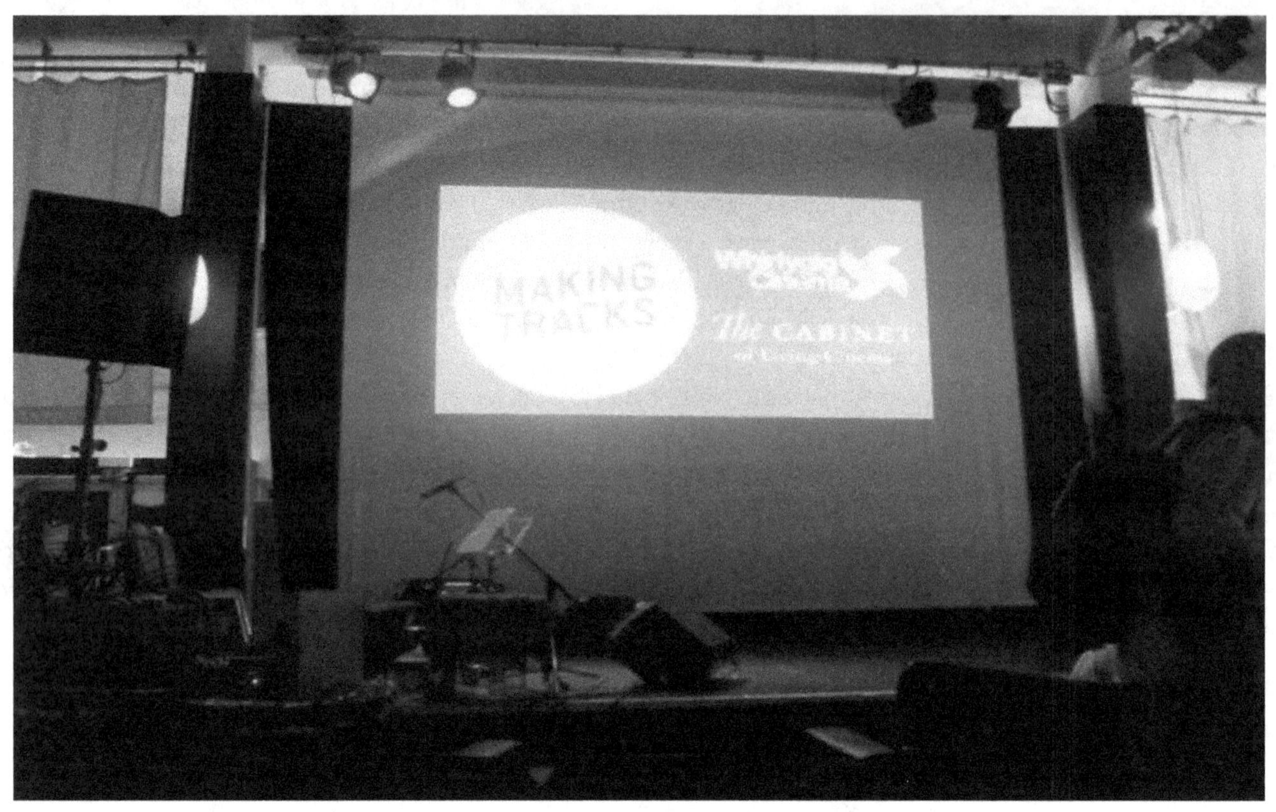

Rich Mix, Bethnal Green, London.

Preperations for the rescoring of "His Haunted Laughter (Reversed Version)"

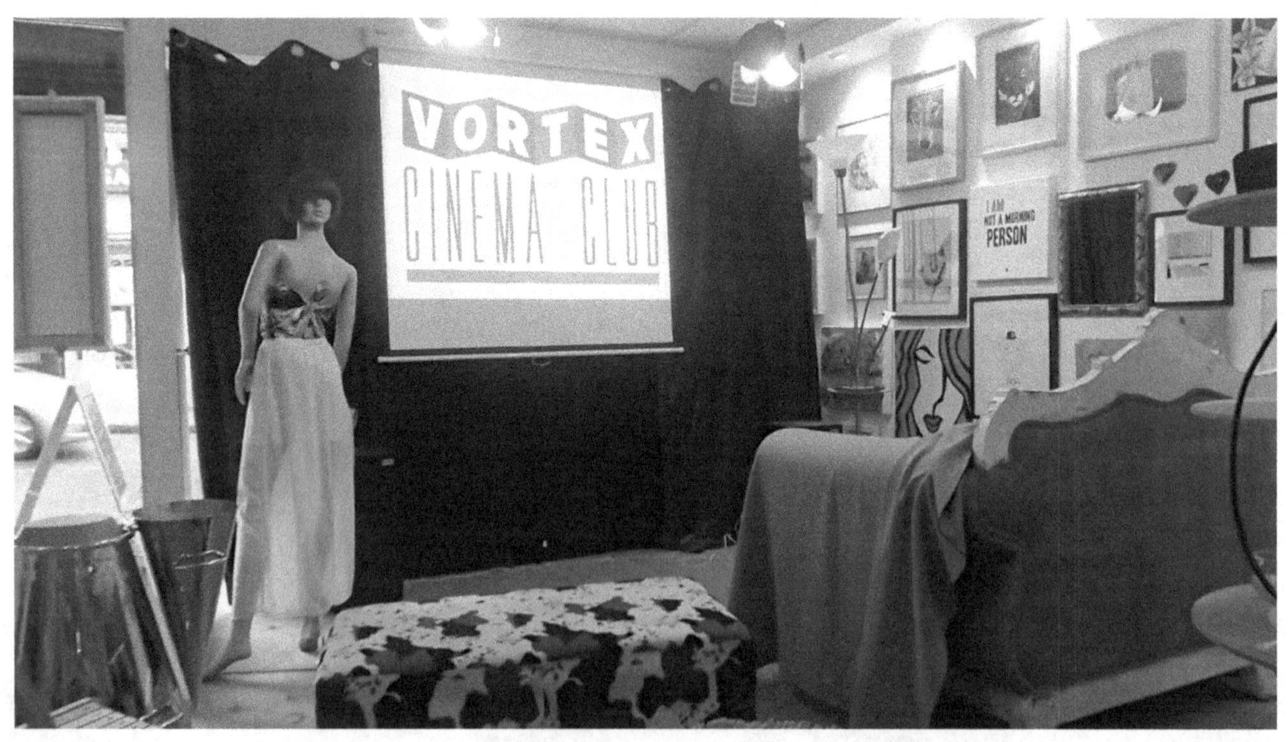

Vortex Cinema Club - Doopo Doopo, Forest Hill, London

Before the screening of "His Haunted Laughter (Reversed Version)" - 1/5/2014.

Mr Anti – Valentines

Forty lousy years we have been together,
I thought our relationship propelled a dream,
But all I got for Valentines,
Was a George Formby Deep Grill Machine!

I thought he would romanticise me with roses and chocolates,
I thought he would mollycoddle me with bliss,
But he didn't appreciate our affection on any substantial level,
Because he is just taking the piss!

This would be the day that he would project his love,
The day we cherish and celebrate,
Well, he is getting nothing from me tonight, he can sleep in the other bed,
and help himself to masturbate!

It just shows that you really do not know your soulmate,
Because he is just an utter tit,
Valentines can diminish into thin smouldering air for all I care,
Because the 14th of February is full of shit!

This anecdote is written from the perspective of a lavish gay man, who undervalues his lover's gifts. This was inspired by many stories I have heard of how partners receive a shit Valentines gift from their better half and in the manner of giving your other half anything, to compensate it as a "gift" on the day. I actually performed this piece at The LUU Spoken Word student event based at The Brudenell WMC in Leeds on Thursday 13th February 2018, as a response to their given "Anti-Valentine's" theme.

SMOGGY SPECTACLES

I wish window wipers were invented for spectacles,
Now that would be the ultimate dream,
I am tired of wiping my lenses every time,
When they fill up with so much steam!

It mainly happens during the bleak winter period,
When I come into contact with blistering ice,
The arctic temperature has a habit of intruding my view,
And I no longer see through my eyes!

My penultimate predicament is when I catch a glimpse,
Of an irritable, turpid smudge,
Yet I am tired of wiping my lenses in order,
To get the obtrusion to budge!

Handkerchiefs are the only tool to rectify the hitch,
Now that is a delinquent taboo,
Piddelling about all day, wiping your specs,
In order to achieve a better view!

I have considered upgrading my pitiable sight,
I have pondered about getting contacts,
At least I will be free from obstacles in my vision,
And my perception will be perfectly intact!

I really do wish that window wipers were invented for spectacles,
It is a concept which is unforeseen,
I am tired of wiping my lenses every time,
When they fill up with so much steam!

This anecdote was inspired by another very good friend of mine named Ian. He works and is a patron based at The Leeds Playhouse. He mentioned about the persistent predicaments spectacle users encounter throughout winter, when their lenses steam up, due to the bitter chill. I went away and wrote this poem. There is a similar poem in relevance to this titled "I should Have Gone to Specsavers," like the saying, the poem does exactly what it says on the tin. I merely perform this piece, with "Smoggy Spectacles" being the prominent feature. I did perform "I Should've Gone to Specsavers" at the Spoken Word events being "Jawdance," in London and "WORD!" based at The Y Theatre in Leicester, both in the spring of 2015, so the piece didn't completely go abandoned. When writing two similar poems, I always veer towards the piece which has a lot more perspective and meaning to it and this is how "Smoggy Spectacles" was birthed.

Wednesday 1st August 2018

I had a surge of creativity this evening, so I began work on a new stop motion animation, titled "Smoggy Spectacles." I had an abundance of energy channelling through me. I returned home and immediately dived into the process. I commenced with the opening titles. I knew that I wanted the title to appear gradually on the screen and disappear through the tracing paper, in the same way that I have done in many previous projects. I love the challenge of producing a distinctive air of mystery. To replicate this effect, I faintly drew out the shapes of the letters so that they would gradually appear and made several photographic shots. It was a repetitive, gruelling process but the result was fantastic, when I collated the individual shots in the form of an animated sequence. I decided to reject the final part of the title sequence, where the text is transformed into the shape of spectacles. This didn't artistically appeal to me during playback on my camera. I kept everything in during the title opening, apart from the spectacles image.

I decided on keeping things simple within this project, by having the spectacles in view and nothing more. At first, I made an image of a face with facial expression wearing the spectacles but during playback, the clip looked disorientated. Having only the spectacles present, was expressive enough. Reverting back to my sketchbook, I used the template of a character's spectacles by placing a piece of A3 tracing paper onto the page and very lightly traced over the image as a guide for my sequence. My spectacles manifested into view, post titles. I used individual shots to produce this visual gradually fading in. I worked consistently on the project for at least four hours. Over the following couple of days, I completed the first two verses of the Poem. For the opening line -

"I wish window wipers were invented for spectacles,
Now that would be the ultimate dream -"

I drew window wipers which would rise up from the bottom of the screen, in lining with the spectacles. I made them appear to operate with a series of four cogs connected to each other. The cog depiction was rotoscoped. When the window wipers moved, so did the cogs. This was be a multi-tasking challenge, as I was co-ordinating every spectrum of the visual at once. This is a process which I challenge myself with, on many of my animations. I then made a pair of cut outs of eyelids, to create a blink movement. This provided a realistic rhythm for the following line -

"I am tired of wiping my lenses every time,
When they fill up with so much steam -"

I cut out six lenses from tracing paper, to replicate the build-up of condensation. I originally decided to smudge the lens with pencil lead, but I found that it unrealistic and still. I reverted to the cut outs and went with this concept. At various points, I did feel sceptical about this current project as a whole, because I was beginning to experience strong emotions of feeling that I was producing this animation, just for the sake of it. Also my expectations had mounted up, as I was comparing this with previous projects.

Today is Saturday 4th August 2018, I feel a lot more engaged with the current project now, which contrasts with how I felt about it a good couple of days ago. In some aspects of producing, I was contemplating how I was going to interpret the second verse -

"It mainly happens during the bleak winter period,
When I come into contact with blistery ice -"

I replicated the spectacle sketch, to have a fresh, original template to work with. I rotoscoped eight snowflakes, to represent the dilemma of spectacles during the arctic, winter solstice. As the snowflakes fell from the sky, I drew an isolated twiggy looking tree, rising upwards, in a dystopian landscape. Jagged icicles formed at the bottom of the spectacle rims and then disappeared with the forlorn tree remaining below. I used a second cut out of lenses, produced on tracing paper, to represent the cracking of the glass as it comes into contact with Siberian temperatures. I simply drew lines on the lenses to show the shattering of the glass. A pair of hands, held open together, appeared from the bottom of the screen, preparing to catch the debris of the lens shattering into pieces. The fragments of glass were simply made from strands of paper which I ripped. I made the hands dip down out of view, as the character's eyes spun around erratically. Again, I produced a cut out of the pupils, so that I could make them move. I erased the pupils to adjust the eyes and move them in a different position.

Sunday 5th August 2018

I made myself a large cup of decaf coffee and resumed work on my current animation, in the living room. I re-produced a third template of the spectacles, to keep it looking fresh for verse 3 -

"My penultimate predicament is when I catch a glimpse,
Of an irritable turpid smudge -"

To portray the smudge, I produced replica of the right-hand side lens, by cutting it out and placed it over the original eye. I very faintly drew the outline of a fingerprint, which appears and disappears from sight, during the sequence. I also drew an aggravated looking frown, to animate the character's eyes, when he discovers the "irritable, turpid smudge."

I then took myself upstairs, to complete this scene, by making photographic shots. I am yet to do the fingerprint effect. I came back downstairs and edited the material I had, into a six second clip, and then added it to the developing animation. I then headed out into the summer sweltering heat at approximately 2:15pm until 3:30pm for a run.

I resumed work on the animation for the next couple of hours after having a bath. I completed the rest of verse 3 -

"I am tired of wiping my lenses in order,
To get the obtrusion to budge -"

This being the fingerprint, emerging on the right-hand side spectacle lens. To conclude this specific verse, I made a hand appear from the right-hand side of the screen, to completely eradicate this obtrusion. The final scene was a reverse playback to the opening clip. I finished work for the day, just before 7pm, feeling content with what I had produced throughout the afternoon.

There were some aspects of the project which made me feel aggravated and feel oppressed, though some moments allowed me to breathe and reign back a balanced wavelength. It is just the triggering moments when I can sense the mental and physical elements of mania seeping within me. They say that being productive in creating, reduces your ability to think. My thinking is the complete opposite. I can be focused on creating something, whilst my mind is reminiscing on memories, or my episodes when my mental health overhauled me. Then I could have a scene from a TV programme or film playing on cycle in my imagination. This is how I feel that the devil makes work for creative hands.

Monday 6th August 2018

I resumed work on my current Animation, when finishing 10am until 2pm Box Office shift based on Eastgate. I managed to complete verse 5 -

"I have considered of upgrading my pitiable sight,
I have pondered about getting contacts,
At least I will be free from obstacles in my vision,
And my perception will be perfectly intact -"

I used the idea of a pair of hands taking off the character's spectacles, replacing his "pitiable sight" with contact lenses. Every object but the eyes, was again, cut out symbolic features. The eyes were the only human form that was fixed onto the A3 tracing paper. The process being, one set of hands would take away the spectacles to the bottom of the visual, whilst a second set of hands would emerge from the top and bottom, venturing towards each eye, to provide the contact lenses. The bottom hand balancing the contact lens on the tip of its finger; the top hand being an aid to lift up the eyelid. Also vice Versa on the left eye. I took myself down into the living room, to jigsaw the individual parts into a sequence.

Tuesday 7th August 2018

I returned home at approximately 8pm, after a shift at the Playhouse, resuming work on my current project. I did a little bit of development of the project, when returning home at 3:30pm but not very much. I ended up having a snooze on the leather couch in the living room, as I felt exhausted. I do not know what from. Anyhow, I continued work on the verse -

"Handkerchiefs are the only tool to rectify the hitch,
Now that is a deliquent taboo,
Piddelling about all day and wiping your specs,
In order to achieve a better view -"

This was a sequence which I subsequently created on Wednesday 8th August 2018. I used the cut out of the spectacles and placed it directly onto the template of the short-sighted eyes. I had placed petite fragments of white masking tape on the bottom and top rims, to keep the replica still. Because dusk was gradually approaching, I used my five-foot something lamp, to maintain the lighting levels for the animation. The lamp light produced shadows of the spectacles. I noticed this during the edit process. So, I used this particular clip as a screentest rather than an official edit.

Wednesday 8th August 2018

I resumed work on the animation at 7:30am. I perched myself in the living room and produced another spectacle template for verse 3. This being the Verse I attempted to work on last night. I didn't know how to represent the "foggy spectacle lens" without the clip looking mundane. I didn't want it to look repetitive either. I sketched out a vintage metal kettle, which I cut out and used a motion stencil, to place on the template, underneath the spectacles. With this, I made the kettle appear into the scene from the bottom of the screen, releasing a cloud of condensation, which made the lenses to steam up. I achieved this, through making several photographic shots. The kettle appeared in view, frame by frame. I produced the cloud of condensation, by gradually adding texture using pencil marks, making it appear to seep out from the tip. I then smudged the marks to produce a swirling vapor effect. Hands gripping a handkerchief came into view from both sides of the screen, to clean the spectacles.

On completing the footage, I went back down to the living room, to edit the sequence together. I finished this at approximately 1:30pm. I had another snooze on the couch, then resumed work on the animation at 4pm. All I had to do was the closing credits. Faintly rotoscoping the slapstick style typography from the surface of my laptop screen, I took myself back up to my bedroom, to work on the final section. I used the same effect of text fading in and out, just like I did for the opening credits. It took me a good hour to create this. I then returned to the living room, to edit the final sequence. I used a royalty free tun that sound humorous and whimsical. It belonged to composer called Jay Man. Wherever necessary, I added relevant sound effects to add another interesting layer to the animation. "Smoggy Spectacles" was completed at approximately 9pm.

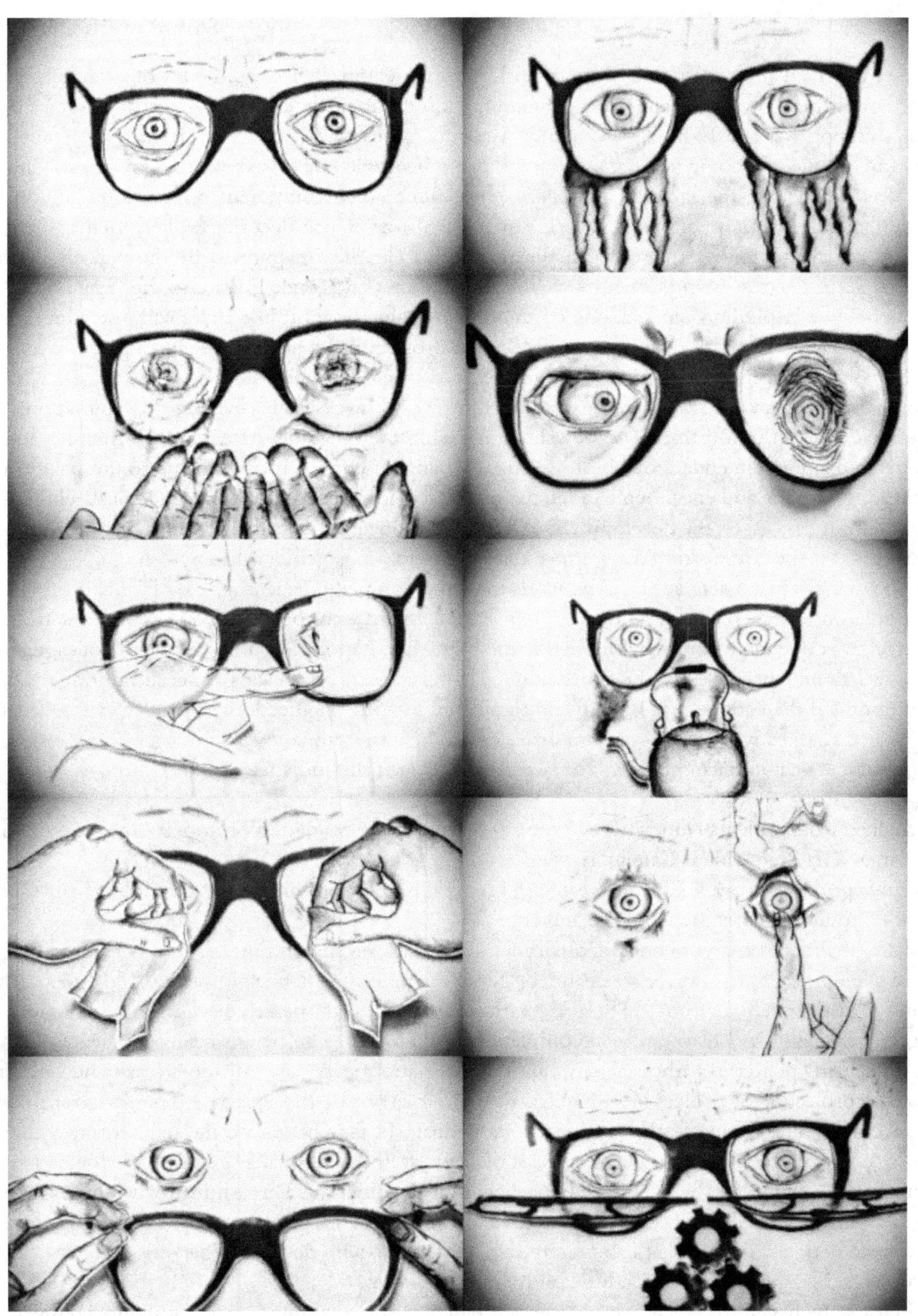

"Smoggy Spectacles"
Animation stills.

Saturday 6th October 2018

I eventually arrived at The Cinema Museum in London at 6:45pm, after a little bit of a farce commuting here. It is that time of year again, where my animation "Smoggy Spectacles" is getting screened at this evening's edition of The Exploding Cinema. Audience wise, it was a very lively turnout. I entered the momentous venue, the home to Charlie Chaplin, being bedazzled by an exhibition of vibrant illuminating projections, serenading the interior. Vintage, archaic filmmaking equipment posed eloquently in almost every dimension. I cannot comment on every spec of history which decorated The Cinema Museum. A repertoire of memorabilia, ranging from the prestigous Charlie Chaplin, to the immensely established celebrated actors, actresses and directors well before my era. I was welcomed into the venue by two male founders of The Exploding Cinema, one of them mentioning how prolific I am, with my commitment in travelling around consistently. I was given a free petite programme, a raffle ticket and a free entry stamp on my right hand. I then made my way into the immense projection space.

A brilliant eclectic, varied programme of short films was showcased this evening. My animation, "Smoggy Spectacles," was the fourth film to be screened during the schedule. After the two minutes and twenty-one second animation ended, Ben Slotover, this evening's compere, invited me up to the stage for an informal Q&A with the audience. Ben handed me over a second microphone for me to speak a little more in depth about my processes, the development of the animation and the inspiration that I had for the project.

"So, how was the Animation created, was it layers of drawings?" Ben asked.

"It was actually just a single sketch, which I drew as a complete piece, frame by frame, through photographic stills, in order to create a sequence." I answered. I then went onto speaking about how the whimsy soundtrack was obtained from the musician named Jay Man. I spoke about how a work colleague told me about how irritable spectacles can be, when condensation appears on the lens, especially during the Siberian winter months. I then added that I had been nominated to write an anecdote about dry eyes. A gentleman in the audience asked what tools I used in order to produce the animation.

"Graphite Pencil on tracing paper," I answered, glancing at the audience with a beaming spotlight blindsiding my sight.

Ben asked what projects I am working on next. I plugged the headline slot Robert Garnham has booked me in for, at The Blue Walnut Cafe in Torquay.

"Sounds good. Well, we will be interested in seeing it here," Ben said, as he rounded off my Q&A session with a round of applause from the audience.

The first half of the event concluded with an interesting seventeen minutes and twenty second documentary by Filmmaker, Ernesto Sarezale, titled "Naked Tongues," which explored the art of poetry through a complete distinctive perspective. There are various spoken word open mic events, predominantly based in London, that allow poets to perform completely naked on stage, in front of a live audience. This is not about sexualizing poetry in a physical way, but it is more about exposing our inner spirit and our sense of freedom by projecting our voices in a unique way. Ernesto is one of the artists who performs and thrives at these specific events, amongst other expressive individuals. In fact, he graced the stage this evening, naked for his Q&A session. Obviously, there was a lot of interest in this particular genre of performance poetry. It is an event which I would be interested in participating in sometime. Performing my whimsical anecdotes naked is definitely a challenge, which I would love to experience. I have actually written an anecdote which will resonate perfectly with this. It's about a retired gentleman, who decides to become a life drawing model, in a way to keep active and earn a little bit of pocket money.

I left after the first film screened in the second half, at approximately 9:45pm, walking 0.6 miles to The Elephant and Castle tube station in the bitter chill air. I caught the 11:30pm National Express service back to Leeds, arriving in the Yorkshire city of Leeds at 5:45am the following day.

"Smoggy Spectacles" was also on the bill at an event called "Video Art Club" based at The Leyden Gallery in London, on the evening of Saturday 13th October 2018. I didn't attend, due to having a low income at the time.

Thursday 18th October 2018

I arrived at The Candid Arts Trust in Angel, London, at approximately 5:15pm, after venturing from London Victoria by foot, through the thriving capital. It took about an hour get there. I met Molly upstairs in the cafe. She was perched in a small chair alone, in the corner of the dining space. We greeted each other as I joined her company. We had an interesting epic conversation about various subjects, such as her registration of becoming a British citizen. She mentioned that the test, which any non-British Citizen has to undergo, included completely irrelevant questions, which are not necessarily important for the British people to answer, like "how much of the British population have grandparents residing outside of the United Kingdom." The answer to that is 10%. The only alternative option would be to marry Brandon, who is a British Citizen. Molly has lived here in the United Kingdom since before I was even conceived. Brandon subsequently arrived, joining us after grabbing a slice of lemon cheesecake from the cafe counter. A waitress lit the venue with candles, to beam a flicker of light around the room. Desiree Lemonde also arrived with her son at 7pm, as Molly, Brandon and I went down into the basement, for this evening's edition of "Kino 99."

Dustin Murphy has apparently taken over the event, from Jonathan Evers, who has immigrated to another country but I am forgetting where. It was a good-sized audience this evening which included some new and old audience attendees. Molly's animation, "Oliver The Werewolf," began the eclectic showcase. My animation, "Smoggy Spectacles," was the third short film to be screened during the second half. I went to the microphone wearing a flowing, chocolate multi-tone shawl, very Clint Eastwood-esque, mentioning that the narrative was inspired by a friend of mine. I then returned to my seat beside Molly on a red velvet couch, with a tacky golden trim, whilst my animation was screened. As always, Kino 99 was a pleasant evening.

The event concluded at 9:35pm, after the UK premier of Dustin Murphy's short film was screened, titled "Averley Road." It was about the prejudices that exist against abortion, being viewed as murderous sin by catholic people. It was a political and thought-provoking piece. His female friend, who collaborated with Dustin on the film, had flown in from L.A especially for the screening. I thought "Averley Road" was brilliant in every retrospect. I bid farewell to Molly, Brandon, Desiree and then Dustin, who stood in the doorway to the basement. Dustin asked me if I was going to attend Kino 100 on Thursday 22nd November 2018. I was undecided, due to other scheduled commitments. I returned to London Victoria by foot, through the bustling capital via Trafalgar Square from Angel, arriving at approximately 11:05pm. I caught the Megabus coach service back to Leeds at 1am, arriving at 6am and then a bus back to Batley.

Saturday 24th November 2018

It is currently 6:45pm and I am perched on a front row chair in The Christ Church, based on Pitsmoor Road in Sheffield, for this evening's edition of "Cheap Thrills Zero Budget Film Festival." I will be performing a live recital of my animation, "Smoggy Spectacles," in the opening of the second half. I introduced myself to Martin, the curator of the event, who is dressed in a distinctive, revolutionary attire, accompanied by a handmade cardboard cut-out hat. The interior of the church is beautiful; a perfect heavenly altar vibe, with plenty of pastel vanilla lighting. Martin showed me where I would be performing alongside my animation, on a half foot raised platform, behind a microphone to the left hand side of the stage and the projection being in the centre.

"Have you brought your spectacles to wear?" Martin subduedly asked, standing beside me.

I answered that I hadn't. Martin had asked me out of pure sarcasm. I laughed.

The audience is beginning to arrive, the time now creeping towards 7pm. The event will initially begin at 7:30pm. The audience approximate age range being forty plus, with children in attendance. The event opened with the sound of the church bells ringing out from the two large speakers on either side of the projection screen. This is when Martin stood on the stage and advised the audience members to stand up and become a revolution, lasting approximately one minute and thirty seconds. The event was as eccentric as it could be. There was a woman on stilts gearing the audience up to exploit a revolutionary change. The short films throughout the first half were captivating, as they opened up with the name of the country that they were created in. The second half of the evening opened up with a six-minute projection of a 16mm film, which was technically operated by a middle-aged fellow, whom I am forgetting the name of. It was a beautiful, interesting, intricate piece which captured the 16mm cinema period. He briefly spoke about his piece, post screening. I was the second creative to grace the stage with a live recital of my animation, "Smoggy Spectacles," which went down brilliantly with the audience. My animation projected onto the big screen with me performing a live rendition beside it. I received a huge round of applause and could hear faint cheers echoing throughout the church. I stepped aside from the microphone and gave a bow. Martin stepped up onto the stage and we both gave each other a hug. I had to quickly dash off back to the train station immediately after my performance. Reverend Hive gave me a lift back to the station, complimenting how unique my performance was, with the accompanying animation. It is the first time that he has seen poetry presented in this way. The adrenaline buzz I received post performance, felt as always, incredible! It was bitterly cold outside and I must have dropped something in the car. My instinctive words I said was "Oh Lord," then "God," and then "Jesus Christ," directly in front of Reverend Hive. I hope he didn't hear my blasphemy in vain. I caught the 10:20pm train back to Leeds and then a second train back to Batley.

Friday 30th November 2018

I arrived at the Temple of Doom music venue at 6:15pm, which is based down in the basement of a grade two listed warehouse, on Millwright Street in Leeds. I will be performing alongside my animation, "Smoggy Spectacles," as well as screening "A Peculiar Imagination," at an event called "In Other Words." The well attended audience, seemed to have been thoroughly captivated by my work, with Lewis and a few other individuals who I connected with this evening, commending me on my delivery and projections. My slot was at 9:30pm, just before the second interval. It was an experience to perform and express my creativity, to an incredibly amiable and supportive audience, contained together in a bitterly cold, dingy rock club, on the final night of November. Kim, who performed in the first half, and her male companion compliment-ed me on how well the two artistic mediums married together, to create the performance I gave tonight. Adekelode, who also performed this evening, and Tai, both from the LUU Spoken Word nights, shook my hand as a congratulatory gesture. Laurence was exceptional as always. He graced the stage directly after me, so this allowed me to congratulate him on his performance, during the second interval. Katie Wallis was another delightful individual who I met this evening, here as an audience member. She is a music therapist, working with dementia patients here in Leeds. She recently moved to Leeds from Huddersfield, a town she is originally from. Unfortunately, Katie had to leave during the first interval, predominantly with the venue being ridiculously cold. I met a whole herd of beautiful spirits whom I hope I can keep in contact with. Angus a writer who recited a little story this evening, travelled all the way down from Edinburgh, to specifically share three of his pieces here. A massive thank you to Jade and Lisa for sharing my material at this event, which concluded at 10:15pm. I said goodbye to Laurence. He had another gig at The Primrose also in Leeds, directly after this one.

Friday 7th December 2018

I am currently sat in a large room, based in Stoke Newington, at a venue called The Others, situated on top of a snooker club, based on Manor Road. The time is approaching 7pm. There are a few artists in attendance at the minute. There is male and female duo band rehearsing for their showcase this eventing, a violinist and a drummer. I am one of the artists also showcasing three stop motion animations of mine, at this evening's edition of "Propaganda." I have already introduced myself to Peter Thomas, this evenings curator and also for The Exploding Cinema. A Burlesque dancer named Belle, also introduced herself to me, asking who she should approach, to introduce herself to. I pointed to Peter, who was preparing the technical inputs and outputs. Everything in due course at the minute is soundchecks. Now, there is a very handsome band in soundcheck. I am sat with Belle, who is now teching. Iris, a female poet has also introduced herself to me. She is based here in London but is originally from France.

The event commenced at approximately 8:50pm, opening up with the first of three of my animations being "Smoggy Spectacles." Propaganda was one of those events where fifty percent of the audience were here for the show and the other fifty percent came to quietly socialise. Iris graced the stage after my first animation, with a small set of her interesting material. One of the poems which she beautifully delivered, was written on an endless shard of narrow paper, which must have been easily eighty feet long. My subsequent animations titled "A Peculiar Imagination" and "My Husband Has Booked Our Funeral" was screened during the opening of the second half. Peter then invited me up to the flat stage, for a five minute Q&A session with the audience.

"How did that come about?" Peter asked me with a smile, referring to the final animation.

"It's a piece inspired by my grandma and grandad," I began. "My grandad always vowed that on the day he retires, he will to take my grandma and himself to book their funeral, which is very optimistic of him."

Subsequent questions from the audience, would be raised about whether the animations were all hand drawn as single sketches, in order to make the sequences. I explained that my earlier animations were developed through making hundreds and hundreds of drawings, which I would then compile to create a moving image. Now, I just rely on one or two sketches which I produce through single frames of photographs. I personally feel that this process is a lot more efficient and effective. I pretty much taught myself the process of animation, a good couple of years ago, when I was in need of delivering something distinctive in style, as opposed to my experimental short films which I created earlier on. It was also an opportunity to channel my inner fine art alter-ego and marry the medium together with my whimsical anecdotes.

"What are you working on next?" a young man asked, sat with a party of people, horizontally to the right of me. I spoke about a project I may be creating for a rock band named "Roof." The lead singer named Noah, approached me via social media, asking if I was interested in producing an animated backdrop for his upcoming show. I agreed but he later found that my distinctive style was too gothic for him. I also mentioned that I recently completed a music video for Laurence, titled "Lence-Loved."

Belle showcased a divine burlesque performance with a theme focussed on women's empowerment through body issues. She delivered a beautiful performance. I left the venue with Belle and her partner named Matthew at approximately 10:40pm. She vowed to pitch my animations to filmmakers working in the industry.

"So, what do you want?" Belle asked, lighting up her cigarette outside. I said anything which would promote my animations through various connections. She added that she is good friends with someone who used to work at the BFI in London, which would be a progress. I returned the favour to her, mentioning I will send her links to potential venues based in Leeds like The Live Art Bistro. I have never been to LAB, as it is formerly known as, but I do know they are besotted with experimental, risque acts, particularly in burlesque. Matthew is a chaperone and also a manager for Belle's act. They both connected in theatre. He complimented how unique and distinctive my animation style is, which was an honour to hear.

"Some people say "unique" meaning "different" but your animations were truly unique." Matthew smiled, as we strolled towards Stoke Newington overground station. We then changed for the underground at Seven Sisters, as I left them at Kings Cross, to venture back to The Albany Hotel. The time being 11:20pm. The capital is still thriving with tourists. A city that never sleeps.

I returned back to Yorkshire the following day, travelling for two hours on the 12:03pm East Coast train service from London Kings Cross station.

Thursday 18th April 2018

Steve introduced me to the petite stage, in the Terrace Courtyard at The LS6 Cafe, being the first featured poet at "Outspoken" to showcase a live recital of my animations, in front of an intimate audience. In my own visual fashion, I performed alongside my animations, "The Day My Grand Rode A Rollercoaster," "Smoggy Spectacles," "My Husband Has Booked Our Funeral" and a standalone screening of "A Peculiar Imagination." As one of the featured poets, I wanted my set to be a combination of Animation fused with live performance. The following featured poets were Eileen Benham, an alternative Poet, and the subtle gothic-esque poet named Rhiannon-Skye Boden. This followed onto five open mic poets, after a fifteen minute or so interval. As always, it was a pleasure to see Laurence, who supported me in the audience and gave us an MC rap performance in the Open Mic, which was an honour to see. Lisa arrived during Eileen's set and Jade arrived during the short break. Great to see them both too.

It was an interesting open mic section. We had a seventy year old, Kevin Flaherty, who doesn't look his age by the way, deliver two very Yorkshire based anecdotal pieces. The second piece was "The Cloth Cap Rap," which erupted hysteria in the room. Kevin was inspired by the new generation of rap, which he encountered at Laurence's event "Blur The Lines," based at The Hyde Park Book Club, back on the evening of Saturday 9th March 2019.

This evening's event commenced at 7:30pm, concluding shortly after 9:30pm. Laurence, Lisa and myself caught the bus into Leeds from Woodhouse Lane and dined at the Caribbean restaurant, Turtle Bay, based in The Light. It was a lovely eating out venue, with a reasonable £10.00 portion. We ate and drank, talking about various subjects. It was 11:05pm when I hugged and bid farewell to them both for the evening. Jade didn't tag along as she couldn't really afford to, but it was still lovely. I ventured home by foot, in the late, glacial evening air.

"Smoggy Spectacles" Animation will be included in an online episode of a Muddy Feet Poetry platform called "That Awesome Poetry Show" on Friday 29th January 2021, organised by Peter Hayhoe.

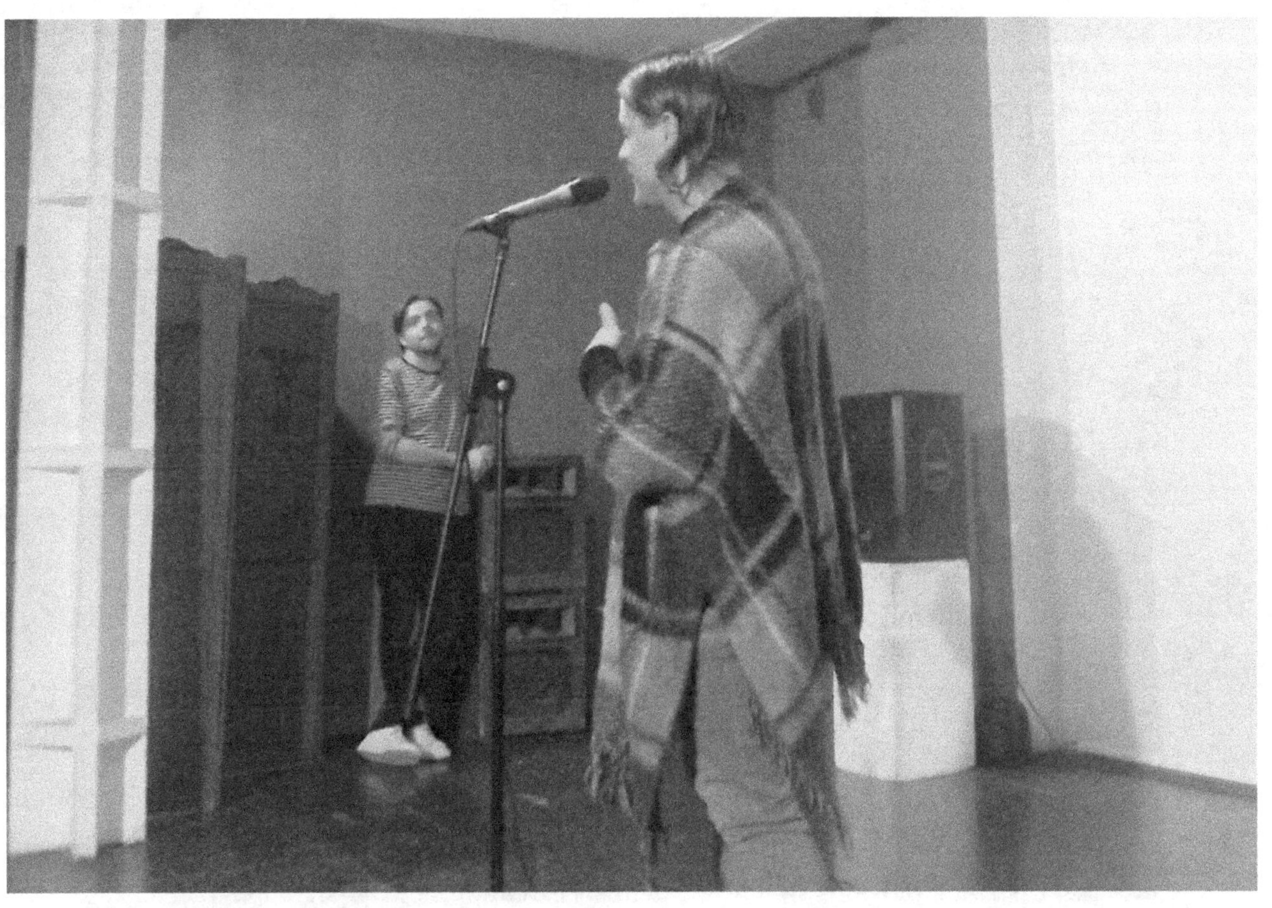

Introducing the Animation "Smoggy Spectacles" at Kino Open Mic Film Night
The Candid Arts Trust - Angel, London
18/10/2018

"I AM WHAT I AM!"

I'm surprised she hasn't run off with the milkman,
She will do knowing my luck,
At my age it is so strenuous to function adequately,
When a man cannot get it up!
I have prepared for this for the last six years,
That is when I knew there was something wrong,
The moment when I wasn't physically aroused,
When she gazed at me wearing a thong!
It really affected my aura,
I thought this was going to be it for the rest of my life,
I thought nothing is going to bedazzle me,
Not even my darling wife!
But I discovered the resolution to this quandary,
I can rectify this temporary malfunction,
Hopefully, I can medicate this obstacle with just one dose,
To eradicate this erectile dysfunction!
My lord it worked a miracle,
This reprised activity is becoming a habit,
It is like Christmas has come every day for me,
Because we are suddenly back shagging like rabbits!
Isn't it a phenomenon how scientists can improve your stamina,
How a nuclear formed pill can prove the trick,
How a generic treatment can enhance your performance,
To cure my dilapidated dick!
I am now a striving seventy-year old gentlemen,
Living life to its fullest peril,
I am like a dog on heat with my devoted dearest,
I am like a ravenous, libidinous devil!
My wife hasn't felt satisfaction for the past six years,
I am now a reproductive man,
I can finally sing at the top of my voice,
"I AM WHAT I AM!"

LIVE AND ANIMATED

I had the incredible opportunity of staging my debut show titled "Live and Animated," which was a live recital of all twelve of my animations, I have independently produced or collaborated on. The performance was held at The Slocken, based on Calls Lane in Leeds. I initially planned for the event to be staged at Wharf Chambers but The Slocken provided me with a better offer. The venue was free and the profits on the bar would be the compensation for the use of electrical equipment and so on. Nina and I was sat down upstairs in the venue having a cocktail, before I had a shift at The Playhouse on the evening of Friday 15th March 2019, when we noticed the beautiful petite stage. I immediately went down to the bar with the encouragement of Nina, to enquire about the space. I spoke with a lovely bartender named Meghan, who hired me out the space for the 5th June 2019. I rehearsed on numerous occasions in my bedroom at Pennington Grove in Leeds, as the animations played in the background on a mobile projector screen and even had a rehearsal at the venue, on the afternoon of Monday 20th April 2019, between 12:15pm until 2:05pm. When the supporting acts had completed their sets and it was my turn to deliver during the second half, I was initially going to start with an anecdote titled "Paler Than My Foundation Paste," which is about an elderly woman's distaste for weak tea. I performed a partial of "Live And Animated" with this original opening at a Jackanory event based in Wakefield on the afternoon of Saturday 23rd March 2019, to see how it would reflect on the audience. A good response. It was at this event where I would met with a bunch of other open minded artists including a transgender, quirky musician by the name of Jessica Rowbottom aka The Bleeding Obvious, who played lyrical numbers on her keyboard, depicting subjects surrounding the LGBQT community in a humorous tone. A song of hers titled "Superglue" was my favourite. She dedicated this to her former to be wife. Reverting back to my initial proposal, I swapped "Paler Than My Foundation Paste" for "Lycra" and you will soon read why.

Wednesday 5th June 2019

I arrived at The Slocken in Leeds at approximately 3:15pm to begin the set up preparations for my show "Live And Animated" this evening, which went brilliantly by the way. Meghan, the venue Manager, arrived at 4pm to de-clutter the stage by taking away the drums and amplifiers, so that I could push the projector screen a little further back to the wall. I wanted to have the 'jackanory' effect, which I think I successfully achieved. An Indi looking guy subsequently popped over to The Slocken and set up the two microphones and the additional amplification for Nina and Kelly's set. Nina arrived at the venue at 5:20pm, with her authentic acoustic guitar, where she quickly performed a soundcheck. Sarah Beavers aka Mrs Housecoat arrived a good half an hour later with her friend Michelle, who I had previously met at Sarah's 50th birthday gathering in York, a couple of years ago, where I also performed. Louisa arrived soon after, to apply make-up to her face in preparation for her drag performance as her inner alter-ego Luca. I have never seen Louisa perform before. She was very impressive and a delight to have as a support act at "Live and Animated." All of the acts were fucking amazing to have, expressing and gracing the intimate, lit stage based upstairs at the venue. The show provided a balance of subjects raised including whimsy, jocular, thought-provoking and often there were segments during the show that gave a deep intensity to what they individually wanted to say, in front of a very well attended audience. I had bouts of apprehension building up inside me, prior to this evening's performances, due to not particularly knowing how the technical flow of the show was going to be. Everything flowed perfectly. It was such a brilliant evening of creativity. My mum, Jenny, grandma and grandad came along to watch and give support this evening. Thomas Dewhirst, whom I met at "In Other Words" based at The Wharf Chambers in Leeds in April, where we both performed, even travelled all the way from Manchester, just to be here this evening. I thoroughly appreciated everyone's support tonight and I cannot thank them enough.

"Live And Animated" began at 7:30pm.

"Are you ready?" I asked the audience. They certainly were.

I pressed play on my laptop, to display the opening sequence of the show - "Welcome to Live and Animated," where a circus number played out in the background. Approximately forty seconds into the opening sequence, I took to the stage with my journal, welcoming the audience to this evening's showcase. I then introduced Nina, already sat and prepared with her acoustic guitar on stage, where she serenaded the crowd with her whimsical songs. The wonderful Mrs Housecoat then came to the stage, wearing a headscarf and holding a walking stick. She was followed up be Kevin Flaherty and then Yvonne Ugarte.

During the twenty-minute interval, I quickly popped upstairs to the toilet and dressed into my cycling lycra attire. Kelly welcomed me to the stage with her organic Yorkshire uniqueness. I put down my pint of Pravha and then delivered the first anecdote of my thirty-minute set being "The Granny Zimmerframe Race." This then followed onto "Lycra" where I stripped down to my lycra attire. I then performed a full set of my animations, as I perched myself on a blue curtain draped chair, beside the projection screen, enthralled with every minute of the delivery, clothed of course.

I subsequently performed a third anecdote being "Thirty Pence To Have a Piss?!" soon after Kelly graced the stage with her electric guitar, soothing us with two beautifully raw original songs with her Cerys Matthews-esq vocal. It was the first time I have heard or seen her perform - beautiful! Lence took to the stage and entertained the room with his brilliantly lyrical voice, after the three final collaborative animation screenings of "Grenfell" (Daren Peary), "Director's Cut" (Eva Curless) and "Lence - Heard."

The talent this evening was incredibly faultless and a privilege to share with the audience. I thank everyone who attended, partook and especially The Slocken, for allowing "Live And Animated" to happen. It was brilliant to see Lisa again, who kindly took photos during the second half of the show.

I stopped for a drink, upstairs in the venue post show, with Ian Brown, Amanda Robinson, Thomas, Lisa, Nina and Laurence until they called for the 11pm last orders at the bar. I dismantled and put away all the technical equipment in the venue's cellar, with the help of Laurence. I was still thrilled about the success of the show, even a good week or so later. It is an elation everyone would experience after a debut show. Fabulous, darling!

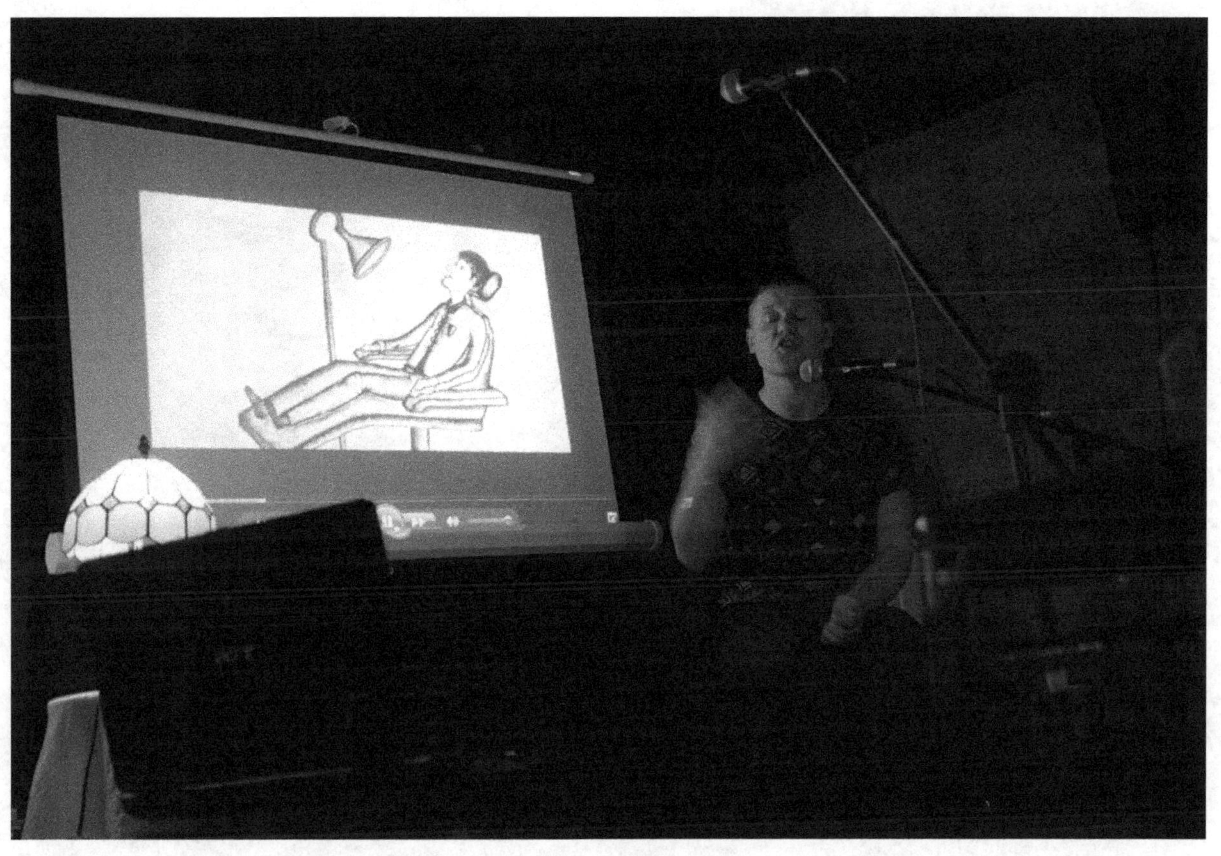

"Live and Animated" - The Slocken Leeds
Performing a live recital of my Animation "A Visit to the Dentist" - 5/6/2019
Photo courtesy of Lisa Boardman.

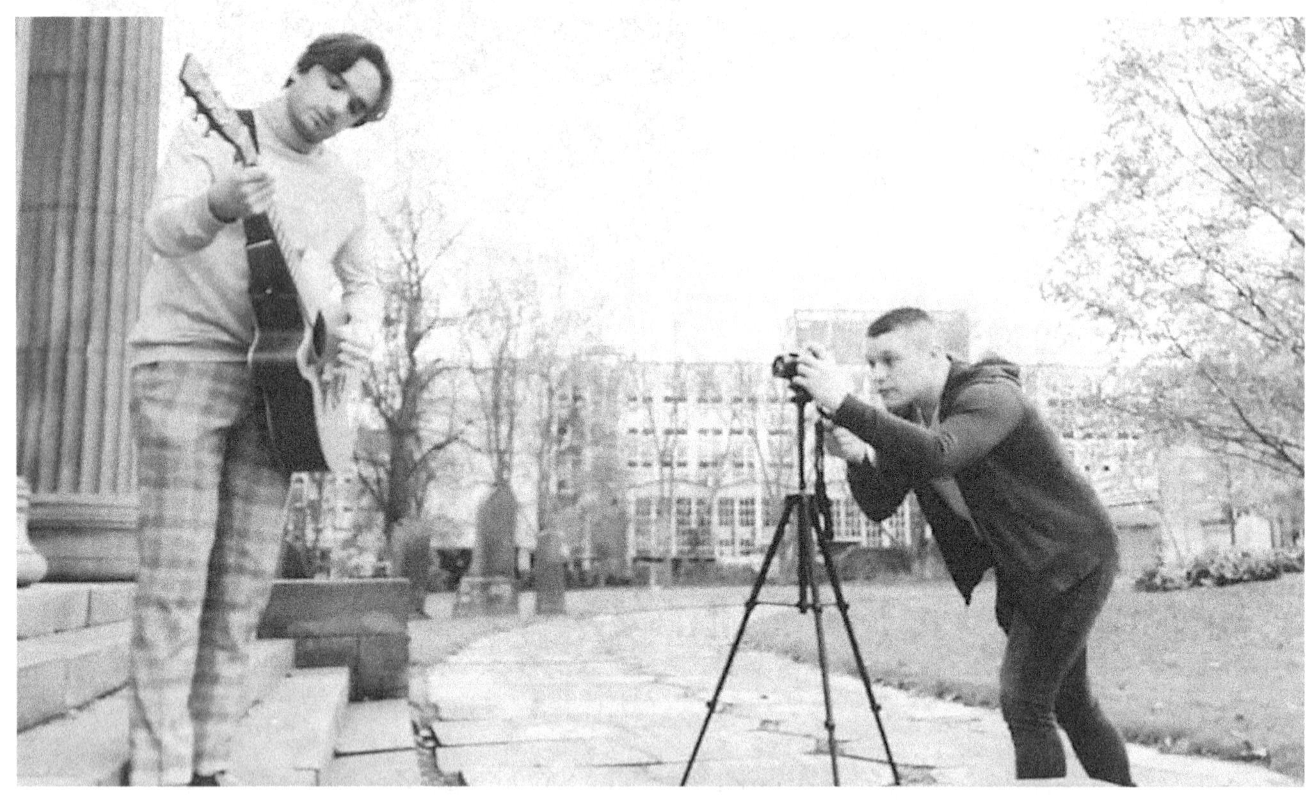

Capturing shots to rotoscope John playing the guitar at the beginning of the Animation.
Saint George's Graveyard

Icarus

(King Among Rascals)

Thursday 5th November 2020

Marc dropped me off outside the tall iron gates of North Lodge House, shortly before 1pm in Leeds, as we kissed each other goodbye in his car. I shall be returning back to his house this weekend. I popped to the shop before sitting down for a cuppa, ready for a run between 2:15pm until 3:05pm.

Between 5pm and 5:30pm, I spoke with a Leeds-based musician by the name of John Harbour Devlin, who has proposed a current track of his, titled "Icarus (King Among Rascals,) which I am going to adapt into an animation for a music video. This was going to be part of a commissioned project. He really likes the idea of the animation being focused on exploration and experimentation, but still having the scope of based on the Greek mythology fable. A sketchbook style ambience, with an artistic, poetic lyrical style to the visuals. I spoke of using rotoscoping, agreeing to meet to shoot live footage, early next Wednesday morning. I had the concept of filming John strumming along to the delicate instrumental acoustic melody, which I would then rotoscope. Within the animation, John would transition into a Greek legend with feathered wings, escaping the unruly Greek Islands but with his modern, English reimagining of the fable. I have yet to research more in depth this particular fable, to grasp a clear understanding its herculean background. John resides in Wortley, but he has agreed to come to me here in Woodhouse for the filming. I am extremely excited about the project, hoping I can fulfil its potential.

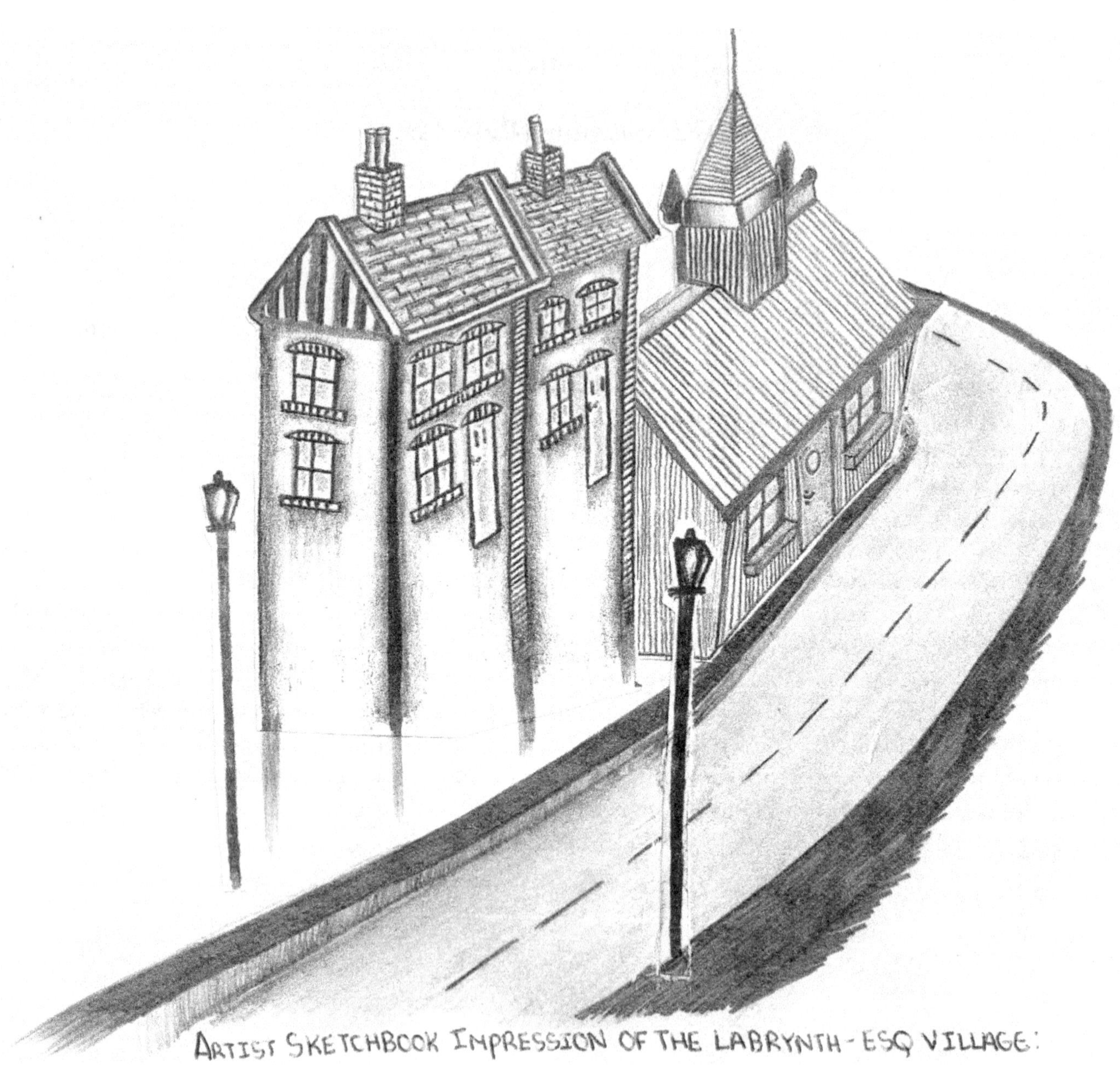

A visual impression of my subsequent 2D paper village model.

Tuesday 10th November 2020

I commenced work on the "Icarus (King Among Rascals) animation at 10am, as I perched at the desk near my unmade bed. I sketched a petite toned portrayal of a railway viaduct on a stretch of six sheets of cartridge paper which I sellotaped together last night. This followed onto a drawing of a church, which later stood as a 2D model with the aid of a paper backing stand. I am undecided about where the small church will be based, so it is ideal for the model to be mobile. I am attempting to create a labyrinth style village or an outer world, to use as part of Icarus's aviation sequence.

The same bipolar effect of becoming creatively inspired and feeling an immediate pessimistic attitude towards the project, really side lined my focus. But I do know that the result will be surprising. It is completely normal for me to be like this. I took a break from the project at 1pm, to energize myself and venture out for a run. I recommenced work on the animation from 3pm until 5:30pm, sketching out a Humber Bridge style structure to add to the 2D "flight" set. To make the 2D models sturdy, I used card to help the cut outs to stand up. I subsequently faintly rotoscoped my original sketch of "The Lighthouse" on an A3 piece of tracing paper. With this project being my first official commission, I am wanting the visual to appeal as magically inspiring as much as possible for John. Giving the animation an poetical tone is the absolute key, as John asked for this. Adding to this entry, I ended up sketching a road on my 2D drawing model between 11pm until 11:40pm. I only nipped downstairs to the loo and found myself going into my dimly lit basement room, picking up my 6H pencil to make additional features. This wasn't forced, I was enthusiastic. Even though the aviation sequence will have a rapid motion to it, it is completely essential to add intricate details to any working project. This is how you adapt and develop, particularly if you are an independent artist.

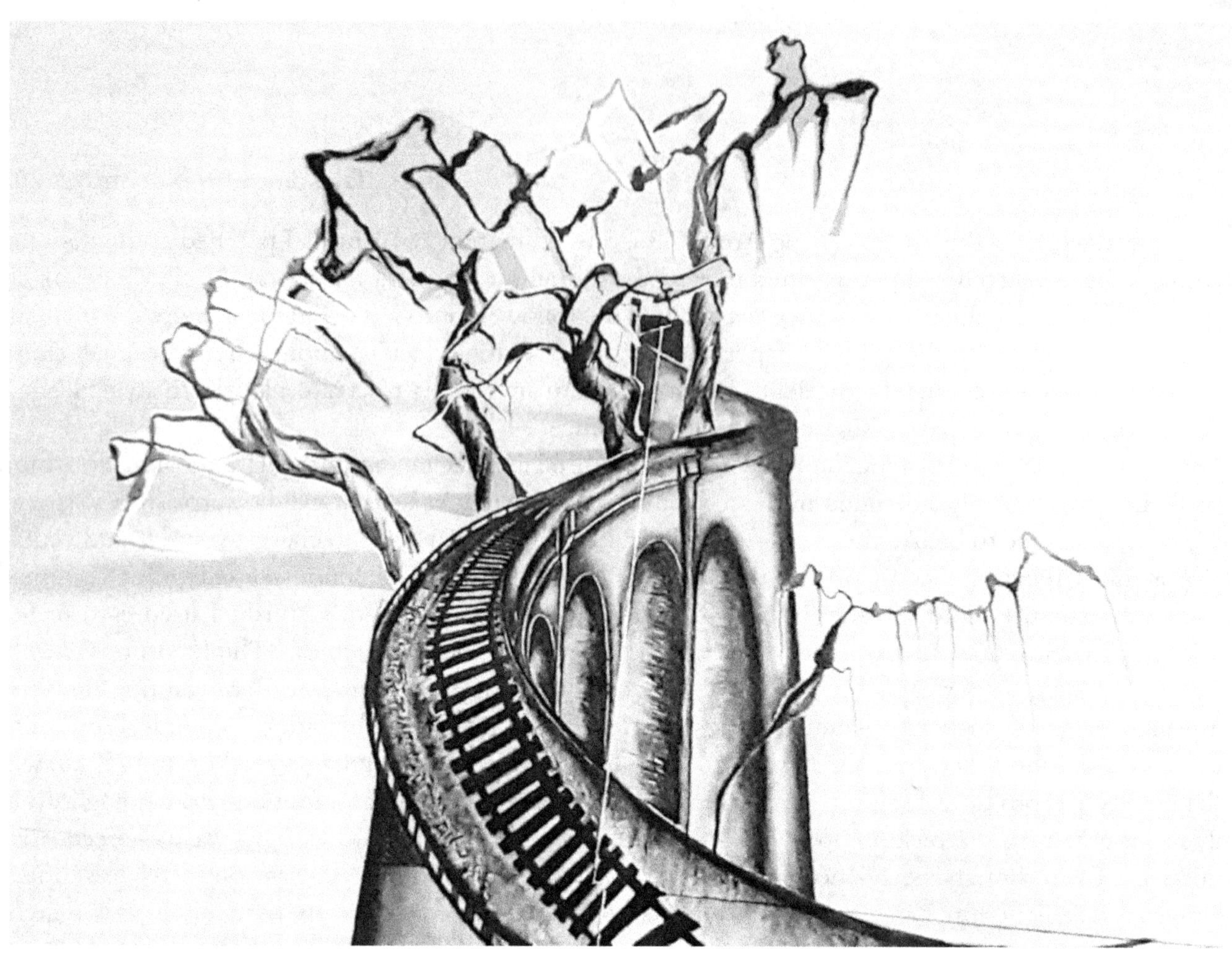

A sketch of a railway viaduct produced onto the surface of the soon to be 2D model.

Wednesday 11th November 2020

Between 9am and 9:30am, I had a short film session with John as he performed the instrumental opening of the animated music video on his acoustic guitar in Saint George's Park, near my flat. I began rotoscoping this particular footage between 6:30pm and 8:25pm, as I perched at my desk beside my hand drawn 2D model, which I also worked on from 10am until 1pm and then 3pm until 5:45pm.

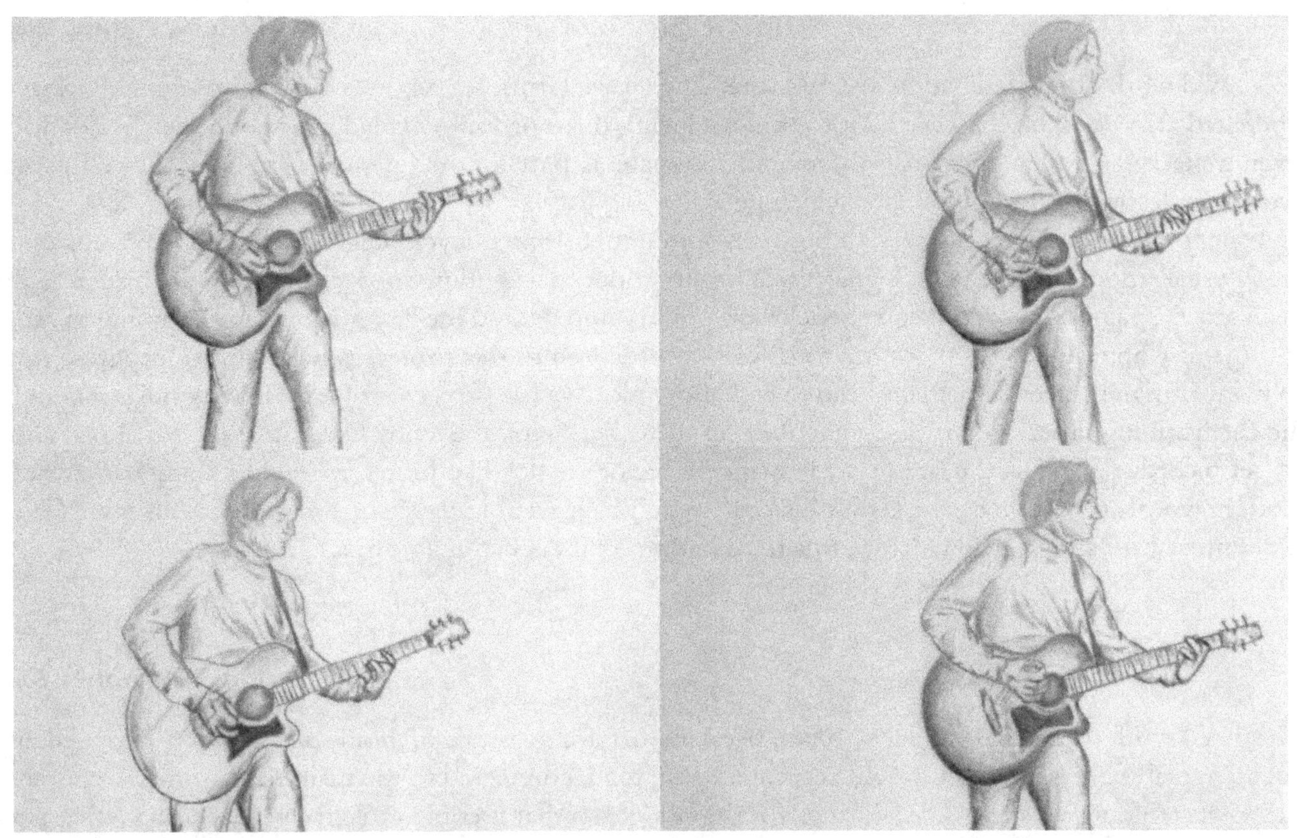

John rotoscoped into the opening of the animation.

The model's additional features were a vintage street lantern, a realistic looking road produced with black graphite pencils and an abundance of foreboding twiggy trees, rooted beside the railway viaduct. Again, I am sensing a form of bipolar attitude towards the 2D model. As I previously mentioned, my sense of perspective will change, and I will regain optimism throughout the project. I did initially invite John to North Lodge House to have a glance at the model until I realised that I had left my front door key inside the flat. Once rearranging another time to meet in a few weeks' time, I took myself around the back of the premises, lifted up the iron grate and climbed down into my basement flat through the window with my camera and tripod.

I personally feel that this current project is slightly slow paced, but my stamina will pick up once it gains momentum. I'm feeling excitedly enticed by this animation so there is nothing to doubt myself on.

"Morgan's Skylight" will now be the artist's name I will be working on for John, although I will use "John" as his name within these entries.

Thursday 12th November 2020

I resumed work on the animation at 10am, breaking away at 1pm for a bowl of porridge and a quick run. I perched at my desk in the basement room, producing three or four detailed rotoscope sketches of John strumming away on his guitar to subsequently animate as part of the opening clip. I also hope this will provide a classic literature book vibe which he is looking for.

I spent the second working session between 3pm until 6:15pm, developing petite additional features on the 2D scale model for example, a graveyard. I also produced a winding road, connecting the bridge to the main street. A single hickory dickory style clock would stand behind the graveyard. I am beginning to sense the mythical appeal that the piece has to offer. My attraction to this project is helping it to progress, with so many intriguing avenues, which I can personally explore as the project evolves. There is still going to be the forthcoming process of rotoscoping, but on the other hand, the animation can really be filmed as an on set recording. This is the beauty with a sincere melodic track like John's, merging together to create a modern lyrical adaptation of the Greek historic myth. I have an abundance of exciting options which I can experiment with and to help enhance this track and make it enchantingly attractive.

Friday 13th November 2020

I resumed work on the 2D model at 10am, breaking off for a couple of hours at 1:15pm. I designed and built a miniature bridge, which would accompany the road, connected to the main road from the church. I had to sketch out two stony side bearings for the bridge, so that it could effectively be seen on either side. I then had to design a small archway to connect the bridge to the road. I discovered that the road was too narrow for it to fit with the bridge, so I placed a black charcoal path, which obliterated any naked white flesh of cartridge paper. It looked effective when I placed the bridge in the model village. I also produced a thirty centimetre railway line freehand, near the viaduct, which I later began to build between 3:30pm and 6:30pm. Even though there is a lot to build, I feel that the resulting model will visually look prominent in the animation. As I have previously mentioned, there is an array of various avenues which I am seeking to explore. The design and form of the viaduct was produced using the same process that I did for the small bridge but at a slightly raised height of approximately thirty centimetres by thirty centimetres. Additional support had to be placed behind the walls to allow them to stand. I added foamboard to the leg frames to make the model sturdy. I have yet to add the curved inlays, to give the viaduct a much more realistic feel. I subsequently scrapped the viaduct concept as the exterior felt slightly out of place in the model village.

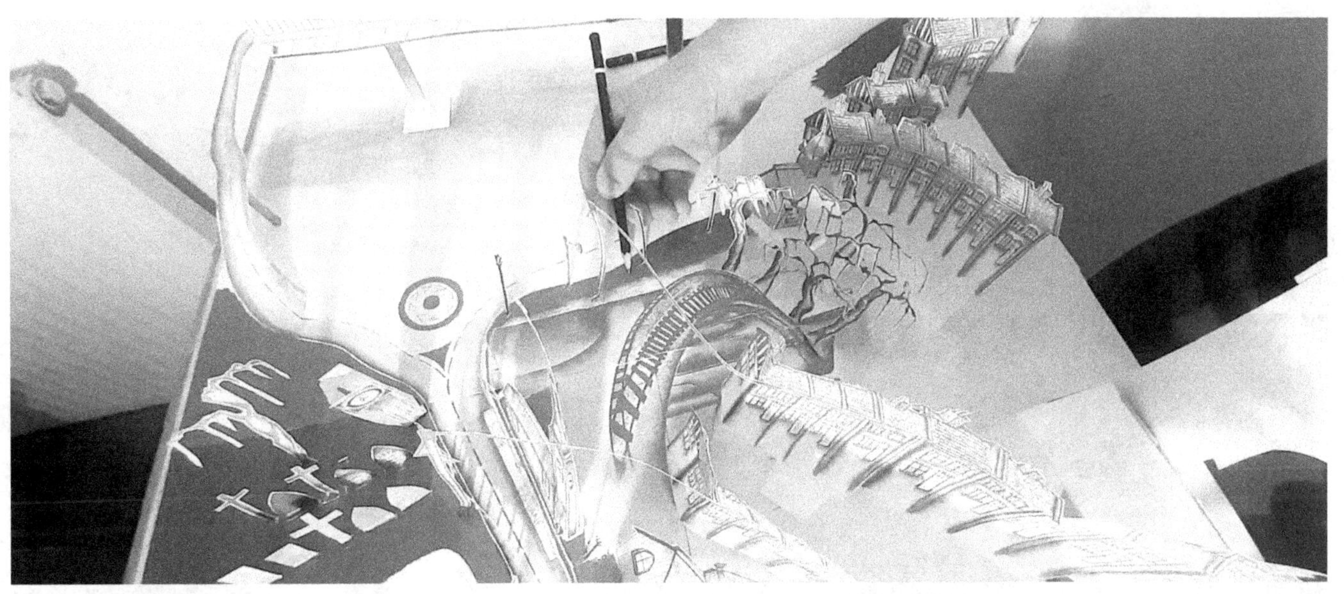

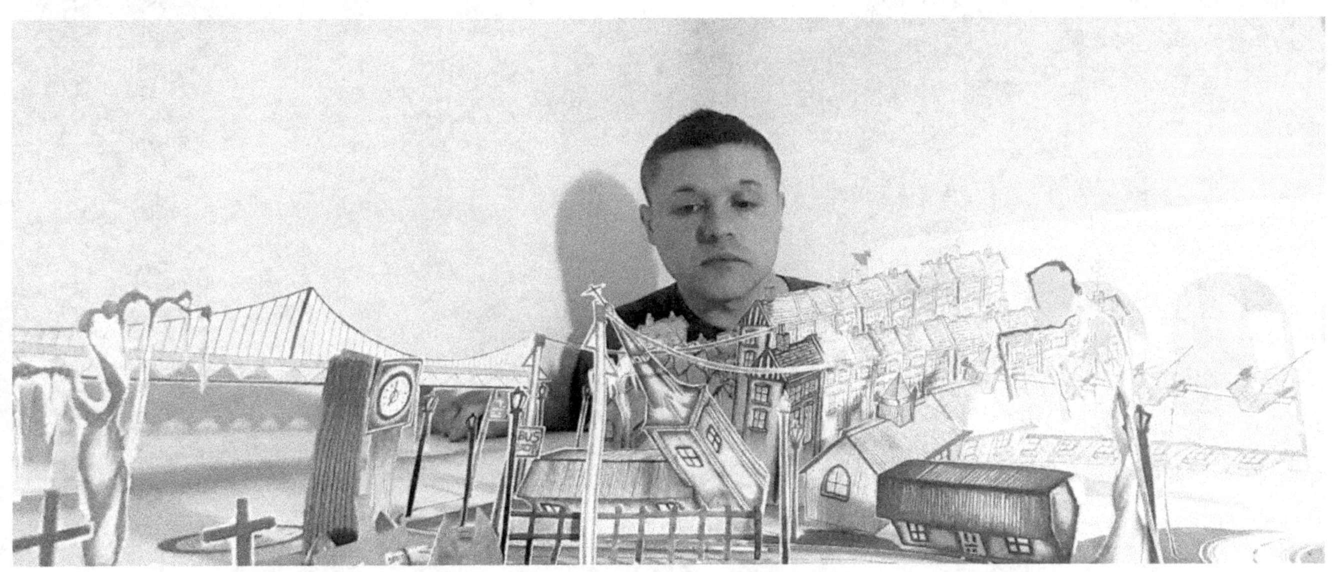

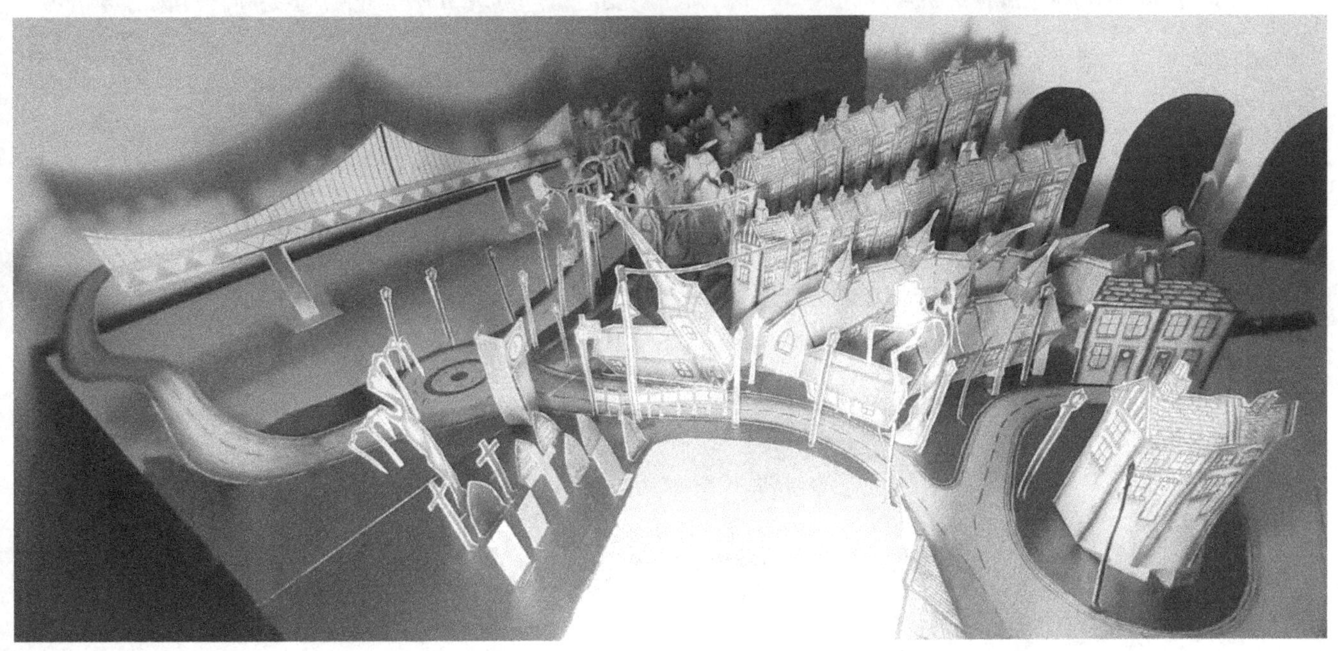

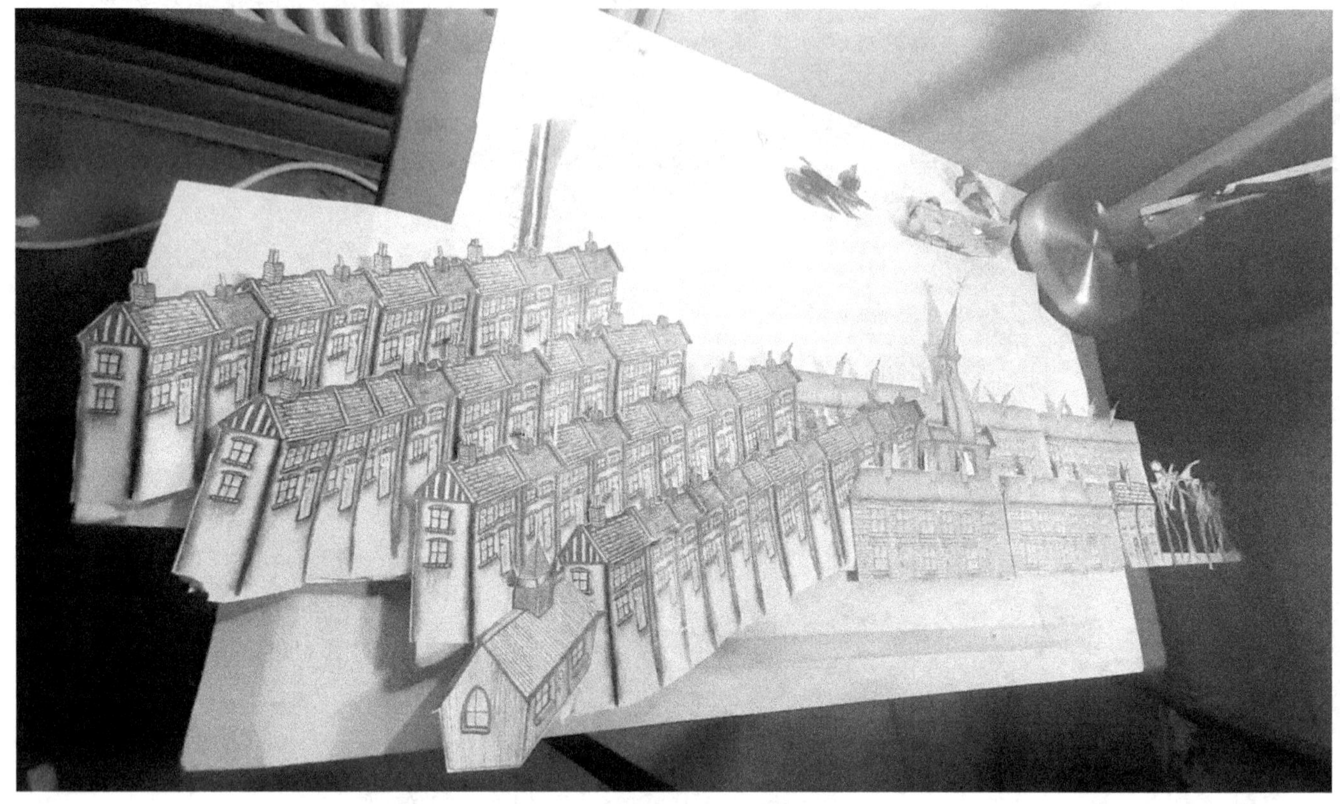

I dismantled the model, creating a town montage, as it would be easier and more effective when filming the aviation scenes.

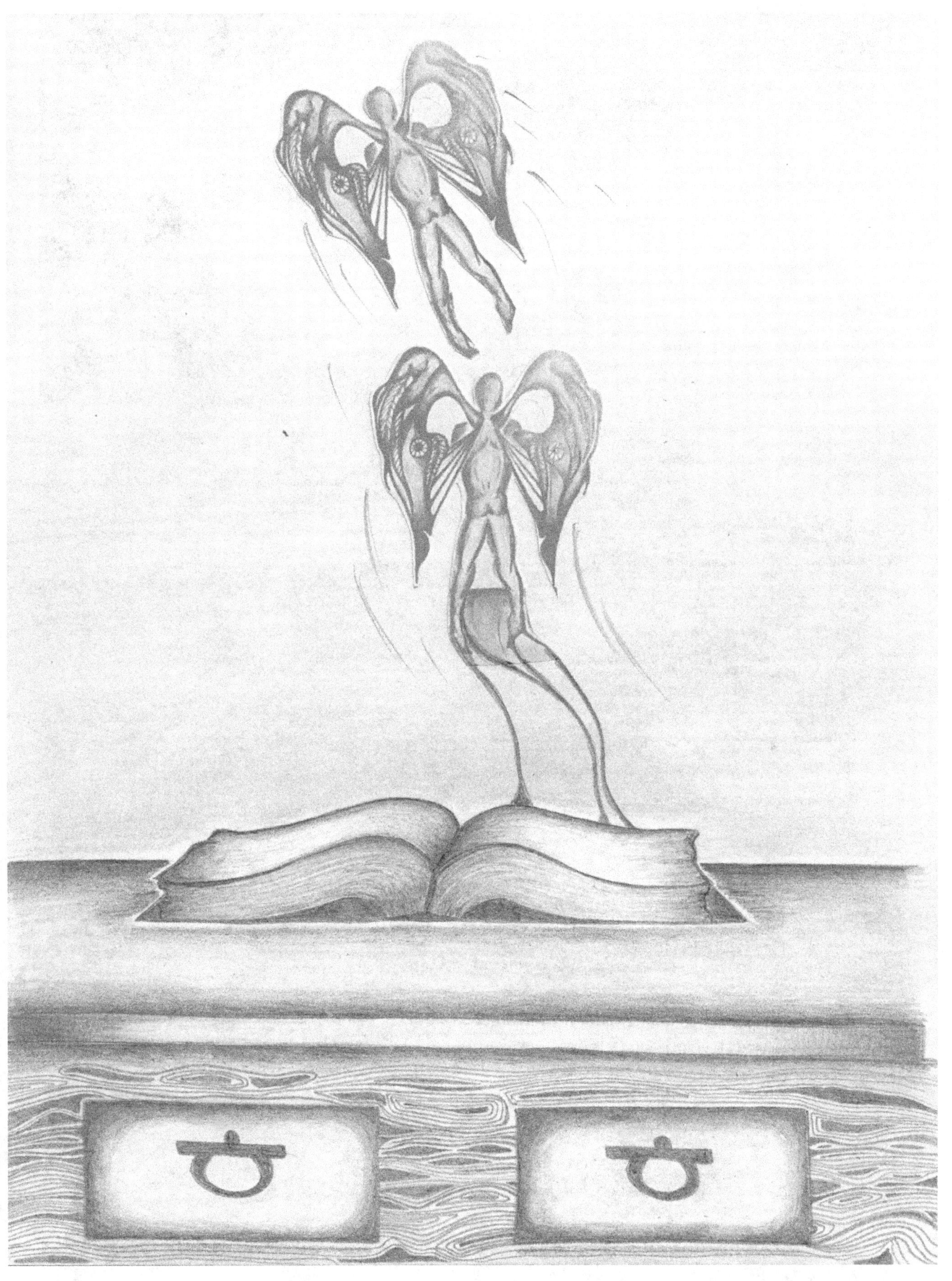

An impression of how I would like the characters to transition from book to aviatio

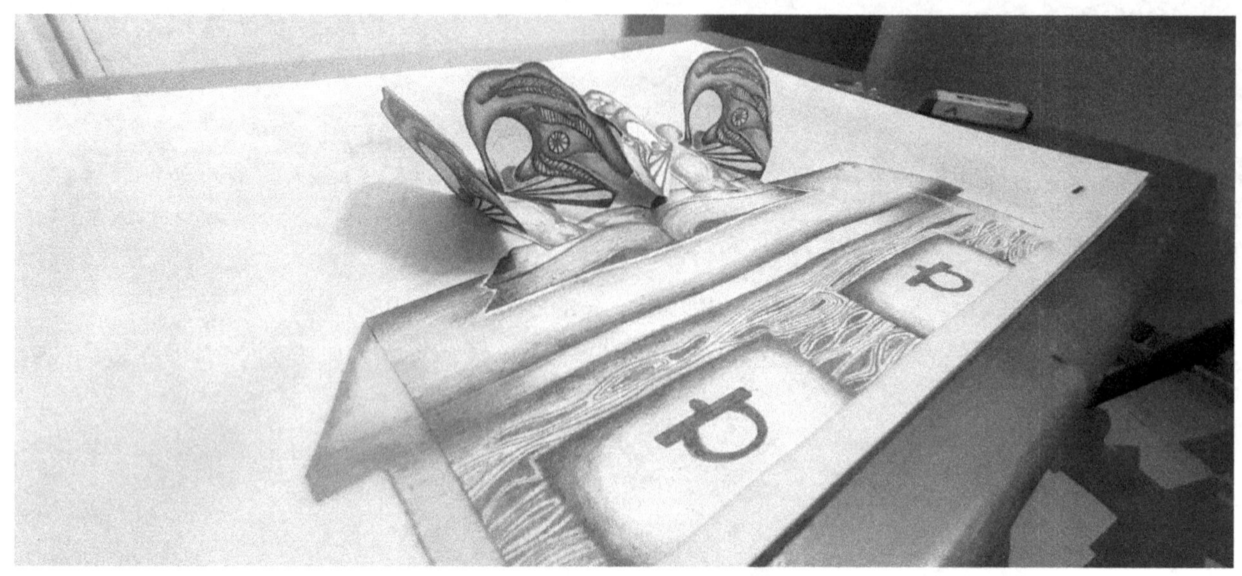

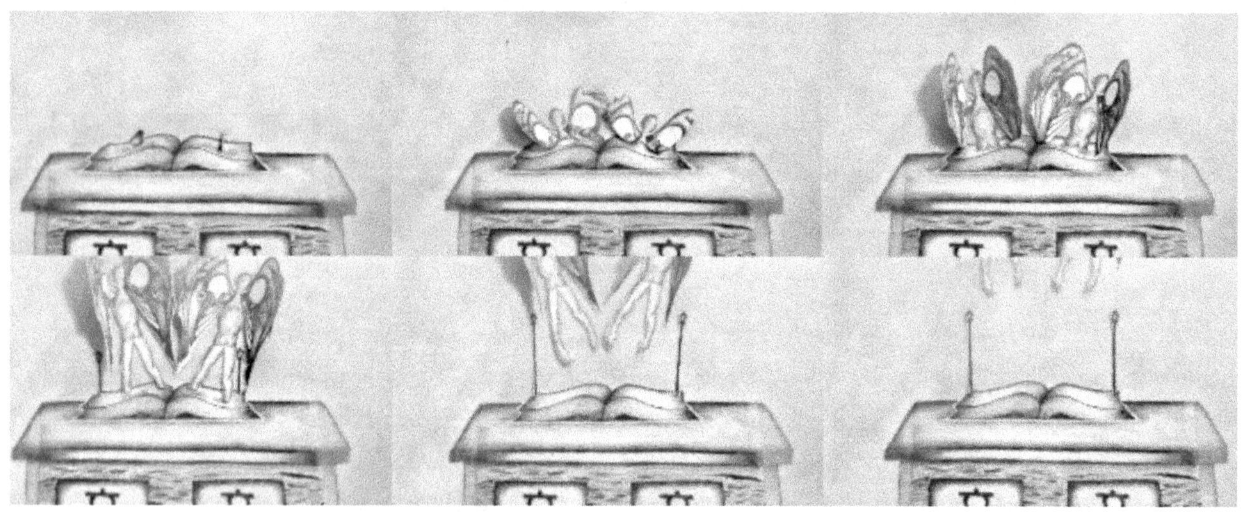

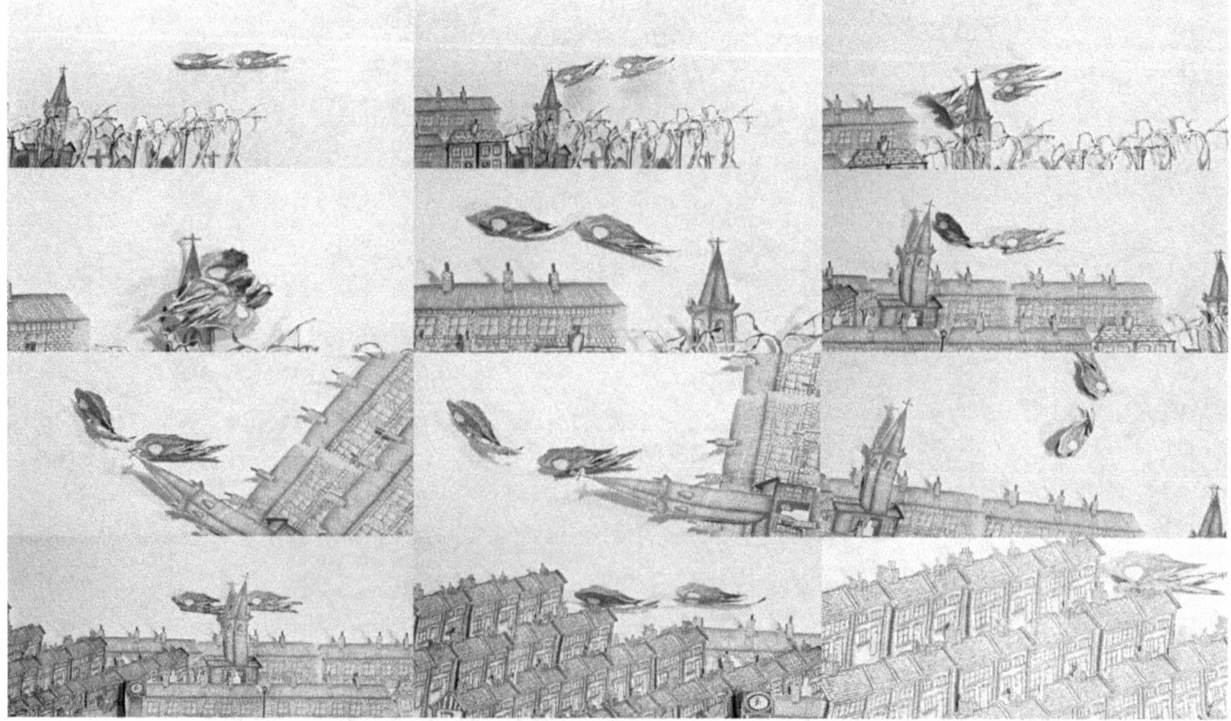

Saturday 14th November 2020

Marc drove me back home to North Lodge House, arriving at approximately 10:30pm. He had a quick coffee before driving back to Huddersfield. Vinnie and Taina were in the kitchen when we arrived, although we went down into my basement room, where I added the additional features to my 2D model, which I sketched out this afternoon whilst at Marc's cottage. The sketch that I did was of a tall terraced Victorian house adjacent to a place of worship. Photocopying these black and white drawings, allowed me to collate and mount a series of houses within the developing village. These sketches allowed me to add more depth to the angelic setting of the labyrinth. I am hoping I can capture the mysterious charm of classic literature and keeping with the reimagined concept of the historic Greek mythology. I am also making it contemporary, to compliment with the accompanying song. This project is coming along nicely so far.

Sunday 15th November 2020

I resumed work on the 2D model this evening, placing additional houses together, just behind the church. I then began to add another constituency containing terraced houses, just behind the mingling trees, next to a drawing of a railway line. This development will make model environment, appear more wonderous and ravishing. Visually the village is extremely attractive when captured through the lens. Additional features such as street lanterns, bus stops and even telegraph poles were planted in the village, throughout the course of the week. I am thinking of making a few more of these to capture the freedom of Icarus and Deadus's venture from various angles. I spent between 7:30pm and 9:15pm adapting the model, over the radiant shine of a lamp light which penetrated the desk. I then settled upstairs in the kitchen for an hour or so, where Vinnie and Taina were, before retiring to bed for the night.

Throughout the course of the subsequent week, I continued to develop new features for the paper model, like trees, street lanterns and winding roads, to add more character to the village before filming starts. On Thursday 19th November, I began to develop the opening to the animation. Through multiple singular shots, I created the appearance of a rotoscoped illustration of John, which then disappeared and turned into an open novel with a flickering candle at either side to give a classic literature vibe. On the right-hand page of the book, John is strumming away on his acoustic guitar. On the left-hand page, the title for the animation fades in and out. The page then turns to display the following text, "Act 1" which is written across two pages along with the opening lyrics of "I know you've always wanted to escape this town." The text appears to melt giving way to the appearance of town. There is murky smog of smoke rising from the chimney of a house, it quickly evolves into an image of a moving sunset with a car driving by. Frame by frame, I slightly erased the curve beneath the sun, to create the illusion of a sunset. I used the torchlight of my mobile phone to represent the headlights of the moving car.

Wednesday 25th November 2020

I resumed work on the current animation, commencing at 11:15 am and breaking for the day at 6:15pm. I developed my scheduled processes, contemplating how I am going to direct the remainder of the first verse. I produced a detailed sketch of John, with wings attached. I am planning on having him briefly lip sync the lyrics. There will be two silhouettes (Icarus and Daedalus) standing behind Georgian style windows, peering out, before the appearing cogs come into view on either side of the screen in the hope that aviation will be possible, during the line - "If you shine our champion in an emblem of hope -"

I will be using my sketch "The Lighthouse" as a representation of emancipation, but this is just a working concept at the minute. I subsequently illustrated how the aviation sequence will work. I am going to have the cut outs of the characters suspended on a piece string or wire, when I begin this specific scene.

Thursday 26th November 2020

At 3:30pm until 11:30pm with a couple of breaks in between, I commenced work on the current project. Pretty successfully, the first verse of the animation has come together beautifully. I still have some visuals to complete, such as the rotoscope illustrations of John strumming away on his guitar. I have completed the cog sequence and the appearance of the town through a Georgian window. The town evolved into the visual of "The Lighthouse", with a seagull ascending into the precarious sky. Whilst the wings were formed, I had to make sure that the cogs were consistently rotating, in order to bring the operation alive. I made the wings flutter so that they appeared realistic. This scene transition back into the pages of the novel, as soon as the cogs disappeared out of view. I simply cut away at the edges of the visual to perfectly fabricate the shape of the book. The book page turned and that was when the two characters ascended majestically from the book. I produced this scene backwards as it involved cutting away at Icarus and Daedalus, in order to make them appear emerging from the page. I positioned the two characters at the top of the screen and frame by frame, they descended closer to the book until they was nothing but a ripple on the page. Two street lanterns appeared on either side of the book, at the same time as the characters did.

Friday 27th November 2020

I resumed work on the animation from 11am to 1:30pm. I somewhat completed the first verse. I decided on having John lip sync the lyrics with wings on his back. The lip syncing was later cut from the take and just had him peering into abyss with the town gliding by to represent as if he was flying. This felt more relevant and authentic. The scene then gradually zoomed onto his face, blurring out the details.

Monday 30th November 2020

Marc dropped me off near the open iron gates of North Lodge House at approximately 10:30am, before he headed off to meet his interpreter at work at Printworks. Throughout the afternoon, I made alterations with the opening of the current Animation, to meet with John's criteria and outlook. The film now begins with him strumming along to the guitar during the acoustic melody. His figure would then disperse into the outline of the novel as he agreed that he wanted to keep this effect of the book. I did keep a second original opening, to have the transition still present but with this new visual introduction merged over the top of the initial clip.

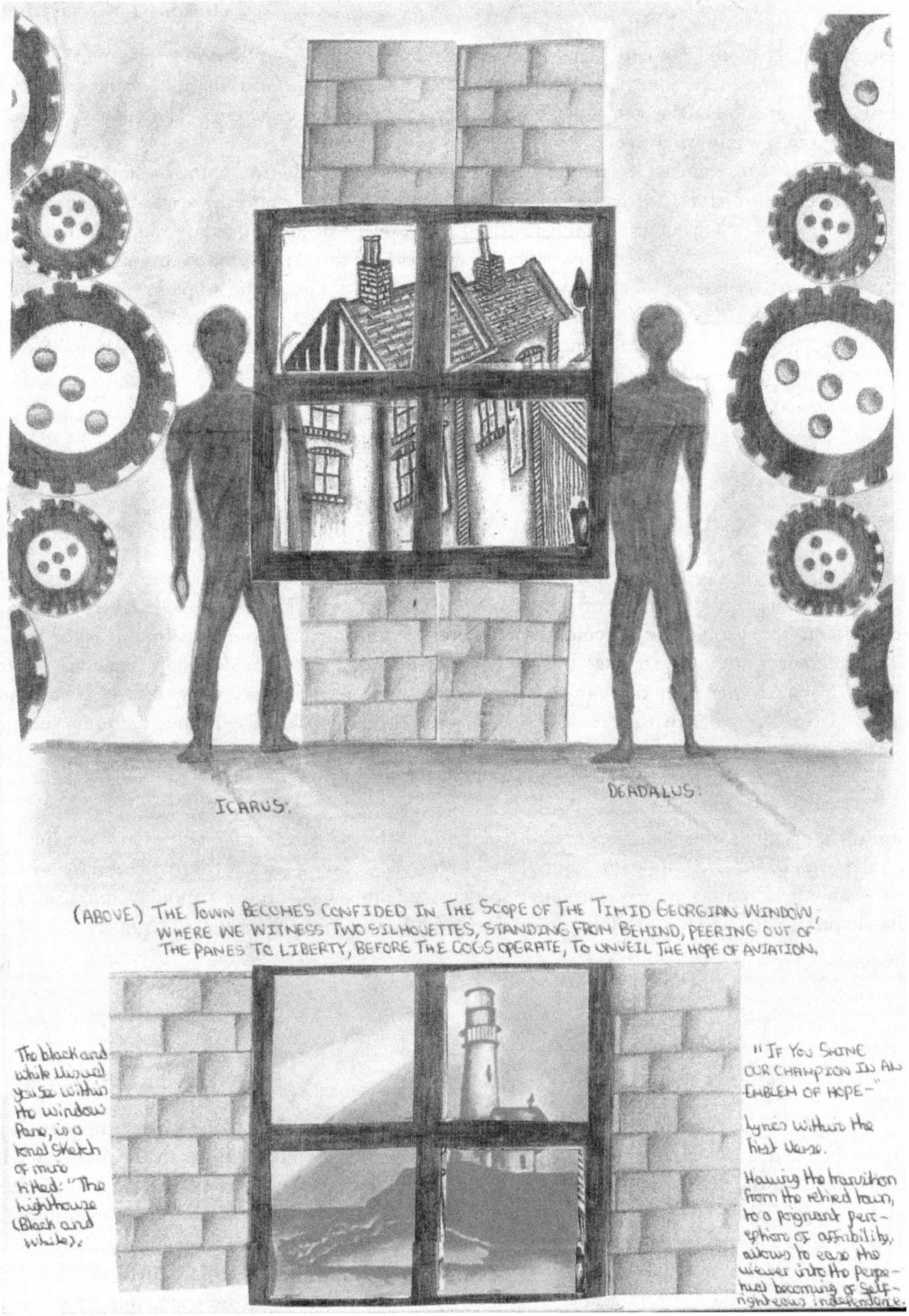

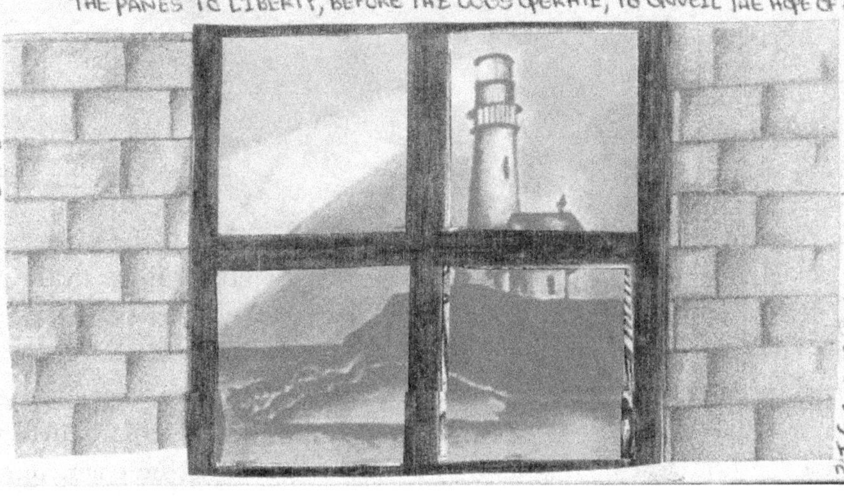

(ABOVE) THE TOWN BECOMES CONFIDED IN THE SCOPE OF THE TIMID GEORGIAN WINDOW, WHERE WE WITNESS TWO SILHOUETTES, STANDING FROM BEHIND, PEERING OUT OF THE PANES TO LIBERTY, BEFORE THE COGS OPERATE, TO UNVEIL THE HOPE OF AVIATION.

The black and white illustration you see within the window Pane, is a tonal sketch of mine titled: "The lighthouse (Black and white).

" IF YOU SHINE OUR CHAMPION IN AN EMBLEM OF HOPE —"

Lyrics within the first verse.

Having the transition from the retired town, to a poignant perception of affability, allows to ease the viewer into the perpetual becoming of self-righteous independence.

Tuesday 1st December 2020

Commencing work on the Animation at approximately 11am, I produced two A4 landscape visuals to proceed with verse two. These represented the earth, a mature angel and God, slightly raising up both hands in harmony. Icarus and Daedus will glide collaboratively through these sketches. The scene would be complete throughout the following week.

In the evening, I reproduced the titles sequence. The titles merged into a robust waterfall and then into a characteristic land of trees, a river and rolling hills. I made Icarus fly into the scene from the right-hand side of the screen and vanishing at the left-hand side. This scene need to speed up to synchronise with the rapid pace of Verse 1. I had to then crop, highlight and conceal the clip to embed this in the original book. Meeting the client's criteria and expectations, pushed me to pull out all the stops in order to complete a winning result. Personally, I feel this is what this entrancing commission has gifted me.

I evaluated today's development in my sketchbook, as I perched on the edge of my bed, based in my dimly lit basement room and then I slept from 1am.

Friday 8th January 2021

Commencing work on the animation at 12noon until 3:20pm, with a slight short break in between, I produced two A4 landscape depictions of a dystopian volcanic setting. This visual will hopefully tie up with the transition to the second chorus, which I took a break from shortly before Christmas. I asked John if he had any preferences on how he wanted the second chorus to look. He provided me with an idea of having Icarus and Daedalus swarming through space with a few stars and planets coming into view and then for the closing lyrics, the wings of the characters melt as they both get too close to the sweltering sun:

"Don't get scared and don't be stupid."

I am working along with this concept and this is where the volcanic setting comes in. I am thinking of having the two characters flying to another planet, before descending back to Earth. The volcano concept was subsequently scrapped and an alternative scene of a fairground and the famous Whitby ruins would see the characters fly over, before gliding over the North Sea and into the tranquill nightsky.

Tuesday 19th January 2021

I spent a good few hours adding, collating and producing the start of the second town template this afternoon, as I perched at the kitchen table top at Marc's cottage. Pretty much similar to the montage which I put together using the 2D paper model but with different structures and a town hall clock. I made some of the buildings slightly taller, to vary from the previous structures. I don't want the animation of flying to be identical to what was seen during the first verse. Last night, I produced a bewitching sketch of Huddersfield's Castle Hill in order to add a local vibe to the animation, and to compliment the music. I also sketched out a steam locomotion accelerating along the railway tracks as the characters fly above and I completed the Tudor houses. I contacted John through messenger to see if he was satisfied with me going ahead with this. He firmly agreed. When I get back to North Lodge House tomorrow, I will focus primarily on the aviation scene and the and make slight adjustments to the transition sections in between the scenes.

Wednesday 20th January 2021

Marc dropped me off at North Lodge House at approximately 2:30pm, we kissed each other goodbye and then he headed to Pat's bungalow for the afternoon. I resumed work on the current animation down in my basement room from 3:30pm until 5:15pm, whilst the rapid sound of rain pattered down on the window. I completed my first attempt at creating the aviation scene featuring Icarus and Daedalus using the second town template. Feeling aggravated, I took a break from the project and resumed a good few hours later. At 8pm until 9:30pm, I reshot this specific scene, after inserting a few more additions to the visuals. I had the characters fly in and out of the town. Again, by placing them both in one position and altering their angles when needed, I moved the landscape along bit by bit by two inches, and captured it frame by frame using my camera, just like I did for the first chorus, to give a sense of movement. The seventy-four photos are ready to be edited and put together into a sequence tomorrow.

Thursday 21st January 2021

I edited the scene which I produced last night, whilst I was perched in the kitchen on the leather couch. I then completed an additional sequence in my basement room, depicting the steam locomotion travelling past the viaduct and the historic Castle Hill. I made Icarus and Daedalus reach the summit of the castle before descending into the setting of the next scene. The train came into view from the right-hand side of the screen and the characters took flight at the same time. Icarus flew through under one of the tunnels, before flying beside his father. I decided on having a couple of houses in passing by, to add a bit of realism and the sense of travelling through the country. Multitasking in various aspects of the scene became aggravating, as every object was a challenge to the eye but visually appealing during playback. Because of my head was rammed with an abundance of stress, I vowed never to make another animation again and retire from the arts. This is something I pledge myself to do, although if you if ask any artist, they would feel the same, when experiencing mental afflictions, it doesn't mean that we are going to cease working as artists. The amount of times I have endeavoured to get rid of this practice, I would be a millionaire by now. I am absolutely blessed to have been gifted the freedom of expression as an artist and I will forever cherish this. Tomorrow, I will be editing today's scene. Throughout next week, I will be animating the remainder of the final chorus, this being the volcano setting and reworking the minor sequences in order to sew the entire video together.

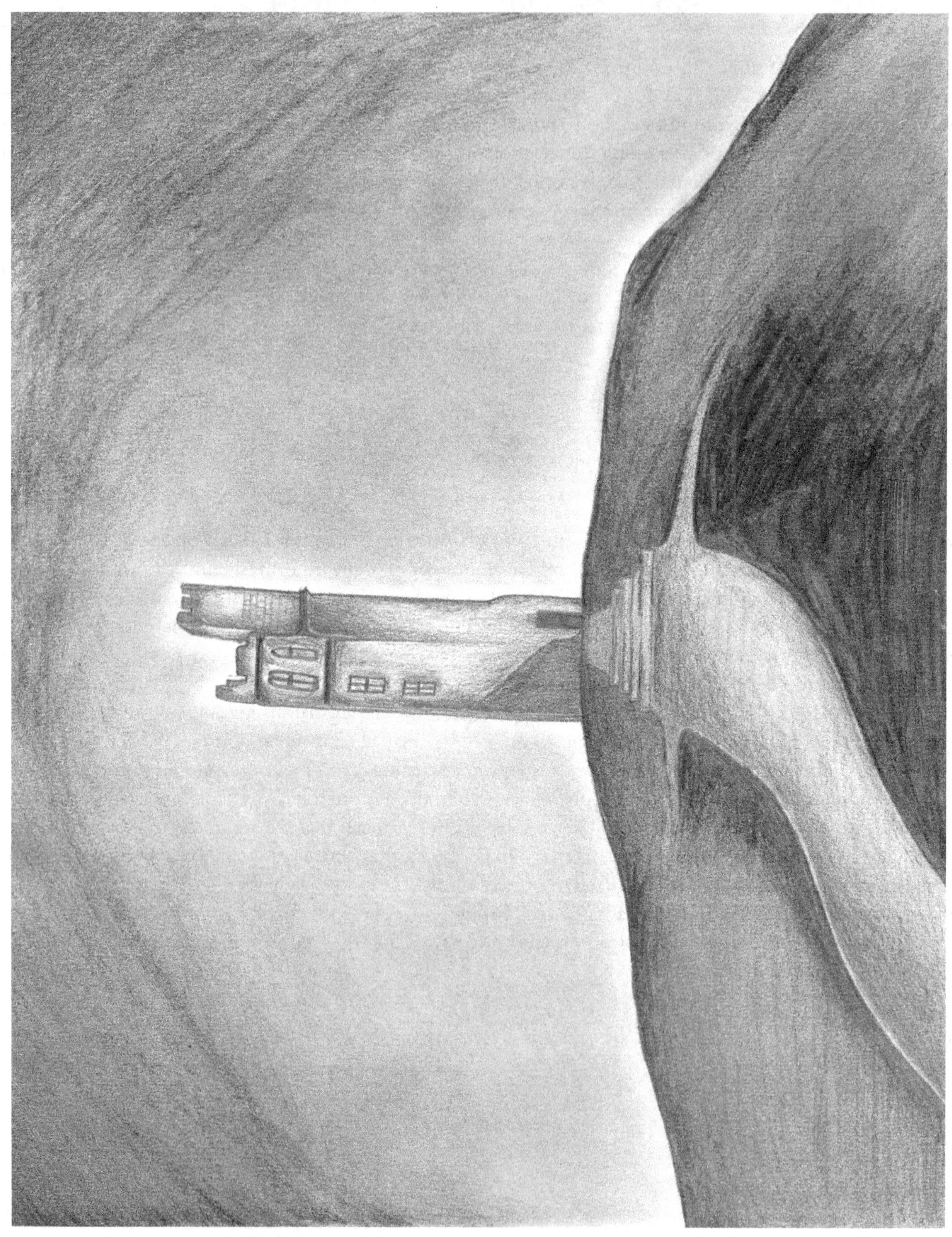

Template for the opening of Chorus 2 - Aviation scene around Castle Hill, Huddersfield.

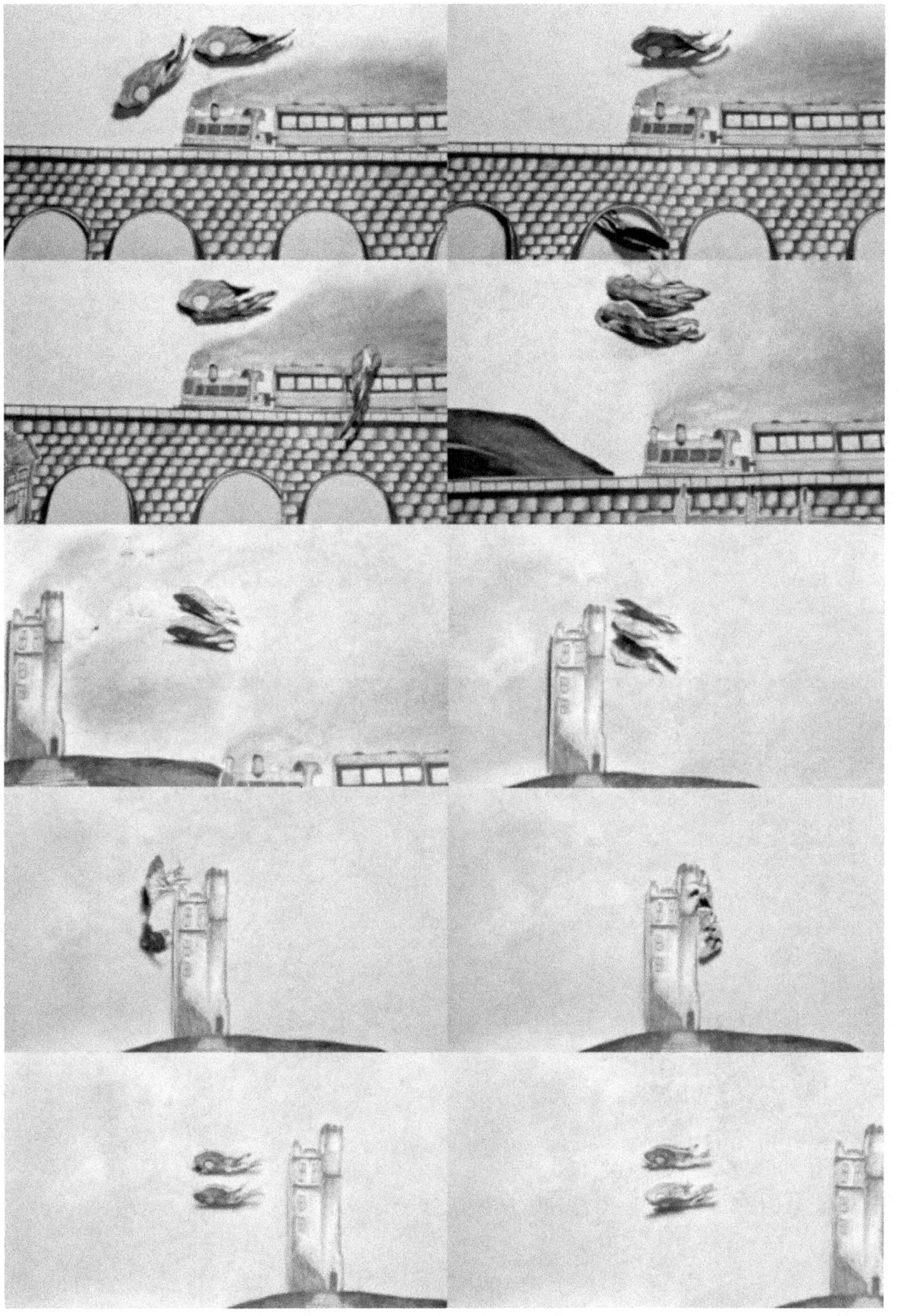

Chorus 2 - Aviation scene around Castle Hill, Huddersfield.

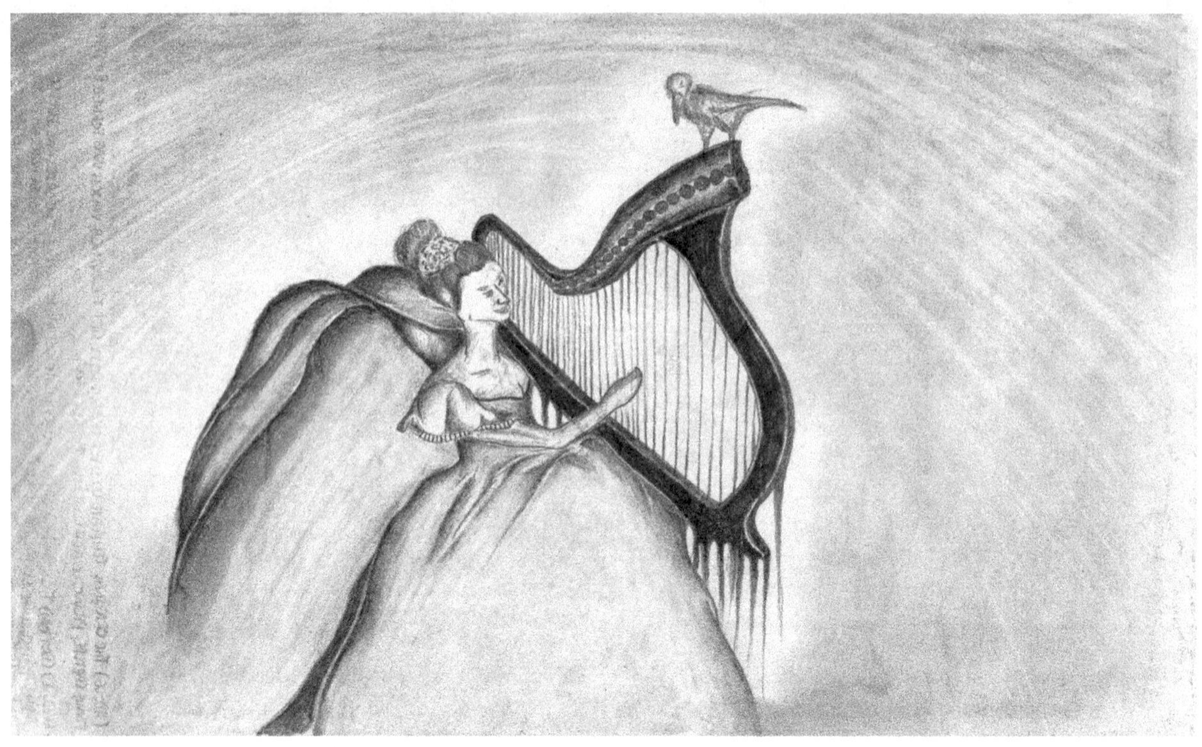

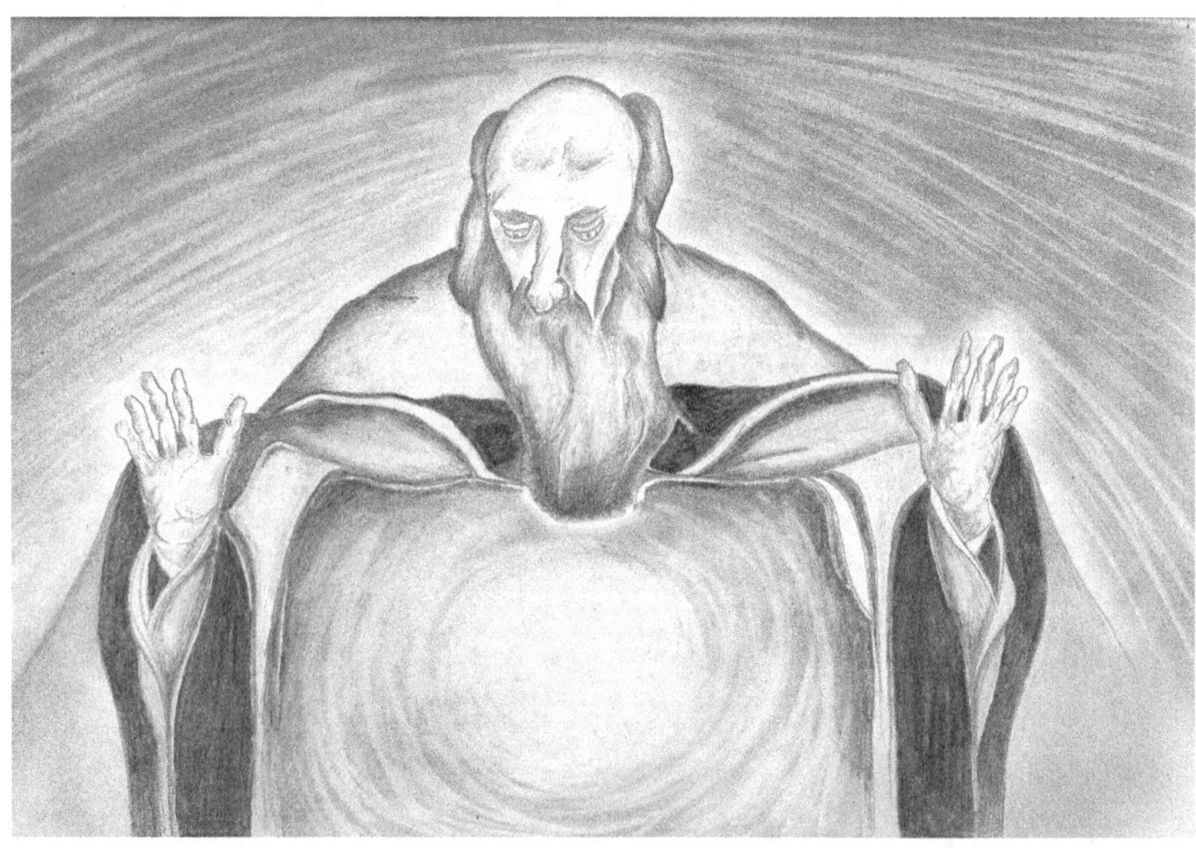

These are templates for the Verse 2 animated sequences.

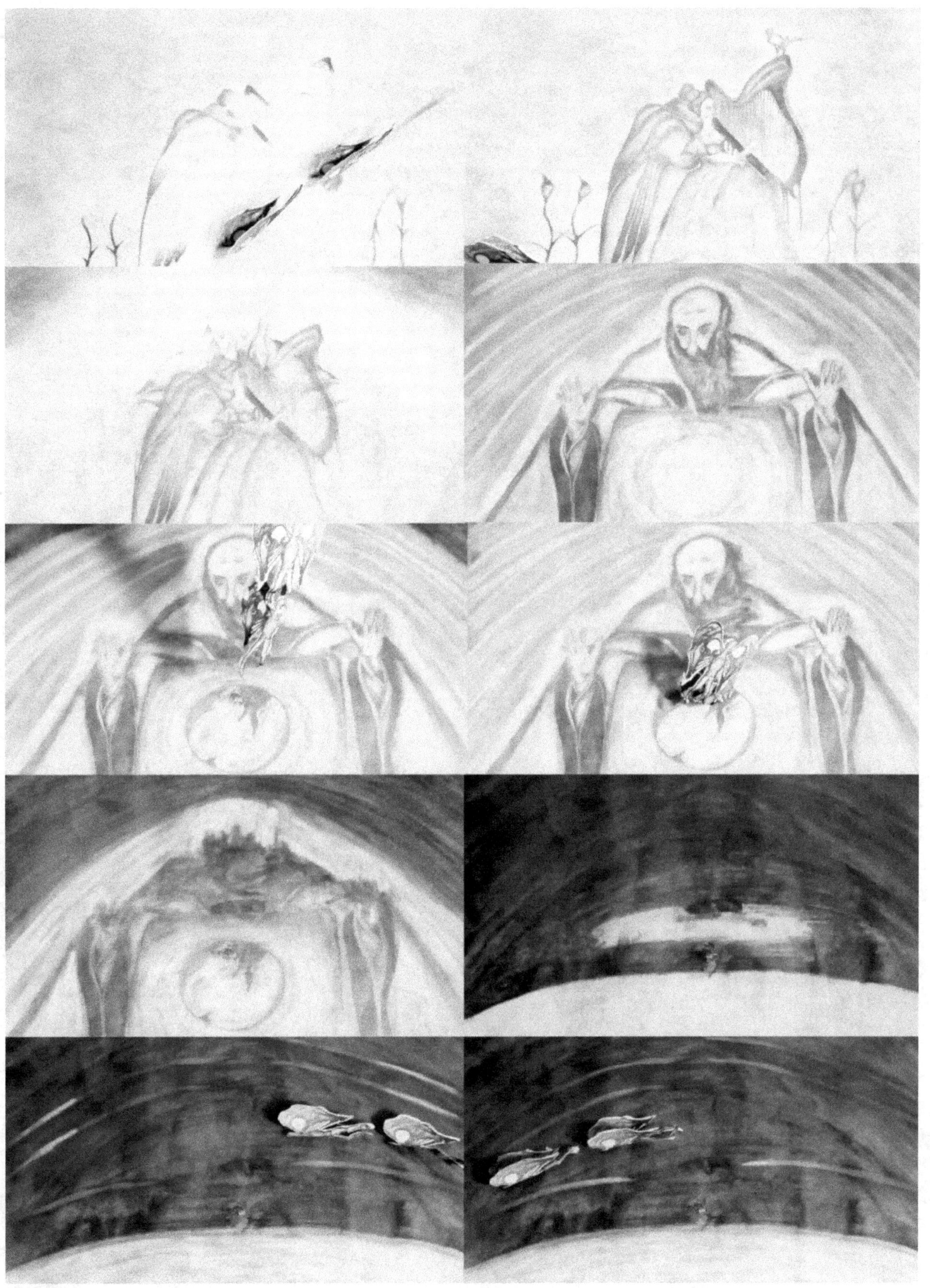

Verse 2 animated sequences.

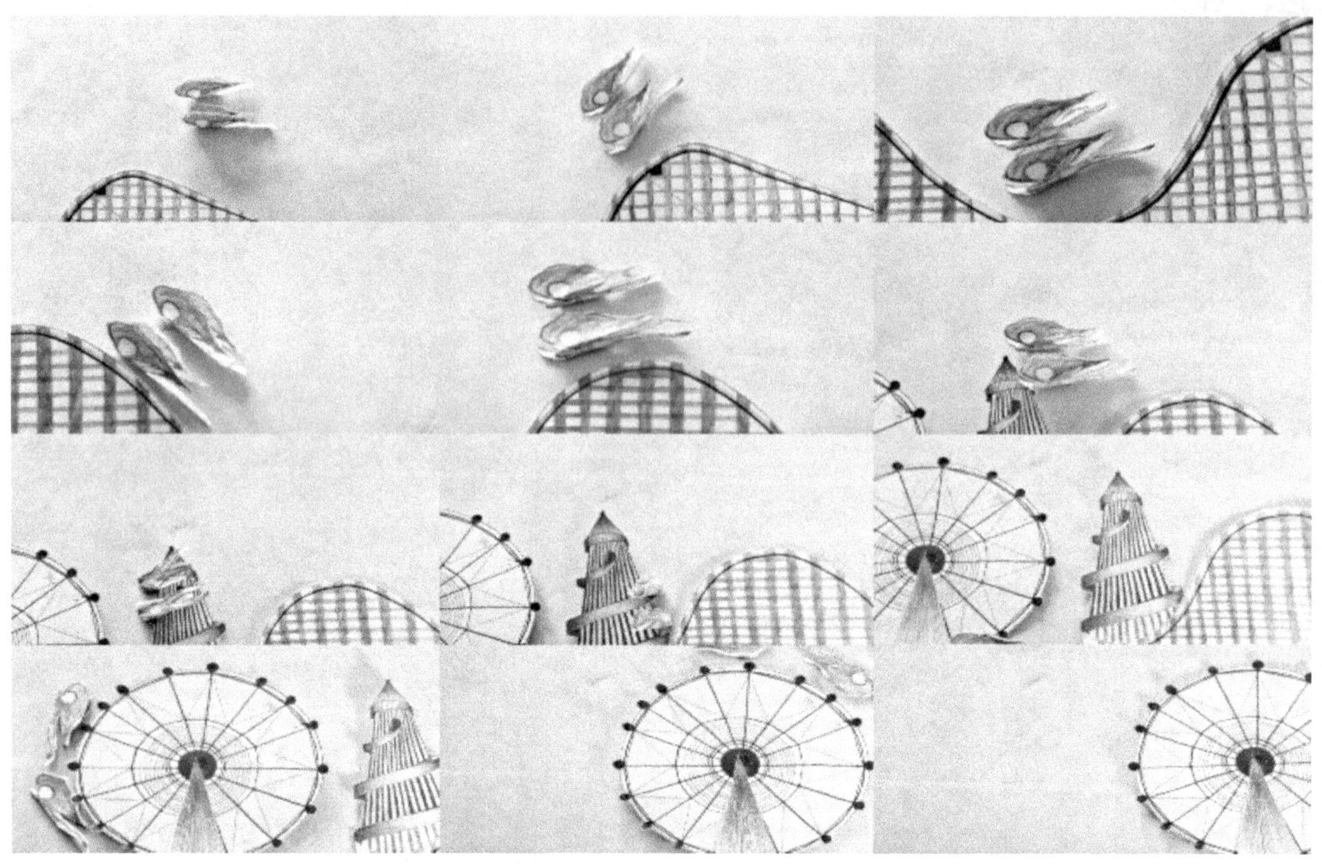

The characters swarm over a Fun Fair during the second bridge, before setting sail into the moonlit sky.

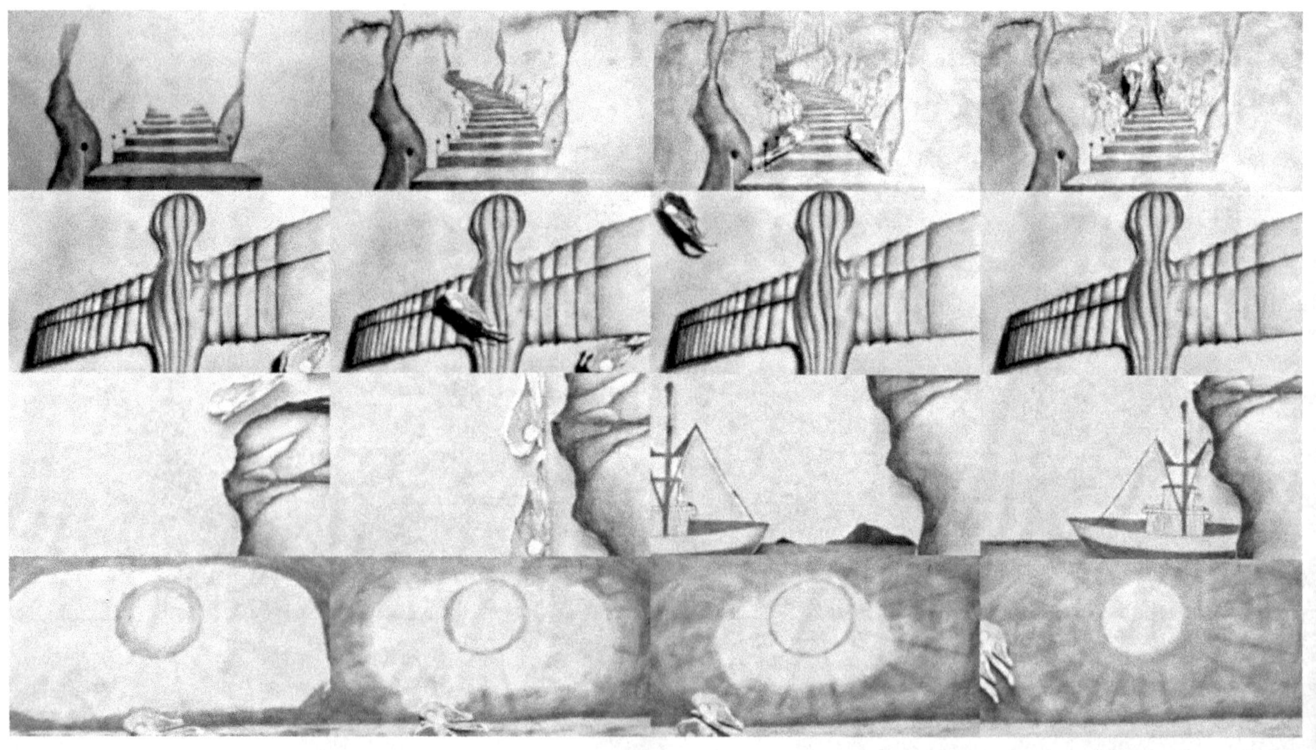

Here are more of the stills included in the Animation

It has been an incredible honour to have been invited to adapt John's pure musical genius as part of my first official commission. It is the first time that I have genuinely felt like a true practicing fine artist. This project has provided me with the stamina, commitment and virtue for future commissions and any solo projects that I work on. I would love to possibly take the music video on the road, hopefully with John, to various film festivals when the nation has been successfully vaccinated and when events are happening again. But for now, I shall continue to breathe, create and be the kooky individual that I am.

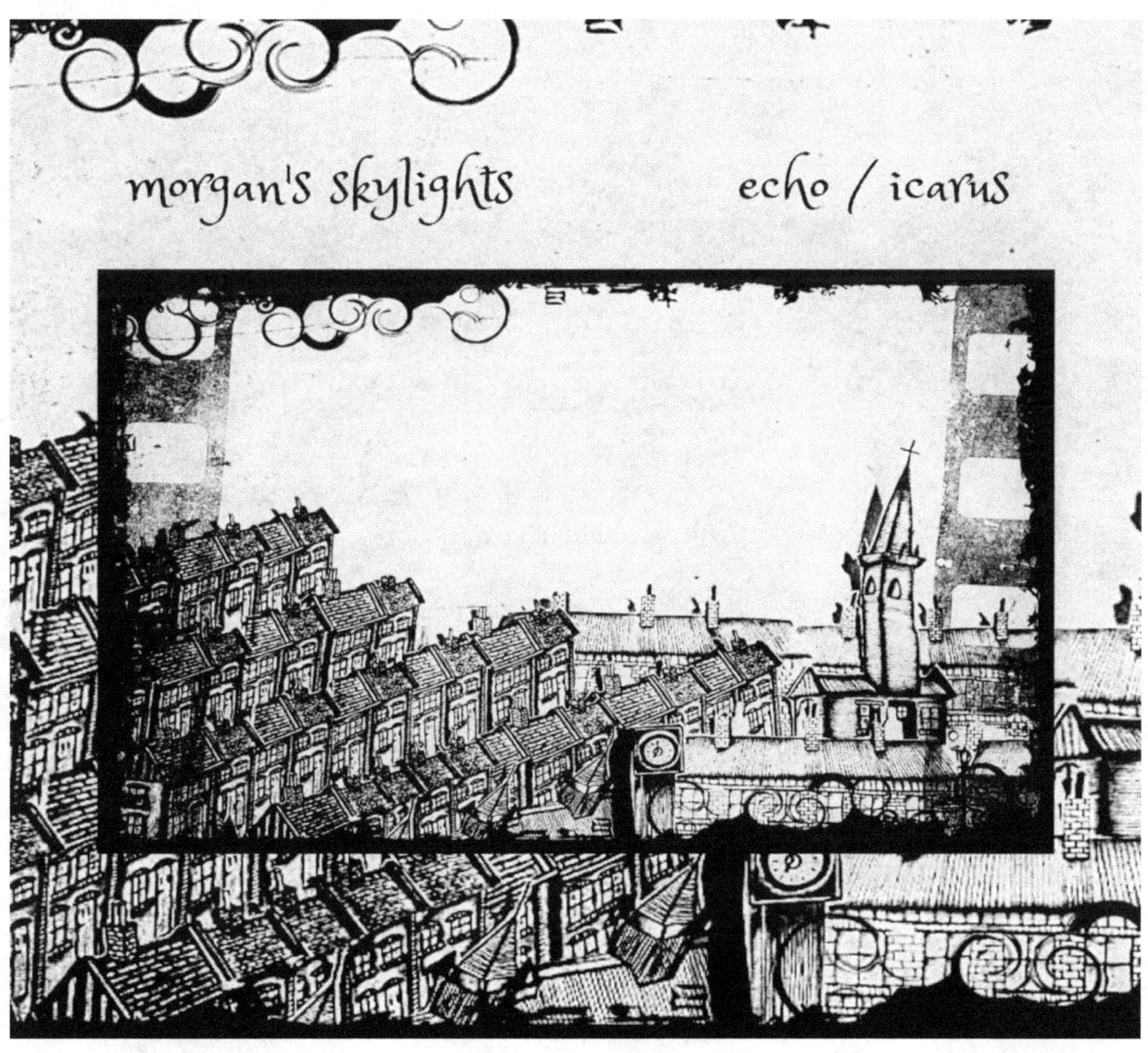

"Icarus (King Among Rascals)" *Promotional Cover.*

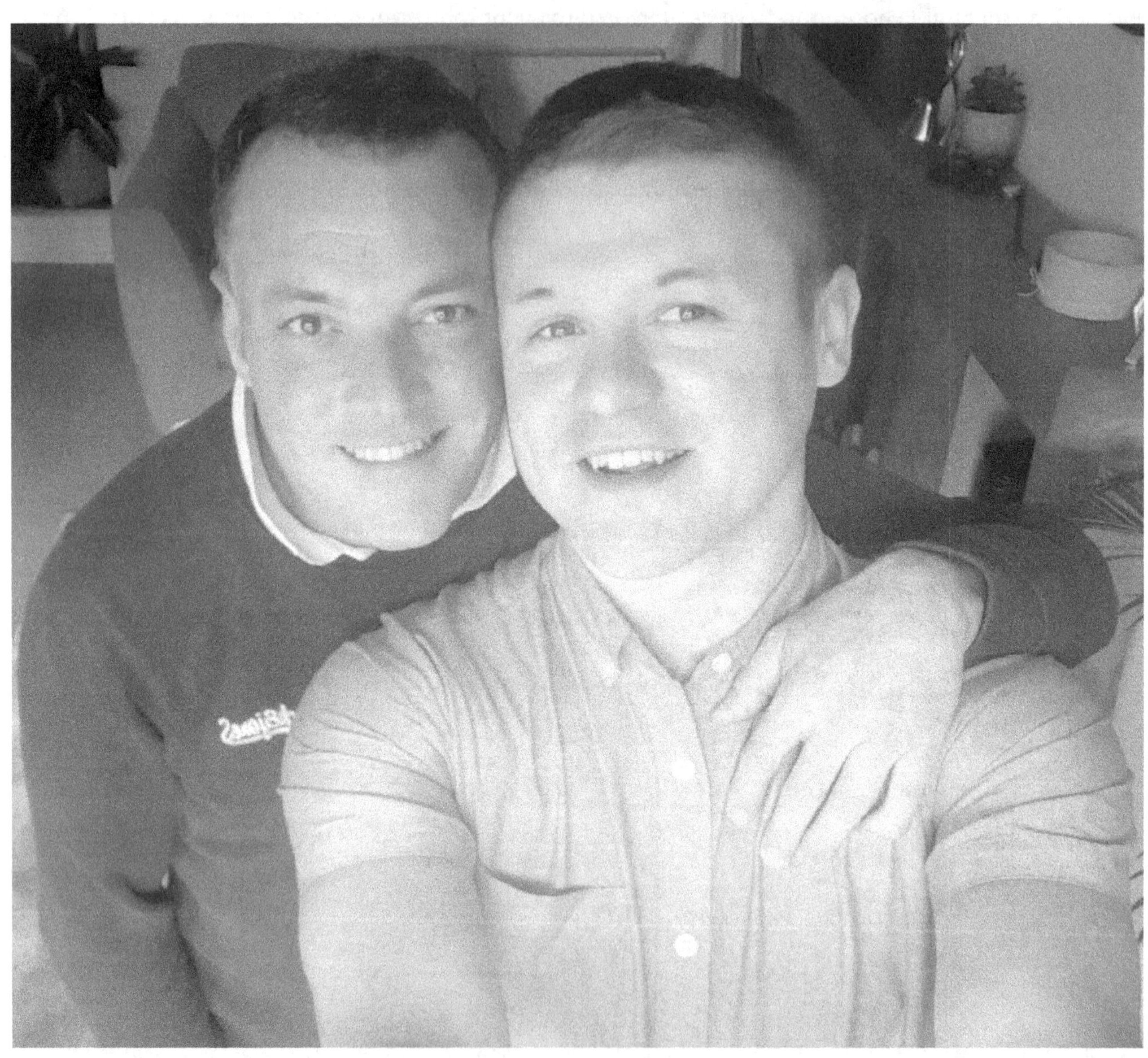

Me and my partner Marc
- 28/6/2020

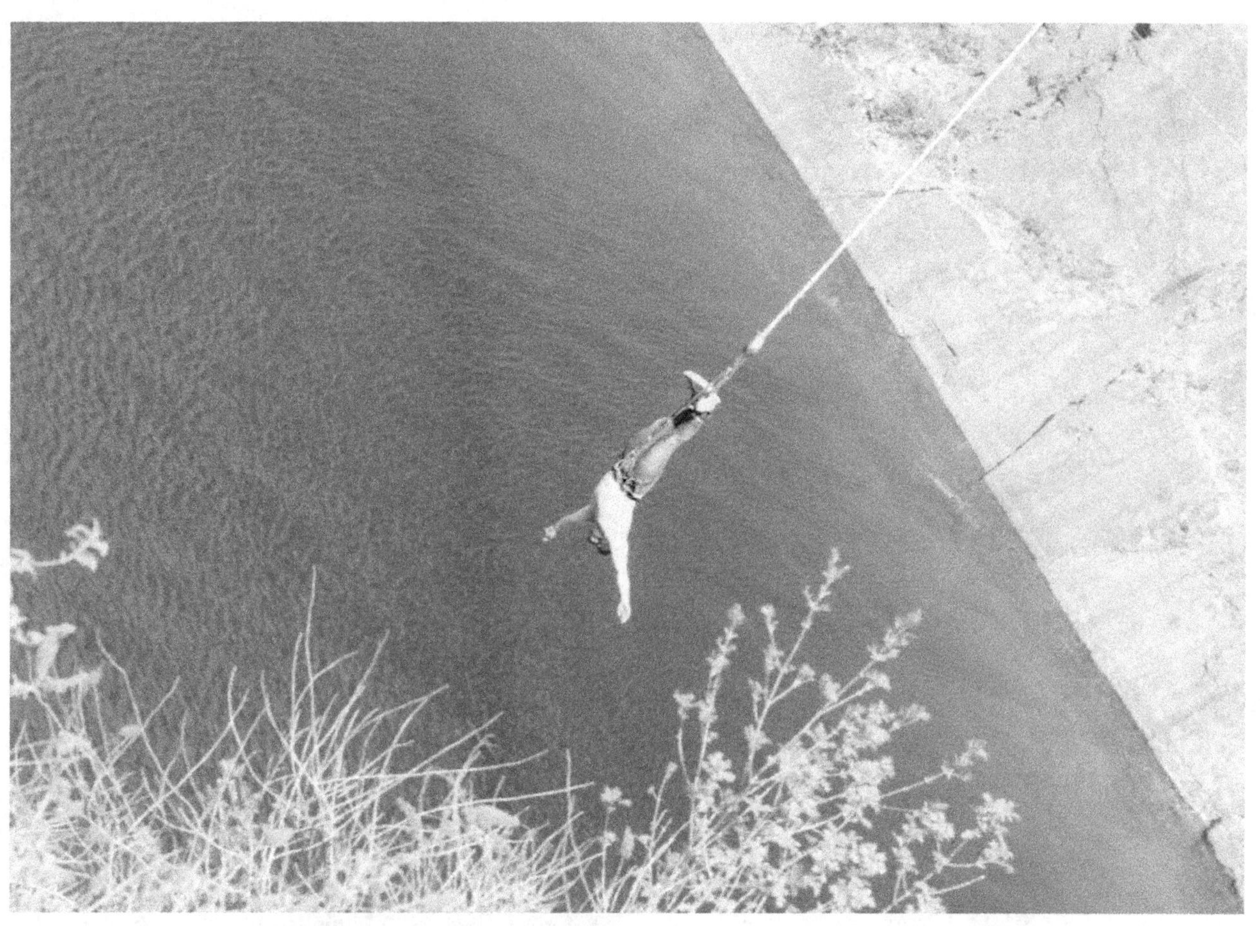

Bungee Jumping from 400ft in Chepstow
- 2/5/2021

CPSIA information can be obtained
at www.ICGtesting.com
Printed in the USA
BVHW010941160621
609641BV00007B/1098